OBSCURED
BY
WAVES

Paul Caffyn. Photo: The Christchurch Press

OBSCURED BY WAVES

South Island Kayak Odyssey

PAUL CAFFYN

To Kathy
best wishes
Paul Caffyn

Kayak Dundee Press

Also by Paul Caffyn:

Dark Side of the Wave - North Island Kayak Odyssey 1986

Cresting the Restless Waves - Stewart Island Kayak Odyssey 1987

The Dreamtime Voyage - Around Australia Kayak Odyssey 1994

Dedicated to the memory of Margot Greenhalgh

First edition published 1979
Second Edition published 2005
by Kayak Dundee Press
P. Caffyn, RD 1, Runanga,
Westland, New Zealand.

ISBN 0-9583584-0-0

Printed by Spectrum Print
134 Antigua St
Christchurch
New Zealand

CONTENTS

Photographs by the author except where noted otherwise
Cover photograph: Dick Strong
Rear cover: photo by Dick Strong
Chapter heading line drawings by Les Holmes

ACKNOWLEDGEMENTS

Equipment:
Arthur Ellis Ltd., for the fibrefill sleeping bags; Jan Cameron, for the fibrefill jackets and sausage bags; Doug Lyon, for the spare paddle; Anne Stephenson, for the spare sprayskirts and numerous stuff sacs; Grahame Sisson, for the Nordkapp modifications.
Food:
Ron Haddock, the Fiordland food order at reduced rates.
Typing and Proofreading:
Thelma Eakin, Marianne Belcher, Dick Strong, Bruce Annabell, and Lesley Hadley.

Line Drawings:
Les Holmes, for his beautiful pen and ink sketches.
Maps:
Shaun Leyland, for his neat and detailed maps.

SECOND EDITION
Proofreading:
L. Ferguson, K. Costley
Map Redrawing:
Lyn Rothery
Photo Scanning:
John Kirk-Anderson

PREFACE to the SECOND EDITION

On 16 January 2003, I enticed most of the original team involved with the Fiordland stage of the South Island kayak odyssey back to Jackson Bay, to celebrate the 25th anniversary of Max Reynolds and myself completing the trip. Following a re-enactment of the final landing, with Julie Reynolds (Max's niece) alongside me in a kayak, we donned formal attire for a great nosh at 'The Craypot' restaurant. Local fishermen, unloading their catch on the jetty, were shocked and stunned by the sight of top hats, flashing bow ties, tiaras, suits and slinky dresses as we strolled along the jetty, but were kind enough to take a group photo (p.78) with a magnificent full moon rising out of the sea in the background.

Well, I had great difficulty in accepting that 25 years had slipped by since Max Reynolds and I landed on a grey, blustery evening at Jackson Bay after paddling around Fiordland. And yet the memories are still so fresh of that first trip which opened up a whole new world to me.

I would like to include a brief update of what has transpired with the main participants of the South Island kayak odyssey since 1978. During the summer of 1978/79 I was desperate for another challenge and headed off around the North Island, completing the odyssey with a crossing of Cook Strait. In August 1979, Max and I teamed up again for a wee paddle across Foveaux Strait and the first circumnavigation of Stewart Island. Fortunately I wrote up the story in late 1979, for on 19 January 1980, Max and another good friend drowned in the flood swollen waters of the Aorere River. Tragically, his girlfriend Ainslie was watching from a bridge downstream and saw two bodies swept underneath, heading for Tasman Bay. Reading the funeral service for Max and John Gray was far more emotionally disturbing than anything we had ever faced at sea.

With Max's enjoyment of life, irrepressible hu-mour and desire for challenges largely responsible, I flew to Britain in 1980 and paddled around England, Scotland and Wales with Nigel Dennis. Even that wasn't enough to satisfy the urge so I set off around Aussie on 21 December 1981, the same date as Max and I began the Fiordland trip, and spent a year paddling around Australia. In 1985 I paddled 4,400 miles around the four main islands of Japan with Lesley Hadley as support crew. Two attempts to paddle across the Tasman Sea from Australia to New Zealand in 1987 and 1989 were thwarted by a combination of rotten weather and the Tasmanian authorities.

Between 1989 and 1991, I completed a 4,700 mile solo mission around the coastline of Alaska. Unfortunately in 1994 I fell foul of abdominable problems. Some wags blamed this on too much dehi-food on previous paddling missions. A perforated colon and peritonitis resulted in a colostomy for nine months and the end of life as I knew it, until a successful hookup led to a slow recovery. In 1997 I teamed up with Wellington paddler Conrad Edwards to paddle around the tropical paradise of New Caledonia, and we paddled 1,400 miles along the iceberg laden waters of West Greenland in the northern summers of 1998 and 1999.

After the Fiordland trip Maestro, supplier of grog and great white hunter of the Fiordland trip, went floosie-chasing, sorry tour bus driving for three seasons, married in 1982 and returned to teaching in Greymouth. Reaching the pinnacle of his 16 year educational career, he became a careers adviser and in 1998 took his own advice and left teaching to take over a small tour bus company in Greymouth. The years haven't been kind to Maestro. As he says himself, "shape, looks and bank account have all deteriorated over the years."

After Max drowned, Ainslie stayed in Nelson looking after their recently acquired house and kittens with the help of many friends. In 1984 she married and moved to a semi-rural area of Cumbria, England for eight years. Her English Nordkapp was used mostly in Scotland's Inner and Outer Hebrides, with a three week circumnavigation of the Lofoten Islands in Arctic Norway prior to her son's birth. They returned to Invercargill in 1991 and moved to a small rural holding grazed by a variety of animals.

Lyn Taylor moved to Wellington some 10 years ago in a valiant attempt to redress the ratio of politicians to sane citizens in that city. She works as an independent contractor writing and editing business documents. Despite the evidence of 20 broken umbrellas, she still denies that Wellington breezes blow with any more force than a good Canterbury nor-wester.

Bruce Annabell's passion for old Peugot's and motorbikes slowly waned, and was replaced by interest in computers. His current vocation as tutor of computing skills in Greymouth allows him to indulge his enjoyment of snowboarding and sailboarding. He now drives a flash four wheel drive Subaru!

Dick Strong joined the people in orange robes who bang drums and cymbals on street corners, and nurtures their large vegetable garden near Christchurch. The famous Keith Dekkers is still adventuring, cave diving, ocean diving and rock climbing, and joined two Nelson paddlers some years ago on a trip from Te Waewae Bay around Puysegur Point to Doubtful Sound. He is currently taking apart or putting together old houses in Christchurch. Pip Aplin retired from the park service and moved to D'Urville Island. Both Paul Dale and Pete Simpson currently work for the Department of Conservation in the big smoke of Wellington. Sadly, Ben the old ship dog succumbed to melanoma in 1990 but was given a good send off at the 12 Mile.

'Obscured by Waves' has been out of print since 1984 and is virtually impossible to track down in second-hand bookshops. Continuing enquiries every year for copies led me to consider publishing a second edition. Discerning readers will notice a few differences from the original edition. Canoe is changed to kayak as paddlers in Australasia no longer refer to a kayak as a canoe. And I have changed much of the present tense text to past tense, in view of automation of all the former manned lighthouses and other changes that have occurred over the past 25 years. Sean Leyland's maps were lost by the original publisher and these have been redrawn from scratch with help from Lyn Rothery. I have included more photographs, including one of the 25th anniversary of the completion of the Fiordland trip.

Paul Caffyn,
12 Mile, July 2005

Paul Caffyn and ship dog Ben at the launching of the first edition in 1979. Photo: Damer Farrell

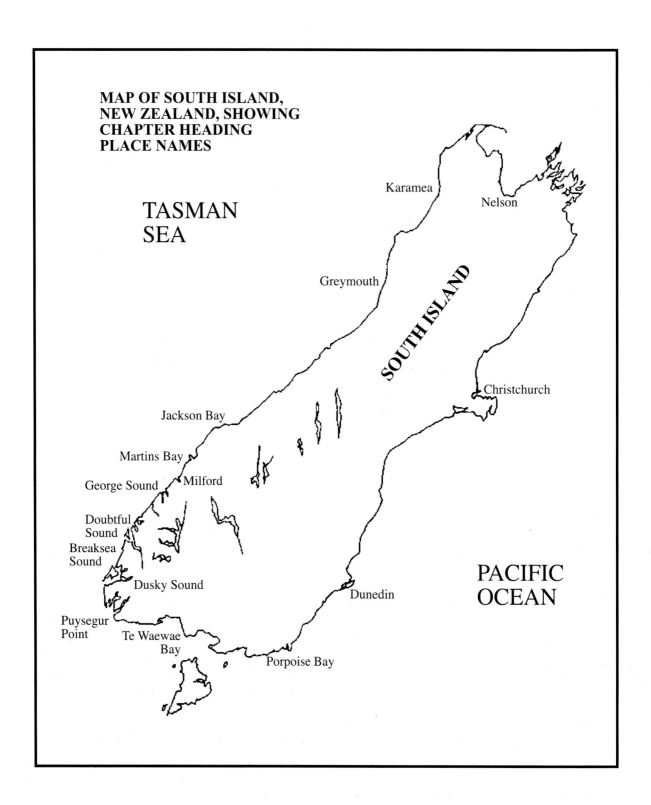

MAP OF SOUTH ISLAND,
NEW ZEALAND, SHOWING
CHAPTER HEADING
PLACE NAMES

TASMAN
SEA

Karamea

Nelson

Greymouth

SOUTH ISLAND

Christchurch

Jackson Bay

Martins Bay

George Sound

Milford

Doubtful
Sound

Breaksea
Sound

Dusky Sound

PACIFIC
OCEAN

Dunedin

Puysegur
Point

Te Waewae
Bay

Porpoise Bay

Chapter 1
CONCEPTION, TRAINING
& PREPARATION

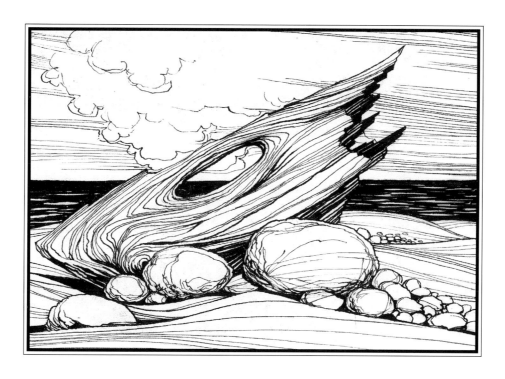

The idea of a South Island circumnavigation by kayak was conceived in 1977 on the banks of the West Coast's Upper Grey River after a bitterly cold midwinter paddle through Gentle Annie Gorge. It had been so cold that during a stop to patch a crack in one of the kayaks, we chased each other around a small island to restore circulation to our numb hands and feet. After finally dragging the kayaks out of the river, we stood shivering by the waiting cars, passing a bottle of port from hand to hand. Shaun Leyland mentioned that he had recently seen a long Eskimo type kayak on top of a car in Greymouth. Called a Nordkapp, it was constructed from fibreglass and designed specifically for sea kayaking. It had airtight compartments for storing gear and a bilge pump mounted on the deck.

Shaun, myself and Max Reynolds went on to talk of long kayak trips we had read about, trans-Atlantic crossings in wide, long kayaks with small sails, and joked about the idea of paddling across the Tasman Sea from New Zealand to Australia. But the thing that appealed to us most was the idea of paddling around the South Island.

Max returned to his job in Christchurch but over the next few weeks, Shaun and I kept the idea in the back of our minds and after much discussion settled on a shakedown paddle around Stewart Island. Shaun ordered marine charts of the area and I wrote to a friend on the island for advice from fishermen on sheltered landings and sea conditions. We spent several evenings discussing the feasibility of the trip and making up lists of equipment, food, repair and medical kits.

In July a news item in the local newspaper announced the intention of three Nelson kayakers to paddle around the Fiordland Coast from Jackson Bay to Te Waewae Bay. The trio were allowing three weeks during August for their proposed 300 mile trip, staging along the rugged coastline in three day bursts, then resting for a day and camping each night on shore.

As this would be the first major trial of Nordkapps in New Zealand waters, I was keen to see how the trio would fare. Three weeks seemed insufficient time and I was puzzled by their choice of paddling south from Jackson Bay instead of setting out from Te Waewae Bay, as the prevailing winds and swell are both from the south-west. However August can be a good month for settled sea and weather conditions in the Fiordland area.

Unbeknown to Shaun and I this trip had been planned since 1976 for in August that year a kayak manufacturer in Nelson, Grahame Sisson, was asked to attend a secret meeting with five other paddlers. The idea of a long expedition was explained to Grahame and he was asked about the possibility of making a mould for a sea kayak - the objective, Fiordland.

Grahame wrote to kayak designer and manufacturer Frank Goodman in England asking about importing a mould to make such a kayak. Frank replied, informing Grahame of his very successful Nordkapp design, 18 feet long, 21 inches wide, a 200 pound load carrying capacity, round bilge hull and designed along the classic lines of a West Greenland Eskimo seal-hunting kayak. It was first conceived as an expedition kayak in 1974 when a team of six paddlers were planning an expedition to the Nordkapp (North Cape) of Norway. Their Anas Acuta kayaks were neither large enough nor fast enough for their expedition, so Frank designed a round bilge kayak that would carry up to 200 pounds of gear and fitted it with hatches, bulkheads and a deck mounted pump to obviate the need for deep water rescues. In July 1975 the expedition successfully paddled 469 miles of Norwegian coastal waters from the edge of the Arctic Circle to Nordkapp, the most northerly point of Europe. Since then the Nordkapp kayaks had been used in successful expeditions (both in 1976) into the coastal waters of Greenland and Spitzbergen.

At the time of the Nelson paddlers' Fiordland expedition in August 1977, a group of us were ski-mountaineering for two weeks at the head of the Tasman and Franz Josef glaciers. We had almost 10 days of perfect weather so I assumed the paddlers had a good chance of completing their trip. After emerging from the mountains I was surprised to find they had stopped at Milford Sound, nearly two weeks after setting off from Jackson Bay.

Their trip report, which appeared in the Nelson Kayak Club newsletter, provided a valuable source of information as to what sort of sea conditions we could expect in Fiordland. The three paddlers involved, Vic Hague (leader), Brian Ogden and Brian Joyce, arrived at Jackson Bay late afternoon of 13 August. Extracts from Brian Joyce's report continue their story:

It seemed a bad omen from the start because the rain poured down and the wind was blowing strongly from the NE straight into the bay. On Aug 14 the wind was still howling into the bay from NE. The fishing fleet stayed at home and so did we. A walk over to the open sea coast revealed surf pounding in up to 20 ft high. Aug 15 again proved

a frustration with the weather even worse and no sign of improvement from the forecasters, both official and unofficial.....

Aug 16 calm in Jackson Bay but the weather had turned to the south and big sea running. We decided to have a go and left at 11am. Locals and Leicester saw us off. After a sortie out into the 20 - 30ft seas, we retreated to the bay - the kayaks were completely different to paddle fully laden. Aug 17 forecast bad and big sea still running - again a frustrating day. Aug 18 off at last with still a big swell from the south. We battled around Jackson Head and soon ran into some wind that proved disconcerting in the heavily laden kayaks. We put into Smoothwater Bay for lunch to see if the wind would drop a bit. It did and we pushed on down the coast towards Cascade Point.

Fishermen from Greymouth advised us against rounding the point because of a big sea running and a big surf on Cascade Beach. We put in at a rocky beach short of the point at a seal colony after 4 hour's paddling. Great feed of pauas but seals kept us awake. Aug 19 forecast fine and weather good. Left beach at 9.30am and quickly rounded Cascade with its beautiful waterfalls. A big sea rolling into Cascade so we decided not to land and headed instead for Barn Bay for lunch.....

We decided on Browns Refuge as our refuge for the night as progress much slower than we hoped. It was going to take us four days to do what we had hoped to do in two, and evident in the conditions that we would never get right round. We arrived at Browns at 5pm after 6.5 hours paddling. Into the swell and with heavy kayaks we were only making just under 3mph. Aug 20 started badly with a big surf roaring into Browns Refuge.

We left the beach finally at 10am after waiting for an hour to see whether it would die down with the incoming tide. It was quite a battle through surf between 12 - 16 feet. The SW swell was still a nuisance and as we neared Awarua Point at the north end of Big Bay it was getting bigger. It was breaking about two miles out to sea on the Awarua Point Reef and we had a long battle to get around the surf. We decided not to stop for lunch but plug on to Martins Bay - just five miles across Big Bay.

It was a long slog across Big Bay into the weather with a rough chop getting rougher. Just short of Long Reef Point at the northern end of Martins Bay Vic cried "shark" and in front of me (about 15 yards) was this eighteen footer basking on the surface. We rafted up and drifted away from him as he lazily swam away. We gave him a wide berth to fight our way round another reef with breaking surf. With the weather worsening and unable to land on Martins Bay beach proper because of the huge surf we battled across the bay to the southern end and a protected landing despite the comments of a Port Chalmers fisherman that we wouldn't make it.

Vic was suffering from sunstroke or exposure short of the beach but we managed to make it safely after 7.5 hours in our kayaks without setting foot on shore. We vowed never again as we stretched our legs. We set up camp high on the beach and after a quick meal fell into our tents and slept....

Aug 21 was a rest day after three day's paddling .... Vic nauseous with headache and unable to eat .... Aug 22 Vic's condition worse and had the cold shakes, but he ate some food. Forecast indifferent and rain in the afternoon. Aug 23 Vic much better and we decided to head for Anita Bay at the entrance to Milford Sound. We buried much of our food because it had become tainted by the plastic bags we were using, and left Martins Bay at 10.30am with Vic feeling a little weak after his two days crook. There was a big swell from the SW but we started getting some help with wind from the NW.

We decided to land again near Yates Point for lunch but big surf rolling in again and plugged on to Anita Bay arriving 3.30pm after five hours in our kayaks. Poor camp sites on many beaches and the sandflies prompted us to use the last of the flood tide to take us into Milford - 10 miles to the lawn in front of the hotel where we parked our kayaks. We made good time up the sound and arrived at 6.50pm - 2 hours and forty minutes for ten miles and about 28 miles altogether for the day....

Aug 24 it was decided to end the trip at Milford. We did not have enough time to get right around and the only other exit place was Doubtful Sound - about four day's paddling down the coast. The weather forecast was bad and as it turned out we would probably be still down there .... Suffice to say that even in good weather you face a battle to break clear of beaches that are exposed to the SW or NW and more than three weeks to attempt 300 miles around that coast.

The size of the seas and surf, not to mention the shark, would be enough to put anyone off contemplating the trip but it didn't deter Shaun and I from our plans for Stewart Island; if anything it made our proposed trip even more of a challenge. We arranged a date with Grahame Sisson for a sea trial of the Nordkapps, and one weekend early in September Shaun and I drove to Nelson and went out to Tahuna Beach with Grahame and two of the 'magic' Nordkapps. I was impressed at first sight with the kayaks, their long graceful lines and the flare of the finely pointed bow.

The blustery grey day, with a cold breeze and showers did not offer the best conditions for a sea trial but the Nordkapps cut cleanly out through a small surf and on to the open sea. I found the kayak rather tippy and unstable on the choppy sea but we were both impressed by their turn of speed, due largely to the shape of the round bilge hull.

On the beach Grahame showed us the 'extras' that make the Nordkapps so good on long trips; two airtight bulkheads (one in front of the footrest and the other immediately behind the cockpit), which form two sealed storage compartments, and a deck mounted bilge pump to clear water from the cockpit.

Shaun and I each ordered a Nordkapp with bulkheads, hatches, decklines, a bilge pump, sprayskirt and a skeg. We asked Grahame about the possibility of sponsorship or a cut in price but apologetically he said no. He had partially sponsored the three Nelson paddlers with their Nordkapps but on their return to Nelson Grahame had not heard a single word about the performance of the kayaks. The absence of feedback meant a halt to further development and refinements to the Nordkapps and accessories. The only publicity after the trip had been destructive as far as Grahame was concerned, as a news item said the kayaks had leaked, although where and how had not been reported. Absence of sponsorship did not change our plans so we both chose medallion yellow for the deck and hull colour as we figured it would be easily visible on a bluey-green sea.

I rang Max in Christchurch to say we had ordered our kayaks and he followed suit. However the anticipated price of about three hundred dollars proved too much for a fourth prospective member of the team, Bruce Annabell who, although keen to join us, did not have that sort of money and as yet no second hand Nordkapps were available. No one else we approached to join us showed the slightest interest in a long trip, leaving the team of Shaun, Max and myself, which we considered to be the absolute minimum number of paddlers, four being preferable.

Back in Greymouth Shaun and I embarked on a training programme to build up arm strength and stamina, paddling for an hour or more on the Grey River each afternoon after work in our 12 foot long whitewater kayaks. In the evenings we pored over maps, tossed around ideas for pieces of equipment, and made the lists of food and gear more detailed. We discussed all the likely situations that might eventuate including having to spend a night at sea in the kayaks, and being caught short well offshore; my mind boggled at the thought of squatting astride the two Nordkapps while they drifted apart. The idea of carrying emergency radio bleepers in the kayaks had to be discarded when we found out how much they cost.

One weekend in Christchurch I talked with Jan Cameron, proprietor of Alpsports, a climbing equipment shop, and she advised me to forget about taking down sleeping bags and jackets in the kayaks but recommended a new synthetic material called fibrefill which didn't absorb water. The only disadvantage was that fibrefill was bulkier than down and not quite as warm.

Jan offered to write to Arthur Ellis and Co., manufacturers of sleeping bags, and ask if the company was prepared to sponsor us with prototype fibrefill bags. A few weeks later Jan wrote to me saying that it was all on and the bags would be available by late November.

I'd written many letters asking for advice on the trip and replies were coming in. One in particular from Brian Joyce of the Nelson Fiordland kayak expedition, brought good news about the kayaks and advice on handling the sea conditions in the far south:

> How do the Nordkapps handle? Excellently in all seas. They paddle pretty true in all but beam wind and then a skeg corrects the tendency to round up. Skegs are a problem. We attached ours with shock cord and rafted up to remove them before hitting a beach. Leaving the beach even in a dumping surf is okay. They knife through the breakers as long as you keep 'em straight. On dumping beaches the landing technique is to let the last of the big ones go under you then paddle like hell or lie sideways on to the breaking wave and dig your paddle into the wave and hang on as it carries you up the beach.

The trio had carried sufficient dehydrated food for the proposed three week duration of the trip. Brian also wrote, 'A fully laden Nordkapp is easier to roll than any slalom kayak I have been in,' which was good news.

However the news from Pete Simpson, a Lands and Survey Department relieving ranger on Stewart Island, wasn't so good. He said he hated painting a 'picture of gloom', but 'it was the opinion of locals that we did not attempt the West Coast or south of Lords River.' His observations were enough to give me second thoughts about carrying out our shakedown trip around the island in case it turned out to be our last.

The completion date for our Nordkapps had been put off for two weeks so Shaun and I continued training in the smaller whitewater kayaks, on the local rivers and in the West Coast surf. But one afternoon as we slogged upstream on the Grey River, Shaun dropped a bombshell. He would not be going on the trip. Although he would go ahead and purchase the Nordkapp and continue training, he would not be joining Max and I. Shaun explained that as he hoped to start building a house soon, he couldn't afford to go. As well as this, I feel there may have been a little pressure from Shaun's wife Lyn, especially after we had read and reread Pete Simpson's letter. This sudden news left me speechless for the rest of the afternoon. Reducing the numbers to two would seem to put an end to the trip.

The same evening I rang Max to break the sad news and to propose a change in plan. Instead of journeying around Stewart Island, I suggested we paddle from Te Waewae Bay up the Fiordland coast to Jackson Bay. There was much umming and ahing over the end of the phone so I told Max about the beautiful fiords we could explore when the sea grew too rough, and that I had first hand knowledge of the Preservation Inlet area. Finally, and to my glee, Max reluctantly agreed to give it a go.

In early November Shaun and I drove up to Nelson and picked up the completed Nordkapps. The final cost came as a shock, $450 instead of the anticipated $300 but Grahame explained the extra was due to the labour involved in fibreglassing the bulkheads and deckline fittings in position.

On our return to Greymouth we drove out to Rapahoe, the beach where we carried out our surf training, eager to try out the kayaks in the fiery West Coast surf. I lowered mine into the sea for the first time and although there was no bottle of champagne, I christened my Nordkapp *Isadora* after the dancer Isadora Duncan.

The two Nordkapps sliced easily out through a moderate surf but my journey back to shore wasn't so successful. A breaker tumbled *Isadora* over in shallow water, which resulted in a grazed elbow and injured pride, not to mention breaking my best laminated wooden paddle whilst trying to roll back upright. In a nearby lagoon we tried to sink the kayaks, but even with the cockpits full of water and us sitting on top we could not submerge them - such was the buoyancy of the two watertight compartments. The bilge pump effectively cleared the cockpit of water in no time. The pump and buoyancy meant that even a paddler on his own could rescue himself after a capsize, whereas in all other kayaks, deep water rescues are only feasible with at least one other kayak.

Not deterred by this first experience I continued training on the Grey River, in the surf at Rapahoe, and on long cruises on Lake Brunner. One weekend I joined Max for a paddle from Sumner to Lyttelton and back. Whilst Max's kayak neared completion,

Paul heading out of Blaketown Lagoon for a training session on the Grey River

he trained in a demonstration model Nordkapp on the waters of Lyttelton Harbour.

To build up stamina I started doing daily body presses and evening runs as well as the usual paddling. As Max and I would be supplementing our diet in Fiordland with fresh fish, I had to re-learn all over again about hooks, lines and sinkers. Library books on fishing in New Zealand waters weren't enough so one weekend when a group of us were barbecuing on a beach by Twelve Mile Bluff, I sat offshore in my kayak holding a fishing rod, the hook baited with a piece of squid. Two small fish took the bait but each time line spun off the reel and I lost them. The third time I had figured out the mysteries of the reel but was totally unprepared for the way the next fish took the bait. The tip of the rod jerked down into the water with such force that I nearly capsized. By the time I recovered, 20 yards of line had unravelled from the reel but I managed to take the strain.

For the next 20 minutes, with the tip of the rod only occasionally surfacing, the fish towed me around offshore. No one on the beach seemed to take any notice of my erratic course; the kayak went in circles, zig-zags and at one stage backwards. It was obvious I would not be able to place a three to four foot long snapping fish between my legs in the cockpit and as my arms and wrists were aching with the strain, I hoped the line would snap. Fortunately, since the rod wasn't mine, the line weakened before my arms finally gave up the ghost. It suddenly snapped, almost sending me over backwards in a capsize. After that little incident I gave up my fishing training!

For several reasons I considered it unwise to carry all our food supplies with us. As the weather would determine the length of the trip, it would be impossible to keep to a tight schedule. Food dumps at various places in the sounds were the logical answer but how to place them was a problem. I wrote to John Ward, Senior Ranger and Master of the Fiordland Park Board vessel the *Renown*, asking if the boat could put in dumps for us, also for advice on the proposed trip. He replied saying the *Renown* was refitting in Bluff and would not be in service until after Christmas. I also wrote to one of the crayfishermen who worked out of Preservation Inlet to see if he would put in a dump, but received no reply.

Fortunately my flatmate Maestro and Max's girlfriend Ainslie came to our rescue and offered to plant the dumps and act as support crew. There were four places that Maestro and Ainslie could reach without too much trouble, either on foot or by floatplane; Supper Cove at the head of Dusky Sound, Deep Cove at the head of Doubtful Sound, the head of George Sound and Milford. We decided to leave from Te Waewae Bay with sufficient food for two weeks. This should last until we reached the first dump at Supper Cove. Each dump would comprise enough food for a further two weeks, which meant we had an outside limit of eight weeks to complete the trip.

A Greymouth store owner, Ron Haddock, kindly agreed to let us have a long list of food at wholesale prices and a friendly Scottish doctor, Jim Eakin, helped assemble a comprehensive medical kit. Poor old Jim was taken aback when I asked for four gallons of shark repellent. He suggested that I should get in some practice at suturing, either on the skin of an orange or a lump of bacon.

I had lots of small jobs to do on *Isadora* in order to make long stints of paddling comfortable. To lock my knees in a brace position on rough seas, I fibreglassed two knee rests in position in the cockpit and covered them with thin closed cell foam mat. The reasons for the mat were twofold, firstly for comfort and to stop the wetsuit material abrading on the hard fibreglass, and secondly because this type of mat doesn't absorb water. Since my posterior was a little too small for the seat, I made up two thigh rests of closed cell foam mat, one for each side of the cockpit. So my back wouldn't suffer, I constructed a back-rest, using mat and pieces of wood, that slid in behind the rear of the seat and rested against the cockpit coaming. Instead of the usual adjustable aluminium bar for a footrest, I cut up a block of polystyrene foam and worked it into position against the forward bulkhead. It was tapered so the soles of my feet could lie flat against it. I found that my closed cell foam sleeping mat, folded in half, lay nicely along the hull, cushioning my heels and legs from the hard cockpit floor.

In Christchurch Pete Richards made special paddles for Max and I with tubular aluminium shafts and fibreglass blades tipped with rivetted aluminium strips. Because the metal was cold to the touch, I glued one thin closed cell foam mat around the shaft where my hands would grip, and wrapped Sleek adhesive tape over the top. In training this kept my hands warm even on the coldest days and I never once suffered from blisters. Just in case we lost or broke the paddles, both Max and I made up spare take-apart ones.

Taking the advice from Jan Cameron, Max and I each ordered a fibrefill duvet or jacket with long sleeves, and Jan made up six long slender nylon bags, or sausage bags, with drawstrings that would slide easily in and out of the hatch openings. We equipped ourselves with surfie type wetsuits, ankle to shoulder with no sleeves, wetsuit booties, life-jackets, whistles and compasses.

For navigation, both the marine charts and Fiordland Park Board map were too small a scale to serve our purposes so I bought the relevant one inch to one mile topographic sheets, cut them into strips, and stuck them back to back under clear adhesive plastic. This made the maps completely waterproof.

By mid December preparation and training were in full swing and I set 21 December as a tentative starting date for leaving Te Waewae Bay. I knew things were starting to get serious when one night I dreamt about taking a party of fourth formers from Greymouth High School around the Fiordland Coast in kayaks.

The few non paddlers whom I sought advice from, or mentioned the prospective trip to, thought Max and I had developed suicidal tendencies. This was really brought home to me one evening in a Greymouth hotel, when a friend introduced me to a fisherman who had worked out of Milford Sound. After shaking hands I said, "I'm seeking advice about sea conditions and currents off the Fiordland Coast."

"What do you want that for?" asked the fisherman.

"Two of us are going to have a crack at paddling from Te Waewae Bay to Jackson Bay this Xmas," I explained.

For a moment the chap stared at me with an incredulous look on his face, then shook my hand again, and said as he turned away, "Well that's the last time I'll be seeing you!" That did nothing for my confidence so I stopped telling people about our trip.

I read and reread all the books about Fiordland that I could lay my hands on, taking notes and drawing maps in the back of a new waterproof paper log book. The most valuable sources of information were: *Fishermen of Fiordland* by Paul Powell, which had several disturbing photographs of cray-boats working in wild seas; *Columbia Cruises South* by Ralph S. Von Kohorn; the two informative books by the Begg brothers *Port Preservation* and *Dusky Bay*, and the *New Zealand Pilot*. The *Pilot* provides a wealth of information on coastlines, sheltered landings, anchorages, currents, reefs and even the weather. In the following description of Fiordland it even mentions the sandflies:

THE SOUNDS.- General Remarks.- The only natural harbours along the whole extent of the western coast of South island, a distance of about 450 miles, are those remarkable sounds or inlets which penetrate its south-western coast between the parallels of 44° 35' and 46° 10' S. The precipitous and iron-bound coast, through which these inlets penetrate, runs in a general north-north-easterly and south-south-westerly direction; and the thirteen sounds are included within a space of little more than a 100 miles. Approaching this part of the coast from seaward there is so much sameness in the appearance of the land that unless a vessel knows her position accurately, it is not easy, at a distance, to distinguish the entrance of a particular sound, and the smaller inlets seen from a distance of 4 or 5 miles have more the appearance of ravines between high and rugged mountains than the entrances of harbours. In moderately clear weather the coast can be made with confidence.

The larger sounds are generally divided into several arms, penetrating the coast, in some instances for 20 miles, with a breadth rarely exceeding one mile, and studded with numerous islets; the smaller sounds run in for a distance of from 6 to 8 miles with a width of about half a mile, and anchorage is seldom found except at their heads. The shores, which rise almost perpendicularly from the water's edge, are, in the immediate neighbourhood of the sounds, covered with trees.

The most remarkable features of the sounds common to all is their great depth; soundings can rarely be obtained under from 80 to 100 fathoms (146m3 to 182m9), and frequently much greater depths are found. Enclosed as the inlets are by high mountains, the sun is rarely visible except for about 2 hours before and after noon. It would be difficult to find an acre of level ground in any part, and that in impenetrable forest.

Excellent fish of several kinds are abundant in the sounds, and may be caught with hook and line close to the rocks at the entrances, or wherever there is a shoal patch; crayfish are plentiful in the southern sounds, also several species of duck, pigeon, and the weka or wood-hen; those rare birds, peculiar to New Zealand, the kakapo parrot and kiwi are found here; the takahe, one of the world's rarest birds, is believed still to exist in the wild regions of the southern sounds.

The sandflies are of the most virulent kind; they do not penetrate the thick foliage a short distance from the beach, and invariably leave a vessel at dusk, not reappearing until the following daylight. Mosquitoes are also a pest.

In my letter to John Ward, I asked about places to watch out for tide races. He replied:

Tide rips are few as far south as Dusky but can put up quite a severe chop from there south. Places to beware of tide rips are Cape Providence, Gulches Head, Puysegur Point and all the other points from Puysegur to Green Islets. They are at their worst when the tide is running in the opposite direction to the wind or swell.

On 18 December Max and Ainslie rode over from Christchurch, with so much gear, including packs, paddles, sleeping bags, and lifejackets, that only the two wheels at the bottom of a mountain of gear and a headlight in front indicated that beneath it all was a motorbike. Only one minor problem stopped us from heading south - Max's kayak had not been delivered from Nelson. Although it had been ready for weeks, an unsigned cheque had held up delivery. We sent a telegram to Nelson and Grahame Sisson replied saying the kayak would arrive at 7am on 28 December. We hoped the telegraph office had made a mistake with the 28th instead of the 20th.

While Max and I completed the last minute touches to our equipment, Ainslie sorted out the large quantities of food into eight separate lots - five for the kayak party and three for the support crew. As we were both taking Nikonos underwater cameras, I rolled 10 colour slide films and 10 black and white films. In one of the compartments I would carry a small compact Rollei 35 camera for shots on shore. For communication Max had hired from Mountain Radio in Christchurch a radio set that would give us a forecast each night and keep the outside world informed of our progress.

Before going any further, I feel it is necessary to introduce more fully the cast of the expedition. Max, a stocky and solidly built figure, was a keen caver, tramper, skier and paddler. He was not so much a stylish paddler but strong, with great stamina, and always reliable in a sticky situation. He liked a wee dram of port and enjoyed singing raucous Irish folk songs. Having worked in a variety of jobs Max was then employed as a storeman in Christchurch.

Ainslie, tall and attractive with long auburn hair and a Princess Anne nose, was a keen tramper, working part time as a teacher and part time at Alpsports.

Maestro, tall dark and handsome, had black hair and a soup-straining moustache; also a teacher, he was known to his pupils as Mr. Lysaght and to his parents as Matthew. According to Maestro the copy of this book received by his parents will have several pages carefully deleted. He only came out training with me once in the whitewater kayaks but spent so much time upside down in the freezing cold waters of the Taipo River that he declared afterwards, "I'm going to write a submariner's guide to the Taipo River." Needless to say he had an excellent sense of humour.

Lastly myself, with the unlikely nickname of Knuckles, whose character should emerge through the pages.

20 December 1977

The first entry in my log book reads: 'Up with the alarm clock at 6am, and we ate a hasty breakfast, then loaded *Isadora* onto the VW's long suffering roofrack, and started cramming food bags and equipment inside. When the car was nearly full, Ainslie squeezed into what was left of the back seat and more gear was piled on top of her. All the light equipment such as sleeping bags had been stuffed into my Nordkapp's cockpit. After a last goodbye to Gertrude, the friendly four legged woolly lawnmower, we drove into Greymouth hoping that Max's kayak had arrived from Nelson.

The transport truck had just arrived at the depot but we had to chase the driver around town to find out if the kayak was on the truck. When we caught up with him he didn't think there was a kayak, but when he thumbed through his delivery dockets it was there to our relief.

Ten minutes later, after we helped untie the tarpaulin over the load, Max's kayak emerged, covered in a long plastic envelope. With the two Nordkapps side by side on the roof rack, we set off for Invercargill, stopping in Hokitika to ring Maestro and tell him when to meet Ainslie in Te Anau next day. We also bought a newspaper. The weather map looked promising, a large anticyclone approaching the South Island from the Tasman Sea.

Apart from a stone which shattered the windscreen near Fox Glacier, the drive south was uneventful and we were able to have the windscreen replaced in Wanaka. On our arrival in Invercargill we went to the Police Station and filled out a 10 Minute Form; a four page document which must be completed by yachts departing on overseas voyages. Small craft going on coastal cruises were also recommended to fill it in. Its main value was in the eventuality of a search and rescue operation, for it contained details of radio equipment, emergency gear, the craft, the crew, and shore contacts.

With the form filled in, there remained nothing else to do; our preparations were complete. Kind friends bedded us down for the night; all three of us a little apprehensive about commencing the journey on the morrow.

Where the trip began.
Te Waewae Bay,
December 1977

Chapter 2
TE WAEWAE BAY to
PUYSEGUR POINT

21 December 1977 - Day 1

The alarm went off at 6am. Outside it was cloudy and calm. We ate breakfast quietly, then drove to Riverton and west along the coastline to Te Waewae Bay. On the horizon to the south, Stewart Island lay as a sombre grey shadow. A small surf was breaking in Colac Bay with a larger surf breaking a long way out from the beach at Orepuki, but beyond the surf the sea appeared to be settled.

A few miles past Orepuki, the road followed the Waiau River to a bridge at Tuatapere, then swung back towards Te Waewae Bay. At Rowallan Burn the road joined the beach and passed beneath cliffs which continued almost to the road end.

With all the dreams, plans, training and preparation of the last six months about to be put to the test, we were both subdued. Driving beside the bay, Max and I cracked a joke or two and quoted snippets from Spike Milligan's writings, but as Max said, "It's merely nervous energy oozing out from the mouth."

At the western end of the bay, I reversed the car down a narrow sandy track to the beach, parking beside a crayfishing boat on a trailer. There were two tractors nearby; a red one which appeared to be in working condition and a rusty relic which lay half buried by rocks and sand. A rubber dinghy came in through the surf and landed. Two chaps, who had been out diving for crays, said the sea around the first point was calm with little swell.

We set about loading the Nordkapps. The hatches on Max's kayak were so tight he had to use his diving knife to force the covers off. Max attached decklines and a skeg was slipped over the stern of each kayak and tied to the bilge pump. Lastly the clothes went on; a longjohn surfie type wetsuit over a wool singlet, wetsuit booties, sprayskirt, lifejacket, fibreglass helmet with visor for my headgear and a red yachting cloth cap with crossed dolphin insignia on the front for Max. Loading the kayaks seemed to take ages. By now the three of us were a trifle edgy. Questions asked received curt replies.

I had hoped to be paddling by 10am at the latest to make the most of the tide. According to the *New Zealand Pilot,* the tidal stream through Foveaux Strait sets westward with a falling tide, and its influence is felt out as far as Long Point, 20 miles paddle to the west.

We watched as a crayboat powered into the beach, dropped off the deckhand who started up the red tractor and reversed the trailer down into the surf.

Max unloading the kayaks at Te Waewae Bay

Within the space of a minute, the boat had powered onto the trailer and been towed to the top of the beach.

It was time to go. Max and Ainslie embraced each other in farewell, then Max slid into his cockpit, pulled the sprayskirt over the cockpit coaming, and paddled out through the surf. I photographed his departure before joining him on the tranquil grey waters of the bay. We found to our delight, that the Nordkapps fully laden with tent, sleeping bags, clothes and two week's tucker, were more stable than they were unladen, and that the turn of speed was still there despite the weight. Ainslie followed us for a while, walking along the foreshore, then with a last shouted farewell and a wave, we pointed the bows to the south. The trip of a lifetime had begun.

It was 10.30am. The sky was overcast but there was no wind and only a very slight swell. For a few minutes we paddled in silence, both preoccupied with thoughts of what lay ahead. Briefly I wondered how it would feel to be paddling in to the beach from the east, having completed a circumnavigation of the South Island.

After leaving us, Ainslie planned to drive up to Te Anau where she would rendezvous with Maestro. They would then take the first food dump into Supper Cove at the head of Dusky Sound and wait until the two of us arrived.

For the first two miles, the kayaks glided through the dark blue-green water, just outside the breaking waves. The foreshore was a jumble of rounded boulders littered with driftwood with a curtain of forest above.

"There's no turning back," said Max.

"No turning back," I agreed.

Round a small rocky point, we paddled into a bay where in the distance could be seen the remains of Port Craig. After an hour's paddling we rafted the kayaks together off Port Craig for a five minute spell. Here was once a thriving timber milling town with one of the largest mills in New Zealand. A tramline was constructed to haul timber to the mill. The line ran out to Sand Hill Point and west to Francis Burn and sawn timber was loaded from a wharf onto ships in Port Craig. The mill commenced operations in the early 1920's and closed down in 1930. The only visible traces of the former settlement were old wharf piles and a schoolhouse which was equipped with bunks and served as a hut for trampers.

Leaving Port Craig astern, we set off along the bare rocky shoreline towards Sand Hill Point. At 11.30am the wind changed from a slight northerly blowing offshore to a strong south-westerly breeze. We were amazed at how quickly a sou-westerly chop picked up, for within 10 minutes the enjoyable paddling had become a slog. It was our first introduction to this wind with its associate which we

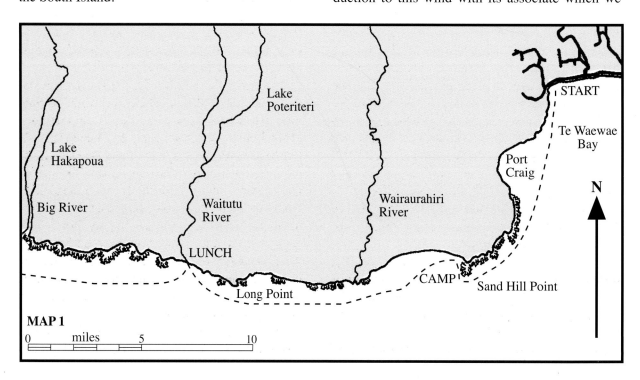

MAP 1

The camp site at Sand Hill Point. Max coaxing a driftwood fire into life

came to call the '11 o'clock chop'.

John Ward, the ranger to whom I had written during the planning of the trip, had sent me some advice on the wind: 'During periods of fine weather you will experience a day breeze off the sea from the westerly quarter. This wind usually comes away about 11am and blows between 15 and 20 knots, putting up a short, steep chop.' How right he was.

For a few moments we found shelter from the wind in the lee of a steep rocky point, before nosing out into it again. We were soon joined by two porpoises who seemed determined to show us how gracefully and effortlessly they could slice through the chop. Our attention was suddenly diverted to a 24 foot long crayboat which overtook us. The two fishermen were heading west to lift their pots.

With short, steep white-capping waves breaking over us, it took over half an hour to cover less than a mile towards the sand-capped top of Sand Hill Point. The crayboat returned in a cloud of spray and the skipper yelled out, "It's too choppy for us." It was too choppy for me too and I tried to convince Max that there would be a good sheltered lunch spot in the lee of Sand Hill Point.

"We're just burning up energy for bugger all distance," I yelled out. Although Max was full of beans and keen to keep on slogging, we poked in through kelp-snagged rocks and reefs, to surf onto a short sandy beach under a vertical cliff.

We climbed around the point looking for a camp-site for although it was only midday the weather appeared to be deteriorating. A grey squall which blotted out the horizon to the south was moving towards us. We found a level spot in the dunes partly sheltered from the wind, then brought the Nord-kapps round the point, through several reefs, to a beach near the campsite.

During lunch a light plane flew over, heading towards Puysegur Point, and half an hour later it landed on a beach a mile to the west of us. A figure left the plane and walked towards us. My immediate thought was, 'that plane's looking for us but we've only just left Te Waewae Bay!' We set off jogging along the beach towards the plane.

There was no cause for alarm however as it was the same chap who had yelled at us from the cray-boat. Alister Sutherland was out for an afternoon shoot. Behind the single seat of the blue Piper Cub, two headless deer carcasses were propped up. In the mornings Alister worked the crays, then if the weather and tide were favourable in the afternoon he took off from Tuatapere, flew along the coast till he spotted a deer, then landed and stalked his prey. What a life!

We chatted for a while about the coastline to the west, then Alister climbed into the cabin, put on a set of headphones, selected a tape cassette, for music while you hunt, then took off into the wind in an amazingly short distance.

In the late afternoon we explored Sand Hill Point, disturbing a sleeping seal in a cave which passed

Max recovering from the effects of seasickness, during a lunch stop at the mouth of the Waitutu River mouth

through the point. Amid the dunes to the west we found the remains of paua feasts from when Maoris stopped over on their way to the Fiords.

At 7.45pm we heard a promising forecast from the Mountain Radio base in Dunedin which reported an anticyclone centred in the Tasman Sea, with south-westerly conditions and occasional showers on the South Coast. Mountain Radio had bases in Christchurch, Dunedin and Invercargill. Small compact radio sets were hired out to tramping and climbing parties. Each evening during the 'sched', an up to date forecast was provided then all parties with sets were called, asked for their location, intentions and if there were any messages.

At 8pm Bill Reynolds at the Mountain Radio (FK) base in Invercargill came on loud and clear. We waited while he rang the met. office for a marine forecast: 'Moderate seas with winds up to 20 knots.'

By 9pm we were snuggled into our new fibrefill sleeping bags, a bit disappointed with only nine miles for the day.

22 December - Day 2

We awoke just as the sun crested the horizon, casting a golden glow on the base of cloud banks to the south. It was a cold morning. South-westerly showers persisted during breakfast and while we packed the kayaks. At 7.40am we paddled out through the reefs to meet the swell. The wind had eased during the night but for the first hour the arms had to push

the kayaks into the chop until the wind died, leaving a long glassy swell rolling up from the Southern Ocean. We were almost a mile offshore heading towards the mouth of the Wairaurahiri River, as the surf was breaking a long way out from shore. South of the river mouth, a shoal of submerged reefs caused the swell to break. For several anxious minutes the kayaks were tossed around with breaking waves showering over us. One swell broke on top of me and I threw in a high brace - holding the paddle blade flat on top of the broken water - before I was left in its wake.

To escape from this shoal area, we pointed the bows south towards the small grey blobs of the Solander Islands on the horizon and when there were no more capping waves around, we resumed course for Long Point, five miles to the west. Approaching the long flat-topped headland with its surrounding cliffs plunging sheer into the surging waves, we could see a white marine beacon on the tip of the point.

After the second hour of paddling we were still half a mile short of the point. We rafted the kayaks together for a spell and Max groaned, "I'm feeling crook. It's probably sea sickness." I was feeling a little woozy in the head but found as long as I didn't look down at the map for too long, I felt all right.

Off Long Point Max's condition worsened. He wanted to land in a bay on the west side of the point but there was no way we could get in through the reefs guarding it as the swell was breaking out level with the point, leaving a cloud of spray as waves pushed half a mile into the bay. We had no option but to push on.

Progress became slower and slower as Max stopped frequently, slumping over the cockpit. Then we spotted a beach by the mouth of the Waitutu River. There was no sign of offshore reefs and the surf looked marginally smaller than what we had paddled past. It was a mile paddle in to the shore before we could ride three foot breakers onto the beach.

On terra firma a nibble of garlic sausage and a few squares of chocolate soon revived our spirits and the symptoms of sea sickness disappeared. To stretch the legs we went looking for a Forest Service hut which I knew lay close to a bridge over the Waitutu River. Half a mile upstream we found a wire rope bridge suspended over the swiftly flowing river and nearby a relatively new but deserted hut.

During the morning the clouds had gradually dispersed until by midday it was beautifully warm and sunny. After a brew on the beach we launched into a near dead low tide. Out from the beach lay a boulder bank over which a small surf was breaking. As Max photographed *Isadora* knifing out through the surf, a wave caught him, carrying his kayak sideways over the boulders but he stayed upright.

The next six miles of coastline revealed rocky reefs extending up to half a mile offshore. We were able to avoid the reefs over which the swell was breaking regularly, by keeping a mile out but now and then a swell would rear up without warning and break where previously there had been no broken water.

Max was 30 yards away when one of those sneaky swells caught me without warning. *Isadora's* bow climbed steeply up the face of the rearing swell, then

it broke over me and I was caught with the paddle on the wave side of the kayak. The kayak flipped over backwards and the paddle flicked out of my hand. In the wake of the departing surge, I was left upside down but still in the cockpit. By dog paddling I was able to keep my nose above water and was happy to see Max turning back towards me.

After what seemed ages I grabbed hold of his kayak's bow and leaning back with my head almost on the deck, I rolled up. The paddle was within reach. I grabbed it and hanging onto Max's bow, I frantically worked the handle of the bilge pump to clear water from the cockpit which had filled when the sprayskirt had partially come adrift with the force of the breaking wave. When another swell almost broke over us, Max pushed me away yelling, "We've got to get clear of this area!" I heeded his advice and further out to sea pumped the cockpit dry. (When the cockpit is partially full, water slops around from side to side, upsetting the kayak's stability.) My confidence shaken, we again turned westwards.

Well offshore, climbing up and over the long swell estimated between seven and eight feet from trough to crest, we approached the entrance to Prices Harbour where for the first time mountains rose up steeply from the rugged coastline. Previously we had been paddling past a low forested coastal terrace with the mountains set back several miles inland.

Only a mile west of Prices Harbour lies the steep sided gorge of Big River which drains out of Lake Hakapoua. Max wanted to head in to the river mouth as he was feeling nauseous and tired. He had also developed a blister on one finger.

Neither of us was too happy. With four hours of daylight left I wanted to push for the boat harbour at Green Islets, seven miles to the west and described in the *New Zealand Pilot*. The harbour would be a

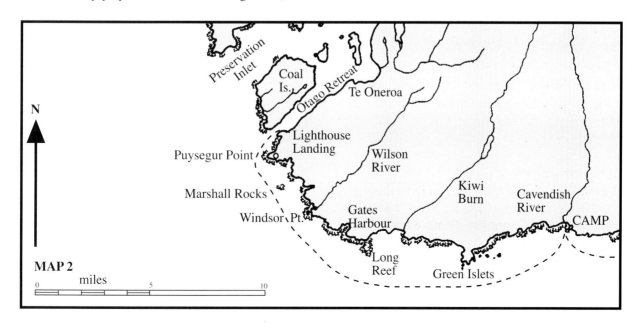

MAP 2

miles

Late evening and low tide, at the Cavendish River mouth

good starting point for the attempt to round Puyse-gur Point. I was feeling fine and rearing to go, and was cheesed off with Max as I thought he wasn't as fit as he should have been. After some unnecessary strong words from me, Max agreed to paddle on until 6pm. "We will never make it at this rate," I grumbled.

West from Big River the coastline consisted of steep rocky bluffs with numerous offshore reefs and rocks over which the swell was surging. The bluffs created a backchop which made paddling unpleas-ant. As we drew level with the Cavendish River, Max had had enough and headed in towards a cove near the river mouth. The cove was protected on one side by a rocky island with numerous reefs and exposed rocks on the other. Leaving the turbulent waters of the reefs, we paddled in to the calm beer-coloured water of the cove, beaching on boulders. There were bluffs on each side of the beach and a dark cascade of the Cavendish River emerged from the forest, tumbling over boulders to the sea.

On a level bank by the edge of the forest, just above high tide mark, we pitched the tent. The amount and size of driftwood in the forest, and steepness of the boulder beach, indicated that huge seas must pound this southern coastline.

Morale picked up as we ate a meal of soup, fried sausages and peas washed down with a hot jelly, and listened to the evening radio sched. FK base in Invercargill said the forecast for next day was for 10 to 15 knot south-easterlies with isolated showers and slight to moderate seas. We couldn't hope for better than that.

As the sun eased down towards its watery grave, the scattered banks of cloud were filled with an intense golden yellow colour. A tapering line of golden light extended from the cove out across the sea to the sun on the horizon. As the sun set, the golden glow turned to red and then to a soft pink colour.

"Well mate," I said to Max, "Red sky at night, paddler's delight."

We pottered among the rock pools, enjoying the cove's beauty in the soft evening light. Only after it was too dark to see any more did we crawl into the sleeping bags.

23 December - Day 3

The attempt to round the notorious Puysegur Point! Conditions were really a paddler's dream; cloudless with no wind and a calm sea. Having read and heard of the wild seas so often experienced off the point and especially since the number of gale days re-corded is the highest for any of the New Zealand weather stations, I regarded this stretch as the first crux of the Fiordland trip. A strong tide race also adds to the difficulties of rounding the point.

I'd already experienced what the seas in the area could be like when in January 1976 I went for a trip on a fishing boat from Preservation Inlet to Chalky Island. I thought my last hours had come but the skipper quietly assured us that it was 'just a normal sea.'

Max and I were so keyed up with the 'aura' of the point that we were slow getting away in the morning. It was 8.30am before we left the boulder beach on top of a surge and headed out towards Green Islets.

There wasn't a breath of wind and the long Southern Ocean swell was almost glassy as the kayaks glided over the crests and down into the troughs. Off Green Islets we rafted up and removed our light nylon parkas. After consuming a glucose sweet we pointed the bows towards Long Reef, four miles to the west.

The first signs of wind were parallel ripples on the swell, then within minutes a strong south-easterly breeze was blowing. It created a confused chop on top of the south-westerly swell. Long Reef is aptly named for in front of us a line of broken white water extended south for almost a mile. I was determined to give the end of the reef a wide berth to avoid a repetition of the previous day's capsize.

The chop grew large enough for the kayaks to start surfing in front of small waves. This gave us little opportunity to look at the rugged shoreline; staying upright and on course for the reddish brown coloured rock of Windsor Point took all our concentration. The Nordkapps were bucking in the chop and occasionally burying their bows.

Off the entrance to Gates Harbour, we paused momentarily to glance in at its temptingly sheltered waters. This half mile deep bay was named after a sealing vessel called the *General Gates*, commanded by a cruel and harsh captain, John Riggs. In 1821 he dropped off a sealing gang in Chalky Inlet. For a while the gang used Gates Harbour as a base, leaving a cache of sealskins before returning to Chalky Inlet. Some 17 months later they were picked up by another vessel but when they returned to pick up the skins, they were driven off by a party of Maoris.

In the late 1800's gold was discovered in the hinterland to the north and for a time the harbour served as a port for the prospectors and a tiny short-lived settlement sprang up.

We made good time along to Windsor Point, the blue sky overhead streaked with long bands of cloud. Even before we rounded the partially submerged rocks off the sloping end of this point, where a few seals were sunning themselves, I could see several small white poles on the next distant headland. They had to be the radio aerials for the Puysegur Point lighthouse. Excitedly I yelled to Max, "Thar she blows, Puysegur Point!"

We sheltered from the chop on the north side of Windsor Point and rafted up. The lighthouse on the tip of the flat-topped headland of Puysegur Point and several small white houses nearby were just discernible. The sea was calmer in the lee of the last point as we paddled inside the barren Marshall Rocks, half a mile offshore.

The swell was surging wildly before crashing on the rocks of Puysegur Point but we pressed on, giving a submerged reef a wide berth. Then we were around and heading towards the entrance of Otago Retreat, situated between the mainland and Coal Island. A section of road leading down from the lighthouse to a landing inside Otago Retreat was visible, but apart from a few sheep and a solitary Friesian cow, there was no sign of life.

Pauline Therkelsen was standing at the window of the principal lighthouse keeper's house when we hove into view. She was startled and momentarily puzzled to see two banana shaped objects closing on Otago Retreat. She called to her husband Robin and with the two relieving keepers, John and Rob, and the two Therkelsen children, they set off down the road to the lighthouse landing.

The tide was against us as we paddled into the entrance of Otago Retreat but the swell was subsiding and after passing through a narrow gap blasted in a reef surrounding the landing, we finally reached calm water. We were no more than 100 yards from the landing when a tractor ferrying several people, emerged from the trees near the end of a long white boat shed. Max and I landed, dragged the kayaks up a sandy beach and had a joyous meeting with Robin, Pauline, John and Rob.

Robin Therkelsen carried a bucket over from the tractor. In it were bottles of cold beer and freshly cooked crayfish. With bottles of beer in one hand and crayfish in the other, we talked nonstop for 20 minutes and discovered we had a number of mutual friends.

"I thought I had seen everything come around the point until today," Robin announced. Then he uttered those magic words, "How about a hot shower and lunch up at the lighthouse?" Without the slightest arm twisting we joined Pauline and her children on a tray attached to the tractor. From the landing the road climbed steeply through a forest covered cutting, then down to the foreshore again for a short distance before climbing again through red flower laden groves of rata trees. From the forest we drove onto the cleared headland, almost surrounded by the ocean, to see the houses and lighthouse.

Pauline served coffee and cakes before starting on a batch of paua patties. While they were cooking Robin gave us a guided tour through the buildings and lighthouse.

The history of the Puysegur Point lighthouse is described in detail in the Begg Brothers' book *Port*

Celebrating our arrival at the Puysegur Point Lighthouse landing in Otago Retreat, with bottles of cold beer. Robin and Pauline Therkelsen, with their children, standing behind the kayaks

Preservation. Preparatory work started on the site in 1875 and in 1879 the light commenced flashing from the top of a 60 foot high wooden tower. During 1908, a telephone line was pushed through the bush from Orepuki to the lighthouse but it ceased to work in 1922 as it was difficult to maintain. A radio station was opened in 1925. In 1942 a prospector living on nearby Coal Island put the radio gear out of action, threatened one of the keepers with a shotgun, then set fire to the lighthouse which was razed to the ground. The burning tower was noticed by the pilot of an RNZAF plane on wartime patrol. The pilot informed authorities and the prospector was arrested by a police patrol two mornings later. By the end of the same year the present structure was completed and commenced operating.

In the porch of Robin's house Max and I were amazed to see a small model of a Hughes 300 helicopter. It stood about three feet high by five feet long, and was built for the children using parts from two helicopters that had crashed nearby in recent years. The console came from a Hiller which crashed while ferrying coal from the hold of a supply ship to the landing. With a red and white aerial projecting forward from the cockpit and a small set of rotor blades on top, it looked like the genuine article. One of the commercial helicopter companies offered Robin a full sized set of blades but he declined the offer. With the consistent strong winds, he could visualize the model chopper autorotating into the air with his children in the cockpit.

Helicopters were used to ferry in food, mail and the relieving keepers who changed over every six weeks. Once there were three families at Puysegur Point but as with all the remaining manned lighthouses on the South Island and the two island lighthouses in Foveaux Strait, there was now only one family. This economy measure had been brought in by the Department of Marine Light Service in a bid to cut costs. Pauline said she regretted the departure of the second family as her children had no contact with other youngsters and the only time she had with other women was when they flew out for their annual leave. Guardians of the point for the previous 18 months, Robin and Pauline had been lighthouse keeping for seven years.

The lighthouse also served as a Post Office, so Robin sent a telegram to the Chief Ranger of the Fiordland National Park at Te Anau, stating that we had arrived safely at Puysegur Point and were heading on to Dusky Sound. We had a look at the radio room from where weather reports were sent out every three hours, 24 hours a day. In one corner of the room was a wooden marker from William Docherty's grave on Cemetery Island, further up Preservation Inlet. Robin had been looking for a way of preserving the timber before replacing the marker at the grave.

In the generator shed were three green generators which provided power for the houses and the light, one going continuously while the other two were in case of a breakdown.

From the 18 foot high lighthouse tower, a single flash every 15 seconds was visible for up to 18 miles out to sea. Passing into the tower, through a steel door, Max and I were intrigued to find curtains drawn around an array of lenses which surrounded a single oval light bulb. Robin explained that during daylight hours the sun's rays, concentrated through the lenses, could create sufficient heat to melt the lamp's mounting.

We must have looked a sight, standing out on the point; Robin in black gumboots with a black beret perched jauntily on his head, Max barefoot, wearing a pair of longjohns that were a few sizes too big so the crutch sagged down to his knees and myself with an ancient pair of pink woollen longjohns which showed more leg through the holes than there was wool.

For fresh venison Robin had to go no further than the edge of the forest. He had a theory that the flashing light at night attracted deer towards the lighthouse.

Pauline's paua patties were fabulous but we weren't able to do justice to the quantity she had made and the leftover patties went into a plastic bag for our lunch next day. An invitation to stay the night was tempting but Robin suggested we should try to round Cape Providence while the spell of settled weather and seas held.

From Puysegur Point, I had planned to paddle up Preservation Inlet to Cuttle Cove and spend a night with crayfishermen based there. In 1829 Cuttle Cove had been the site of one of the first two whaling stations established in the South Island. In January 1976 Keith Dekkers, a long-standing canoeing/climbing/caving friend, and I had used it as a base camp during a caving expedition. We had walked overland into the head of Long Sound (Preservation Inlet is one of the two entrances to this sound, Otago Retreat is the other) from the West Arm of Lake Manapouri, via the Spey and Seaforth rivers to Loch Maree, thence via the Pleasant, Heath and Dark Cloud ranges. We'd organized dinghy transport from the head of the sound to Cuttle Cove. There we spent another week exploring old gold mines, a Maori pa on Spit Island and caves on Chalky Island. Much of the success of the expedition was due to Paatu King, skipper of the crayboat *Cordillera* as he took us on numerous trips around the sounds and out to Chalky Island.

Robin told us that because it was the Christmas New Year period, there were no fishermen in Preservation Inlet. So we changed our plans and hoped by evening to make Cape Providence, 13 miles to the north-west.

At 5pm, with bodies showered clean of encrusted salt spray and sated appetites, we thanked Pauline for her wonderful hospitality then jolted down on the tractor with Robin and John to the landing, clutching the bag of paua patties and some fresh fruit. John gave us a couple of cans of beer for the 'road' then he and Robin motored out beside us in an aluminium dinghy to bid farewell at the gap in the reef.

For Max and I it was a reluctant, almost sad farewell, for we were paddling away from friends, warmth, food and music at the lighthouse and there had seemed so little time to talk. In front of us lay a black overcast sky, an inky sea, the thought of the big swell outside and a near desperate urge to get past Cape Providence.

This was to be the first of many occasions during the Fiordland trip when we would turn our backs on the security of shelter and new found friends, heading ever northwards into the swell. With each farewell came a gut feeling of apprehension and foreboding.

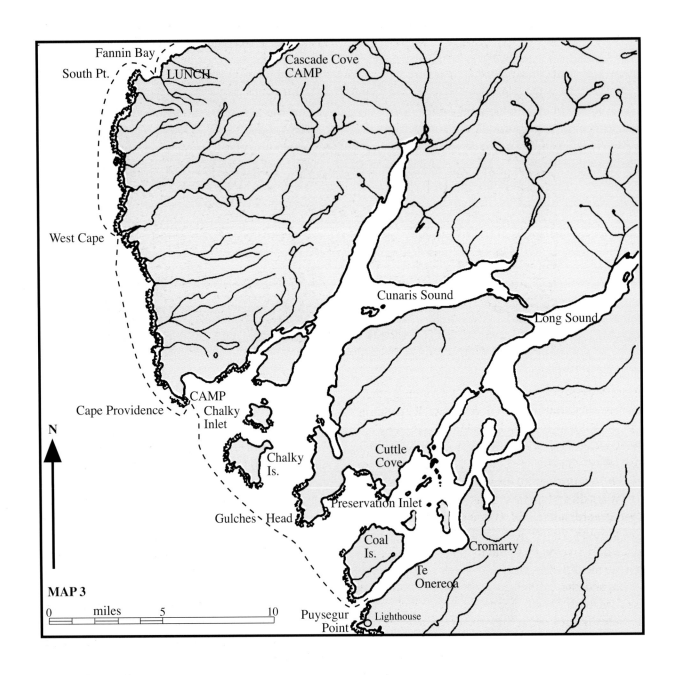

Fannin Bay
South Pt.
LUNCH
Cascade Cove
CAMP
West Cape
Cunaris Sound
Long Sound
CAMP
Chalky
Inlet
Cape Providence
Chalky
Is.
Cuttle
Cove
N
Preservation Inlet
Cromarty
Gulches Head
Coal
Is.
Te
Onereoa
MAP 3
miles
0   5   10
Puysegur
Point
Lighthouse

Chapter 3
PUYSEGUR POINT
to DUSKY SOUND

From Puysegur Point to Cape Providence, there were two possible routes we could take. By paddling inside of Coal and Chalky islands, we would be sheltered from the open sea, apart from an exposed section off Gulches Head between the two islands which is called Broke-adrift Passage. The alternative was a direct line from point to cape, paddling on the seaward side of the two islands. However the inside route would have doubled the distance and since only five hours of daylight remained, we had to take the direct route.

Beyond the calm waters of Otago Retreat we paddled onto a long south-westerly swell to the southern tip of Coal Island, then turned north. The swell was now abeam as we paddled with legs braced and passed the rocky shoreline of the island. With the island astern we moved across Broke-adrift Passage, passing the grey cliffs of Gulches Head, and on towards the white cliffs of Chalky Island which provided a pleasant contrast to the grey of the rocks, sea and sky.

When we were dropped off in Sealers Bay on Chalky Island during the caving expedition, three of us scrub-bashed across the island to Boat Cove where I photographed the seals. Although there were several hundred in the rookery, they must have numbered into the tens of thousands before their near extermination by the sealing gangs. The first Europeans to kill the seals were Captain Cook's crewmen. Full use was made of the carcasses; the skin in the rigging, fat in the oil lamps and the meat for eating. In 1792 the first sealing gang arrived in Fiordland and they took only the skins from the carcasses for the fur trade in Europe and North America. Such was the methodical searching and slaughter that by the 1820s the seals were nearly wiped out.

As we passed in the Nordkapps, keeping well out from the surge and backchop by Boat Cove, the seals were visible as small dark objects stark against the white rock.

From Chalky Island we paddled across the Western Passage entrance to Chalky Inlet, aiming for the numerous rocks and partially exposed reefs that protect Cape Providence. We attributed our swift progress to paua power.

After manoeuvring in through the rocks we crunched the bows onto a short stretch of gravel beach on the tip of the cape. It was 8.45pm, too late for both the 8pm sched with FK base and an 8.30pm sched we had arranged with Robin, to say that we had arrived safely at the cape.

A cave behind the beach appeared to offer a camp site but we soon discovered its floor was a pool of water. We contented ourselves by pitching the tent close by and cooking a meal of sausages and paua patties. Out on the horizon a large tanker moved slowly north. The setting sun suddenly reappeared from behind clouds, tinging the sky with pink. With the promise of a fine day on the morrow, we eventually drifted off to sleep; a 30 mile paddle and a day to remember behind us.

24 December - Day 4

At dawn there wasn't a cloud in the sky and the sea was calm with no wind. What more could we have asked for? I considered the section of coastline from Cape Providence to Dusky Sound to be the second crux of the trip as I had been warned to look out for a tide race off the cape. The *New Zealand Pilot* notes:

> From South point the coast continues high for about 12 miles southward to Cape Providence ... West cape, which projects half a mile westward, lies about midway between them. Shoal ground, with heavy overfalls, is reported to extend one mile offshore between South point and West cape, and vessels should not approach within 2 miles of this stretch of coast.

By 8am we had downed the ritual bowl of porridge, packed and slid down the gravel beach into the sea. As we weaved in and out amongst a maze of reefs and rocks I told Max to keep an eye out for Grono's Cave. One of the sealing gangs had spent considerable time there and in recent years John Hall-Jones, a Southland historian, had uncovered a cache of sealskins. I had explicit directions on how to locate the cave entrance but as we headed north past near vertical bush-topped cliffs, the sun was directly in our eyes and we didn't spot the cave.

We were fortunate to have such a perfect day as there was no sign of a tide race off the cape. For the first two hours it was easy going over a gentle swell as we paddled north towards West Cape on the horizon but as we approached the most westerly tip of New Zealand, a south-westerly sea breeze came away, announcing an early arrival of the 11 o'clock chop. We rafted up and put the skegs down.

The skeg is designed to do for a kayak, what the centreboard or keel does for a yacht, that is keep the craft running in a straight line with a following or beam wind. Since we knew some landings would be on boulders, fixed skegs were set aside in favour of retractable ones. These slid over the kayak sterns like a moulded sleeve, and were attached by a tight line to the bilge pump. The retractable 'keel' section, hinged about a small bolt, was four inches long, two inches wide and quarter of an inch thick. In the 'up' position it lay flush with the hull, while in the 'down' position it projected three and a half inches below the kayak stern. We found the skegs weren't long enough, for in choppy seas they were out of the water for a third of the time. The skegs became permanent fixtures on the kayaks as we never took them off. From a beach we launched with the skegs up and if a wind came away we rafted up and turned them down.

Amongst the rocks off West Cape I could just make out a crayboat and was looking forward to greeting the crew when there was a sudden shout from Max.

Even with the skegs down in the choppy sea, the Nordkapps were broaching side on to the swell. Occasional waves were breaking over us from astern and we had to brace with support strokes to stay upright. Despite this we had been making good progress, surfing now and then in front of the waves. I seemed to be going faster than Max, with a 50 yard lead, when I heard an anxious shout, "I'm sinking. I'll have to land."

Somehow that morning, Max's rear hatch had not sealed properly and waves breaking over the stern had gradually filled his rear compartment with sea water. The stability of a sea kayak is lost when full of water. Max felt certain he was going to capsize at any moment.

Luckily we were level with a small cove on the south side of the cape, with a narrow inlet at its head. The outer edges of the inlet were steep cliffs but where it narrowed I could see a landing of sorts amongst a mess of large boulders under a cliff. Working the surges until *Isadora* was wedged on the boulders, I leapt out and dragged the kayak until it was clear of the sea. I slithered across green slimy boulders to steady Max as he laboured in on the surging swell. He seemed unnecessarily shaken by the incident until I realized what he was so concerned about. Along with Max's half of the food in his rear compartment, was the radio. Max took the hatch cover off and pulled out the plastic bags containing the radio. He untied them, then we watched sadly as sea water drained out of the radio.

I was really cheesed off as we had experienced difficulty in obtaining a set for the trip. With an assurance to Mountain Radio that the radio would stay dry, Max hired a Tait 500 set a week before the trip began. With it there was a feeling of security, knowing we could radio for help in the event of an emergency and receive the radio forecast each evening. Before the trip I was torn between taking a set and relying on our own instincts as a guide to the weather as the Maoris and early sailors had done. Now there was no contact to the outside world. However Max was distressed enough without me saying anything.

After emptying the compartment and repacking the sodden gear, I helped Max launch on top of a surge. As I scraped off *Isadora* left a few patches of yellow gel coat on the rocks.

Beyond West Cape, named by Captain Cook during his first voyage of discovery in 1770, there was no sign of the crayboat we had seen earlier. With the wind, waves and swell combining to push the kayaks along, we made good time along the rocky foreshore. On the northern horizon lay the grey line of Five Fingers Peninsula at the entrance to Dusky Sound.

Max stopped for a moment to take a photograph and his paddle slipped off the deck, drifting quickly out of his reach. He yelled to me to retrieve it but by the time I had slowly turned *Isadora* into the wind, he had backpaddled with his hands until he was able to grab it.

Two miles before South Point, on the southern side of the entrance to Dusky, we passed inside two rocky islands where we found shelter from the chop. The steep rocky foreshore and islands were home to hundreds of seals. From their ledges they barked defiant warnings, sliding into the sea if the yellow kayaks came too close. In contrast to their awkward movement on the rocks, they were gracefully lithe in the sea as they cavorted around the kayaks, poking their sleek, bewhiskered faces up less than a yard away.

I didn't want to leave as the antics of the seals engrossed me as much as trying to capture them on film. The Nikonos underwater camera came into its own when I held it beneath the kayak taking several shots as the seals swam close by.

Max lured me away at last by mentioning 'food' and 'cup of tea'. The sun overhead, with clear water below, allowed us to watch the weed-covered rocks slip by as we paddled towards South Point. Wishing to take a photograph I stopped to sneak up on a large snoozing bull seal sprawled across a rock, as Max paddled into a large cavern beneath a cliff only to hastily backpaddle out as the surge threatened to suck him into the darkness.

With its four mile wide opening, between Five Fingers Peninsula and South Point, Dusky Sound has the widest entrance of all the sounds. We rounded the point and stopped to gaze into the splendour of this Queen of the sounds. A small stream bouncing onto a boulder beach in Fannin Bay beckoned as a lunch spot. At last we were in Dusky Sound.

Soon after we landed, the boulders were draped with drying clothes and sleeping bags. In the sparkling waters of the mountain fed stream Max washed salt out of the radio set and left it in the sun to dry.

Some of Max's food which had also been in the rear compartment, we buried but we figured the peas, pre-soaked and pre-salted, would be fine for the evening meal. A large brew of sweet tea with the last of Pauline's paua patties restored Max's spirits and with the thought of no more open sea for a few days, we relaxed on the boulders, soaking up the marvellous sunshine.

The sound was named 'Duskey Bay' by Captain Cook as he sailed northwards on his first voyage. During his second voyage of 1773 Captain Cook sailed the first vessel into the sound. The most comprehensive book I found on the history of the sound was *Dusky Bay* by the Begg brothers and I had sketched several of the book's historical site maps into the back of my log book.

Our evening destination was a small hut in Cascade Cove, six miles up the sound. As it would be our second evening without a radio sched, I told Max we should try and find a crayboat so that we could get a message out saying our radio was stuffed. I knew Luncheon Cove on the south side of Anchor Island was a base for some of the crayboats working out of Dusky and that sometimes boats worked out of Cascade Cove. Although a trip across to Luncheon Cove involved a few more hour's paddling, I felt we would find crayfishermen at home in Luncheon Cove.

At 4pm *Isadora* left the beach cleanly on top of a surge but Max's kayak stranded on a large boulder as the surge died. His Nordkapp rolled down the side of the rock with Max struggling to stay upright as the next surge came in. It hadn't been Max's day and he let fly with a few choice words before finally floating free. By this time I was hunched up, looking in the opposite direction, choking and snorting whilst trying to suppress my mirth at Max's antics. Still you get days like that on the big trips.

From the shelter of Fannin Bay we paddled out into a bracing easterly wind, slogging into the accompanying chop. Ahead lay Anchor Island, to the south lay Seal Islands while half way across lay Many Islands which shield the entrance to Luncheon Cove.

By paddling into the lee of Many Islands we were able to escape the chop. In one of the narrow channels we spotted a line of cray pot floats and knew the fishermen shouldn't be far away.

The forest grew down to the high tide level on the islands. Beech and rata trees stretched over the water and in some places almost formed a full canopy over the narrower channels. With paddles nearly grazing the rocky walls, our kayaks glided through tranquil sunlit waters until we turned into a narrow passage leading towards the centre of Anchor Island.

For several minutes we paddled northwards until a small beach at the head of Luncheon Cove came into view. Old mooring lines in the trees were evidence of crayboats but there wasn't a sign of one. I was a little disappointed but then around a small point three boats moored side by side appeared. We paddled around behind the *William John, Capricorn* and *Aries*. There was no sign of life until a shouted, "Anybody home?" brought a small boy on deck, closely followed by Russell, a fisherman from Invercargill.

Puzzled, red-haired Russell looked around for another boat until our call of, "We're down here," drew his eyes down to the kayaks.

"Where did you spring from?" he asked with a huge grin.

"Te Waewae Bay. We've paddled around Puysegur."

"I bet you fellas could do with a beer then."

In a flash we climbed onto the crayboat and Russell filled our clutching hands with brown bottles. Waiting for his mates to fly in after the Christmas break to resume fishing, he promised to send a message to Awarua Radio in Invercargill, asking them to notify FK base that we were safe and our radio was out of action.

Luncheon Cove was discovered and named by Captain Cook in 1773 when he lunched there on crayfish. The cove and nearby area are associated with a number of New Zealand firsts. The first house constructed in this country was built to accommodate a sealing gang left at the head of the cove by Captain Raven. In the 10 months before Raven's return, the first ship to be built was nearly completed. Three years later it was used to replace the *Endeavour* (not Cook's ship) which sank during a gale in Facile Harbour, five miles north of Luncheon Cove.

We left Russell worrying how he would convince the other fishermen that he had seen two kayaks in the cove, and paddled out through Many Islands and across a short stretch of water to Stop Island. Here in 1910, the *S.S.Waikare* which was on a West Coast cruise struck an uncharted rock while steaming between Indian Island and Passage Islands. As water rushed in to the boiler room, the captain steered the ship onto the rocky foreshore of Stop Island. All the passengers and crew were safely rescued after a launch carried a message to the Puysegur Point lighthouse.

From Stop Island we headed for the western tip of Indian Island where Captain Cook met a small group of Maoris in Indian Cove, which lies on the eastern tip of the island.

The easterly wind had eased as we rounded Indian

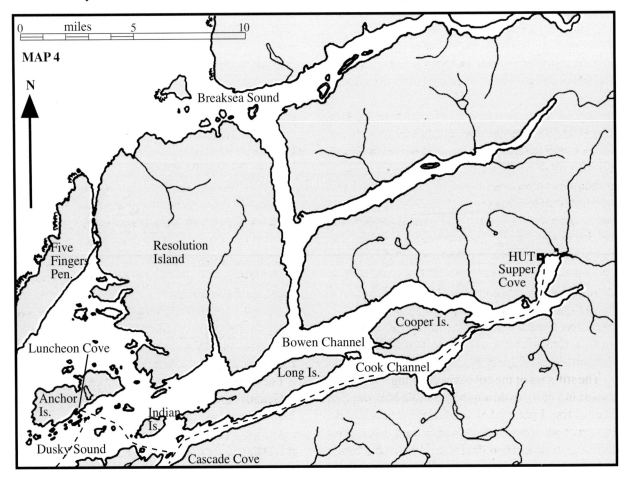

Cascade Cove at dusk, in Dusky Sound

Island, making the paddling easier as we passed the entrance to Pickersgill Harbour where Cook had moored the *Resolution* for over a month in 1773 while his scientists fixed the position of Dusky Bay by star and moon observations. Stumps of trees felled on Astronomer Point are reported to be still evident today. Unfortunately it was too late in the evening for us to explore Pickersgill and we pointed the bows towards Wales Point at the entrance to Cascade Cove.

As the sun disappeared behind steep forested ridges to the west, the wind eased to a whisper, leaving the surface of the cove gently ruffled with only the rhythmic splashing of paddles to disturb the tranquillity of the evening.

The hut which lies on a gravel fan halfway along the southern side of the elongated cove was not visible in the fading light until we were only 300 yards away. At 9pm the Nordkapp bows gently ground onto a gravel beach in front of the hut. Although it was a cramped tin box with four bunks and a fireplace, the hut's setting was sublime. Overhead beech trees spread their foliage while on the surface of the sound, reflections of the mountains to the north were slightly rippled by the breeze.

The stillness of the cove was catching. Neither of us was in a hurry to do anything. While Max thought about a fire, I pottered along the gravel beach looking for fresh water and a Maori cave dwelling that the Begg brothers had described. Where the beach

ended against a rock face, I found a small stream which I followed into the forest to beneath a high grey cliff with a series of overhangs and ledges. Human bones and artefacts had been discovered here and removed for identification. Now only a solitary mussel shell hinted at the former Maori occupation.

As the evening light faded, the heavy green, blue, brown and black colours of forest, water and rock faded into soft yellow, brown and grey autumnal tones. The moon, large and full, rose up slowly above the mountains. It required little imagination to understand why Captain Cook called this sound 'Duskey Bay'.

The stillness of the evening was broken by the noise of a motor and we glanced up to see an aluminium crayboat barrelling down the cove. Attracted by a wisp of smoke from Max's fire, the boat changed course and ran onto the beach in front of us. We introduced ourselves and met Gerard Murphy and Brian McCarthy.

Gerard gestured towards the hut. "You're not going to spend the night in this dump?"

Brian agreed. "Grab your sleeping bags and come and spend the night on our barge."

I hesitated. "What about some tucker?"

Gerard dismissed the objection. "We've got plenty. All you need is your sleeping bags."

We had a fast ride around to the other side of the gravel fan, in their 24 foot long boat driven by twin

80 horsepower Mercury outboards. Max and I had visions of a rusty old barge with a shed on top and were amazed as Gerard powered alongside a 130 foot long former tugboat, now called the *Kiore*. Serving under the name *Awarua* as a tugboat at the port of Bluff, she was bought by tender for $5,000, the same amount that it cost to have her towed around to Cascade Cove. *Kiore* had three freezers for crayfish tails, cooking facilities and sleeping accommodation for the crews who worked out of the cove.

Under the light of a tilly lamp, Gerard and Brian finished tailing their day's catch of crayfish, throwing the tails into a mesh basket attached to the side of the boat. Then after a five minute trip around the cove to wash them, the bags of crayfish were stored in a freezer. The boat's name was printed on the outside of each plastic bag. Eventually the frozen tails were flown out to Te Anau by float plane or by helicopter, the latter landing on a helipad built on *Kiore's* stern.

The fishermen apologized for a lack of lighting and hot water for a shower as the generator had broken down. Down in the depths of the galley, Brian lit a gas stove and whipped up a meal of spaghetti, tomatoes, crayfish and corned meat. We learned the boat we had seen earlier off West Cape was the 40 foot long *Hercules* which was tied up alongside another boat called *Bucko*. The other fishermen had flown out for the holiday period.

It was Gerard and Brian's first season crayfishing out of Dusky. Gerard was a builder by trade but for the past few years he had been crayfishing and hunting deer from a base in Big Bay. His nightmare was of a large wave breaking over their boat. For the past seven years Brian had been with Environmental Forestry in Queenstown, culling chamois and goats.

Their boat *Mac*, with a sealed bulkhead between the hull and the self draining deck, was considered unsinkable. It had no wheelhouse or cabin, just a shield or windscreen to keep the wind and spray off them. Gerard explained that working close in to rocks, they needed the power of the outboards to sometimes escape from being swamped by waves. Craypots were expensive at $40 each so Gerard and Brian economized by making 108 of their own which they dropped off as far south as West Cape. Although I thought Luncheon Cove would be completely sheltered from all seas, Brian said during a recent 60 to 80 knot south-westerly blow, it became too rough for the boats and they moved across to Cascade Cove.

We talked about kayaking, crayfishing, hanggliding and skiing until the early hours before climbing into a bunk with an alarm clock set for 7am. It was a fine way to spend Christmas Eve and I could think of nowhere else in the world where I would rather be.

25 December - Day 5

After the clanging of the horrible alarm clock woke me, I roused the rest of the troops with a rowdy rendition of 'Jingle Bells.'

The day's objective for Max and I was a Park Board hut in Supper Cove at the head of Dusky Sound, some 20 miles to the east, where we hoped our support party would be waiting; for Brian and Gerard a normal day's crayfishing.

Breakfast completed Brian and Gerard gave us a ride round to the kayaks. With a parting gift of a sack of crayfish for Christmas dinner they wished us, "good kayaking" and we wished them, "good fishing."

Shortly after 10am on this perfect morning we glided the kayaks over the mirror surface of the cove, our destination Cook Channel which would lead us to Supper Cove. The noise of an airborne motor became audible then we saw a float plane fly overhead in the direction of *Kiore* but by an abrupt turn above us, the pilot had spotted us. We heard the plane land near the tug and soon after take off again. To our surprise it glided down and landed in front of us and the motor stopped. We paddled over to meet the pilot.

"It's a great day for it," I said. Mike Neison agreed but said he would rather be with his wife and family in Te Anau. The previous August, Mike had flown myself and three other climbers into the head of the Tasman Glacier for a ski mountaineering trip. Mike had just dropped off food and mail to *Kiore* and on the previous day had flown Maestro and Ainslie with our food dump into Supper Cove. We wished him a merry Christmas and watched as he took off in a cloud of spray.

We continued paddling into a light easterly wind blowing along Cook Channel, with the steep forested mass of Long Island to our left blocking a view of Acheron Passage, up which we planned to paddle in a few day's time.

After an hour the wind swung around to the southwest and it soon had the kayaks barrelling along, surfing occasionally in front of small waves. The combination of following wind and the hot sun on the sack of crays tied to *Isadora's* stern deck caused it to smell more like a crayboat than a kayak.

With Long Island astern, we paddled by Cooper Island passing through a narrow gap called Nine Fathoms Passage. From the gap we could see the entrance to Supper Cove and without a word being spoken, the pace gradually stepped up as we were both keen to meet our support party. However neither kayak could stay in front for long as first one then the other would take off in front of a wave, surfing past for 50 yards or more. While one was getting back on course after dropping off a wave, the other kayak would shoot past.

There are two coves at the head of Dusky Sound, the narrow elongated Shark Cove which continues an easterly trend of the sound, and the broader north-south trending Supper Cove into which the Seaforth River drains. From the moment we turned into Supper Cove our eyes were searching the shore for a sign of the hut, either a white wisp of smoke or a grey cloud of sandflies lurking above the door. Only when we were less than half a mile away did the green painted door of the hut become apparent, but our excited shouts and yodels of greeting echoed unanswered from the cove's steep walls.

Side by side we slid past a grey rocky promontory where the hut sat in a cleared area, to nose the kayaks onto a gravel beach. We found food and wine in the hut with the support party's gear but no sign of them and no mention of their intentions in the log book. The sou-sou-westerly wind was still pushing a chop into the cove and we were concerned that our friends may have rowed down the sound to meet us.

Trees and bushes were soon draped with our sleeping bags and damp clothes. After tailing the crayfish as Gerard and Brian had shown us, we settled down in the bunks for an afternoon siesta.

A shout from the cove woke us. The kayaks had been spotted. Then Maestro burst out of the trees singing:

We wish you a merry Christmas
We wish you a merry Christmas
We wish you a merry Christmas
And a happy New Year.

Ainslie and Maestro had gone to meet us all right but they had rowed past Nine Fathoms Passage into a broader channel on the north side of Cooper Island. While Maestro was taking his rifle for a walk in the forest, we had slipped by.

For the next hour we talked nonstop; yarns, stories, incidents, all interspersed with sips from cans of beer. The float plane flight with Mike had been thrilling, highlighted for Maestro when Mike put on his thigh waders and insisted on carrying them to shore in piggyback fashion. The four of us were feeling on top of the world, revelling in the isolation and beauty of the cove.

The description of Christmas dinner is taken more or less straight from 'Dear Diary':

MENU

Thirstquenchers	- Leopard Export Lager
Dinner wine	- Sylvaner Riesling 1977 (a good year for riesling)
Main course	- Crayfish a la kayak
	Peas, undehydrated and salted in the Tasman Sea, Tomatoes, carrots
Dessert	- Fruit salad a la Ainslie with a topping of instant pud
Fourth course	- More Sylvaner Riesling

The social reporter for the *Fiordland Times* would have described the scene as follows:

'Ainslie is looking extremely demure in orange hot pants with matching wool singlet and ankle length leather gumboots, decorated with steel D rings. Maestro is wearing the latest creation from Te Anau, the all natural hairy leg look, in smelly faded blue shorts with a touch of paint primer, and topped off with a black woollen singlet, also a bit smelly, his accessories including a leather sheath knife. In a sporting wool outfit, Knuckles is wearing baggy trousers with specially ventilated holes for the knees and chest hugging singlet. Outfitted with the latest woollen outfit from Christchurch opportunity shops, Max is wearing a pink singlet and drooping longjohns.'

The meal progressed satisfactorily. Toasts were drunk to Gertrude, the pet sheep at home in Runanga, and the women on our minds. Maestro disgraced himself with a rather naughty version of 'Partridge in a Pear Tree' and this was followed by numerous versions of 'We wish you a merry Christmas'.

"Where's the Christmas cake then?" asked Max.

From her pack Ainslie produced a delicious looking fruit cake which was promptly devoured without undue ceremony.

"Where the roast venison then?" I asked, looking at Maestro.

Maestro waved a vague direction with his hand, "Over in the next valley." Prior to the trip Maestro had circulated rumours that he was a great white hunter and had boasted that the Fiordland venison recovery helicopters wouldn't be able to compete with him. Maestro continued, "You've done nothing but moan since you arrived here. For three days I struggled over the mountains carrying all this food and booze for you ungrateful lot."

Max picked up the axe, quipping over his shoulder as he went out the door, "I'm going to cut this conversation short."

"There's no wine left," I sobbed draining the dregs from a flagon.

Maestro commiserated. "I should've flown in another dozen. But I tell you what, there'll be piss rolling down the fiord in George Sound."

By late evening the wind had died away. Maestro and I fished from the Park Board dinghy on the smooth surface of the cove, with perfect reflections all around. Beneath the dinghy the water was so clear we could watch the fish swimming around our fishing lines and darting in to steal the bait. I was happy lounging back in the bow, dangling a bare hook and gazing at the peaks while Maestro had the time of his life catching three blue cod and a baby groper. The previous day at Supper Cove, Maestro had caught his first fish ever. Later at the hut he was chastised for using the baby groper for bait.

"You're groping for words," said Max.

26 December - Day 6

By unanimous vote, Boxing Day was declared a day of rest. Gear was repaired and dried in the sun and food was sorted out for the next stage of the trip to Doubtful Sound. Mid-morning Maestro noticed from the hut window, "some large fish jumping out there." Armed with cameras we gave chase by kayak and dinghy but the Dusky dolphins were feeding and not willing to play, and soon outdistanced us.

Supper Cove was also named by Captain Cook during his survey of the sound in 1773. A party from his ship *Resolution* spent a night on the banks of the Seaforth River. Next morning they fired at some wildfowl and disturbed a party of Maoris also camped by the river, which was thenceforth called the Alarm River until it was subsequently renamed the Seaforth.

In 1910, ten moose were liberated from a steamship at Supper Cove. The small herd was protected until 1923 but the first trophy was not taken until 1929. The last recorded kill was in 1952 when a bull was shot in the Wet Jacket Arm area. Since then there have been no recorded sightings of moose.

By kayak and dinghy Maestro and I travelled to Shark Cove where the Begg brothers had found the site of Docherty's hut. In 1877 William Docherty discovered a small copper deposit on a steep ridge above the entrance to Shark Cove but within a short time the ore ran out. In the years following the failure of the mining venture, Docherty lived a hermit's life in the hut he had built on the south shore of the cove, prospecting and surviving on fish and birds that he and his dog caught. In 1894 he journeyed in a small dinghy to Cromarty to join the Preservation Inlet gold rush. Two years later he died there and was buried on Cemetery Island by his fellow miners. It was the marker from his grave which we saw in the radio room of the Puysegur Point lighthouse.

We spent a pleasant afternoon exploring. Maestro even took his rifle into the forest for some exercise but although there was plenty of sign, hoof prints and droppings, roast venison was not to be on our evening's menu.

When the time came to head back, Maestro was introduced to the 11 o'clock chop which had come away with a vengeance especially for dinghies. Off one rock Maestro stayed in the same position for several minutes unable to make progress into the chop, sweat dripping off his face.

"You'll have to give up smoking," I told him.

He ignored my comment and asked, "Is there anything hanging beneath the dinghy?" With a puzzled expression on my face, I paddled alongside but couldn't see anything dragging beneath the dinghy.

"No," I replied.

"That's all right," said Maestro, "I thought my ring had fallen out."

After dinner, during which we were treated to a tin of ham, Ainslie produced a bottle of port which she had kept carefully hidden from the three males. Maestro then told us a bedtime story.

When he was working as a shepherd on a high country station out the back of Kaikoura, the other shepherd who lived in an adjacent room of the whare had a problem with mice getting into his dog biscuits. After several nights, Maestro was sick of hearing, "chew, chew, I'll teach you to chew, chew, chew on my dog biscuits", followed by the sounds of thumping and crashing as various objects were hurled at the offending mice, who seemed to lead a charmed life, emerging unscathed from the battle only to rip into the dog biscuits the following night.

Eventually a solution was reached. Maestro would go around next door the next time he heard, "chew, chew, chew", with his .22 rifle loaded with blanks.

The showdown came one night but although the solitary mouse may have been deafened by the noise of the fired blanks he was as lively as ever. So Maestro began firing live rounds at the mouse, pulling over bookcases and cupboards for a better field of fire (well it wasn't his room after all). Still the mouse survived.

Sadly to relate the poor mouse finally succumbed to the great white hunter when Maestro cornered him and stood on him. Such a gallant stand against overwhelming odds deserved a fitting funeral. At 1.30 in the morning, while the other shepherd played the last post on his piano accordion, Maestro ceremoniously threw the mouse out the window.

The boss's attitude later that morning was most unpleasant. Disturbed sleep and bullet holes in the walls of the whare did not go down well.

From his prone position in his bunk, Max threw one of the corroded batteries from the drowned radio at Maestro. Then he reached out to the table, picked up a plastic salt container and sent that flying at the recumbent position of Maestro in his bunk.

"What was that for?" asked Maestro.

"Assault and battery," grinned Max.

Chapter 4

DUSKY SOUND
to BREAKSEA SOUND

27 December - Day 7

At first light the air was still and the sky overcast. Our next stage was to paddle up Acheron Passage into Breaksea Sound. From there we would venture onto the open sea again for the journey to Doubtful Sound, where the support party had arranged for our second food dump to be left on a tourist launch. Based at Deep Cove, *Friendship* journeyed daily down the sound during the tourist season. We arranged a tentative rendezvous with Maestro and Ainslie on *Friendship* in three day's time.

Neither member of the support party was cheerful at the prospect of a two day impending tramp out to Lake Manapouri. Maestro had to carry the extra weight of the drowned radio and despite assurances that 'the scenery is terrific' and 'the track is easy to follow,' he was desperately hoping for a float plane to drop a party at Supper Cove and the pilot to offer to fly Ainslie and himself out to Te Anau.

All four of us were packed and ready to go at 8.30am. We made a last dash out of the hut, through clouds of ever present sandflies that were waiting in ambush just outside the door. Maestro and Ainslie stood on the rocks in front of the hut and said goodbye.

"See you in Doubtful Sound," were the parting words from Maestro. Max, determined to get in a last pun said, "That's doubtful." We had no idea then of how nearly prophetic those words were.

As the kayaks knifed through the glassy surface of the cove, the echoes of our parting shouts disturbed the tranquillity of the morning. We were almost mesmerized by mirror reflections of each other as we paddled side by side and stroke for stroke. As we turned west out of the cove four sleek Dusky dolphins swam gracefully past, showing no sign of interest in the kayaks.

I stayed in close by the shore with my paddle almost grazing the rock walls, the branches of southern rata spreading its foliage overhead. By the time we reached Cooper Island a breeze had come away, in our faces for a while then from astern.

With bladders about to burst from the early morning cups of tea, we stopped by a rocky shelf on the north side of Cooper Island. I suffered a short bout of 'eye of needle country' diarrhoea which must have resulted from all the rich food consumed at Supper Cove. Two miles later, in Bowen Channel, Max said, "Guess what I forgot?" I just looked at him assuming he had left something at Supper Cove.

Max and Paul setting off from Supper Cove. Photo: Ainslie Lamb

"My camera is back on Cooper Island where we stopped for a leak!" Max turned back after we agreed to meet at Passage Point, at the southern entrance to Acheron Passage.

I continued down the sound staying close to the forest edge, looking for deer and giving cheek to a pair of pied oyster catchers who became rather noisy if I paddled too close.

On two rocky points I saw chicks of some sort of sea bird. At first I thought I had discovered the elusive takahe but they had webbed feet. Their buff colour blended perfectly with the rock ledge they stood on, and it was only their movements that gave them away.

I felt like a rest so I stopped on a rock ledge and waited for Max. The sandflies and I had a game of tennis. They scored a point every time one of them bit me while I got one each time I consigned one of their number to oblivion. I developed a mean smash. It wasn't long before I spotted a tiny black dot making rapid progress down the sound towards me. Happily it was Max and not the grand-daddy of all sandflies.

During the morning dark grey clouds in rolls and folds had ominously enveloped the mountains to the west. Although there was only an eight knot breeze

behind us, the swirling waves of cloud around the peaks suggested much stronger winds aloft. All the indications were of a cold front coming in from the Tasman Sea. Little did we know what was waiting for us in Acheron Passage.

As we approached Passage Point, there appeared to be a surf running southwards into Dusky Sound. It was hard to imagine why there were whitecaps in front of us when we were paddling in relatively calm water. On rounding the tree-covered rocky point we suddenly found ourselves battling to make headway into a strong wind, which was kicking up a chop, two to three feet in height. It seemed that the north-westerly wind was concentrated in the northerly trending passage. For half an hour the Nordkapps bucked into the chop and we made only half a mile progress. Frequent strong wind gusts buffeted our bodies and whipped spray off the whitecaps, stinging our faces. All we could do during these gusts was a sculling stroke, keeping one end of the paddle moving over the surface of the water to stop us from being flipped over. We had paddled past a small cove on our right and were barely making progress by steep rock bluffs when I yelled to Max, "This is pointless. It's tired arm country." Max agreed, so we gingerly turned around and ran back into the cove we

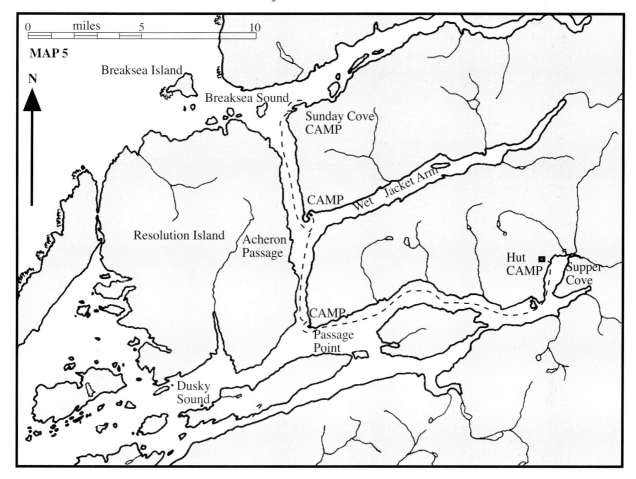

had passed, the wind chasing us along.

Deep in the cove was a sheltered gravel beach and we ran the bows of the kayaks onto it. A mountain stream fed into the cove and over the years it had built up a gravel fan or delta, providing the only small area of level ground for miles around.

A few drops of rain fell from the dark sky overhead and we pitched the tent under trees in record time.

While Max rummaged around for some food I sat out on a rocky ledge and dangled a piece of bacon rind on a hook in the water. Before long Max brought over two steaming bowls of apples, rice and raisins. The occasional rain squall passed down the sound as we sat huddled on the rock, the warm bowls on our laps.

"It's getting beyond the beyond, when you have to spoon the sandflies out of your dinner before you can eat it," I said ruefully.

We agreed that we would much rather be aground on the bar of the Milford Hotel, looking out at the sea from bar stools. For a brief moment the sun found a gap in the clouds, scattering its rays through the foliage of rimu, rata and beech trees that leaned over the sea. Then it was gone and our gaze returned to the whitecaps rolling down the passage. Max hit the sack but I stayed on the ledge, watching the tide come in until it was too dark to see the water's edge.

28 December - Day 8

Acute lethargy confined us to the sleeping bags until 6.30am when we emerged into the sandflies to find an overcast sky and a choppy sea still running down the passage. Despite the inclemency of the weather, we decided to try and reach Breaksea Sound.

The *New Zealand Pilot* describes the passage as follows:

> Acheron passage, the arm connecting Dusky and Breaksea sounds, lies between the eastern side of Resolution island and the mainland. High, precipitous, wooded mountains rise on either side to elevations of 3,000 to 4,000 feet. There are depths of 200 fathoms in mid-channel, and so perpendicular are the sides of this passage that depths of 80 fathoms are found within a few feet of the shore.

We left the shelter of the cove and paddled onto the chop, finding that it wasn't as bad as it had been the previous afternoon. We must have started during a lull, for within half an hour the wind had increased to such an intensity that we were scarcely making headway. Spray was whipped off the wave crests into our faces, and during one particularly violent wind gust, Max's paddle was flicked out of his left hand, athough he didn't lose grip with his right. Fortunately the strong gusts were visible, barrelling down the passage as a dark band on the water's surface and we were able to brace ourselves, using the paddles for support. All we could do at these times was watch the loss of precious ground covered as the kayaks drifted backwards without the forward momentum of paddling.

Points jutting out only a few yards into the passage afforded noticeable shelter on their downwind side but as though to make up for this, the wind seemed to be twice as strong on the upwind side, where it turned the chop into a breaking surf. By hugging the rock walls in an attempt to escape from the full force of the violent seas, we had to contend with a back chop which added to the confusion of the surface of the passage.

There was only one possible landing spot, a narrow rocky beach fed by a tumbling stream between Passage Point and Wet Jacket Arm. My leg which had gone to sleep was sufficient excuse for me to call out to Max that I wanted to land, and we went in through a small surf onto the rocks. Wet Jacket Arm is the only side arm in the passage and is roughly halfway between Dusky and Breaksea sounds, on the mainland side. On the Park Board map a sea plane landing was shown in a cove on the northern side of the entrance to the arm. Max was keen to try to reach it as we assumed it would afford a sheltered landing. I wasn't looking forward to a second dose of northerly chop, but since we had stopped in such an unpleasant, bleak and windswept spot, we agreed to push on.

Slowly we worked northwards into the chop until with aching shoulders we drew level with Wet Jacket Arm, and headed for the cove which was set behind a long forested headland. Once in the shelter of the headland we were able to relax and watch willy willies whipped up in the centre of the passage, snaking their way over the sea as moving columns of spray.

At the head of the easterly trending arm, a tall peak stood out against a grey sky, patches of last winter's snow on its western slopes. From the arm we paddled into a beautiful cove with a bush-clad island on our left and at its head a sandy beach where a stream fed into the sea. Although the water in the cove was barely ruffled, the wind hadn't eased, for from the beach we could see spray flying out in the passage and the trees on the skyline were writhing and swaying with the wind gusts.

Since it had taken two and a quarter hours to paddle only five miles, we decided to wait until late evening before attempting to reach Breaksea Sound. As we explored the forest we found an old bungi shelter and the remains of a fire place, probably a shooter's camp from long ago.

Alongside the island, I tried to catch fish on a hook baited with a fatty piece of bacon. To my surprise I felt a nibble and pulled in a red cod. I dropped it flapping in Max's cockpit between his legs and before he had time to object, told him to take it ashore and deal with it. I didn't want to kill it. Between us we caught enough cod for the evening meal. We could have stayed fishing but the sandflies won in the end, they were biting faster than the fish.

The grilled fish, with a parsley sauce topping, were delicious. The manner in which we had to eat was not so pleasant. Our bodies swathed in socks, longjohns, bushshirts and parkas, leaving only hands and mouths exposed, we stood side by side in the smoke from the fire, all in an attempt to escape the incessant biting of the sandflies. I commented in my diary: 'The wind is still blowing from the north, but it is easing slightly. It's clear to the south apart from the clouds of bloody sandflies.'

At 7.30pm we set off for Breaksea, happy to be paddling out of 'Sandfly Cove.' It wasn't until we rounded the headland that we felt the full force of the wind. The gusts were as violent as ever. We crouched low in the cockpits, scarcely making headway. During one particularly strong, buffeting gust I caught a glimpse of Max as he nearly capsized. 'Here we go,' I thought but he recovered and without a word being spoken we slowly turned the kayaks and let the waves surf us back to the shelter of the headland.

We tried again an hour later but still couldn't make headway up the windswept waters of the passage. Delighted to see us return to the beach, the sandflies did their darndest to deprive us of as much blood as possible before we could pitch the tent and dive into our sleeping bags.

29 December - Day 9

At first light Max braved the sandflies and paddled over to a chasm where he was able to look into the passage. There was no change and we had a good sleep in. Later when I was about to leave the tent I attempted to distract and disperse the sandflies lurking outside the zipper by pushing out my wetsuit, socks and sleeping bag. Then I made a spirited dash for the beach where I skipped around on the sand, furiously fanning the sandflies while I tried to ease my bladder. The alternative to this was to use insect repellent. We carried with us a bottle of dimethyl phalate, the basic ingredient of the commercial product 'Dimp' and although the liquid was effective in keeping the insects away, its application on the tender parts of the body or as Max stated, "Putting Dimp on your donga," was extremely painful.

The wind seemed to have eased slightly by midday and with a little persuasion Max conned me into making yet another attempt to reach Breaksea. This time we managed to slowly fight past the headland. I found the paddling slightly easier close under the cliffs but still had to contend with a back chop off the grey walls.

As we struggled northwards, conditions deteriorated. On the downwind side of each small rocky point there was a lull then a real fight to struggle past the point. With only half the distance to Breaksea behind us, the situation was pretty grim. I kept glancing at the passage walls hoping to find a landing. I didn't mind how long we had to wait for the wind to drop, as long as we could get ashore safely. A jumble of rocks with a stream tumbling out of the forest into the sea caught my attention and I pointed out to Max the possible landing.

"We'll smash the kayaks on the rocks if we try to land there," he yelled.

While I tried to rest my arms for a moment in the lee of a point, Max pushed on for a reconnoitre, then drifted back and called, "There's nothing better." For a minute or two we rafted the kayaks together and pumped the cockpits dry, for with the chop breaking continually over the Nordkapps we had taken some water.

Less than a mile up Breaksea Sound from the northern end of Acheron Passage is Sunday Cove where I knew there was a freezer barge for the crayboats working out of the sound. With this thought in mind we again turned into the chop. Our progress was painfully slow. The Nordkapps rose over the wave crests then thumped down into the troughs, sending a shower of spray back in our faces.

Crouching or rather cringing low in the cockpits, we held the paddle shafts at a low angle to avoid being flipped over by the strong gusts. The visor on my helmet was nearly blown off during one violent gust. My arms and shoulders ached with the strain of continuous paddling.

In the next shallow bay I yelled to Max and pointed at a narrow, vertical sided chasm with a steep boulder beach at its head. We both nosed in for a look but it was out of the question to attempt to land as waves were dumping heavily on the boulders. To our horror we found the wind and waves were driving us further into the chasm, despite our frantic efforts to backpaddle out. I was hard up against the left hand wall and could not make progress backwards even after pushing against the rock wall with the paddle. Max manoeuvred to turn around and in doing so jammed *Isadora* hard against the sheer rock wall. I was drawn closer and closer to the bumper dumpers but with Max clear, I was able to slowly turn and, with the bow scraping on the rocks,

inch my way out of danger. It was a close shave and I was none too happy with Max for using me as a turning point but by the time I turned northwards he was 100 yards away.

My glasses were a real curse. Droplets of spray stuck to the lenses and distorted my vision. I wished that like some modern fishing boats I had revolving windows to flick the water droplets off. Finally after struggling up to one last point, we were able to turn eastwards into Breaksea Sound, leaving the willy willies out in the passage astern. The chop eased off as we paddled towards Sunday Cove and half a mile west of it, we turned into a long narrow cove, the thought of a sheltered landing before us. At its head we reached a steep boulder beach, littered with what appeared to be the remains of a fishing boat. Waves were dumping onto large rounded boulders but we both landed safely on top of a wave, leaping out of the cockpits before the surge could drag the kayaks back.

I stretched out on a flat piece of ground, happy to be alive and on dry ground. Too tired to say much, we sucked on glucose sweets in an effort to restore some of our burned up energy.

Very faintly I could hear the rhythmic thumping of a motor, the sound appearing to come from Sunday Cove. A steep sided valley, half a mile long, was shown on the map linking this cove with Sunday Cove. Rather than paddle around, we decided to walk through to see if anyone was home. We followed deer trails through the forest, littered with fresh sign, until the masts of two fishing boats were visible through the trees. The noise of a motor on a large barge was enough incentive to retrieve the Nordkapps and paddle around.

Captain Cook left Pickersgill Harbour in late April 1773, and sailed *Resolution* up 'New Passage', which was later renamed Acheron Passage, into Breaksea Sound. He continued up the outside coast leaving the sound unexplored but thought there may have been an inland connection between Breaksea and Doubtful sounds. In 1791 Breaksea was first mapped and explored by two British naval vessels under the command of Captain Vancouver. No inside connection with Doubtful Sound was found.

In the shelter of Sunday Cove we found a large modern barge with three crayfishing boats tied up alongside and a rocket shaped fuel tank anchored astern. A smaller barge with two more crayboats was moored 200 yards away. While Max held *Isadora* I checked the larger barge for signs of life but apart from a freezer motor thumping away, no one was home.

A little disappointed not to meet any fishermen we paddled into a black sandy beach and pulled the kayaks up under the trees. Old food dumps, rusting craypots, discarded sea boots and an old kerosene heater were strewn across the beach. A Park Board sign stating, 'This is a fishermen's storage area' had been thrown into the ferns behind the 'stored rubbish'. Although the Park Board had full control over crayfishermen's actions on land, it had no jurisdiction at sea which is why the crayfishing bases were all afloat.

We had a brew of soup after pitching the tent but morale wasn't too buoyant as we stood in a shower or rain, trying to extract some warmth from the bowls.

Dear diary noted: 'With the rain, the wind died and it's calm at the moment; more like the Fiordland I know; grey seas, grey sky, dark grey forest and misty squalls of rain passing over.'

Late evening Max was in the tent while I was walking along the beach trying to make out the fishing boat names for dear diary. A different sounding motor caught my ear and I watched a big beautiful crayboat cruise into the cove. After mooring, one of the fishermen rowed over in a dinghy and took us out to the barge. We were pleased to meet Richard Squires and Don Hamilton, both from Stewart Island. In August they brought *Ocean Ranger* up from 'The Island' as they called home, where they had been crayfishing for the past few seasons.

Richard told us that during the previous two days the sea had been so rough that they had managed to lift only one craypot. Earlier in the day they set off to visit *Kiore* down in Dusky Sound. After a few games of pool with Gerard and Brian, Richard cruised up to Supper Cove to have a look at the two madmen in the yellow kayaks. They saw our note in the hut log book that we had headed for Doubtful Sound.

They offered us a beer and a gloriously hot shower with shampoo for the matted hair. An entree of fried sweetbreads was followed by a mouth watering feed of roast chops, fresh potatoes and fresh cabbage. If that wasn't enough to make us eternally grateful, Richard opened a can of peaches after fetching a block of ice cream from the freezer. What a treat! It was no comparison to our skimpy feed of dehi-beef curry which we had earlier tried to convince our stomachs was the evening meal.

If I seem to dwell on the subject of food, it is because on such a trip where the influences of the rat race, pressures of society, and the temptations of wine women and song were not present, we were reduced to the very basic ingredients for human survival, food and shelter. A steaming bowl of rice and beef curry was something to look forward to at the end of the day. Any change from the 'hard tack'

was indeed a bonus.

Don and Richard's home during the crayfishing season was a 40 foot long by 25 foot wide fibreglass barge, with fuel stored below in the flat hull section. A diesel fired stove also heated the shower water. The crayfish freezer was centrally situated with bunk rooms, kitchen and toilet at one end of the barge and the shower and storage area at the other. The motor which maintained the freezing temperatures in the walk-in freezer also charged a set of batteries which powered the lights, radio and cassette when the motor was turned off. The broad flat barge roof served as a landing pad for helicopters which flew in supplies and flew out frozen bags of crayfish tails.

In the early hours of the morning as I lay snuggled inside a sleeping bag on a top bunk, with the noise of rain drumming on the roof just above my head and the wind outside, my basic survival needs were more than satisfied.

30 December - Day 10
Awarua Radio's early morning forecast was not encouraging: 'A south-westerly change with 15 to 20 knots winds and moderate to rough seas.' Richard tried unsuccessfully to pass on a radio message to Te Anau that we had arrived safely in Breaksea Sound.

As Richard was keen to see how much gear had been lost during the last two days of rough seas, he offered to take our kayaks on *Ocean Ranger's* deck and drop us along the coast. Regretfully I told him, "Thanks but we have to start from here again, otherwise it wouldn't be right." However the prospect of joining Don and Richard and seeing the crayfishermen in action was much more appealing than the thought of paddling into the wind and rain.

Ocean Ranger was a modern 36 foot long aluminium boat, equipped with radar, depth sounder and two rotating windows at the front of the wheelhouse. Richard explained that visibility was impaired with glass windows for the water from a wave breaking over the wheelhouse took some seconds to run off. When the boat was working close to reefs, those brief moments of blurry vision were critical. The rotating windows spun at high speed, flicking water off as soon as it hit the glass. Richard switched on the radar set as we cruised past Entry Island, and headed for the northern side of rugged Breaksea Island where the first pot was set. Between the island and Oliver Point, on the northern side of the sound's entrance, the boat began ploughing into a moderate northerly swell. The wind had swung to the south-west and was creating a lively chop on top of the swell.

Approaching the first brightly coloured float bobbing on the grey waves, Richard brought the boat into the wind with the float on the starboard side. Don was waiting with a small grappling hook and with a single practised throw hooked the line. Hauling in enough slack until he was able to wrap the rope three times around a side winch, like a small capstan winch, Don pulled the rope in until it was taut against the craypot on the sea bed below. Then he flicked the rope over a snatch block, mounted on an arm extending over the side of the boat, and ran the rope through a pot hauler winch. This labour saving device took in the rope without assistance, Richard working a clutch in the wheelhouse. The rope whizzed through the winch, flicking water off in an arc until the black netting of the craypot broke the surface.

Richard then threw the clutch and helped Don swing the pot around so the door or gate opened inboard. A rubber strap holding the door closed was released and the pot tipped onto its side, sending an extremely lively catch of crayfish and fish cascading onto the deck. While Don replaced a 'sniffer' pot containing mackerel, Richard wired two bait fish inside the pot and the door was fastened.

Using the echo sounder to find a good position for the craypot, Richard yelled to Don who pushed it overboard, watching carefully that the line fed out without tangling.

As Richard turned the boat northwards, searching for the next float, Don squatted down amongst the excited crayfish and began measuring the length of their tails, throwing the undersize ones nonchalantly over his shoulder into the sea.

Rain squalls blowing up from the south-west, reduced visibility to less than two miles. A huge surf pounded against the bleak grey cliffs as Richard and Don lifted their string of pots. Some were close to reefs over which the sea was surging, others were out in the open sea. Several pots contained fish called Maori chieftains, one had a resident octopus which was sent smartly over the side and in another a starfish. A conger eel in one pot was kept for bait.

As the wind strengthened and the chop worsened I started to feel seasick. Max stayed in the shelter of the wheelhouse while I stood with feet braced and spread wide apart to combat the rolling of the boat. I had as much of my body as possible wrapped around the exhaust funnel from the engine room, trying to extract a little warmth. The southerly change had brought a marked drop in air temperature. Although I was cold and feeling queasy, my sympathy was for Don working on the exposed stern and buffeted by the full force of wind and spray. He was wearing a huge yellow, hooded parka, almost two sizes too large for him and it reached almost to the deck.

Richard Squires and Don Hamilton loading a bag of crayfish tails, at Sunday Cove in Breaksea Sound

There had been so much heavy rain overnight, the steep coastline was alive with a myriad of mighty torrents, small cascades and leaping waterfalls, all racing each other through the cliffs, rocks and trees to burst on the foreshore below in showers of spray.

The catch was patchy; several pots contained five or six mature crayfish, some had only one or two, and a few were empty. One pot lay in very close to a rocky reef over which the swell was breaking continuously. *Ocean Ranger's* bow was almost in the broken white water when Don snared the float with the grappling hook. With motor in reverse, Richard called to Don, "Be quick with this one," as he watched over his shoulder for a sneaky swell. For a brief moment the rope ran in cleanly, then it stopped with the winch groaning under the strain. The pot was firmly held by rocks on the sea bed below. For what seemed an eternity but must have been closer to 30 seconds or so, Richard edged closer to the reef, the pot hauler winch straining to tear the pot loose. I wished I was back on the barge, or in the Milford bar, anywhere other than on *Ocean Ranger*.

Suddenly Richard flicked the rope free from the winch and the boat surged seawards with the motor at full revs in reverse. "It's not worth it," he declared. I had decided that minutes before as we approached the reef.

By now I was feeling decidedly ill. Fortunately

there were only 12 more pots to lift before Richard turned the bow for Breaksea Sound, opening *Ocean Ranger* up to her top speed of 18 knots. Leaving a huge wake astern, the boat surged over the swell crests, dropping with a stomach lifting thump into the troughs. Don wasn't feeling too good either so Richard called it a day despite having another 30 pots set south of Breaksea. From the wheel he called to me, "Could you find your way back to Sunday Cove?"

"No worries," I replied, taking the wheel as Richard joined Don on the stern, measuring and tailing their catch.

All thoughts of sea sickness were forgotten as I stood with feet braced behind the wheel, a grin from ear to ear, totally engrossed in keeping *Ocean Ranger* on a straight course for the entrance to Breaksea. Richard and Don were happy with a bag and a half of tails for four hour's fishing.

During the afternoon, Gerard, Brian and Russell came up from Dusky Sound for a social visit. A combination of monopoly and drinking games kept us busy until dinner time. After the seven of us tore apart two roast chickens, I retired to the solitude of my sleeping bag and drifted off to sleep while a spirited argument continued to rage as to who was the world's greatest boxer.

Chapter 5

BREAKSEA SOUND
to DOUBTFUL SOUND

31 December 1977 - Day 11

Max and I rowed ashore at first light, dropped the tent and packed the kayaks. Although the sky was overcast with occasional showers of rain, there was no wind in the cove. Max wanted a more substantial breakfast than just a cup of coffee but I wanted to be well underway at sea before the wind came away.

From the cove we had four miles to paddle to Breaksea's entrance, then 14 miles of open sea to Dagg Sound. On the map there appeared to be one possible landing place if sea conditions deteriorated, a mile wide by a mile deep bay halfway between the two sounds where Coal River entered the sea.

Gerard, Brian and Russell had spent the night on the barge as no one had been capable of finding their way home in the dark after all the drinking games. We thanked Richard for putting up with and feeding the two madmen in the kayaks and said goodbye to the fishermen from Dusky. Richard assured us that he would transmit a message that we were leaving Breaksea and heading for Doubtful. Don was still in his bunk at 8am when we paddled away from the barge.

From the still, dark waters of the cove we paddled into a light south-westerly breeze and pointed the bows towards the grey mist-wreathed outline of

Breaksea Island. Beyond the lee of the island, a big swell was running and rain drops were splattering on my helmet as we headed northwards, keeping well out from the rocks and reefs. Although we were making reasonable progress with the swell pushing the Nordkapps along, we were none too happy. The swell, crashing against the rocks and reefs, created a strong back chop which added to the general lumpiness of the sea, and threw the Nordkapps around.

Each rocky point along the steep inhospitable coastline first appeared as a grey shadow in the murky distance. Point followed point until at last a deep bay opened up in front of us, into which we could run and escape off the swell. Although we had reached shelter it soon became apparent as we closed on the beach that we would have a struggle to reach shore. A huge surf was running onto the beach. The wind was whipping spray off the wave crests like a 'dream of white horses'. I did not like the idea of landing as the surf was frighteningly large but Max didn't want to push on to Dagg Sound. "The south end will be best," I shouted, but Max wanted to try paddling in over the Coal River bar. While Max went for a look, I waited and tried to reassure my

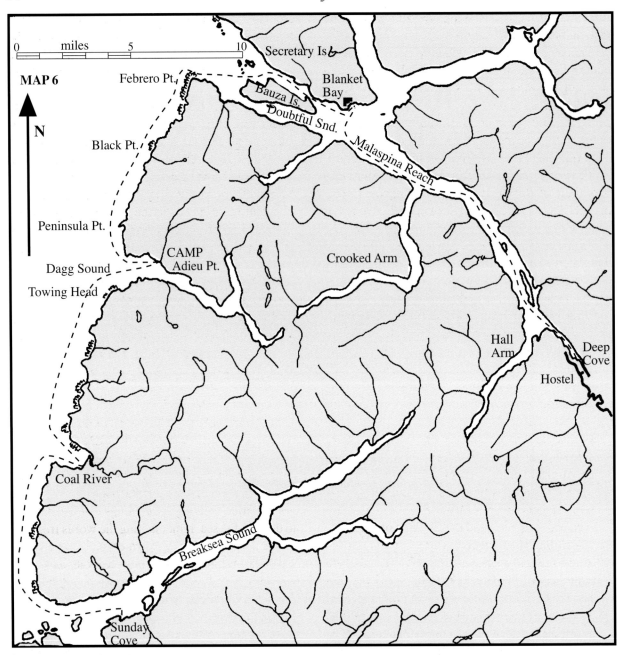

MAP 6

thumb that it wasn't really that cold. Despite a wetsuit, wool singlet, parka and thin plastic gloves over my hands, I was cold. Max returned after retreating from the bar and we paddled slowly along to the south end of the bay, watching for a break in the surf. Max was in closer than me when a set of three large waves began smoking towards the beach.

In retrospect I know that waves are reaching nine or ten feet in height when they start smoking. Heart in mouth I watched Max disappear behind the leading wave of the set, then his stern broke through the crest of the wave as it was about to break. He paddled hard to turn and face the second wave of the set. Again I lost sight of him, only to see his Nordkapp shoot over the crest, leaving the sea completely and describing a graceful arc before plunging into a trough. On the last wave of the set, he took to the air again, landing with a great splash. Paddling furi-

ously he continued out to sea before turning and joining me. "I felt the bottom of the kayak flex," he declared.

The surf was smaller at the very southern end of the beach where sand met the rocky bluffs of the southern shore of the bay. We waited for a lull between sets. It arrived suddenly and we both set off paddling rapidly for the beach. For a time I surfed in on the face of a steepening wave, broaching right just before it broke, then bounced shorewards buried in foam, with a high brace keeping me upright. Left in its turbulent wake, I rode a second foaming wave sideways onto the beach. Max broached left and reached the sand after two exciting rides. It had been quite a frightening experience.

The wind was bitterly cold and I shivered as we carried the kayaks up into the dunes. To warm up, I slipped into the top half of my wetsuit, which had full length arms, and tried to thaw out my hands by placing them in my armpits.

Sheltered in a belt of withered trees we sat on either side of the white spirit stove, slurping a body warming brew of soup. Max pointed along the shore and I looked up to see a deer casually walk onto the beach. Silently we watched the doe walk gracefully to the water's edge before returning to the dunes.

In fine weather Coal River would be a beautiful spot to camp, with a black sandy strip in front of a wide belt of dunes, with a broad lagoon further inland. Amongst the dunes we found barren flat areas with stones spaced around on top of the sand as if some visitor from ages past had carefully placed them there. Straw coloured grass with patches of a darker green variety grew on the dunes facing the beach, a stark contrast to the black sand.

While we warmed up on shore, the wind strengthened offshore. Whitecaps which were not offshore when we arrived at 11am were now plainly visible. I wanted to sit tight until the sea settled but Max wanted to push on to Dagg Sound. I was sure the wind was too strong but was silly enough to agree to paddle out for a look.

We sat in the Nordkapps on the damp sand, waiting for a wave to lift us off. I was reluctant to part with the top half of my wetsuit, and decided to leave it on, even though I anticipated it would restrict my arm movements. What a mistake!

Even before we cleared the first line of breakers, Max was upside down and struggling to right his kayak. I managed to plough through the wave that had capsized Max but backpaddled through the slop to help him empty out. During a second attempt, and only after a struggle, we both cleared the lines of breakers. To the west the sky was ominously dark, almost as black as the sand on the beach we had just left astern.

Before leaving the bay we struck a large south-westerly swell which was complicated by a short, steep chop. Cutting into the swell as we paddled out of the bay wasn't too bad but as soon as we turned northwards, the conditions were worse than I had anticipated. During the morning the seas had been marginal for paddling. Now they were angry and dangerous. The wind was over 25 knots and gusting to much higher speeds. Although the bay was only half a mile astern, there wasn't a show of reaching it by turning back. It was now a survival situation. We were totally committed to reaching Dagg Sound.

As the first large swell broke over me from astern, *Isadora* was buried in a white broken surge. I slapped the paddle hard down on the surface of the sea and managed to stay upright, but in my stomach welled a sudden tight feeling that this was nearly the finish.

Not daring to look over my shoulder to see what the next swell was about to do, I steered *Isadora* as she surfed in front of the seas, using the paddle as a rudder to stay on a semblance of a course parallel to the coast.

Succeeding crests did not break for a while and I glanced quickly over my shoulder, only to be horrified by the size and steepness of the seas. After a while I could tell from the angle of *Isadora* on the face of a wave whether or not it was going to break. Max and I never got very close to each other; he would be surfing towards the grey cliffs desperately hanging in a left rudder with his paddle while I was shooting out to sea, my paddle straining in the right rudder position. Only in the brief moments as a swell crest dropped me backwards into its wake, could I slip in a few quick paddle strokes.

We rafted the kayaks together only once to pump out the cockpits. As we clutched grimly on to each other's decklines, the conversation was brief.

"I'm willing my cheeks to stick to the seat of the kayak," said Max.

"I'm scared shitless!"

We were able to give the partially submerged reefs a wide berth as perpetual clouds of spray and broken white water made them easily visible. The concentration involved in staying upright was so intense that I was unable to keep a train of thought going. I tried thinking about things that had nothing to do with the sea; remembering the words from the song, 'Don't Cry for me Argentina', but I could never get past the second line without having to concentrate on either a slap support or a high brace. The wetsuit was constricting my arm movement and making me more tired than I should have been.

During the really strong gusts all we could do was crouch as low as possible in the cockpits, supporting ourselves with one end of the paddle on the water and the other end up in the air, acting as a sail. One recurring thought I had was, 'If we ever get out of this, I will never venture out to sea again unless it's a veritable millpond.'

I can remember little of what the coastline looked like, apart from a few glimpses of grey rock bluffs shrouded in mist, and steep forested hillsides climbing into the cloud. Although the swell was breaking all around, not every crest capped on top of us. Once a wave broke there was usually a break of ten unbroken waves before the next one broke.

After what seemed an eternity, we paddled into Dagg Sound. It was named after Captain William Dagg who in order to pick up a load of sealskins, had sailed *H.M.S. Scorpion* into Dusky Sound in 1804.

The size of the swell diminished as we ran eastwards, searching for a sheltered landing. The map showed a long narrow cove on the northern shore of the sound, near Adieu Point, with two streams draining into it. Entering the cove we found a shingle beach at its head with a dumping surf. Exhausted I watched Max who was 100 yards in front, paddle towards a gap between the beach and steep rock walls on the east side of the cove. Through a narrow gap, where a stream entered the sea, I watched Max ride in through a small surf and paddle out of sight behind the beach.

I relaxed with only a short distance to go, content to keep my tired arms going around slowly, paddling towards where Max had disappeared. Without warning a strong gust hammered into the cove, driving *Isadora* towards the rock walls. Slowly she came around as I paddled hard on the left side, until we were parallel to the beach. I had almost reached the stream mouth when something made me glance to the right. A steep wave was about to break over me. I barely had time to get into a high brace position before it buried me and hurtled the kayak shorewards. To my eternal amazement I was left high and dry on top of the beach as the wave receded, Max grabbing hold of *Isadora* before we could slide down the steep face of gravel.

Max had paddled upstream to reach a lagoon behind the beach. After landing he climbed on top of the beach, just in time to see the wave break over *Isadora*.

High tide had banked up the lagoon and we were able to paddle upstream to an island which had the only flat ground in the area. On each side of the stream, the forested hillsides were steep and soggy underfoot. The trees were being tossed around by the wind as we struggled to pitch a flapping tent.

For me the last straw was to find that the top had come off the honey pot in my food bag, creating a sticky goey mess. At 9pm after a meal of beef curry, we crawled into our sleeping bags. By the light of a candle stub, I noted in my diary: 'What a way to spend New Year's eve!'

1 January 1978 - Day 12

My diary declared: 'The New Year. Big deal!' We slept in until mid morning as the previous day's paddle had really sapped our physical and nervous energy. By traversing around a line of bluffs we were able to reach a rocky point and gaze out to sea. The waters of the sound were quiet; at sea a large swell but as yet no whitecaps. Eight miles of open water separates Dagg Sound from the entrance to Doubtful Sound, a mere two hours' paddle in good conditions.

Although it was approaching 11 o'clock chop time, we decided to have a look outside. The ritual

The beaut wee campsite on the north side of Dagg Sound

morning bowls of porridge were bolted down in between packing and dressing. From the lagoon we nosed out through the gap and through a low surf. Max cut in close under the rocky point which had served as our lookout and was bombed by a breaking swell. He emerged unscathed but dripping water from the broken wave.

But our run was too late. Off Castoff Point, on the northern side of the entrance to Dagg Sound, a south-westerly breeze had come away. To the south a squall blotted out the horizon and above us the sky was overcast. I had sprained my wrist during the previous evening's landing and despite an elastic bandage for support, the tendons were aching with the strain of paddling.

"It's marginal," I called to Max as we drew level with Castoff Point. The breeze was freshening and whitecaps had already started to form. With memories of the previous afternoon's paddle, vivid and fresh, we turned and paddled back to our island campsite.

Morale sank to a low ebb for it was now obvious we would not be able to keep our rendezvous with Maestro and Ainslie in Doubtful Sound. The sandflies were not helping either as they attempted to carry out blood transfusions, from us to them. As a last resort to restore morale, we resorted to food. It's marvellous how a feed of pancakes smothered in butter and peach jam can lift kayaker's spirits.

The sun suddenly reappeared after several day's absence and we covered sunny patches beneath the

Paddling out over the bar of the small stream on the north side of Dagg Sound

trees with the blue, orange, red and yellow colours of drying clothes.

Dear dairy noted: 'It's a beaut wee campsite; the sounds of surf and running water all around; an overweight native pigeon has been flopping around in the trees; had an early tea just in case the chop dies down and we can split to Doubtful.'

Late afternoon we sat out on the rocky point and watched the clouds disperse. Out to the horizon the sea sparkled, almost as if it was as happy as we were to see the sun. The sullen grey mood of the overcast morning was replaced by a warm serenity.

In an attempt to beat the 11 o'clock chop next day, the porridge was set to soak on top of the stove which was ready to light.

2 January - Day 13

We paddled out over the bar of the stream at 7am, less than an hour after waking up; our earliest start yet. The sky had returned to normal, overcast. Off Castoff Point the long south-westerly swell was glassy and we turned the bows northwards towards the jagged grey rocks of Peninsula Point.

Long ribbons of bull kelp swirled around the rocks of the point, rising and falling with the surge. As we neared Black Point, ripples on the glassy swell announced the arrival of a northerly breeze. Our speed dropped as the wind and chop picked up.

Beyond this gloomy point, where the forest rises up steeply to the tops at a height of 3,200 feet, we could see the seaward edge of Secretary Island which forms the northern shore of Doubtful Sound. After three hours of paddling, we rounded Febrero Point, passing well inside of the two rocky islands called the Hares Ears, and entered Doubtful Sound.

Half a mile up the sound we rafted the kayaks together in the lee of a large rock and celebrated our safe arrival with a few squares of chocolate. The elastic bandage around my wrist, while allowing me to paddle painlessly, had restricted the flow of blood to my fingers. I transferred the chill of my fingers to my armpits waiting until the normal flesh pink colour had chased the white numbness away.

We were relieved and happy to be inside Doubtful Sound with the knowledge that seven miles of easy paddling would take us to the Blanket Bay Hotel where hopefully we would find crayfishing boats and fishermen. The tension that had hung over us like a bad dream since Breaksea Sound disappeared, marked by a bout of verbal diarrhoea and renewed attempts to find the worst pun of the trip.

Captain Cook named 'Doubtful Harbour' as he sailed northwards along the coast in 1770 but the first European didn't enter the sound until February 1793 when two Spanish sailing vessels under the command of Alessandro Malaspina anchored off

Febrero Point. From a longboat Don Felipe Bauza explored and compiled the first map of Doubtful Sound. Landing on Bauza Island he encountered the Fiordland sandflies and promptly named it 'the island of Bauza or of mosquitoes'. The sandflies must have created quite an impression.

We paddled along the northern shore of Bauza Island, enjoying the pleasant change of not having to worry about capsizing and to be able to soak up the scenery, the calm waters of the sound, the tree daisies in bloom and the trees, rocks and occasional fishing boat gliding past.

As the Nordkapps neared the entrance of 'The Gut', a 200 yard wide channel separating Bauza and Secretary islands, we saw a gravel beach at the head of Grono Bay. Here in 1890 Captain John Grono established a base for his programme of seal extermination. He explored and named Thompson Sound, which joins Doubtful Sound to the sea on the northern side of Secretary Island.

The tide was ebbing and flowing swiftly through The Gut and we ferry-glided across to the shore of Secretary Island. (Ferry-gliding involves turning a kayak at 45° to the current which helps push it towards the opposite bank.)

From The Gut it was less than two miles to the Blanket Bay Hotel, which is situated near the eastern tip of Secretary Island. In several books I had read of the famous hospitality found at the 'hotel', a base for many of the crayboats working out of Doubtful Sound. I was also keen to see what the establishment looked like and also if beer was on tap.

But at midday as we paddled into the bay's entrance there was no sign of the building. We were definitely in the right place as two fishing boats lay at anchor on the far side of the bay. Our eyes scanned the foreshore and our noses sniffed for the whiff of a beer. To our delight the hotel came into view on the back of a small island. It was certainly a sight for sore paddlers' eyes as we gazed at the green corrugated iron 'Hilton of the Wilderness'. In accordance with Park Board policy it was perched on piles above the bay. Three boats were moored alongside a wharf which was covered with stacks of craypots.

Side by side the Nordkapps powered towards the hotel and we ran the bows onto an old wooden slipway, beneath a picture window in one wall of the hotel. Someone shouted and the window filled with faces showing a variety of expressions; some surprised, a few bleary eyed and several looks of utter astonishment.

We climbed a ladder to the deck and introduced ourselves to Gilo and Caddy and several other fishermen. I asked Gilo if the tourist launch *Friendship* usually steamed this far down the sound from Deep

Cove, but he told us it went only a few miles into Hall Arm. Our food dump was on the launch but Gilo said a fishing boat was heading that way in a few minutes and we would be welcome for the ride.

Max and I had earlier decided that if the weather forecast was favourable we would forego the food dump and push on to George Sound where our next re-supply was waiting. However the lunchtime forecast was for 20 to 25 knot north-westerly winds and since we had lost some food when Max's rear compartment flooded off West Cape, our supplies were running low.

Delicious ham and tomato sandwiches clutched in one hand, we dragged the Nordkapps onto the stern of Graham Well's boat *Rangi* and within half an hour of arriving, we were waving goodbye to the fishermen on the wharf.

Rangi, a 50 foot long wooden boat, was one of the largest crayfishing boats we came across in Fiordland. Graham had been fishing for 15 years, initially out of Nelson and Westport and for the last two years out of Doubtful Sound. He was more than satisfied with what most people would say was a dangerous and lonely way to earn a living and told us he was determined to keep on fishing as long as he could.

The surface of the sound was calm as *Rangi* cruised out of Blanket Bay but the north-westerly soon came away and chased the boat up Malaspina Reach. For Max and I it was a change to be able to look at the scenery without having to make the arms go round. Accepting a ride with the kayaks had not been an easy decision for me as I was determined from the start not to take any short cuts or accept any lifts, but as the overall trip would not be disrupted I felt the decision was justifiable. Four dolphins surfed in front of the boat, taking turns to ride the bow wave. Graham told us their movement through the water by the bow could slightly increase the boat's speed. It had something to do with reducing friction or drag of water on the boat.

As we cruised past Hall Arm Graham pointed to a white boat and told us it was *Friendship* showing tourists some of the waterfalls near the head of the arm. When we reached Deep Cove Graham cruised alongside several fishing boats and we helped him moor *Rangi* against a huge cantilevered wharf. Graham intended heading out to Manapouri for a visit to the big smoke.

We didn't have to wait long before *Friendship* returned and after the tourists had disembarked, we went down a gangway onto the launch and introduced ourselves to the skipper, Les Hutchins.

"You wouldn't happen to have a box of food on board for a couple of kayakers?"

Les promptly pulled out a cardboard box from

1. *The South Island kayak odyssey begins. Max Reynolds paddling out from Te Waewae Bay*

2. *Low tide has exposed the massive boulder beach by the Cavendish River mouth.*
Late evening, with calm sea conditions fortunately for the landing, and launching next morning

3. Max at the sheltered campsite on the north side of the entrance to Wet Jacket Arm

4. Max at sunset off the entrance to Looking Glass Bay, after a late evening paddle from Caswell Sound

underneath a bench where it had remained for the last week.

We watched two laden tourist buses depart for the 12.5 mile drive over Wilmot Pass and down to the power station at the West Arm of Lake Manapouri, where fast launches waited to convey the tourists across to the township of Manapouri. The road was built to enable transport of equipment and heavy machinery from cargo ships in Deep Cove to the power station site at West Arm.

The controversial Manapouri power scheme was designed primarily to supply cheap electricity to Comalco's aluminium smelter near Bluff. Work commenced on the scheme in 1963 and was completed in 1971. From Lake Manapouri, water drops down through vertical shafts to spin the turbines of an underground power station, from where the water continues down a six mile long tail race tunnel to discharge into Deep Cove. A former trans-Tasman liner, *Wanganella,* was moored in the cove in 1963 where it served as a floating home for the workmen.

The original scheme involved raising the level of Lake Manapouri. Only after a protracted major battle between conservationists and the Government was a considerable reduction made in the proposed rise. The low price Comalco pays for power is still a source of contention with a great many New Zealanders.

Opening the cardboard box, we began sorting the food dump. As always one of us would sort the packets, bags and containers into two piles of roughly the same weight and volume, then the other would choose which pile he thought was marginally smaller and lighter. A half eaten bar of chocolate turned up and we wondered if a hungry tourist had succumbed to temptation. We found out later that Maestro and Ainslie were the culprits. By the time we had tucked the food bags into the stern compartments, Les had finished washing down the decks of *Friendship* and we waited for him by his small Mini van.

"Any chance of taking the two kayaks on your roof to Manapouri?" I asked.

I'm sure Les thought we were serious for he replied, "I could take the two of you but you'll have to leave your kayaks behind." We laughingly declined his offer and he sped off in a cloud of dust, hurrying to catch the last launch from West Arm.

Then there was just Max and I walking around the old hostel which had been used in recent years as an outdoor education centre for schoolchildren until cracks appeared in the ground above the foundations and it was condemned. Above us patches of drizzle darkened the sky and limited visibility down the sound. Without the voices and motors, the cove had a desolate inhospitable feel as we walked past locked

Fishing boats moored to the wharf at Deep Cove, in Doubtful Sound

buildings and the deserted fishing boats.

We paddled out of the cove into a short, steep chop. Hugging the southern shore of the sound, we made reasonable progress into the wind until we reached Hall Arm. The full force of the chop now hit us and I caught only a glimpse of the arm's sheer walls disappearing gloomily up into the clouds. A fishing boat materialized out of the grey squally distance of the sound and headed past for Deep Cove. Level with Crooked Arm we rafted the kayaks together for a spell. I was feeling tired and Max attempted to revive me with a few squares of chocolate.

When we heard the sound of a motor we turned to see *Towai* cruising back down the sound. Max paddled out to see if we could hitch a ride but the few squares of chocolate seemed to have given me a second lease of energy and I was determined to reach Blanket Bay under my own steam. As Caddy brought *Towai* in towards me, I waved him away, yelling, "I'll race you." Caddy shadowed me down to Espinosa Point where the wind eased to a light breeze, a welcome relief for my tired arms. I crossed the two mile wide Pendulo Reach and with shoulders aching, I arrived back at the hotel at 8pm, pleased to have made it under paddle power.

The troops at the hotel had kept warm a feed of crayfish for us, and that was just the entree. The meal that followed, roast lamb chops, salad, peas and fresh potatoes confirmed the reputation of the famous hospitality to be found at Blanket Bay. During the evening radio sched with Te Anau, Gilo passed on a message that we had arrived safely at Blanket Bay. He also arranged a radio sched with Maestro and Ainslie at the Mt. Cook Airlines office next morning.

Max and I enjoyed the exquisite pleasure of a hot shower after which we chatted with Gilo into the early hours of the morning. We learned the large tanks behind the hotel were not for beer but contained diesel for the fishing boats. *Endeavour*, a 72 foot long oyster boat, brought the fuel around from Bluff. Built some ten years ago, the hotel served as a refuelling depot for the crayboats and also as a storage depot for the catches of crayfish. At the time the tails were flown out to Te Anau by float plane but there were plans to add an extension to the wharf to allow helicopters to land. Fresh water reached the hotel through a hose which passed beneath the bay and was fed by a stream which had been dammed on Secretary Island.

Above the dining room table it was hard not to notice a long, tightly wound coil of wire which was attached near the light to the ceiling. The coil was from a broken down freezer unit. Some hotel visitors are told that at night, when sandflies are attracted to the light, they fly up inside the coil and get so dizzy, they fall down onto the table and knock themselves out.

For the past year Gilo had been manager of the Blanket Bay Hotel, working crays as well from his 30 foot long wooden boat *Tania*. Max and I were on the verge of dropping off to sleep when Gilo led us out to his boat and bunked us down for the night.

3 January - Day 14
Gilo was up at 7.30am to catch a forecast of 10 to 15 knot north-westerlies with a change to south-westerlies in the afternoon. The synoptic situation placed a low pressure system moving across the Tasman towards New Zealand at 30 knots. We stayed listening to the Mt. Cook Airlines frequency, expecting our sched with the support crew.

Whilst waiting for the sched, we learned how *Empress 1* had narrowly averted disaster on New Year's Day. Off the entrance to Doubtful Sound for a day's cod fishing, a large wave broke over the stern, shorting out the electrical system, including the radio and starter motor. The situation was desperate as she was being pushed by the swell towards the rocky shoreline of Secretary Island. With 110 metres of water below the boat, the anchor chain was far too short to reach bottom. The two fishermen tied a codline onto the end of the anchor chain and lowered it until, with the boat almost in the white water of waves

breaking on the rocks, the anchor held.

For ten hours, the codline held them off the rocks. Late afternoon a temporary power supply allowed the fishermen to transmit a MAYDAY signal on the radio. This emergency signal was received by Awarua Radio in Invercargill and shortly afterwards, a message reached Blanket Bay. The troops had been celebrating New Year's Day in grand style so it was a slightly tiddly crew that manned *Victor Hugo* and successfully towed *Empress 1* back to Blanket Bay in the dark.

It must have been a hard night also for the support crew in the Te Anau tavern for they didn't show up for the radio sched, much to our disappointment. We later learned Maestro and three cobbers had done a 'down trou' in the tavern on New Year's Eve. During this lapse from his normal righteous behaviour, Maesto's wallet had spilled from his trouser pocket. He didn't realize he'd lost it until next morning and he approached one of the local police constables.

"You wouldn't have had a wallet handed in by any chance?"

"What's your name?"

"Matthew Lysaght."

"You can collect it from the police station. It probably fell out of your trousers while you were doing that down trou on stage last night."

Taken aback, Maestro mumbled, "My belt broke and my trousers slipped." Still you get excuses like that with support parties on the big trips.

Max and I figured to paddle up Thompson Sound while the wind continued from the north-west, then slip into Nancy Sound in the lull before the south-westerly change arrived. That's what we figured.

Max and I had just finished loading the kayaks and were thanking Gilo for his hospitality when a fisherman called out, "Awarua Radio is asking fishing vessels to watch out for two kayaks between Breaksea and Doubtful sounds, as they haven't been sighted for three days."

I immediately asked Gilo if he could contact Awarua Radio but his set wasn't very powerful, so we quickly went aboard *Victor Hugo* and managed to pass a message that we were quite OK and had spent the night at Blanket Bay.

I hoped the commercial radio stations had not picked up Awarua Radio's message as it would cause our friends much undue worry. Since we had advised our arrival the previous evening there should have been no cause for concern.

At 10am we bid farewell to Caddy, Gilo and the other fisherfolk and climbed into our cockpits. With a wave we turned away from the Blanket Bay Hotel to set out on the next stage of our trip, to George Sound.

Chapter 6

DOUBTFUL SOUND
to GEORGE SOUND

In the lee of Secretary Island we had a mile of calm water before us to Common Head at the island's eastern most tip. For a while I mistook the grey vista of Bradshaw Sound for Thompson Sound but as we rounded Common Head there was no mistaking the whitecaps that a bracing north-westerly breeze was pushing down Thompson Sound. We kept the Nordkapps in as close as possible to the sheer walls of Secretary Island, trying to avoid the chop. I marvelled at the way vegetation clung to the steep rock faces. 'There's no shortage of water,' I decided.

We passed a beautiful waterfall which drops from Secretary Lake, 1800 feet up in a basin on the island and by the clean rock walls of Lieutenant Head we decided to look at the misty mountains from the other side of the sound. During lulls between wind gusts, we paddled hard into the chop, only easing off during the strong gusts, content to maintain position as we slowly angled across the sound.

Our immediate objective was the shelter of Deas Cove, well inside the sound's entrance. Crayfishing boats sometimes anchored there for the night. I was passing beneath a grey cliff when a grunting noise startled me. It wasn't Max who was 50 yards ahead and apprehensively I looked over my shoulder and

was relieved to see on a shelf, 15 feet above the sea, a large bull seal with his harem of two females and a wee pup. I inferred from his aggressive grunting that he was rather possessive of his harem and would tolerate no untoward advances towards them.

I drifted back with the wind until I was close enough for a photograph. It was hard to imagine how they had climbed onto the shelf with only a tail and two flippers. It was obvious that man had never frightened or attempted to disturb the seals. The old bull kept an eye on me while the females and pup kept snoozing.

From the whitecaps we escaped into the sheltered water of Deas Cove where a solitary fishing boat lay at anchor. The cove lies on the south side of a T shaped peninsula of rock with Neck Cove on its seaward side. No one was at home on *Marilyn* but a dinghy on the beach indicated the crew were ashore. Walking along the beach we were puzzled by a neat gravelled path leading over a recently built wooden bridge for 100 yards into the clearing in the forest where the track stopped. Later we learned the Fiordland National Park Board intended building a hut with money provided by the Fiordland Game Fishing Club. Along a blazed track we walked through the forest to Neck Cove for a view of the sound's entrance. The north-westerly was still hunting whitecaps down the sound so we decided to wait in Deas Cove for a south-westerly change.

Late afternoon when Caddy motored *Towai* into the cove, mooring alongside *Marilyn*, I paddled out to listen to the evening forecast from Awarua Radio and to see if I could borrow a book from *Towai's* library.

Sid, owner and sole crew of *Marilyn*, had been out trying to supplement his diet with some fresh venison. One of the oldest fishermen we met, he preferred to fish the sounds on his own. Sid had a wife and family in Invercargill and sought not to make a fortune from crayfishing but just enough for a comfortable living. Like many of the older and larger crayboats *Marilyn* had its own freezer and was not reliant on a shore base to store cray tails.

During the evening forecast we heard a 50 knot north-westerly was blowing at Puysegur Point, and that the south-west change was not due until next day. Keen to pass on a message to Maestro and Ainslie, I asked Caddy if it was possible to sched with Carley Burnby in Te Anau. For many years Carley has provided morning and evening forecasts for the crayboats between Dusky Sound and Milford. Carley

noted the location of each boat, passed on requests and messages, and provided an up to date forecast.

Caddy switched the radio onto Carley's frequency and when there was a break in traffic, I said, "ZLCE this is *Towai*, do you copy?"

"Roger *Towai*." Carley's voice came clearly through the speaker.

"The kayak party is safe in Deas Cove," I informed her.

Carley acknowledged and said, "The support party has been calling in to see me each day."

"Carley would you tell the support party that we will be in George Sound in two to four days depending on the weather."

"In that case watch out for a purple-hulled boat *Tainui* in George Sound."

"Thanks Carley. Over and out."

Caddy's deckhand Gary switched to the frequency operated by Maureen Harvey at Waikawa on the east coast. She asked all boats in contact with her to watch out for two kayaks between Breaksea and Doubtful sounds, as they hadn't been sighted for three days. Before Gary could respond we heard Gilo inform Maureen that we had spent the previous night at Blanket Bay and had contacted Te Anau. As soon as

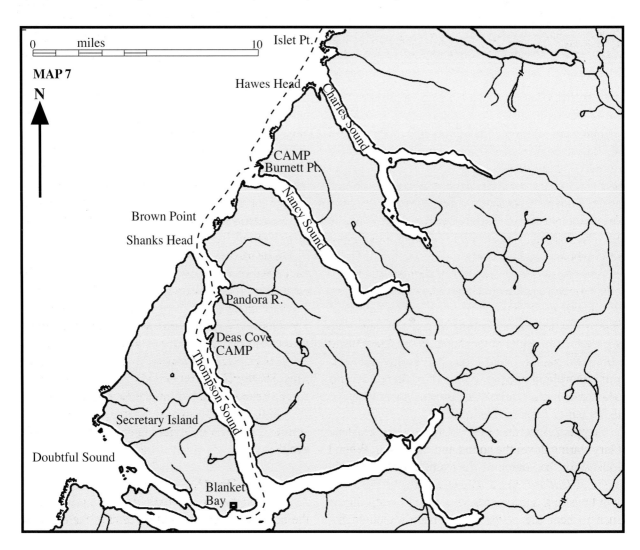

Marilyn *and* Towai *moored in Deas Cove, Thompson Sound. Max is loading his aft compartment*

Gilo finished Gary advised Maureen we were safe in Deas Cove.

The forecast over, Max paddled ashore while I stayed yarning with Caddy and Sid. We discussed the merits of small scoop boats which unlike the larger and slower crayboats, can work in closer to rocks and reefs. Built of fibreglass or aluminium, they work from a mother ship or floating freezer barge. "They're certainly making it more difficult for the older types of crayboat," Caddy told me.

As I untied *Isadora* from the stern of one of the boats to return to shore, Gary called out, "There's a news item about you on the radio." I leapt back into *Towai's* wheelhouse, hoping it wasn't about two kayakers missing in Fiordland. Instead we heard about two paddlers who were halfway through a 400 mile Fiordland trip, paddling Nordkapp kayaks. Maestro must have made an announcement to one of the commercial radio stations.

Stepping out of the wheelhouse I found Caddy and Gary staring down the sound and chuckling. When I looked for the source of their amusement, I caught sight of *Isadora* 20 yards away with the northerly wind pushing her towards Thompson Sound. In my rush to hear the news item, I hadn't secured her

properly. Aboard Sid's aluminium dinghy I gave chase, putting on a terrible display of rowing until I caught up with the kayak.

Max, after hearing the commotion, paddled out and helped me manoeuvre *Isadora* back alongside the boats. Naturally the fishermen thought this was a terrific joke, still chortling as we paddled towards shore. I thanked the powers of wind and wave that there were no cameras around at the time.

We set up the tent beneath the forest in the rain and had a feed of beef curry diluted with vermicelli. The evening was cold with the normal Fiordland overcast sky. My entry in the diary reads: 'Stripped off the wetsuits, dived starkers into the tent before the sand-flies could descend and wriggled into the fibrefill sleeping bags. We both borrowed a book from *Towai*; Max has *Battle Cry* by Leon Uris. I'm writing dear diary by candlelight with rain beating against the tent fly and the wind gusting in the trees above. Read a Wilbur Smith novel till midnight. Pretty good book, aye?'

4 January - Day 15
At first light the wind was still blowing strongly from the north-west. Of the south-westerly change there

The entrance to Thompson Sound from the Pandora River mouth, on a grey north-westerly morning

was no sign, just the familiar overcast sky although the rain had stopped. The inclemency of the weather was sufficient excuse for a sleep in.

By 8am the wind appeared to have eased and we decided to paddle out for a look. Sid had already set off for Deep Cove for a break while Caddy and Gary were just surfacing as we paddled out to *Towai*. Caddy had been on the radio to *Pamir* already out at sea working its pots. Her crew said the north-westerly was blowing 20 to 25 knots and that they would be sheltering in Nancy Sound for the night, if we got that far.

With a wave to *Towai's* crew, we headed out of Deas Cove and turned north into Thompson Sound. Slow progress into the wind and chop, it took us an hour to cover two miles. Since there was no sign of the wind easing, we pulled into a small bay where the Pandora River entered the sound. Surfing over a shallow bar, we paddled upstream and around a corner into a beautiful lagoon. A low forest-covered belt of dunes separated the lagoon from the beach. Of all the places we landed in Fiordland this to me was the most beautiful. Tall black-trunked beech trees protected the lagoon from the wind; beneath these ancient trees the grassy forest floor was so smooth, it appeared to have been recently mown.

We had heard from several fishermen that weather changes often accompanied a turn of the tide. Since the tide was ebbing we hoped the awaited south-westerly change would arrive at dead low water. By mid afternoon I had finished my novel and was settled comfortably in a hollow amongst the grassy dunes. Max was lost in the jungles of Guadalcanal, fighting the Japanese army with the American marines. To my disbelief he was only a third of the way through the book. It did not pay to be a fast reader in Fiordland.

The northerly had eased noticeably by 7pm and clouds were beginning to drift over from the west. After two days of hesitation, the south-westerly change had finally decided to arrive. For the next 15 minutes we gazed intently at the sea and sky; walking up onto the dunes for a better view, then down onto the beach again. Some would call it procrastination but for Max and I, it was 'Big decision making time.'

We decided to paddle out as far as Shanks Head on the northern side of the entrance to Thompson Sound for a look at the condition of the sea; if conditions were favourable we move on to Nancy Sound, if not we'd paddle back to Pandora River. The tide was almost full when we slipped out through a surf on the river bar into a slight headwind. Off Shanks Head a large south-westerly swell was rolling north from the Southern Ocean and this was complicated by the leftovers of a northerly chop. On the horizon to the west we could see a clear band of sky with the sun trying hard to burst through the surrounding cloud banks.

"It's the best sea we've had since the South Coast," declared Max. We were both raring to go, almost as if straining against a leash, waiting for one of us to say, 'Let's go.'

"Nancy Sound then," I said and we slipped our leashes.

From Shanks Head we had to paddle three miles to reach Anxiety Point at the southern entrance to Nancy Sound. For the first time we both felt completely at home in the Nordkapps as we surfed down the face of the large swell. Our minds were totally in harmony with the sea. Previously I had always dreaded the thought of paddling out from the security of the sounds onto the open sea. The size and motion of the swell, the feeling of commitment after leaving one sound with no option once at sea but to reach the next sound, and the intense feeling of isolation with the two of us alone on the Tasman Sea, took a bit of getting used to. Although I sometimes describe the sea as angry or friendly, it is in truth unemotional and has no feelings; if we completed the trip the sea wouldn't care; if we failed it would merely cast our bodies and kayaks onto the boulders as if to be rid of us. To be able to enjoy what I am doing, whether it is on a steep face climb, deep in a cave or paddling down a rapid, I gain the greatest enjoyment when my mind is relaxed and in harmony with the surroundings. On such occasions, initial feelings of fright are replaced by a healthy respect. And so it was this particular evening, with both of us fit and accustomed to the swell. It was exciting to be out there.

A backchop off Brown Point threw us around and the sun then broke through the clouds, casting a dark yellow tinge over sea and forest. The mood of the landscape changed, almost as if the sun was reawakening the rocks and trees from a long sleep. A warm, fresh glowing mood matched our own feelings perfectly.

"I'd love to see a red sunset," I called to Max.

"How about I poke you in the eye with a burnt stick; then you'll see a red sunset," chuckled Max.

I kept glancing over my shoulder to watch the red orb of the sun as it descended into its overnight watery grave, with its beautiful red trail across the surface of the sea. As the sun sank lower I realized how large the sea was, for in the troughs *Isadora* and I were completely in shadow, with no sign of the sunset. As we closed on Anxiety Point the sun disappeared below the horizon.

This point is aptly named for off its rocky tip, the swell appeared to be higher than elsewhere and we turned out to sea. Suddenly I felt the Nordkapp lifted by a huge swell and dropped down onto its face below the crest. As I surfed out to sea I caught a glimpse of Max shooting out backwards from the swell as it broke. Needless to say, we gave Anxiety Point a wide berth.

Just on 10pm we paddled in towards the steep sided entrance of Nancy Sound. The light was fading quickly and rather than paddle up the sound until we located a landing, I wanted to head across to Burnett Point on the northern side of the sound where the map showed an 'L' shaped cove. I was sure we would find a sheltered landing around a 90° bend in the cove.

In the gathering gloom we headed towards the cove's entrance. Max could only see a line of surf on the steep rocks ahead and his voice had a note of alarm when he called, "Which way?"

"Straight ahead," I replied.

Max wanted to head up the sound. I tried to reassure him by saying, "There's a sheltered cove ahead." We paddled into a large area of foam by the rocky entrance to the cove. All the normal kayaking sounds, water dripping off the blades, waves slapping against the bow, were stifled in the foam. It was almost an ethereal feeling.

Scarce minutes of dusk were left before it would be dark and even in the cove's entrance there was no sign of a beach in the fading light. "I can see a beach, but I don't like it," declared Max.

"Come on," I yelled for I had spotted a craypot float and paddled hard for the beach before Max could change his mind. I landed through a small surf on a steep beach of large, round boulders. Before the surge could drag *Isadora* backwards, I was out of the cockpit and dragged the kayak up the boulders. As Max surfed in on top of a broken wave, I grabbed his bow. Even on terra firma Max was still worried about the landing. "We won't be able to get out of here if the swell comes up," he grumbled.

We split up, searching for fresh water and a level campsite. Max found a small stream at the northern end of the boulder beach and I found a vaguely level spot between two large rocks in the forest. With insufficient room to pitch the tent, we spread the sleeping bags over the tent and fly. It was such a relief to pull off the wetsuits for we had been spending so much time in them, we had both developed an uncomfortable nappy rash.

By candlelight I brought my diary up to date: 'Max is in his sleeping bag making his presence known by a string of Z's emerging from the tightly drawn up hood of his sleeping bag. Loud surf noises from the beach. Hope it doesn't rain tonight. I can actually see a few stars.'

5 January - Day 16

I was woken at 5.40am by a sandfly who had found its way in through the hood of my sleeping bag. The red sunset of the previous evening had justified the saying, 'red sky at night, paddler's delight', for there were large patches of clear sky and just a few banks of cloud. A gentle breeze ruffled the surface of the cove and we wasted no time in bolting down the ritual bowls of porridge. We wanted to be in the shelter of Charles or Caswell sounds before the 11 o'clock chop came away.

The most unpleasant task of the morning was getting dressed. A cold wet woollen singlet pulled over a goose bumpy chest, a clammy wetsuit pulled over the legs then a hunch forward as the cold neoprene came in contact with the groin.

The sleeping bags were damp from the ever present water sloshing around on the cockpit floors during the day however the synthetic fibrefill was always warm after the initial clammy contact with the damp fabric.

We launched off the boulders and paddled out onto the Tasman where to our disappointment the swell was waiting with a light chop from a south-westerly breeze. Hawes Head at the entrance to Caswell Sound lay four miles ahead. We made good time, occasionally surfing the Nordkapps in front of the swell crests. We were in the shadow of Turn Peak, a 3,650 foot high peak only a mile inland from the coast.

Half a mile from Hawes Head we watched a white-hulled crayfishing boat plough into the swell towards us. When the crew finally spotted us bobbing on the swell, we waved and the boat changed course towards us. We paddled into the lee side of *Pamir*, the boat which Carley Burnby had told us to look out for in Nancy Sound.

"Have you heard a forecast," I asked the skipper.

From the rolling deck of *Pamir* the skipper called back, "The forecast is for south-easterly winds. There's a huge high coming over the Tasman. It looks more like south-westerly winds."

"Could you pass on a message to Carley Burnby that the kayak party is heading for Caswell?"

"Haven't got her frequency."

"What about Gilo at Blanket Bay?"

The skipper said he would radio Gilo with the message and ask him to pass it on to Carley.

We thanked the crew of *Pamir* and pointed the bows to the north-east. As we drew level with Hawes Head we looked into the enticingly sheltered waters of Charles Sound. Although the occasional swell was starting to break, as the south-westerly breeze picked up, we decided during a raft-up to make a break for Caswell.

Ahead we could see the sharp, bare rocky crags of Islet Point with one prominent fang poking out of the sea off the point. But as we passed 100 yards to seawards of the fang, the 11 o'clock chop had come away with a vengeance. The wind was gusting strongly and the swell crests were capping more frequently. The time when we could paddle grew shorter and shorter as the chop built up. Mostly we were surfing in front of the swell, either in towards the bluffs or out to sea. Only when a swell crest left us in its wake could we attempt a few quick paddle strokes.

With marked relief, as we surfed past Nugget Point, we saw the entrance to Caswell Sound, not around the distant headland as had appeared further to the south, but just around the rocks and reefs of McKerr Point, less than a mile away. One swell broke over my head and for a moment *Isadora's* deck disappeared beneath white surging water, but I hung in a high brace and she skated out onto the surface of the wave, shaking the water off.

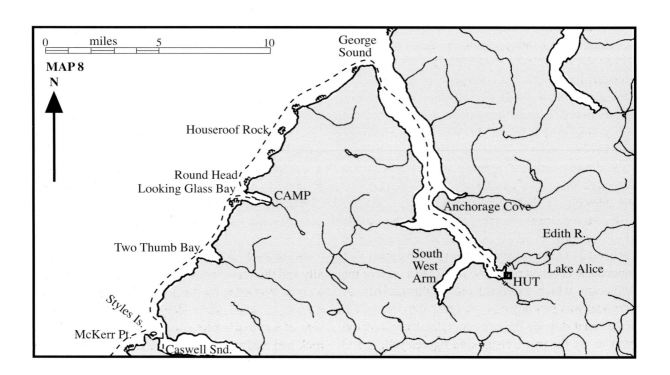

During the planning stages of the trip, one of the books I had read several times was Paul Powell's *Fishermen of Fiordland*. The two photographs of the roughest seas were both of crayboats off Styles Island in the entrance to Caswell Sound. I was sure a wild sea was lurking for us off Styles Island, just like in the photographs. I would be a lot happier once we were north of Caswell.

The numerous rocks and reefs south of McKerr Point provided little shelter from the chop. As the Nordkapps slewed and surfed towards the bare rocky foreshore of Styles Island I thought, 'This Fiordland coastline is not going to give up easily to the kayaks; it's going to make us fight for every section.'

We aimed for a narrow channel shown on the map between the island and the point. In the calmer waters of the channel Max was paddling ahead of me when the sun broke through the clouds at the head of the sound. The deck of his kayak and the sea around him momentarily appeared to be on fire, with the sun's rays dancing and sparkling on the waves.

We paddled over a shallow bar and entered the calm waters of the sound. Slowly we pottered around the lee side of Styles Island, searching for a landing. Nothing invited so we continued along the shore of the sound, following a line of craypot floats to where a stream tumbled out of a narrow forested gorge and splashed onto a boulder beach.

In a flash the wetsuits were stripped off, washed in fresh water and set on the rocks to dry. It was good to be alive as the sun streamed down onto our pale bodies that hadn't glimpsed sunshine since Dusky Sound. "After the last couple of days, this is almost idyllic," commented Max as we sat naked on either side of a tea billy which was bubbling over a driftwood fire. The beautiful blue waters of the sound sparkled in the morning light with the steep 4,000 foot high rocky sentinels on both sides. Trees on the ridges above, whipping around in the strong south-westerly breeze, and the ever-present sandflies were the only reminders that we were in Fiordland. The awareness of isolation was with us not as a worry but as a feeling so good that it is hard to explain or attempt to describe.

Mid-afternoon we decided to paddle out for a look at the sea. Inside the sound, the sea was unruffled but the trees on the skyline indicated the wind had not died. On the north side of Styles Island a sizeable chop and strong south-westerly wind gusts soon deterred us from venturing further. In a rocky gut we landed and climbed round the rocks for a view of the whitecaps which extended out to the horizon. A crayboat was making slow progress into the sound, but when it stopped in calm water, the crew were too busy to see the two wetsuit clad figures yelling and waving from Styles Island.

The boat cruised slowly around towards our lunch spot and we gave chase in the Nordkapps, soon catching up with *Dismas*. The skipper Dave Mackay and his son Andrew had been lifting pots during the morning when a rope snagged around the rudder. In a full wetsuit and face mask, Andrew made a series of dives before finally surfacing with a length of rope attached to a buoy. Dave told us Andrew had only recently bought the wetsuit and had been hoping for a rope to foul the propeller so he could try it out.

Earlier in the day as *Dismas* made her way down from George Sound, a rubber oil hose had burst. Dave carried a spare now as once before when the same hose had broken, he'd had to send out a MAYDAY signal on the radio and had been towed into shelter.

Dave told us about the crayboats in George Sound, the largest being *Xanadu* which was moored in Anchorage Cove. He promised to pass on a message to Carley Burnby on the evening sched that we had arrived in Caswell and were heading for George Sound. We thanked Dave for a bag of crayfish which he dropped into my cockpit and paddled over to our lunch spot.

George Sound lay 17 miles up the coast. We hoped the sea would drop by evening so we could make a break for the sound. On the intervening stretch of coast, both Two Thumb and Looking Glass bays looked on the map to be probable landing places.

My attempt to cook an early meal met with disaster. I managed to boil the crayfish but just as a full billy of rice, raisins and dehydrated apples was ready, it fell off the stick holding it over the fire, spilling the lot onto the rocks and embers. With a fresh start I served out two steaming bowls of rice but as Max picked up his bowl, mine was knocked over. After a few choice words to the world at large, Max gave me half his rice. To top off the evening, my legs were slightly sunburnt and sore, not to mention Max noticing the tip of my paddle was broken. Still as the saying goes, 'You get days like that on the big trips.'

At 7.30pm we decided to have another look at the sea. The entrance of the sound had lost its whitecaps and the wind was no longer gusting in the skyline trees. To the north-east a cloud was continuously forming on the seaward slope of Mt. Tanilba and streaming over its summit to the east. Optimistic at our chances of leaving the sound, we paddled out further.

Off Styles Island the swell was breaking occasionally and the south-westerly breeze was still creating a chop. Wavering on the point of turning back, we gingerly paddled out to a large rock off the northern side of Caswell's entrance. Despite the fact that a rock had wedged my skeg into the up position and that conditions were marginal, we decided to push on. We committed ourselves to the sea for once the full force of the breeze caught us, there was no chance of paddling back into Caswell.

The wind drove the Nordkapps swiftly along towards the next steep rocky cape, surfing past an occasional craypot. Several times we were buried by a breaking swell as the kayaks surfed one way, then the other. The thought of a possible capsize made my mouth dry as we surfed on, my knees locked up tightly in the knee rests, and my feet pushing hard against the foot rest.

Off the entrance to Two Thumb Bay the seas were fiery enough for Max to consider putting in there for the night. In the middle of the bay's entrance two rocky islands stood out of the sea like sore thumbs. "Looking Glass Bay then?" I called to Max. After one last lingering glance into the sheltered depths of the bay, we paddled on for the yet indiscernible entrance to George Sound.

Dear diary: 'The sun was getting down close to the horizon. You could tell when a large swell was approaching from astern because you were suddenly in the shadow of a deep trough. I tried to convince myself that once a wave broke over the kayak, I had a spell of at least five minutes before the next wave broke.'

As the sun was about to set, we turned into Looking Glass Bay, paddling past the rocky islands and archways which mark the southern side of the entrance. The last of the dying sun's rays, glowing through one of the archways, was so beautiful that we both stopped paddling long enough to try and capture the scene on film. The bay is over a mile deep and it seemed to take ages before we reached the beach. Gently rising and falling on the swell, we raced the last light of dusk into a beautiful sandy beach, where we surfed onto the sand beside a stream outlet. It was a pleasant change not to have to search for a level place to camp as there appeared to be acres of flat ground behind the beach.

Five cheeky keas soon screeched their presence. Since I knew how destructive their sharp beaks could be, two keas once destroyed the vinyl seat of my motor bike when I left it uncovered for five minutes at Arthurs Pass, we placed our lifejackets, sprayskirts and wetsuits in the cockpits and turned the kayaks over. We slept under the stars as the sky was clear, in order to save time in the morning by not having to pack the tent.

6 January - Day 17

Even if we had taken an alarm clock with us, there would have been no need to set it. In Fiordland the sandfly alarm at first light is very effective for disturbing the sleep of tired paddlers. Joining in a dawn chorus, the keas screeched away mercilessly from a distance of three yards until we stirred.

The surface of the bay was calm but I received a facefull of cold water from a breaker as we left the beach and paddled onto the pastel coloured water of the bay. Just before we reached the open sea the sun crested the mountains behind us; its rays streaming through the swell breaking on the rocks by the entrance. Our faithful travelling companion was waiting but the swell was glassy, and almost as good as during our first two day's paddle on the South Coast. For the first time in days there was no wind.

Over the bows, the coastline stretched away into the distance, shrouded in spray from the surf with only the rocky points standing out. Apart from the porridge sitting heavy in the pit of my stomach, it was great to be making steady progress northwards.

As we closed on Houseroof Rock, a bare rugged island 400 yards offshore, a black-hulled fishing boat passed us heading south-westwards. The skipper of *Ake Ake* ignored us but one of the deckhands on the stern was more sociable and returned our waves. From the rock it took us an hour to paddle the 4.5 miles to the entrance of George Sound. My arms and shoulders were complaining about the three hour paddle from the bay, so once inside the sound we landed on its western shore for a pit stop.

Only 10 miles separated us from our next food dump at the head of the sound. With this in mind we abandoned our strict rationing of the rasberry cream biscuits and happily consumed those remaining in the food bag. These delicious biscuits were the tastiest delights in our mainly dehydrated food rations, so we had to limit ourselves to one or two per day.

It seemed a pity to forgo this perfect day by paddling up the sound to join the support crew when we could be pushing on to Milford Sound but after an hour, we continued up the sound, passing beneath a huge slip which reached from the bushline on Mt. Elder to the water's edge.

Five miles from the pit stop we came to the edge of the topographic map sheet and had to resort to a sketch map of the head of the sound. Paddling side by side, I said to Max, "We're about to go off the map. Watch for a line on the water."

"Bump," said Max. "I just went over it."

Six miles remained to a hut at the head of the sound where Maestro and Ainslie should be waiting with our food dump. As we passed Anchorage Cove we could see no sign of *Xanadu* but we found out later that five boats were moored out of sight behind an island in the cove.

Beyond a point with shadowy bluffs rising steeply from the water's edge, we were able to see the head of the sound, some four miles away.

"There's the hut," I called excitedly.

Max strained his eyes into the sun. "Where?"

"By that beech tree at the head of the sound."

Frowning, Max again strained his eyes, then the penny dropped.

"Just to the left of the other beech tree?"

"That's the one."

Max wasn't long in making up for that. As we drew level with the Whitewater River valley he said, "We're in for a spot of weather. There's cloud coming in."

I looked at him, the blue sky all around and back to Max. Then I followed his gaze and detected a tiny wisp of cloud high up on one of the mountains in front of us, but by then he was out of paddle hitting distance.

My arms were tiring as we surfed in front of a chop and I wondered if the support party would be waiting for us at the hut. Not long after passing South Arm, we were startled by the sound of three rifle shots. The echoes reverberated down the sound almost as if there was a war going on. "We're being shot at, ooh mate!"

I figured Maestro was out his with Mauser rifle trying to enhance his image as a great white hunter with a George Sound wapiti bull. However Max could see a tiny figure leaping around by the forest edge in the distance. We yelled out at the top of our voices but the hut was still invisible, over a mile away.

As we paddled closer, I was able to make out a figure on a beach. At Dusky Sound Maestro had assured us that beer would be flowing down George Sound, so Max and I kept an eye out for partially submerged kegs and Max called, "Don't run aground on a floating can of export lager."

"Do you want a beer boys?" asked Maestro. We paddled through a dozen cans of beer that were bobbing in the chop and powered onto a shingle beach. Maestro had lived up to his promise.

When Maestro emerged from the hut late morning, he wandered out to the beach and pondered whether or not to take a photograph. Two tiny red dots caught his eye, way down in the sound. "They're too big to be buoys, it must be ..... the boys!"

With the telescopic sight on his rifle, Maestro verified it was the boys and let off three shots, partly to let us know we had been spotted and partly to let Ainslie, who had gone for a walk, know we had arrived.

Max and I were tired but extremely pleased to see Maestro waiting on the beach, not to mention the floating cans of beer. For the next hour we talked and drank without let up. When one person ran of breath the other would come in with another exciting episode of the paddle from Dusky to George.

As we walked through the trees towards the Park Board hut, Maestro pointed to the track that led to Lake Te Anau. Max was off like a shot, bolting towards civilization. "Come back Max, come back," called Maestro to the fast disappearing back of the longjohn and wool singlet clad figure. Only when Maestro promised to fly his kayak out by float plane did Max emerge from the trees.

From the North-West Arm of Middle Fiord of Lake Te Anau, the Fiordland National Park Board maintains a track over Henry Saddle and down to the George Sound hut. The track which involves dinghy travel on two lakes was first used by Europeans when Richard Henry set out with a companion in 1879, taking 26 days to explore and map the route. The men used a canvas canoe to paddle along the lakes. Richard Henry, for many years, lived on Pigeon Island in Dusky Sound and transported kakapos out to a sanctuary on Resolution Island.

Through Carley Burnby in Te Anau, Maestro met Vic King-Turner who skippered a 28 foot long fibre-glass scoop boat. Vic was heading down to George Sound from Milford on *Truxton* and offered Maestro and Ainslie a lift. In company with another scoop boat *Tainui II*, Vic considered turning back off St. Anne Point at the entrance to Milford Sound, for the sea was sloppy with a 15 knot headwind. He radioed to some boats working at sea further south, then asked Maestro, "What do you reckon?" Maestro threw his arm forward and said, "Let's go."

"Right, we're away," replied Vic and opened up the throttle of the six cylinder diesel motor.

At a speed of 15 knots, give or take a bit, *Truxton* bounced into the swell, stopping a few times to let the skipper of *Tainui II* feed the fish with his breakfast. At one stage when Vic was chatting to a fishing boat further south on the radio, he asked the skipper if he had seen the two jokers in the kayaks. Vic was asked to repeat the question. A stunned silence followed, then came the question, "Who the hell do they think they are; Marco Polo and his mate?"

After a cup of tea on board *Xanadu* and a guided tour of George Sound, Vic dropped the support party at the hut. That evening Maestro took his rifle for a walk in the forest but failed to bring home any venison for 'the boys'.

When our thirsts were quenched and the tongues had stopped wagging, we set off to search for Ainslie. From a boatshed set back in the trees, we launched a park board aluminium dinghy and Maestro attempted to row us towards Alice Falls. The rowlocks were missing and pieces of number 8 fencing wire held the oars in position.

Max was sitting on the bow, dangling his feet in the water. Maestro, peering over his shoulder, said, "Max are you trying to slow us down?"

"I'm water skiing," he replied.

Despite several 360° turns, the dinghy arrived safely in the cove below the falls. The Edith River tumbles down from Lake Alice in a spectacular white cascade, leaping from a ledge over water worn rock beneath overhanging beech trees. It was here in the forest by the lake we met Ainslie and the chattering began all over again.

Ainslie cooked up a tasty meal of vegetables and mince, most delectable to Max and I who were heartily sick of beef curry. Maestro then drew attention to the 18 empty beer cans. However each of the males assured the others that he had only drunk three cans. Unsuccessfully we tried to talk Maestro into going out for a dusk shot with his 8mm Mauser but the great white hunter said, "The light is too bad."

We spent a wonderfully relaxed and nostalgic evening in the hut, a fire flickering beneath the chimney. As the fire died, we retired to our sleeping bags to swap yarns and relate stories by candlelight.

7 January - Day 18

Early next morning Max and I went out to look at the weather. Grey clouds were scudding over from the north-west and a strong breeze ruffled the surface of the sound, indicating a cold front on its way from the Tasman. There was every justification for declaring a rest day. Returning to our sleeping bags, we tried for two hours to cajole Maestro into going out for a morning shot, as the image of 'the great white hunter' was fast disappearing. He ignored our jibes, pretending to be engrossed in a paperback or asleep. Appropriately enough, I was reading a book *Storm Warning*. Since 'the boys' had been doing so well, Ainslie served us pancakes and bowls of tea while we lay in bed.

Mid-morning I spotted a boat cruising up the sound towards the hut. Great excitement, visitors! We waited on the beach to say good day. As the blue-hulled boat approached, we made our presence known with appropriate words from the book of nautical expressions: 'Avast ye swabs', 'Splice the mainbrace', 'Hoist the mizzen sail', and so on. When the boat dropped anchor we conned Maestro into rowing us out to meet the crew.

On board *Samara* we met Ralph Brown from Queenstown, Robert Brown a cameraman for the TV1 wildlife unit and John Verboeket, a dentist from Dunedin. All three belonged to the Fiordland Game Fishing Club. *Samara* a 32 foot long fibreglass boat was rigged for game fishing.

Ralph explained that game fish drove smaller fish to the sea surface where sea birds, sooty shearwaters, terns, mollymawks and black backed gulls, soon congregated for a meal. Deck chairs bolted to the top

Maestro in the dinghy, at the head of George Sound

of the wheelhouse were used to spot flocks of birds or any sign of game fish, particularly the southern blue-fin tuna.

The fishermen attempted to hook game fish by trolling up to five lures behind the boat; two attached to outrigger poles which stood vertically by the wheelhouse like whip aerials when not in use, and three attached to the stern. Among the lures hanging on a wall in the cabin, we noticed a life-sized replica of a mouse with several hooks near its tail.

"What do you catch with the mouse lure?" I asked.

Before Ralph could reply, Max and I chorused, "Catfish."

We assumed that such lures could well prove an irresistible attraction to the sea run trout which dwell in many of the sounds. By all accounts there are some beauties hanging around the outlet of the tail race tunnel in Deep Cove. We imagined frustrated, randy old brown trout trying to reach their breeding grounds in Lake Manapouri but being defeated by the turbine blades of the power station.

The conversation turned to hunting after a brew of soup. Maestro advised prospective hunters of an assured method for sighting a deer. "You go up the track to the saddle, then climb up through the bush to the white rock, and there'll you'll find deer sign."

Max piped up, "Deer 200 yards, is that what the sign says?"

Unperturbed Maestro continued, "Wait there by

the rock and you'll see a deer. You may have to wait for two years, but you'll see one eventually."

In 1905 a herd of 18 wapati was liberated at the head of George Sound, after a long trip from the United States. These animals grow up to eight and a half feet in length and can weigh up to 1000 pounds. Wapiti hunting is strictly controlled in New Zealand, and hunters have to put their names into a ballot for an opportunity to score a trophy.

Five years ago in George Sound Ralph shot a 17 point wapiti near the tops in the watershed of White-water River. It was during the roaring season when bull wapiti charge without hesitation if they think their territory is being invaded. Ralph and his mate heard a wapiti bull roar down-river. The roar is described as a low note, rising in pitch to a shrill scream with short grunts. Ralph was carrying the antlers of the 17 point bull on his back as they walked down the valley and a second wapiti heard the sound of Ralph's antlers scraping against bushes and trees. Without warning he charged the two hunters, no doubt thinking another bull was in his territory. Luckily Ralph's mate shot the 16 point bull from the hip at 20 yards. Ralph's trophy now hangs in the A Line Motor Lodge at Queenstown.

Max and I were keen to advise Awarua Radio that we were safe in George Sound but Ralph was unable to contact the station. We invited Ralph, Robert and John to the hut for pancakes that evening and had to drag Maestro away from the boat's stern where he was having a marvellous time catching tiddlers on one of *Samara's* large game fishing rods.

A north-wester was blowing hard as we climbed into the dinghy. Grey squalls were driving up the sound, forcing whitecaps in front of them. A crayfishing boat appeared out of the murk and anchored in the cove. Maestro rowed us over to *Alias,* a 32 foot long wooden boat, and we met John Barber, the skipper. John gave us advice for the next stage up to Milford Sound and said he would notify both Awarua Radio and Carley Burnby that we were safe in George Sound. After a brew and an invitation to *Alias's* crew for pancakes after dark, Maestro attempted to row us back to the hut. A strong chop and headwind defeated Maestro. He was just about to give up and make us walk back along the shore when *Alias* cruised past and John threw us a towline. After casting us off by the hut, he moored in the cove beneath the falls. Maestro said, "I was just giving *Alias* a push start."

Late afternoon Ainslie made a brew of tea that had an unusual grey colour. Maestro was lying in a bottom bunk, immersed in a book, when I climbed onto the top bunk above him with a bowl of hot tea in one hand. My toe slipped on the window sill and I sloshed a pint of grey tea over Maestro. He was not amused and made a grab for my legs. Max grinned and said, "You should mind your T's and Q's," to which I added, "That grey colour suits you to a T."

Later when we encouraged Maestro to go out for an evening shot, we again met with failure. His excuse this time was, "The rain will be keeping the deer inside."

It was a dark and stormy night as the saying goes, when we heard the sound of a motor out in the sound. *Samara* with *Alias's* crew on board had arrived for pancakes. They experienced difficulty in anchoring the boat in the chop but eventually the anchor stopped dragging and a stern line was fastened to shore.

When everyone was inside the hut, Robert and John mentioned that they had gone for an evening shot up by Lake Alice. "We've brought you some venison Maestro," said John, trying hard to hide a smile.

"You little beauties," exclaimed Maestro.

But his smile gave way to a bewildered frown as John handed him a can. The label read 'Venison Casserole'. For a moment Maestro was speechless. That takes some doing, but he picked up his rifle and, can in hand, headed for the door stating, "I'll put a bullet through it and then I'll be able to say I shot some venison in Fiordland."

The fishermen had brought a wide selection of tongue looseners ashore, sherry, spirits and beer. In front of a roaring fire, we yarned till midnight, eating Ainslie's delicious pancakes and slices of toasted bread, courtesy of the freezer on *Alias*. It was past midnight when they rowed back out to *Samara*.

The hut at the head of George Sound

Maestro, saluting on the flying bridge, and Ainslie on the stern, as Samara *up anchors en-route to Milford Sound*

Max, with liquid refreshment, in the park board dinghy at the head of George Sound

Chapter 7

GEORGE SOUND to MILFORD

8 January - Day 19

At first light the sky was its usual overcast, and whitecaps were plainly visible in the sound. We remained pit-ridden, absorbed in paperback thrillers. A rifle shot mid-morning had the four of us sitting bolt upright in our bunks. *Samara's* crew was trying to attract our attention, and when we arrived on the beach in various states of undress, Ralph informed us that *Samara* was leaving for Milford within the hour and offered to take the support party with them. Maestro had booked a floatplane for Tuesday from George Sound out to Te Anau but it was not for another two days, and no one could really afford the flight.

With a shouted "Yes please", we returned to the hut and began a frenzied rush to pack and sort out what food Max and I needed for the next stage to Milford Sound. We rowed Maestro and Ainslie out to *Samara* and bid a sad farewell to our support party. It was a change for the paddlers to be seeing off the support party. Usually it was the other way round. From the park board dinghy, Max and I watched the boat up anchor and move off down the sound with Ainslie watching forlornly from the stern and Maestro firmly ensconced in one of the deck chairs on top of *Samara's* cabin.

Alias had set off an hour earlier, so once more we were on our own. Eventually we decided to paddle down to Anchorage Cove for a look at the open sea. The morning forecast on *Samara's* radio had been for a north-westerly change in the afternoon. Ralph hoped to reach Milford before the change arrived.

We left the beach at 1pm and I persuaded Max to paddle over to the base of Alice falls for a photograph. Overnight rain had swollen the amount of water cascading down to the sea and provided an impressive sight as Max cut into the white water at the base of the falls. From the shelter of the cove we paddled out into the sound proper and met a slight headwind. It was a grey Fiordland afternoon as we passed by the near vertical rock walls climbing sheer up into the clouds.

We made reasonable progress down to Anchorage Cove where we found the large orange-hulled *Xanadu* moored in the lee of a small forest-covered island. Three small scoop boats, *Skippy*, *Xaviera*, and *Fernando* were tied up alongside. *Xanadu* didn't venture out crayfishing but remained moored in the cove, serving as a floating home and freezer barge for the fishermen who worked up and down the coast from George Sound.

The fishermen told us we could land in Catseye Bay two miles along the coast from George Sound and that we would have to go up Bligh Sound as far as Turn Around Point to find a sheltered landing. We waited in the Nordkapps to hear the 3pm marine forecast: 'From Puysegur Point to Cape Foulwind - winds 15 to 25 knots from the westerly quarter.'

As soon as we left the shelter of *Xanadu's* anchorage, we started to feel the effect of the ocean swell. Staying in close to the northern shore of the sound we tried to find some shelter from the wind. Slowly as we worked our way seawards, the sea grew rougher. There didn't seem to be much chance of leaving the sound for a while yet. By a vertical rock bluff on the northern side of the sound's entrance, we were barely making headway into the swell and chop. Although the Nordkapps were being tossed around, we decided to push out another 200 yards. Finally at the seaward end of the bluff we agreed, "It's not worth it," and plugged across to our lunch spot of two days ago on

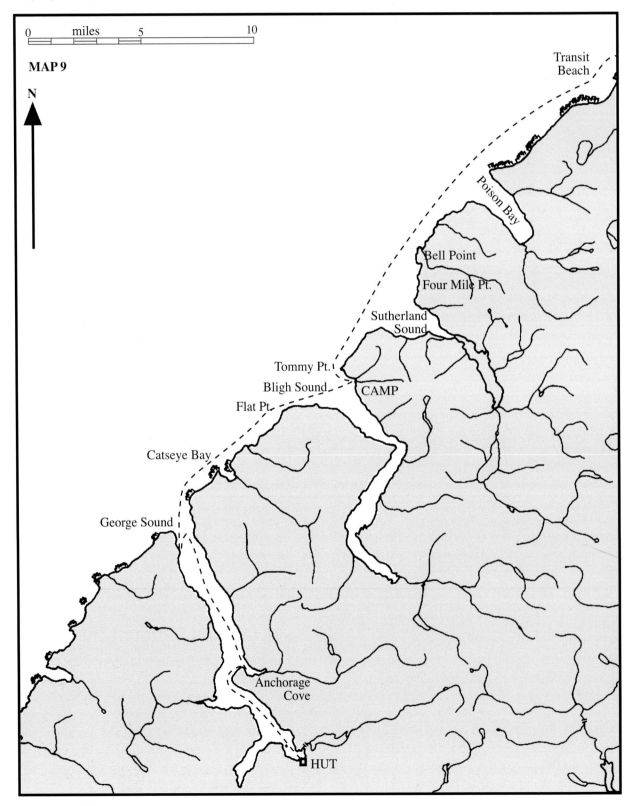

5. *Anchorage Cove, on the north side of George Sound, with small crayfishing boats moored alongside* Xanadu

6. *A meeting with* Samara *off the entrance to Sutherland Sound*

7. *Max about to enter the shelter of Milford Sound, with Dale Point on the left*

8. *Our campsite by the boat landing at the south end of Martins Bay*

the south side of the sound. There were no landing places on the north shore.

In a strong surge we had difficulty landing amongst the weed covered boulders. It was 4.15pm and we had an early dinner just in case the wind dropped.

The wind did ease by evening. We packed quickly and launched sternfirst from the boulders at 7.25pm. A large swell was running off the entrance and the wind was gusting occasionally. *Xanadu's* crew has warned us to give Catseye Bay a wide berth as there were numerous reefs guarding its entrance. As we approached the bay, the swell was breaking wildly over reefs and sending up clouds of spray. Max was tempted to put into the bay for the night but since the sea was settling as the evening wore on, I said, "Bligh Sound then?" Max reluctantly agreed to keep paddling. I had no idea that this decision was to nearly cost me my life.

A south-westerly breeze pushed the Nordkapps along in the right direction, but the backwash from the swell breaking on the shoreline created an unpleasant chop. We had three miles to paddle from Catseye Bay to Flat Point where the coastline turned eastward towards the entrance of Bligh Sound. As the evening progressed the cloud banks gradually dispersed, leaving the sun to cast a soft golden glow over the mountains. By the time we drew level with Flat Point the sun had set. In the gathering gloom we hastened towards Chasland Head on the southern side of the entrance to Bligh Sound. The chop had disappeared when we drew level with the head and the swell had eased noticeably.

We had no chance of landing on the rocks by Chasland Head as the swell was surging viciously onto the shore. Two miles away on the northern side of the sound there appeared to be a sandy beach, one mile inside the entrance from Tommy Point. We paddled hard across Bligh Sound, fighting a losing battle with the growing darkness. Clouds clung to the peaks above the grey, uninviting depths of the sound.

As we approached the beach, the surf didn't appear to be all that large, although judging by the noise it was a dumping surf. Just outside the breakers we stopped to size up the sets of waves that we now could barely make out in the dusk. I counted the large waves and thought they were coming through in sets of two. Max was behind me as I took off behind the second wave of a set, paddling furiously for the beach. In the near darkness I made two mistakes; the first was that I underestimated the distance to the beach and the second that I should have been closer in by the breakers when I made the sprint shorewards.

I was still yards out from the beach, paddling into the backwash from the previous broken wave, when I felt the next swell about to break. I glanced up over my shoulder and was horrified to see the face of an eight to nine foot high dumper about to break on top of me. Then *Isadora's* stern flicked up as though lifted by a giant hand. The bow dug in at the base of the wave and as it broke the wave hurled the kayak stern over bow. The manoeuvre is called a forward loop when done for pleasure. For a fraction of a second, the 18 foot length of Nordkapp was vertical, then I was upside down, still in the cockpit, and hurtling backwards towards the beach, totally at the mercy of the wave.

'This is it,' I thought, 'the finish.' There was a sharp blow on my helmet. My shoulders were being pounded on boulders. From a distance the beach had appeared to be sandy but through contact I discovered that it was made up of large rounded boulders. With the force of the water wrenching my body in all directions, it felt like being torn apart limb from limb. I couldn't see myself surviving, nor *Isadora* reaching the shore in one piece, such was the battering we were taking on the boulders. In retrospect, I realized it was my shoulders that took the brunt of the battering, not the kayak!

Then I was on the beach, and still alive. My glasses were missing - I felt them torn off - and my helmet had disappeared. I can't remember if I was in or out of the cockpit when *Isadora* and I stranded on the boulders. To my amazement each limb still functioned, although there were numerous painful spots, and the kayak was in one piece.

The surge retreating down the boulders in the aftermath of the dumper threatened to drag *Isadora* back into the face of the next wave. By bracing my feet against the boulders I managed to prevent that but as the cockpit was full of water and the beach was steep, I couldn't budge the kayak. Each time a wave broke I had to fight to keep Isadora from being sucked back with the surge. I tried to scoop out the water with my hands, to lighten the weight of the kayak. After a desperate struggle I dragged *Isadora* three feet up the boulders. I located my glasses which had stayed attached around my neck by a piece of hat elastic and, with them on, spotted my paddle in the surge and retrieved it.

In the gloom I could just make out the shape of Max's kayak waiting outside the line of dumpers. When I was sure *Isadora* was high enough out of the surge, I signalled Max to paddle along the beach to the east where the dumpers appeared to be not as high and violent. I staggered along the boulders until there as a brief lull, then I shouted, "Paddle!" at the top of my voice. Max powered in behind a breaker and I grabbed his bow before the surge could drag him backwards.

We managed to drag both Nordkapps up the beach

and unpacked them among large piles of driftwood. By torchlight Max found a flat spot to lay out the sleeping bags. As I stumbled over rocks towards him, carrying my fibrefill bag, I fell onto what appeared to be a patch of grass. It wasn't grass at all but stinging nettle. By that stage I was too dispirited to say anything. It wasn't my night at all. Still you have evenings like that on the big trips!

Max placed a piece of chocolate in my mouth and noticed blood oozing down my chin from a cut in my lip. A tooth must have gone through it. I wondered if Max realized how sore I was. I was worried that a little delayed shock might set in and mumbled, "Got to have a hot jelly."

I heated up a hot lemon jelly and shared a bowl with Max. He helped me out of my parka and wetsuit and examined my back. The skin by my left shoulder was broken and bleeding but all the bones seemed to be intact. When I flipped over, I was wearing a wool singlet, wetsuit, parka, lifejacket and sprayskirt. Five layers of material hadn't stopped the skin being abraded.

Awkwardly I crawled into my sleeping bag after swallowing a couple of panadeine tablets to try and ease the pain. Along with the helmet, I had lost a camera lens cap and a pair of sandshoes. I couldn't see how I would be paddling next day.

The thump of waves dumping on the beach and the graunching noise as boulders washed back with the surge, were not the most pleasant noises to go to sleep by.

9 January - Day 20

Next morning Max wanted to get under way as soon as possible before the wind came away. "There's no wind and the tide is lower than last night," he said. For a while I tried to keep sandflies out of the small opening in the hood of the sleeping bag, but gave up. Stiff and sore I slowly pulled on the cold wetsuit and singlet. Max had a brew of porridge simmering on the white spirit stove.

After breakfast we watched the surf and picked the best spot to launch from. We chose opposite ends of the boulder beach and together carried Max's kayak to the east end and mine to the west. A last search along the beach turned up my sandshoes and helmet, the latter holed through the fibreglass and minus the harness and chin-strap. *Isadora* had also sustained some damage. Beneath the cockpit two five inch long cracks extended through the gel coat and layers of fibreglass but it didn't seem likely they would let any water into the cockpit.

When we were all set to go, Max pushed me off into a broken wave. I paddled out fast, just climbing over the next wave before it broke. Going out through the surf after the previous night's near disaster was a traumatic experience. I was on the verge of tears as I waited for Max beyond the breakers.

As Max paddled away from the boulders, a four foot high wave broke over him. It shook him but he stayed on course. He took off at our usual paddling speed, but I was paddling painfully slowly, hindered by a sore arm and an aching shoulder. "Stick with me Max," I yelled as my confidence was shaken. I didn't want to be left alone. I couldn't see myself getting any further than Sutherland Sound, the entrance of which lay three miles north-east from Tommy Point. We paddled into a light northerly under an overcast sky, the kayaks rising and falling on the familiar south-westerly swell.

Level with the broad entrance of Sutherland Sound I was feeling all right, although paddling at a slower rate than normal, so we plugged on towards Milford. An orange scoop boat caught up with us and we said gidday to Curly on the *Fernando*. From the time he left *Xanadu* at Anchorage Cove earlier in the morning, Curly had been keeping an eye out for us. "The weather forecast is for 15 to 20 knot south-westerly winds but it should stay like this for most of the day," he told us. He and his offsider were going to work a string of pots up as far as Four Mile Point, one mile north of Sutherland Sound, and he would look out for us on his way back to George Sound.

Soon after Curly had left us, we saw a familiar blue-hulled boat cruising towards us. *Samara* with Ralph, Rob and John on board, drew alongside. They had dropped the support party off at Milford the day before and had decided to have one more day looking for elusive game fish.

"Seen any fish?" John asked hopefully.

"Only a penguin," I replied.

Max related the story of the previous evening's big dumper and John offered us a cup of soup.

"Thanks, but we'd better press on while the sea is OK."

Samara was returning to Milford that night and the crew promised to keep an eye out for us.

From Bligh Sound, we had 19 miles to paddle to St. Anne Point at the entrance of Milford Sound. We gave Bell Point a wide berth and met up again with Curly as he cruised south. He climbed onto the bow of *Fernando* and cast his eyes around the horizon.

"I can't see any wind yet. Should stay like this for a few hours. Poison Bay is just around the next point. You could land in there."

Curly was heading up to Milford next day and Max said to him, "See you in the Milford bar." Sadly Curly shook his head and muttered, "I've been banned from the pub." He offered us a bottle of beer, but Max declined the offer saying, "We'd better stay sober until we reach Milford." With a wave, Curly headed south.

Bligh Sound. The morning after the disastrous loop onto the boulder beach

We paddled north-eastwards, the long swell passing beneath the Nordkapps, until we drew level with the entrance of Poison Bay. Max was keen to enter the bay and land for we were both busting for a leak. Although it would be a welcome rest for my tired and sore body, I knew we would lose at least two hours by paddling into the two mile deep bay. "That's another two hours from Milford," Max commented, so we continued towards St. Anne Point. My arms and shoulders were aching but I was determined to make the most of the settled spell of weather. We agreed to land at the first opportunity.

Around the next sharp, craggy point the swell crashed onto rocks and short sections of boulder beach; there wasn't a show of landing. In the distance we could see two points but I doubted if I had the strength to make it to the nearest one. Max had been tired off Poison Bay but now with a second wind, was powering along in front. We rafted up once for a lolly break but Max couldn't find the sweets in his cockpit.

As we paddled, I watched the small capes on shore, making first one then another my next goal. A slight south-westerly breeze came away and helped the Nordkapps along. Finally behind one of the numerous small points we found Transit Beach. The southern end was rocky with a big surf rolling in, whilst the northern end was sandy, also with a big surf.

Then I realized that the point less than two miles

away was St. Anne Point. Milford was almost within reach. Max was 300 yards in front and couldn't hear my shouts. Fortunately he stopped well out from the surf on Transit Beach and I managed to catch up with him. "That next point is St. Anne Point," I exclaimed.

"The surf looks pretty fiery on the beach," Max frowned. I was relieved to hear him say this because I didn't want another dose of big breakers so soon after the previous night's battering.

My progress was becoming slower and slower. I was close to exhaustion. As we watched from the rafted-up kayaks a fishing boat headed in behind the next point confirming that it was the entrance to Milford. After a five minute spell we decided to try to reach Anita Bay just inside the entrance to the sound.

Max shot off in front again and I was smitten with a bout of tears. The combination of fatigue and sore limbs had taken its toll. I tried to reassure myself, 'Not far to go; no use giving up out here my boy.' Never before whilst climbing, caving or kayaking had I been so tired and exhausted that I was reduced to tears. For a moment I wondered how far the poor old body can be pushed and where the drive comes from that keeps the body functioning when the mind is all ready to give up.

Mitre Peak was hiding in clouds as Max closed on the automatic light situated on the tip of St. Anne Point. He was so far in front by now that he was only visible as a red dot as we simultaneously rose over crests of the swell; in the troughs there was no sign of him. Max waited for me in the lee of the point and side by side we paddled into Milford Sound.

I was immensely relieved to have reached sheltered waters. For the first mile up the sound there was no sign of a landing until we reached the boulder beach of Anita Bay, beaching six hours and 20 minutes after leaving Bligh Sound, our longest stint in the Nordkapps without a break.

It took me a while to ease myself out of the cockpit. When I attempted to walk it must have looked like I was staggering around in a drunken stupor. The first priority after landing was always to relieve the pressure of the bladder. With that accomplished, our thoughts invariably turned to the second priority, food and a cup of tea. Max found a bar of chocolate in his food bag. Of all the flavours, its name was 'Ice Breaker'.

One large brew of tea loaded with sugar later, I began to feel a little more human. Within minutes of our arrival in Anita Bay, a large cloud of sandflies had gathered as a welcoming committee. We both wore our parkas with hoods over our heads and I even pulled a sprayskirt over my face in an effort to stop them biting.

On my closed cell foam mat, spread out over the boulders, I lay down for just a moment and within minutes was asleep. After a few hour's snooze I woke feeling a little rejuvenated in spirit and ready to face the 10 mile paddle to Milford township at the head of the sound. Max was worried that we might run aground on the Milford bar.

At 5.45pm we left Anita Bay and made a beeline for Dale Point on the northern side of the sound. The swell was now only slight and a light north-westerly pushed us in the right direction. From Dale Point we

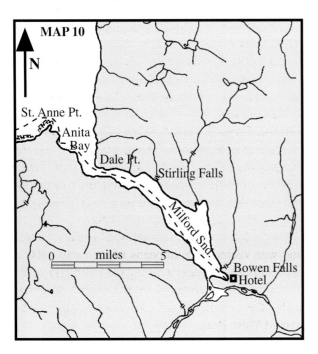

MAP 10
N
St. Anne Pt.
Anita Bay
Dale Pt.
Stirling Falls
Milford Snd.
0   miles   5
Bowen Falls
Hotel

were able to gaze into the brooding dignity of this grand-daddy of all the sounds. High up on our left were the cliffs and crags of the Palisades, their grey verticality broken by the white cascade of Stirling Falls. On our right lay sheer rock walls and moist buttresses, disappearing upwards to the cloud-wreathed summit of Mitre Peak.

Although relieved and happy to be less than two hours paddle from Milford, I couldn't help but feel overawed by the immensity of this sound. With its walls higher and steeper than any of the other sounds we visited, Milford has a forbidding, solemn character all of its own, almost as if it watched while the other sounds were being carved out by the glaciers.

We rounded a corner and could see the Milford Hotel. The cloud base around the mountains gradually lifted, until finally the sharp summit of Mitre Peak was revealed. By Harrison Cove, with only two miles to go, I was tired and had no energy left. Then from the head of the sound a light flashed on and off several times, and we realized our support party had spotted us.

As we neared the spectacular Bowen Falls, we could just make out a figure on the rocks. It was Ainslie who had been using the telescopic sight on the rifle to monitor our progress. Passing the falls we continued into the cove called Freshwater Basin where four or five tourist launches were tied up to the wharf.

Max spotted Maestro on the wharf, waving a can of beer with one hand and a bottle of wine with the other, and took off like a rocket. I didn't have any energy left to put on a spurt and was content just to reach the wharf. Maestro presented Max with a can of beer and held out the bottle of wine as I glided in beside Max's kayak. "Nothing's too good for the boys," Maestro declared. I wrapped a tired hand around the wine bottle and for several minutes we sat in the Nordkapps, happy to be once more reunited with our support party and away from 'those big seas outside.'

On their return from a shopping trip to Te Anau, Ainslie and Maestro pitched a tent on a grassy flat overlooking the sound. Maestro peered down the sound with the telescopic sight mounted on his rifle. Excitedly he called to Ainslie, "My God, they're out there. There's two of them. It's the boys." The Nordkapps still weren't visible to the naked eye but Ainslie flashed the car headlights on and off several times. This was the flashing light that Max and I saw.

The support party found an accommodation shortage at Milford as the motor camp was fully booked and there was only one spare room available at the hotel.

"How much is the room?" I asked Maestro as we drove along to the hotel. "Seventeen Dollars," he said.

I rolled my eyes and groaned, as our finances were running low. "It's my shout for the boys!"

Max on the beach, exposed by low tide, at Anita Bay, Milford Sound

Both Max and I were in urgent need of a shower, to wash away the accumulated layers of salt, sweat and grime. Our last hot shower had been at the Blanket Bay hotel. In the end we decided to fork out the money for one night and cram the four of us into a room.

By a stroke of luck while trying to find a shed to house the kayaks, we met Keith Dent who worked as an air traffic controller for the Department of Civil Aviation. Keith was run to ground in the bar and took us to a double garage where the kayaks would be safe.

"Where are you boys staying?" asked Keith.

"In one of those $17 a night rooms at the pub."

"Why don't you crash at my place?"

"There's four of us," replied Maestro.

"No worries," replied Keith, "move in and make yourselves at home." He showed us the kitchen and the shower and returned to the bar.

I am sure he had no idea of what he was letting himself in for. It's marvellous just how much pleasure and bliss a tired paddler, with a few bruises and abrasions, can find during a half hour soak in a hot bath.

10 January - Day 21

A cloudless sky and beaming sun tempted us to start the last stage of the trip to Jackson Bay. It seemed a pity to waste perfect weather but we both needed a rest day and

a chance for my aches and pains to subside.

Max and I washed our wetsuits and hung them over a fence in front of Keith's flat. Before long there was no sign of the fence; it disappeared beneath a tent, tent fly, sleeping bags, duvets, and drying clothes. The mood of the sound was warmer in sunlight than on the previous grey evening. Mitre Peak dominated the skyline, rising steeply to its sharp summit. On the northern side of the sound, the permanent snowfield on Mt. Pembroke was dazzlingly bright. A strong sea breeze came away in the afternoon and the surface of the sound sparkled with a chop whipped up by the wind.

We were joined by Lyn Taylor from Christchurch who had flown in with Mt. Cook Airlines pilot, Mike Neison. (Mike had flown the support party into Cascade Cove on Christmas Day). On the plane Lyn mentioned to Mike that she was hoping to meet the two kayakers. As she was the only passenger, Mike flew down Milford Sound and along the coast as far as Poison Bay but there was no sign of the Nordkapps, they were hiding in a garage at Milford.

Milford Sound was first named 'Milford haven' and was visited by Europeans in the early 1800's, especially seal hunters working the Fiordland coast. The sound was surveyed by the vessel *Acheron* under the command of Captain John Stokes who named Mitre Peak.

11 January - Day 22

The early morning forecast predicted a cold front moving in from the Tasman, passing over at about 1500 hours. Max and I peered down the sound. Already the weather was starting to deteriorate with clouds scudding over from the north-west, announcing the impending arrival of the cold front. This was sufficient excuse for 'the boys' to declare another day of rest.

Without success we tried to talk Maestro into going for a morning shot. But he was as enthusiastic about hunting as we were about paddling. He had been to a gambling evening the previous night that Keith had organized, and had lost a few dollars. Maestro didn't want to remember the night before.

I knew *Isadora* had sustained a little damage to her hull during the Bligh Sound landing but on close inspection, I found two five inch long cracks, one on either side of the cockpit. They were right through the yellow gel coat and layers of fibreglass but during the paddle up to Milford, the cracks had not let in noticeable amounts of water. Poor old *Isadora* must have come close to breaking in half when she hit that boulder beach.

In the rear compartment I carried a repair kit for occasions such as these. It contained a square yard of fibreglass cloth, a container of polyester laminating resin and a plastic squeeze bottle of catalyst.

I roughed the inner and outer surfaces of the cracks clean with a piece of sandpaper and cut out pieces of the cloth to amply cover the cracks. A few drops of catalyst were mixed with some resin to make a 'brew', which I painted over the areas for the patches. Finally I placed the pieces of cloth over the cracks and daubed more of the brew on top. The time it takes for the brew to harden or 'go off' depends on the amount of catalyst added to the resin; the more catalyst, the faster the brew hardens. Within 20 minutes, *Isadora* was patched inside and out which says a lot for the ease and convenience of repairing fibreglass kayaks after a major ding.

For Max and I there was one last stage to go, from Milford to Jackson Bay. From the experiences of the three Nelson paddlers we knew it would not be an easy section of coastline. Sheltered landings were virtually nonexistent with no more sounds to escape into if the sea became angry. On the maps it looked like a three day paddle; Milford to Martins Bay on the first day, to Browns Refuge or Barn Bay on the second and Jackson Bay on the third; three days in perfect conditions.

During the afternoon we slowly got things in order for the morrow, replenishing our depleted food bags, restocking the raspberry cream biscuit supply, and lightening our loads where possible. I decided to leave the fishing tackle, a few clothes which I had not used and the mouth organ which was not easy to play with a painful split lip.

The evening meal included a special tin of venison casserole, the one Maestro nearly shot in George Sound, washed down with liberal quantities of wine. As it was to be our last night in Milford, Keith persuaded us to adjourn to the hotel bar. As we left his flat, Keith picked up a roll of red and white twine and fastened one end of it to the porch, then he and Max proceeded to unroll the twine in the direction of the bar. "So we can find our way home," grinned Keith.

The twine passed around a petrol tanker and across the road to a petrol pump. Keith played the part of a life-saver, standing in the middle of the road as he fed out the twine to Maestro who tied it taut inside the hotel porch. We all sat by a window in the bar where we would keep an eye on the twine. Our cheeks were sore from continuous grinning and smiling. To some of the drinkers, the barman commented that the twine was a navigational aid for the two kayakers who got lost on the bar the other evening.

A New Zealand Road Services bus was the first vehicle to brake sharply in front of the twine, stretched tightly three foot above the road. Maestro dashed out into the drizzle and held the line down while the bus drove over it. The bus driver was invited to join us for a drink, which he did. In fading light we watched a camper van drive into the twine and break it. "All the toll circuits are down," Maestro told the poor driver, "This radio aerial is the only contact with the outside world." Not suspecting that Maestro was pulling his leg, the van driver climbed under the petrol tanker and joined together the broken ends of the 'aerial', Maestro's watchful eye upon him.

Keith suggested we hijack one of the loopie launches for a 'burn down the sound'. "We could trail our D.N.A. (drunken navigational aid) behind us," I chuckled.

"If we towed the twine behind us," asked Max with a twinkle in his eye, "how many knots would we be doing?"

When a Tourist Hotel Corporation minibus stopped at the twine, Maestro was a little concerned, "What'll I do, What'll I do?" he asked.

"Not to worry, it's only the trainee manager," declared Keith pushing Maestro towards the door.

When Maestro returned, he had almost convinced the trainee manager that the twine was a radio aerial; "The only link with those two poor kayakers who have been out of touch for days." At 10.30pm we were unceremoniously bundled out of the bar, fortunate to have our navigational aid to follow back to Keith's flat. Still you get nights like that on the big trips!

Chapter 8

MILFORD
to MARTINS BAY

12 January - Day 23

At 6.30am the phone rang to remind Keith he had to send out a weather situation from the control tower. After he went out the door clutching his forehead, Maestro tried to galvanise the boys into action. He tried friendly persuasion and cajoling without success; but with the threat of a saucepan of cold water down my neck, I got up and squinted down the sound - a clear sky with a dusting of fresh snow on Mitre Peak and Pembroke.

I had hoped to find inclement weather so we could declare another rest day. I felt much better suited to a life of ease aground on the Milford bar than to the rigours of the open sea. Max wasn't keen to move either. He lay very quietly in his sleeping bag, hoping no one would notice him.

Reluctant as we were to leave Milford, we couldn't waste another perfect day by snoozing and reading; or could we? Maestro thought otherwise and supervised our packing. At 8.30am Max and I were ready to depart with the laden kayaks sitting on a sandbank in Freshwater Basin. An hour of ebbing tide remained to hasten our progress down the sound.

Keith drove up with a weather forecast, "There's a two knot southerly blowing at Haast. The barometer has risen a bit to 1001 millibars. Should be fine boys!" We thanked Keith for his mighty hospitality and he returned to the control tower. When the support party left Milford, they left enough beer, wine and smokes to keep Keith out of the bar for many a night.

Max and I slid off the sandbank at 8.45am after sadly saying goodbye to our support party. A reflection of Mitre Peak, bathed in soft morning light, lay on the mirror surface of the sound. At the entrance to the basin we stopped for a final wave to our friends on the wharf and paddled out into the sound.

Level with Harrison Cove we slid out of the shadows into bright sunlight. With a combination of bodies rejuvenated from two day's rest and the ebbing tide, we covered the ten miles to Anita Bay in an hour and a half, a speed of over six knots.

Turning north out of the sound around Dale Point, we kept the Nordkapps close to shore along to Stripe Point. For the next few miles we were sheltered from the swell by St. Anne Point. The wind was blowing at four to six knots from the north but as we approached Stripe Point it swung to the south-west, as punctual as ever, our old friend the 11 o'clock chop. Before long I could see whitecaps out on the sea to the west, and I had a growing feeling of apprehension. Beyond

Max and Ainslie at Freshwater Basin, Milford Sound

Stripe Point a shallowing of the seabed was apparent as we paddled from the normally dark green sea into pale green coloured water. By now we were out of the lee of St. Anne Point and feeling the full effect of the Southern Ocean swell.

A mile south of Yates Point we were making heavy weather, paddling parallel to the occasionally capping swell. At least we could see when one of the swell crests was going to break, which was far better than having them break from astern without warning. One swell crest larger than the rest broke over Max. As his Nordkapp was forced sideways in front of the breaking wave, Max hung halfway over for a moment, desperately bracing with his paddle in the white surging foam, then he capsized.

Slowly I turned *Isadora* towards where the flat yellow hull was left in the wave's wake. Max's red paddle came up alongside his kayak for the start of a screw roll. He came halfway up with the roll but lost momentum and went under again. A second attempt was successful. With water cascading off his head and shoulders, Max returned to the 'right way up' position.

Screw rolling uses the paddle, skimming over the surface of the sea, to pull the body out of the water. From the inverted or 'submarine' position the paddle blade is laid flat on the surface beside the kayak, and the hand nearest the bow pulls the paddle back over the shoulder. To lower the body's centre of gravity for the roll, the shoulders are arched over backwards so that the head almost touches the rear deck.

Before the trip Max and I had joked about the title

of an account of the Fiordland expedition; 'Submariner's guide to the Fiordland Coastline,' seemed most appropriate as we counted on spending a little time upside down.

By Yates Point we had to turn directly into the swell for the whitecaps were trying to push us onto the rocky reefs of the point. In the lee of the point we rafted up to pull on parkas and put down the skegs. My hands were so cold, I had difficulty pulling off my sprayskirt to get out my parka.

For the first time I was going to try out a fixed skeg which was longer than the retractable ones. Whilst I held onto the bow of Max's kayak, he slid the skeg over *Isadora's* stern.

In a calm sea, pulling on a parka is easy but on a choppy swell we had to keep both hands on our paddles to prevent capsizing. It was much easier to raft up and it was always good to have an excuse to hang onto each other's decklines, not having to worry about balancing the kayak for a few moments. But in those tippy moments as the Nordkapps drifted apart after rafting up, before there was sufficient distance between them to resume paddling, I always felt decidedly unstable. Gingerly, the first stroke was attempted, then another and another until the old natural paddling rhythm was regained.

A small crayboat bounced across the chop towards us and the fishermen were amazed to see the two Nordkapps. Their boat was rolling violently as the skipper called out to us, "There are no landings along the coast until Martins Bay and that's about 12 miles off."

As we approached the next rocky point at the end of a section of sandy beach, I found I was falling further and further behind Max and experiencing difficulty in pointing *Isadora's* bow out to sea to miss several rocky islands off the point. Even by paddling continually on the right hand side, the kayak was very slow to respond. She felt unstable and her movements sluggish. Only when I noticed the bow higher in the air than normal did the penny drop. I looked back at the stern and was horrified to find that it was completely awash. My stern compartment was flooded.

After attracting Max's attention I yelled, "I'll have to land." He asked if I could make for the rocky islands and land in their lee. But the stern was now underwater and the compartment was filling rapidly. *Isadora* was becoming increasingly tippy and hard to manoeuvre. Although we were fortunate to be off a sandy beach, a huge surf was booming in from a long way out. I had no option but to go in.

Max yelled, "I'll try and get through the surf and give you a hand from the beach." During a brief lull he took off and fortunately caught a small wave which carried him out of my sight and almost to the beach. As I struggled shorewards I tried to work out how many waves comprised the sets of higher than average breakers rolling beachwards. Left alone with another set building up astern and not able to paddle fast or turn in a hurry, I was worried at the prospect of being hammered in the surf. Waves in the sets appeared to be at least nine feet high. From behind I heard a loud thumping as the first wave of a set broke. I braced in anticipation of tumbling end over end in a forward loop.

As the breaker pounded over me, we were completely buried momentarily but instead of forward looping, I was surprised as *Isadora* shot out in front of the wall of white water like a projectile from a gun. Normally in such a situation the Nordkapp would have looped but the weight of water in the flooded compartment was holding the stern in the wave. I used the paddle as a flail on both sides to stay upright.

From shore all Max could see was 'a small insignificant yellow and orange blob at the base of an enormous wall of broken white water.' After a fast ride of 100 yards, the wave died and I was left with a 20 yard paddle to the sand. However the shore dump didn't let me off so lightly. It picked up *Isadora* like a matchstick and thumped us upside down on the beach.

When the retreating surge threatened to drag *Isadora* back into the face of the next dumper, I held onto the decklines and called to Max for help. He rescued my paddle from the surge and together we dragged the waterlogged Nordkapp up the beach. The map and the plastic envelope on the deck in front of the cockpit had been torn off. I also lost a pair of sandshoes and the hat which Maestro had given me that morning. Maestro would not be pleased!

The rear compartment was full of water, with bags of food and clothes completely saturated. The cause of the flooding was obvious when I removed the hatch cover. Two inches of the rubber 'O' ring, which formed a pressure seal between the cover and hatch opening had slipped out of its containing groove when I closed the hatch at Milford. Although in calm flat water nothing would have happened, water cascading over the deck from the choppy sea off Yates Point caught in the recessed groove around the hatch cover, dribbling in slowly at first until there was sufficient weight of water to hold the stern submerged. The compartment then filled rapidly.

From our vantage point on the beach, the surf appeared far worse than the foreshortened view we had seen from outside the breakers. I was thankful that both *Isadora* and I had reached the beach unscathed. It would not be easy regaining the open sea, but it was no use worrying about it, so we brewed up a billy of tea to restore morale. My clothes and food bags were hung on pieces of driftwood and spread

Setting off from Milford on the last stage to Jackson Bay. Mitre Peak in the background. Photo: Ainslie Lamb

over flax bushes to dry. To see what a landing would have been like in the lee of the next point, we walked north along the beach to where the Wolf River spilled out of a narrow valley onto the beach. A startled, solitary seal, who had been dozing behind a rock, showed us how easy it was to launch into a dumping surf.

By 5.30pm Max was impatient to leave the beach before the sea grew any wilder. I procrastinated, not looking forward to a dash out in a lull between sets. In sets of three, there was only 60 seconds or so between the last wave of one set and the first wave of the following set. Not much time to paddle 200 yards through surf. The sun disappeared behind banks of cloud and to the south the view was obscured by rain and mist.

At least while we waited the tide was dropping. It was close to full tide when we landed at midday and now the surf was marginally smaller. Although the waves often broke further out from shore at low tide, breakers were never as high as at high tide.

By 6pm I had run out of excuses. We made a final search of the beach for the missing map, the sandshoes and Maestro's hat; not a sign of them. Some future visitor to Wolf River beach may well find an old seal wearing a pair of sandshoes and faded cloth cap, peering at a plastic coated map of the area.

Max pushed me into the shore dump at 6.15pm *Isadora* was battered by the broken water of the last two waves of a set. In the lull that followed I paddled as hard and fast as I could for the open sea. The first wave of the next set reared up in front of me, appearing to cap before I could reach it. But *Isadora's* bow punched through its crest and we crashed into the trough behind. With the Nordkapp climbing up the face of the wave, it felt at least 20 feet high but was probably only nine to ten feet.

I was airborne over the crests of the second and third waves of the set, but with a dry mouth and my pulse racing, I safely reached the open sea.

From the swell crests I caught an occasional glimpse of Max biding his time on the beach, waiting for the

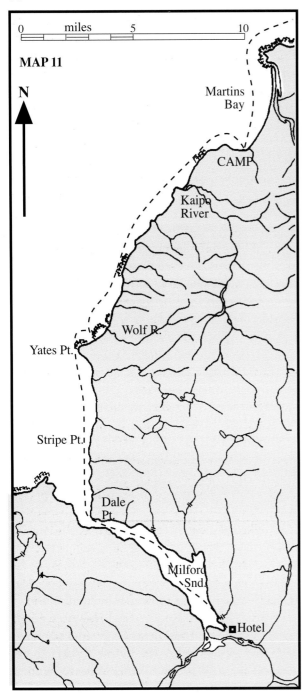

0   miles   5   10

MAP 11

N

Martins
Bay

CAMP

Kaipo
River

Wolf R.

Yates Pt.

Stripe Pt.

Dale
Pt.

Milford
Snd.

■Hotel

A light plane flew south above us, showing no sign that it had spotted us. As we approached the Kaipo River mouth, the plane returned. It flew in circles around us and made several low passes about 200 feet up. Our support party had been keen to see 'the boys' in action on the high seas and had hoped to charter a plane from Milford. Unfortunately the lighting was very poor for photographs but the troops enjoyed the flight. From the plane the two Nordkapps, side by side, appeared as 'two tiny yellow matchsticks on a grey sea.'

Not long after the plane flew off to the south, the weather closed in. Light patches of drizzle drifted by from the north as we rose and fell over the long swell. Just as the light was starting to fade we rounded a rocky point and the grey vista of Martins Bay lay before us. Through misty rain we could just make out Long Reef at the northern end of the bay where the mighty Hollyford River entered the sea.

Max wanted to push on to the Hollyford bar and paddle upriver to the old Martins Bay settlement. But the bar had claimed several lives since it was first visited by Europeans and I considered there was insufficient time to reach it before we lost the last light of day. Between two low rocky points on the south side of the bay, we found a short strip of sandy beach that appeared to be a feasible landing spot. The surf was moderate in size but several sharp rocks were exposed amongst the breakers. On the map I remembered that a boat landing was shown somewhere near here. Half a mile to the west we could see and hear a large surf booming onto the four mile long beach of Martins Bay. When we thought we were level with the boat landing, we waited for a lull and powered in through a line of breakers to graunch the bows onto a steep, gravel beach. After an eventful day, we were both happy to be back on shore again.

There were no decent camping spots in the scrub and forest behind the beach so we pitched the tent on a gravel berm on top of the beach. A Hughes 300 helicopter flew over at dusk, heading towards the Hollyford River.

It was a cold bleak north-westerly evening. 'The boys' were feeling a little miserable at 11pm We sat in the tent spooning down beef curry and peas by the light of a candle stub, rain drumming on the taut fabric of the tent fly, the tent vibrating in the wind.

13 January - Day 24
Heavy rain during the night caused the tent poles to sink into the wet gravel. This allowed the fly to come in contact with the tent and as a result Max and I woke up lying in pools of rain water that had soaked through the fabric. The waterproof tent floor was doing an admirable job of keeping water in. Our fibrefill sleeping bags, although damp, were still warm. If they'd

right moment to launch. He didn't have the benefit of a shove into the waves. Then he was gone and for several minutes there was no sign of him. I dreaded the thought of going back in through the surf if he had canned out.

The bow of his Nordkapp appeared cresting a wave about to break and I was greatly relieved as Max paddled out to join me. He had been knocked sideways twice but hadn't capsized.

Fortunately the south-westerly breeze had died and it was replaced after a brief period of calm by a light northerly. The wind change was accompanied by a darkening of the sky as the cloud base thickened and gradually lowered towards the sea. We paddled by several small islands and a cliff with a tunnel passing right through it.

been down, we would have been cold and wet.

Without getting up, we peered out onto the grey, white-flecked waters of the bay and then quickly closed the door of the tent before the sandflies realized we were there. A strong north-westerly was blowing. Mid-morning, as a cold front passed over, the wind swung to the south-west and the air temperature dropped a degree or two. There didn't seem to be a show of paddling in such rotten weather so we set off to investigate the Hollyford bar. All along the wide sandy beach the surf was booming in, breaking from over half a mile out.

Along the northern half of the beach, the broad slow moving waters of the Hollyford River run parallel to the surf and are separated from the breakers by a narrow belt of dunes. The river entered the sea at the northern end of the beach, hard up against the rocks of Long Reef. It was obvious that we wouldn't have stood a chance of paddling over the bar, for the swell was breaking out by the tip of the point with breakers rolling up the river. The river waters ran swiftly into the sea through a narrow channel, surging and swirling around several sharp rocks exposed in mid-channel. No place for Nordkapps.

We walked back over the dunes, gazing onto the unruffled waters of the river. Wooden poles in the channel were evidence of the previous whitebait season, and three whitebaiter's shacks on top of the dunes were almost completely covered by drifting sand. Across the Hollyford River we could see a house and sheds but there was no sign of life and no response to our calls.

Where the river turns inland from the dunes towards its outlet from Lake McKerrow, we continued south through the dunes until we came across a stand of eucalypts and a few old macrocarpa trees. We found the remains of an old coal range, a few pieces of broken crockery, an old wooden rail stockyard and the rusty remnants of barbed wire fences. They and the exotic trees were all that remained of the old McKenzie homestead.

Early explorers to Martins Bay found an old Maori chief named Tutoko, living with his wife and two children amongst the sandhills between the Hollyford and the sea. In 1870 sections were surveyed on the shores of Lake McKerrow for a town which was called Jamestown. The first ship transporting settlers to the bay was wrecked on the Hollyford bar and the life of Jamestown was to be short-lived, with only a few hardy families staying on.

In her book *Pioneers of Martins Bay*, Alice McKenzie relates the story of her parents settling at Jamestown and later moving home to the dunes by the south end of the bay. Food and mail were brought to the isolated settlers by Government steamship,

over the Hollyford bar if the tide and seas were favourable, otherwise the stores were taken by surf-boat to the landing where our tent was pitched. Alice's three brothers built a 23 foot long surfboat from pit-sawn timber. It was used for two voyages to Okuru, 70 miles to the north-east along the coast, to visit their married sister. The first trip went smoothly but in 1889, after leaving the bay in calm conditions for a second trip, the seas grew worse as the day wore on. The party was fortunate to make a landing through the reefs and surf at Barn Bay where they had to wait three days for the seas to subside before continuing on. That was Alice's last trip to Okuru.

In 1887, four prospectors drowned on the Hollyford Bar after a trip down the coast from Browns Refuge. Their ill-fated lifeboat was from the *S.S. Tararua* which was wrecked on Waipapa Point on the South Coast in 1881 with tragic loss of life. Alice relates a time when a fishing trip nearly ended in disaster on the bar. She, two of her brothers and another three people were fishing at sea one morning. The seas grew rough but they had to wait for low tide before attempting to cross the bar. As the boat crossed the bar a large wave stood it on end. It capsized but all six were fortunate to reach shore safely.

As we were walking back towards the tent something made me turn around. A group of people were standing by the remains of the old McKenzie homestead. Max and I jogged over and caught them up as they walked along the beach. A party of six tourists led by guide Anne Edmonds was on a day trip from Martins Bay lodge. I had met Anne previously at Arthurs Pass, and she explained that a jetboat had dropped her party at the head of the lagoon, a narrow, southerly trending offshoot of the Hollyford River which lies not far inland from the homestead.

Max and I must have cut a dashing pair as we walked along with the group, and we were asked to pose for a photograph. We were clad in holey woollen long johns, bush shirts and knee length orange parkas. We arrived at the Hollyford in time to see a shiny aluminium jetboat pull into the bank. Gerald Williams, the boat's driver, was a tall, middle-aged gaunt looking chap. He asked us back to the lodge for a cuppa. We joined the tourists in the sleek looking jet boat for the fastest ride of our trip, but after only minutes on the plane upriver, Gerald pulled the boat in by a wee jetty on the northern bank. A green-painted lodge was set back from the bank by the end of an airstrip.

Over a cup of tea, while Max and I surreptitiously demolished a plate of chocolate biscuits, we met the cooks, guides and bottlewashers who worked for the Hollyford Tourist and Travel Company. The company was run by Jules Tapper who, at the time, was out in the big smoke. We met Geoff Toner, who the

Max at the landing in Martins Bay

previous evening, had flown our support party up from Milford to photograph 'the boys' at sea.

Scudding clouds and drizzle indicated that another nor-wester was brewing during the afternoon so we helped Gerald prepare one of the jet boats for an engine transplant. Gerald's wife Rachel worked as a cook at the lodge. They used to own a farm in the central Hawkes Bay district but sold it after their children grew up so they could see more of New Zealand before they were too old. Before taking up jet boat driving on the Hollyford, Gerald worked for a season as manager of the Quinton hut on the Milford Track. I couldn't help but admire the decision, made by a couple advanced in years, to give up their livelihood and seek new challenges.

For dinner, the cooks served a superb casserole with a large bowl of coleslaw. We both had ravenous appetites. I had second and third helpings.

After dinner I went over to a deer shooter's camp, 200 yards away from the lodge, to see if they had a recent forecast. When I entered the house, Evan Brunton, his wife Annette and Dave, a chopper pilot, were smitten with fit of the giggles and tried hard to stifle laughing out loud. With knobbly knees peering through tattered remnants of what were once a pair of pink longjohns, and trying to pull the front of my green bush shirt down as low as possible, I must have provided quite a spectacle. I explained that I was a kayaker. Dave said that when they were flying along the beaches the previous evening, they were puzzled by what they thought was a set of helicopter skid marks on the beach by the Wolf River mouth. "They were the drag marks of our kayaks," I explained. Dave and Evan were amazed that we had managed to get in and out through the surf there.

The evening forecast was for a south-westerly change. Evan and Dave were preparing for their evening inspection of slips and beaches from the Hughes 300 helicopter which was parked near the house. For four years Evan was ground shooting from

a hut on Elizabeth Island at the head of Doubtful Sound, rowing the deer he shot back by dinghy to his freezer. He had been ground shooting at Martins Bay for the past three years.

When hunting, Evan took along his dog Reef, a fawn coloured Weimaraner or German Pointer. Poor old Reef had only three legs. Evan explained that he was out shooting with Reef up Hokuri Creek which drains into Lake McKerrow. It was a typical Fiord-land day, rain, mist and poor visibility. Evan saw a deer coloured object moving in the forest and fired. To his horror, whining and yelping indicated that he had shot his dog. "The dog was furious and tried to bite me," Evan related. "But he had a soft mouth." For several hours he carried Reef until he reached the lodge from where Jules Tapper flew the hunter and his dog out to a vet at Queenstown. The bone of one of the dog's hind legs was so badly shattered that the whole leg had to be amputated.

Reef still goes out hunting with Evan, ground shooting, in the jet boat and sometimes in the helicopter. But one thing that the only licensed dog in the Fiordland National Park can't do now, is what his breed is noted for, pointing at game. If Reef was to raise one of his front paws, he would topple over.

Just on dark the chopper returned with two loads of deer. Evan and Dave had checked our campsite to see if the tent and kayaks were standing up to the wind. I watched Evan as he cleaned up the deer. From the deers' top jaws he removed two small tusks which were used in making ladies' jewellery. The carcasses were hung until the body heat had gone before they were moved into the freezer.

The evening's tally included a stag and several yearlings. Velvet covered the stag's antlers. This is a soft furry substance which protects the antlers from injury whilst they are growing and it also contains blood vessels. Between the months of November and January, the hunters bring back the antlers, for the velvet is worth many dollars per pound when used as an aphrodisiac.

In December, the hinds were dropping their fawns and before mum gave birth, she drove her yearling away to fend for itself. Without mum to guide and protect them, the yearlings fell easy victims to Evan's .308 semi-automatic rifle. From Martins Bay, the deer carcasses were flown by helicopter or plane out to the Upper Hollyford road end, where they were trucked to Mossburn in Southland.

Max and I slept in one of the bunkrooms of the Martins Bay lodge. Lying in a top bunk, warm and dry after a supper of Annie's pikelets, was far more pleasant than in a damp sleeping bag on the beach.

Chapter 9

MARTINS BAY to JACKSON BAY

14 January - Day 25

The morning forecast from Awarua Radio was not encouraging: 'A high of 1024 millibars centred 150 miles NNW of North Cape, moving ENE at 20 knots. South of the high, a strong disturbed westerly air stream covers the Tasman Sea and New Zealand. Winds: west to south-west 20 to 30 knots. Seas: moderate to rough, with a moderate to heavy swell. Outlook: Westerly winds 15 to 20 knots with scattered showers.'

When Gerald set off to pick up a party of trampers from a parks board hut near Long Reef, Max and I accompanied him downriver in the jet boat to see what state the sea was in. Gerald planed the boat down to near the bar, then throttled back and turned upstream just before reaching the breakers. The boat was barely holding its own into the swiftly flowing Hollyford. Max had turned a whiter shade of pale but Gerald had the motor only on half throttle, and when he opened it up, we ploughed out of the narrow channel to go onto the plane where the river widened and slowed.

Although a large swell was running there was no sign of whitecaps out to sea, and only a light breeze blowing. I was keen to push on while the wind was

light, so Gerald dropped us off at the head of the lagoon. We arranged a tentative rendezvous for 5pm in case we didn't like the look of the sea. As we walked through the dunes and onto the beach, we startled a pair of small penguins. With an awkward waddling gait, they set off for the security of the sea.

The orange dot of our tent looked rather lonely and forlorn, almost as if it was out of place, as we walked over the rocks to the boat landing. A large bull seal, whom we disturbed from a snooze, kept a wary eye on us until we had passed by.

Apart from the large swell the sea looked OK for paddling but since it was nearing high water, we decided to wait half an hour to see if the wind was going to come away on the turn of the tide. The half hour lost was to result in a disastrous landing that evening.

I was worried about the marked lack of sheltered landings to the north. Once we left Martins Bay, we had no option but to make for either the south side of Big Bay, 10 miles away, or Barn Bay, 28 miles to the north-east as the seagull flies.

As we dropped the tent, I pulled up the tent pegs and in the disturbed gravel found a sealed plastic bag containing porridge. Further digging revealed several more bags containing dehydrated food. Initially

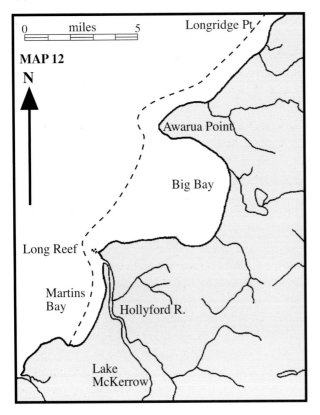

I thought that the food had been abandoned by a tramping party but realized that it must have been where the three Nelson kayakers camped in August on their Fiordland kayaking expedition. They had remained here for two days while Vic Hague was sick. The trio paddled to Anita Bay inside Milford Sound after burying much of their food at Martins Bay.

We finally paddled out through a small surf at 2.20pm onto a long, rolling south-westerly swell, and pointed the Nordkapp bows towards Long Reef. Twice I was horrified to see long white objects lurking in the sea, for I assumed they were sharks. Earlier that day Evan Brunton had shown me a photograph of a 12 foot long white pointer shark which Mike Berry had caught in a set net off the beach which we had just left. (On 11 November 1977 Mike and Allison Clark set out from Milford in a 17 foot long crayfishing boat to go fishing. Next day, Mike's body was found south along the coast from Milford Sound and Allison's body was discovered near Yates Point. No trace of their boat was ever found).

An 18 foot long basking shark had frightened the Nelson kayakers off Long Reef. They rafted up until it swam away. Because of these two shark stories, I was naturally a little jumpy. Basking sharks, although as long as Nordkapps, are plankton eaters and harmless to man. White pointers however, are carnivorous and those caught off the West Coast often contain one or two entire seals in their stomachs. I convinced myself that the long white shapes that I had seen were only patches of seaweed, but paddled a little bit faster anyway.

For an hour we paddled by Martins Bay, staying a quarter of a mile out from the surf. Nearing Long Reef we had to turn out to sea for the swell was breaking a long way out over the submerged reef that gives this headland its very apt name. I was feeling particularly windy as we paddled out parallel to the reef. Waves breaking on the reef were as high, if not higher, than any others we had seen in the open sea. Approaching the reef, the swell steepened with spray smoking off the wave crests, then with a dull roar and an upsurge of spray, the waves broke. Max was 100 yards in closer towards the reef for I was determined to take no chances. About a mile out from the point I headed around two cray pots, thinking that, 'this must be far enough out from the breakers.' Up till then I had caught an occasional glimpse of Max when we both climbed together over swell crests. But now with *Isadora's* bow pointing for the fuzzy grey outline of Awarua Point, six miles away, there was no sign of him.

A larger than normal wave rearing up caused me to paddle hard to face the steep wall of water and climb over its smoking crest. In its wake, I breathed slower with relief. 'If in doubt, stay out,' I decided and paddled out to sea for another 200 yards before turning north again. It was now 10 minutes or more since I last sighted Max and I was feeling decidedly lonely, with just the long grey swell for company.

For a few minutes I continued north, worried that Max had been caught in a reef breaker. I heard a shout, caught a glimpse of Max and was immensely relieved to see him. He was 150 yards away and paddling back to look for me. This was to be the only time on the trip when we completely lost touch with each other. "Jeez, that was a bit foolhardy going in so close," I grumbled. Max merely shrugged his shoulders and without another word we turned towards Awarua Point.

Months later when I again met up with Anne Edmonds at Arthurs Pass, she said that the seas on this day were breaking so violently on Long Reef that she was unable to take a tourist party out to see the seal colony there. The route she normally took was covered by breaking waves.

As we paddled by the five mile wide entrance to Big Bay, nothing could be seen of its distant beaches, four miles away to the east. The sky was overcast but the breeze remained a light northerly. It wasn't strong enough to slow our progress. We made good time across to Awarua Point on the northern side of Big Bay but I was horrified to see another long white line of breakers extending out to sea. It wasn't until we were nearly a mile offshore that I felt we were far enough out to round the point without being caught among the waves smoking in towards it.

Beyond the point and well away from the 'smokies',

I relaxed a little. It was now 5.30pm and we could make out the rocky island off Gorge River in the distance. From our one and a half mile distance offshore, we set course for the island so we could gradually work closer to the coast.

When the wind died, the clouds began to thin. The surface of the swell became glassy and the sea lost its gloomy grey colour, replaced by a beautiful pale blue-green. For half an hour there wasn't the faintest ripple on the sea and the following swell helped to push the Nordkapps along.

The sea had claimed our map of this section of the coastline at Wolf River, so we were relying on our memories to recognize landmarks. Before leaving Martins Bay, we had studied the relevant topographic sheets at the lodge and we also had a smaller scale map of the Aspiring National Park. My next plastic covered map did not start until Browns Refuge.

A mile short of the Gorge River, a northerly breeze came away, gently rippling the surface of the swell at first, but a short time later, we were making painfully slow progress into small whitecaps. By the river mouth we could make out a hut. It was tempting to land but the surf did not appear at all friendly to tired kayakers.

I worked out that the most distant point was Cascade Point, with Barn Bay this side of it, sheltered by a group of rocky islands. There I knew we would find Lou Brown, a crayfisherman, and a sheltered landing. If only we could reach there before nightfall. When we drew level with Browns Refuge, Max was tempted to try and get in through the surf and spend the night there. I thought we might just be able to reach Barn Bay before nightfall. It was a few minutes before 9pm as we paddled by Browne Island, a low barren isolated rock, half a mile offshore.

The light was fading when we considered landing in Cascade Bay two miles further on, where a large surf was thundering in. Worried by the sheer size of the surf, we turned seawards, climbing over rapidly steepening waves to escape from the bay. Now there was no alternative but to reach Barn Bay, still two miles away.

With only 20 minutes of light left, it seemed a hopeless race against time. All stops were out as we paddled hard for the bay's entrance. Our arms were aching with the strain of sustained paddling when we finally rounded a low rocky point at the southern end of the bay. However there were no gaps in a continuous line of smoking waves that were pounding onto a rocky shore. Numerous rocky reefs and exposed rocks added to the confusion of the surf. Although we were about to lose sight of shore with the onset of night, we were both convinced we had to keep pushing northwards to find a break in the surf.

Then it was too dark to go any further. We had to go in. As we turned the Nordkapps towards the line of breakers, there was a glimmer of hope when we both spotted a pinprick of light in the darkness behind the beach. Slowly we nosed towards the beach, eyes frequently searching over our shoulders for approaching waves. A large wave appeared. It picked up *Isadora* and I hung in a right rudder as we sped down the face of the wave. Max was about 20 yards away to my right when the wave picked us up. Unfortunately he'd taken off on the same wave and hung in a left rudder as he careered down the face of the wave.

Both of us thought we were home and hosed. Then came the horrifying realization that we were racing towards each other on a collision course. There was no time to take evasive action. I was a little higher up the face of the wave than Max and shot over the deck of his kayak, just in front of the cockpit. I flicked the paddle up to miss his head and Max had to arch his body over backwards to that my skeg didn't cut him.

Next moment I was upside down and gasping for air in the aftermath of the wave. The paddle had gone and the force of the water had pushed the sprayskirt partially off. Max backpaddled to me and I was using the stern of his Nordkapp to roll back up when the next wave struck. Max had to go with it. Short of air inside this wave, I came out of the cockpit and in the wake of it retrieved the paddle. I was swimming shorewards towing *Isadora* by her bow when Max attempted to tow me in. Yet another large wave tore my grip from his decklines. This wave flipped Max stern over bow in a forward loop. For a fraction of a second, I glimpsed the yellow hull of his kayak standing on end, contrasted against the black of a night sky.

Max attempted to roll but gave up after a struggle in the broken waves. He slipped out of his cockpit and joined me in the water. In the dark, we towed our capsized Nordkapps shorewards, the broken waves helping to push us in until at last my wetsuit bootie touched a rock. We could walk in the rest of the way, but we still had 150 yards to go before collapsing in a heap amongst the large boulders of the beach, exhausted, but thankful to there in one piece with the Nordkapps intact.

"If only you hadn't hooked left," I groaned.

"If only you hadn't hooked right," Max replied.

It was low tide. A wide strip of boulder beach provided our tired bodies with a soul-destroying struggle to carry the heavy Nordkapps to the edge of a wall of flax bushes above the high water level. Slipping and staggering over the large round boulders, occasionally calling, "Rest," to ease the aching arms, we slowly moved both kayaks. Then with a torch and a parka each, we set off in the direction in which we had last seen the pinprick of light.

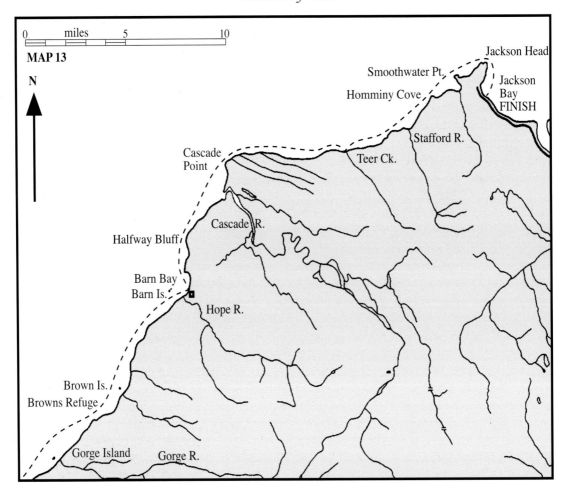

Within 200 yards we came to the end of the boulders, at the edge of the knee deep waters of Hope River. In the torchlight we could see sandy beach stretching away to the north from the river. If only we had paddled another 200 yards. Still, you get landings like that on the big trips!

From the top floor of a two storied house, set back from the northern river bank, lights blazed out onto two crayboats on trailers.

Attracted by the wavering beams of our torches, Lou Brown came down the back stairs to find two bedraggled, dripping kayakers. "We've just had a most unpleasant encounter with the surf," we told him. We introduced ourselves and explained that we had just arrived from Martins Bay, by kayak. Lou told us that he hadn't gone out to check his cray pots that morning as the swell was too big, so we felt a little better. Then Lou said those magic words, "What about a cup of tea and a hot shower?"

Showered and wearing some of Lou's old clothes, we met Maureen, Chris and Ewan, and enjoyed a beautiful cup of tea. Max and Lou discovered that they had met previously on Takaka Hill when they were both trying hang-gliding for the first time.

After a seven and a half hour stint in the Nordka-pps, Max and I were more than happy to crash in a bunkroom behind the house.

15 January - Day 26

The morning forecast could not have been much worse: 'From Puysegur Point to Jackson Bay: Winds: north-westerly 35 to 45 knots; Seas: very rough with a WNW swell; Outlook: north-west winds 25 to 35 knots.'

For breakfast Lou and Maureen cooked up a fabulous feed of large pancakes with a delicious syrup. This was their regular Sunday morning treat. From the dining table we were able to look out through a long picture window onto the windswept waters of the bay. The *New Zealand Pilot* has the following description of the bay:

> Barn bay lies about three miles south-westward of
> the mouth of Cascade river; Hope river flows into
> this bay and Barn islets, a small group with
> Sugarloaf, a rock lying close northward of them,
> are situated about half a mile northward of its
> mouth; Boulder bank extends from the northern
> shore of the bay halfway to Sugarloaf rock. The
> land immediately over this part of the coast is steep
> and of moderate height, but is backed by lofty and
> rugged mountain ranges...

A moderate northerly was sweeping across the bay, allowing no chance for the large pounding surf to settle. Definitely a rest day for the boys. At 9.30am a Piper cub landed on a narrow 250 yard long airstrip, which led away from the house like a corridor through the flax bushes. Maureen and Chris flew out to Jackson Bay with the pilot, promising to pass on a message to our support party. "They should be waiting for us at the bay," we informed Maureen.

Lou and Ewan helped Max and I retrieve the Nordkapps from their overnight bed of boulders and carry them up to the house. There we attempted to dry out some of our wet gear, which was still saturated from the wet nights at Martins Bay. We spent a restful day yarning with Lou, reading and drinking endless cups of tea. I was glad we weren't at sea in the afternoon for the rain was drumming on the iron roof of the house and the leaves of the flax bushes outside were being whipped by the wind. The windsock by the end of the airstrip was streamed out horizontally. Heavy rain during the morning caused Hope River, over a period of four hours, to grow from a knee deep channel to a wide, brown, timber-strewn torrent.

This was Lou's third season crayfishing out of Barn Bay. During the previous winter, he built *Scratch*, a 20 foot long snub-nosed aluminium boat in Cromwell. An enormous caterpillar diesel motor in the stern powered a commercial jet unit, pushing the boat up to a top speed of 33 m.p.h. He kept *Scratch* moored to a rock in a deep pool of Hope River. When Lou checked his cray pots, he was limited to four hour sessions, since there was only sufficient water over the bar of the river for two hours either side of high tide. If the bar was too rough or too shallow, he moored *Scratch* in a lagoon behind a boulder bank on the northern side of the bay. Lou, with Maureen as deckhand, set his pots from Gorge River in the south to Cascade Point in the north. The only other land-based crayboat between Milford Sound and Jackson Bay was at the south end of Big Bay.

Behind the house, Maureen had a fine vegetable garden, growing some of the largest cabbages that I had seen. Black plastic mesh from old cray pots served as a fence. The garden was fertilized with long strands of bull kelp washed up after rough seas and crayfish bodies that were left after Lou finished tailing the day's catch.

One day while Maureen was digging her garden, Lou overhauled the diesel generating plant. This provided power for the lights, radio and maintained cool temperatures in the crayfish tail freezer. He replaced the brushes in the generator but when it was all back together, the ammeter in the house wouldn't register a charge while the motor was running. Lou pulled down the generator and reassembled it, only to find it still wasn't producing current at the house. Again he dismantled the generator and put it together; still no success. Lou radioed for advice and was told to excite the generator with a 12 volt battery. He did this but again no current.

In desperation he flew the generator out to Queenstown where it functioned perfectly. When it arrived back, Lou installed it but there was still no current at the house. He was just about to use the generator as an anchor for *Scratch* when he dug up the cable in the garden between the generator shed and the house. While all the previous events were taking place, two of Maureen's cabbages had mysteriously died.

Lou discovered that a prong of Maureen's garden fork had penetrated the cable sheathing, which in the damp sand, was causing a short circuit. With the cable replaced and the generator excited, current was once again produced at the house. The two dead cabbages had been electrocuted!

Lou had a half share in the Piper Cub which had landed earlier in the day. He used this to fly out bags of frozen cray tails, returning with food supplies. He and Maureen were more than happy with their isolated existence which was occasionally relieved by tramping parties calling to say gidday, after walking in from Jackson Bay via the Jackson and Cascade rivers.

16 January - Day 27

The morning forecast from Awarua Radio was a slight improvement on the previous day's: 'Puysegur Point to Jackson Bay; Winds: north to north-west 25 to 35 knots; Seas: rough with moderate westerly swell, changing gradually to a north-westerly swell. Rain at times; Outlook: northerly winds 30 to 40 knots.'

Overnight the surf had settled. Beyond Barn Islands there wasn't a sign of whitecaps. Max wanted to sit out this spell of grey weather but I saw the day as a chance to try for Jackson Bay otherwise we'd be stuck at Barn Bay for several days. After some persuasion Max agreed to paddle the six miles to Cascade Point. We could turn back from there if the sea was too rough. A light northerly breeze was occasionally lifting the windsock on the airstrip as Lou drove us down to the beach with the Nordkapps on a trailer behind his tractor.

Lou pointed out a narrow channel on the north side of Sugarloaf Rock where he often took *Scratch* out to sea. After thanking Lou for his hospitality, we paddled out onto the sheltered waters of the bay at 10.40am. The channel by Sugarloaf Rock wasn't as easy as Lou had implied. Only after waiting for a lull between breaking waves could we make a run through the surging water of the channel, fending off weed and kelp-covered rocks with our paddles.

At sea a moderate south-westerly swell was running and a light northerly breeze was barely ruffling the surface of the long swell. Naturally the sky was overcast.

All the way from Dusky Sound, crayfishermen we met had told us that we were past the worst of the trip,

Max rounding Cascade Point

for the weather and the seas would improve the further we went north. Max and I joked about this several times for we had not noticed an improvement in neither the weather nor sea conditions. In fact, the best conditions so far were on those first few day's paddle to Puysegur Point and along to Dusky Sound.

We paddled past Barn Bay Bluff and Iota Bluff before drawing level with the Cascade River mouth. A large, noisy surf was pounding onto the sandy beach which extends from the river mouth along to Cascade Point. As we closed on the point, the northerly wind freshened and started to kick up an annoying chop.

A large white-hulled fishing boat cruised around the point towards us. The crew of *Jeanette* was surprised to see the long yellow kayaks.

"Not a very good day for it," I called out.

"What's the sea like around Cascade Point?" Max asked the skipper

"I don't think the sea will get much worse," the skipper replied from the rolling boat. "The glass is steady, and has actually risen a point during the morning. You should make it all right. How do your boats handle a big sea?"

"Pretty good," I answered, "until the swell starts capping."

Jeanette was going to shelter for the night in Big Bay provided the wind didn't pick up too much.

After she moved away to the south, we struggled towards the point. By now the wind was knocking

down the south-westerly swell and creating its own whitecaps. Spray stung our faces as the Nordkapps bucked into the chop. No time to admire the view, just the intense concentration that was required to stay upright on the lumpy, angry sea and on course for the spray-shrouded point.

When Captain Cook sailed past this point in 1770, he chose a very apt name for it. On the northern side of Cascade Point, Dougal Creek tumbles over a cliff edge, falling free for over 200 feet to land in a cloud of spray on the rocks by the beach. As we closed on the point the sea appeared to be making a last concerted effort to stop us reaching Jackson Bay. The nasty, steep northerly chop was aided and abetted by backwash from the cliffs. Progress around the point was extremely slow.

The cloud base was down level with the cliff tops which stretched away to the misty east, gaining in height until the clouds hid them. Beyond the point we saw two more large, spectacular waterfalls, fed by Donald and Duncan creeks, with small waterfalls scattered between them. Whoever named the three streams feeding the large waterfalls had a thing for names starting with the letter D.

A bare, low rocky island lay a mile west of the point, with a 300 yard gap between it and the coast. As I passed by the sharp rocky cliffs of the island, I seemed to be only inching my way forward into the chop.

However there was one sight to spur our slow progress. Ten miles away to the east, we could just make out a rocky point by the entrance to Smoothwater Bay. There we would find shelter from the wind and chop. Beyond this was Jackson Head, the last headland, and around it lay our final destination.

After another hour of paddling by vertical rock bluffs, Max had opened up quite a lead on *Isadora*. I was feeling tired by the time I caught up with him where he waited by the mouth of Teer Creek.

"Is my stern low?" I asked Max, looking for an excuse for my slow progress. I thought my rear compartment may been flooded.

"No, it looks all right," Max replied.

"I think I need a spell." There was no excuse, I was tired and getting a little scratchy.

Just south of Teer Creek, Max paddled in through a low surf to crunch onto a steep gravel beach. Minutes later when I came in, absolutely knackered, a wave stranded *Isadora* on a large rock, where we remained in a precarious state until the next wave lifted us off. Rather uncivilly, I yelled to Max to grab *Isadoras's* bow.

"Keep your hair on," he replied, and dragged the bow up onto the gravel.

My uncivility was due to overtiredness, not just physical fatigue, but also mental fatigue from the sustained concentration of paddling on the choppy sea. Max was in much better shape than me. He had been paddling steadily all morning.

It was now 2.50pm. Offshore there was a moderate white-capping north-westerly swell. I pulled the hatch cover off the stern compartment but it was bone dry inside. I decided a lack of food was the cause of my tiredness. We hadn't eaten anything since the bowls of porridge at 8am. At least Max hadn't lost his sense of humour for on a flat area of gravel above the beach, he set up several weather-beaten wooden fishing crates complete with foam rubber-strips for cushions. After a big bowl of tea sweetened with loads of sugar, I felt much better.

At 4.30pm, feeling ready for another stint of paddling, we climbed into the Nordkapps on top of the beach. A slight push with the hands, and the kayaks tilted down the steep gravel face to splash into the sea, a racing start. We both copped a few face high waves before reaching the open sea. By staying just outside of the surf, I tried to cadge a little shelter from the chop. With the brew of the tea sitting warmly in my stomach, I had no trouble keeping up with Max. On Seal Rocks we saw many of those sleek mammals, some high and dry on top of the rocks, others lower down with waves breaking over them.

Off the Stafford River mouth, we heard the buzz of an aircraft motor long before we saw the plane. It was a wee Piper Cub flying about 500 feet above the sea. I was thinking the pilot must have his eyes closed for he gave no sign that he had seen us. Then the plane made a low pass before continuing southwards. He definitely had spotted us. Not long after, the plane flew back towards Jackson Bay above the beach.

By the reefs and rocks at the entrance to Homminy Cove, the sea was horribly choppy. I was starting to feel tired again and was dropping behind Max. When the Nordkapps drew level with the entrance to the enticingly sheltered waters of Smoothwater Bay, Max stopped and waited for me to catch up.

"Do you want to pull in here?" he asked.

On the map, Jackson Head lay only two choppy miles away with one last long mile then to go into Jackson Bay.

"Let's push on, aye?" I replied.

It was more like a slalom course than a sea cruise as we manoeuvred the Nordkapps through the reefs and rocks towards Smoothwater Point. I was dog tired but determined to keep going. With half a mile to go to the dark grey forested mass of Jackson Head, the wind eased off and stopped gusting. The chop died quickly, leaving a regular short steep swell, much to my relief. For some time we had both been trying to will the wind away, not that it had anything to do with the wind dying away; it was good for the boys' morale though. It was almost as if, within two miles of our final landing, the Fiordland Coast was finally admitting defeat to the Nordkapps.

Off the steep white cliffs of the head, we saw an island called Hapuka Rock and wondered if we could take a short cut through the gap between it and the head. The Greymouth fishing boat *Georgina* that was chugging back into Jackson Bay from the north, spotted the kayaks and changed course towards us.

The boat hove to and waited for us to paddle near. It was rolling violently in the swell and occasionally showing its hull. The skipper said we could pass through the gap.

"Watch out for submerged rock in the middle," he called.

"How far to go?" I yelled.

"Three quarters of a mile to the wharf, not far. Go left from the wharf when you get there."

Georgina chugged around the tip of the low bare rocky island and waited for us while we paddled through the gap. We turned the bows south and saw distant fishing boats rocking at anchor in the bay. For the first time that day, the swell was behind us. *Georgina* escorted the two Nordkapps until we were in amongst the fishing fleet.

It was now 8pm and because of the overcast sky, it was growing dark already. I could see the wharf and a few lights, but no sign of the support party. As we paddled through the fishing fleet several crewmen came out on deck to wave and say gidday.

Max about to land at Jackson Bay; Paul out near the fishing boats. Photo: Lyn Taylor

To the left of the wharf, above the beach, the lights of a vehicle flashed on and off several times. Max changed into top gear and took off. I had no energy left, and was content to plug on slowly towards the waiting support party.

Max paddled in through a low surf to land for the last time of the trip. He was greeted by Ainslie with a hug and by Maestro with a bottle of beer. I took some photos and a few minutes later nosed in through the surf to where Maestro and Lyn waited with a bottle of bubbly.

An excited group stood on the beach, passing bottles of beer and wine from hand to hand. I was happy to be alive and to have completed the trip. My feeling was not of accomplishing something that had never been done before, but of intense relief; relief that we didn't have to paddle out into those 'big seas outside' any more and relief that we had challenged the Fiordland coastline and survived.

Where the cars were parked by the roadside, the support party had arranged a circle of wooden fish crates around a fire. In a prominent position on top of a gravel bank behind the beach, stood a six foot high, wooden stake. On a cross piece, the word 'HOTEL' had been carved. Maestro went to a lot of trouble to have that sign waiting for 'the boys.'

Lyn and Ainslie cooked two soles which they had bought from the fishermen, served up with fresh tomatoes; fine fare for Max and me. Just to make us feel completely at home, the odd irrepressible sandfly

hovered close by, and then it started raining! Still, you get that at the end of the big trips!

Max pulled a yellow crayfishing pot float from the cockpit of his Nordkapp and attached it by a piece of rope to Maestro's leg. Maestro was delighted and pretended that he was a convict, dragging a ball and chain behind him.

For several days, the support party had been waiting for the boys to arrive. Maureen from Barn Bay passed on the message that we had arrived there, but the party didn't have much idea when we would finally reach Jackson Bay. After the Piper Cub spotted the kayaks off the Stafford River mouth, the pilot flew low over the waiting support party and landed on a strip nearby at Neils Beach. Maestro with Pete Simpson, to whom I had written for information on Stewart Island before the trip, drove over to meet the pilot.

"The kayakers are about an hour's paddle away," he told them.

With glum faces, Maestro and Pete returned to Lyn and Ainslie, telling them that, "the pilot had to turn back because of bad weather. The boys won't make it tonight." But they couldn't keep their glum faces for long and admitted that we were only an hour away.

Max wanted to meet some of the local fishermen and wind down over a few beers. I didn't care what we did, as long as my arms didn't have to go round any more, and I didn't have to sit in a kayak. However Maestro was very keen to leave straight away for the

A happy reunion at Jackson Bay; from left, Ainslie, Paul, Max and Lyn. Photo: Maestro

drive up to Greymouth.

"I've got to earn some money," he explained, but we knew better. He wanted to visit a lady friend in Christchurch! As Maestro had been so good to us during the trip, we gave way to his desires and loaded the Nordkapps onto my car. At 4am next morning, we reached Greymouth.

In retrospect, Max and I made a good combination. Although I was fitter at the start of the trip, during the last few days Max had the edge on me with overall staying power. We both experienced ups and downs, but when one was feeling blue, the other was invariably bright. Max never lost his cool with me although on two occasions I said a few uncivil words.

We seldom disagreed when it came to decision making. From the start we were both determined to complete the trip. Although we joked about pulling out at Doubtful, George and Milford sounds, we never seriously contemplated giving up. But at Jackson Bay, there was no way I wanted to continue paddling around the South Island. I never wanted to sit in a kayak again!

The Nordkapps proved to be perfect for the trip, handling the large seas with ease, despite the heavy loads. We had only two complaints: the first was the rubber O rings around the hatch covers. These kept slipping out, and on two occasions caused serious predicaments when the stern compartments flooded.

The second was the skegs; these could have been much longer, for we found on the choppy seas, the short retractable ones were out of the water much of the time and ineffective.

As a result of the planning and trials prior to the trip, our food, gear and equipment were more than adequate, though there could have been twice as many raspberry cream biscuits.

In the role of support party, Maestro and Ainslie performed a mighty job. Their reliability and morale boosting played an important part in the overall success of the expedition. After Dusky Sound, Maestro took on the job of informing the press and radio of our progress and whereabouts. We called him our Press Orifice. Max and I knew however, that the true reason for the press releases was that Maestro liked to see his name in print, '... said Mr. Lysaght,' or 'Mr. Lysaght said...'

The help and hospitality of the Fiordland fishermen and lighthouse keepers goes without saying, especially their passing on radio messages to Awarua Radio and Carley Burnby in Te Anau, and uttering those magic words, "how about a hot shower and a beer boys?" Although we could never repay their kindness and help, I'm sure we gave them something to yarn about in their wheelhouses for many years to come, "Do you remember those two crazy buggers in the kayaks?"

17 January 2003, Jackson Bay wharf.
The 25th anniversay of the completion of the 1977/78 Fiordland Expedition.
Paul managed to entice the original support crew of Maestro and Ainslie back to the bay, along with Julie
Reynolds (Max's niece), and paddling friends to support this auspicious occasion.
From left: Nettie, AJ, James Lamb, Julie Reynolds, Maestro, Ainslie, Peter Simpson, Cathye Haddock, and Paul
Caffyn in front. In the background, a full moon rising over Jackson Bay.

Chapter 10

JACKSON BAY
to GREYMOUTH

I thought this story had finished on a cold, grey drizzly evening at Jackson Bay. However less than two weeks later, the memories of those last few gruelling days had faded and I was trying to contact Max to see if he wanted to continue paddling up the West Coast.

When I returned home after the Fiordland trip I hoped to find a letter with word about teaching outdoor education in the Nelson Lakes area. When I filled out the application form, I had decided to have a crack at paddling around the South Island if the job didn't eventuate. But there was no letter and I rang the headmaster only to find he had forgotten to advise me someone else had the job.

I was not at all sure of what to do next, so I headed over to the big smoke of Christchurch. However a few days of traffic lights, exhaust smells and harassed people was enough and I lit out for the peace and quiet of the West Coast. Five marvellous days of music, sunshine and pleasant company slipped by at the Punakaiki Festival of Plentitude, but I was still restless.

In those two anticlimactic weeks after the trip finished, I couldn't settle down to a quiet life at Runanga. During the four weeks of the Fiordland trip,

Max and I fell into a very satisfying natural rhythm of life, rising with the dawn, bedding down at dusk, an intensified awareness of the environment, the tingling excitement of discovery, the stomach churning chill of fear, curiosity as to what lay around the next point and a strong sense of isolation and commitment. Rather than feeling glad to be away from it, strangely I missed it all. Those experiences, combined with a need to rely on my basic instinct for survival and the challenge of not quite knowing where it all would end, seemed to provide much of the essence or purpose in my life.

In late January the weather was very settled on the West Coast. There had been one spell of five days without rain which for the 'Wet Coast' was a drought. I felt frustrated because Max and I could have been paddling along the coast and making the most of the perfect weather. It seemed such a pity to waste those glorious days thinking about how I was going to renew the old verandah on my house at Runanga.

Finally I found Max. Although keen to accompany me, he told me sadly that he would have to work for some time to pay off his debts. No one else I spoke to showed the slightest interest in a long paddle, so I began contemplating the idea of going solo.

During the planning of the Fiordland trip we considered four paddlers to be the optimum number and three the minimum. As it turned out two proved to be an ideal number. With a larger party I am sure the trip would have taken longer. However alone, there would be no one to discuss decisions with, no one to raft up alongside for a spell, and no one to share whinges and worries with when the going was tough. Despite all these thoughts, I couldn't get rid of a nagging desire or ambition to keep paddling.

The description of the West Coast in the *New Zealand Pilot* did not inspire my confidence:

> From Cape Farewell to the entrance of Milford sound, the western coast of the South island is particularly inhospitable; there is no anchorage or shelter for even a small vessel in westerly weather when the only harbours, Westport and Greymouth, situated about 90 and 135 miles south-south-westward of Cape Farewell, become impossible to enter. These are harbours at the entrances of rivers and, after heavy westerly weather, the bars silt up and dredging may be impossible for days; these bars are dangerous if there is much swell, as the sand and stream cause a heavy break across the entrance.

However there were several points in my favour. 'The current runs in a predominantly north-north-east direction, following the coast, at rates of about half to one knot.' This current combined with the prevailing south-westerly winds and swell would help to speed progress. Also I had first hand knowledge of the coastline from Jackson Bay to Karamea from my days as a geologist working with a mining company that was searching for ilmenite in the West Coast beach sands. I had taken samples of sand all the way along the coast; on foot, by landrover, on horseback, and even from helicopters. Numerous times I had flown along the coast in light planes, and had a good idea of what to expect in the way of landings and seas.

There was nothing to stop me attempting the trip solo provided my mind and body were willing. The design of the Nordkapp kayak was such that even if I canned out a long way off shore and didn't roll successfully, I could right the kayak, climb back into the cockpit and pump out the water using the bilge pump. I had practised this often in a swimming pool and knew I could do it.

For several days I tried to find someone who was willing to drive my car along the coast, look after my black Labrador Ben, and meet me at night: 'Knowledge of weather, map reading, and sea conditions essential.' It had to be someone whom I could trust implicitly and rely on.

One afternoon while Dick Strong was helping me demolish the remains of my front verandah, we got to talking about the kayak trip and Dick offered to take on the role of support crew. Dick worked as a ski-guide at Mt. Cook in winter and spent the summers tending his large vegetable garden in Dunollie near Runanga. Although I didn't know Dick all that well, I readily accepted his offer. Once a gun climber and superb skier, Dick had always impressed me with his steadiness. He was never ruffled or hurried, and had a peaceful outlook towards life, with a strong affinity for the outdoors. There would be lots of time for fishing and sunbathing.

That night I was still debating in my mind whether or not to have a crack at paddling solo. About 1am I decided to give it a go, then rolled over and fell asleep. With the decision made, all I had to do was obtain a set of maps and buy some food. The marine forecast on the local radio station couldn't have been better and the weather map in *The Press*, showed one high pressure system to the east of New Zealand and another coming over from Tasmania. 'No end in sight to the dry spell,' stated the Christchurch newspaper.

When I finished cutting up the one inch to one mile topographic maps and sticking them under plastic, we loaded the car, tied *Isadora* on the roof rack and set off for Jackson Bay. At midnight we reached the Haast River and slept beneath the bridge.

4 February - Day 28

Dear diary: 'Woke up bleary eyed after a fitful sleep, disturbed by annoying mosquitoes and apprehension of the journey that I was about to start out on. We drove down to Jackson Bay and parked beside the ring of fishing crates, standing around the ashes of a fire that had remained undisturbed since Max and I landed there two weeks previously.'

In contrast to the cold blustery evening when we landed through a two to three foot high surf at Jackson Bay after completing the Fiordland trip, the sea was now as calm as a veritable millpond. Waves were lapping quietly on the beach and the sun was shining brightly with only a few banks of cloud clinging to the mountain ranges. The spell of settled seas and weather was marked by the absence of the fishing boat fleet. Only two boats were moored out in the bay with a third tied up alongside the wharf, whereas when we arrived on the evening of 16 January, upwards of 20 boats were rolling in a northerly swell.

I decided to travel light, carrying a change of clothes, medical kit, repair kit, fibrefill duvet and a torch in the compartments of the Nordkapp and some lunch tucker in the cockpit. Dick would keep the tent, sleeping bags and food with him in the car.

To start the day's paddle without a bowl of porridge would not have been right, so we brewed a billy-full and tried to convince our stomachs that it was an adequate breakfast.

When I was dressed and ready to go, we arranged to meet for lunch in front of Carter's timber mill, 16 miles along the coast to the west. We carried *Isadora* down to the water's edge and I slid into the cockpit. "Might have to wait for a bit of a lull," I grinned. Ben tried to swim after the Nordkapp when first I paddled away from the beach so I had to return to shore. With the dog held firmly by Dick, I paddled out onto a beautifully calm sea. *Isadora* felt more unstable and tippy than when she was fully laden for the Fiordland trip as there was now less hull area in the water. However this meant she was a little faster through the water.

I fell quickly back into a natural paddling rhythm and became acutely aware of the smell of salt air, also the sounds that accompany each stroke with the paddle. I felt relieved and happy to have made the decision to keep paddling.

In less than an hour I had passed the mouth of the Arawhata River and pointed the bow for the Waiatoto River mouth. The continuous cream coloured sandy beach with flat forested land behind was such a contrast to the rugged Fiordland coastline. It was a good feeling to know that I could land wherever I liked. I used the isolated forested bulk of the 2,260 foot high Mt. McLean as a reference point to check progress by, for there were no distinctive features along the beach apart from the widely spaced river mouths.

Such was the heat of the sun and glare off the sea that sweat was dripping off my face, and my body steamed inside the wetsuit. I was pleased when the sun disappeared for a while behind a cloud bank. It wasn't like that in Fiordland. Level with the Waiatoto mouth I could just make out the low rocky projection of Mussel Point on the horizon, and the grey buildings of Carter's mill behind the beach, a little southwest of the point.

The old familiar south-westerly breeze started to stir the glassy surface of the sea at 11 o'clock, as regular as ever the old 11 o'clock chop. To my relief the breeze didn't seem to be as strong as further to the south. As I approached the mill, a fisherman on shore returned my wave, and at 11.30, I landed through a small surf in front of the mill. The chop created by the breeze had just started to cap. After dragging *Isadora* up the beach I went looking for Dick, but there was no sign of him.

Two hours later he still hadn't arrived. Mill workers and local residents had seen no sign of a red VW with a roof rack. I thought that either Ben had run off into the scrub and was lost, or the car had broken down, so I started hitching back to Jackson Bay.

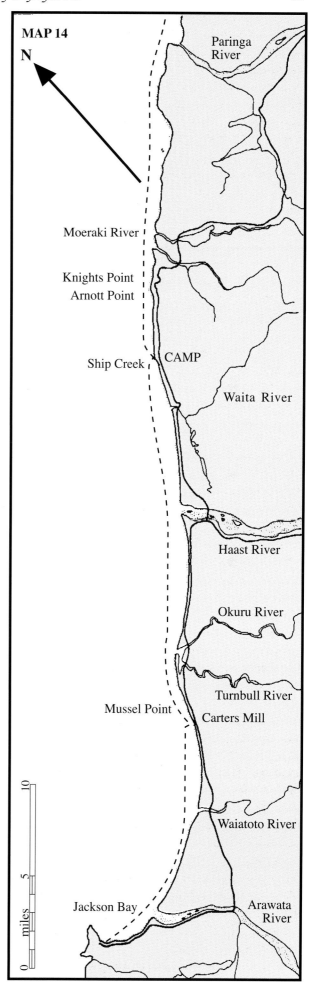

Luckily the first driver that stopped had seen the car a few miles up the road near where logs were being rafted together for towing to Greymouth. A Maori resident told me that this was occurring near the Okuru River mouth, three miles beyond Mussel Point. I asked him to keep an eye out for the VW and left for the beach.

As there was now a reasonable chop offshore I tried to launch stern first with the skeg down but took a fair bit of water into the cockpit during the process before giving up in disgust. I had to launch bow first with the skeg up. Although the south-westerly breeze was helping to push *Isadora* in the right direction, I paddled along to Mussel Point cursing the fact that the skeg wasn't down. She would not run true with the following wind and chop but persisted in slewing left or right.

Once around the point I could see in the distance a fishing boat not far out from shore. Drawing closer I watched a jet boat cruise in over the Okuru River bar after taking a tow line from shore out to the fishing boat. On the beach stood a group of people who were watching a tractor and a bulldozer move long logs into position to form a log raft. One of the figures waved to me and since there was a small black object racing around him, it had to be Dick and Ben. I landed feeling a little peeved that three hours of paddling with the settled conditions had been wasted waiting at Carter's Mill. When I asked Dick why he was here instead of there, he replied, "But you're here now which is the most important thing."

Between Jackson Bay and Greymouth there is only one group of offshore islands and they were plainly visible about three miles out to sea from the lunch spot. When Captain Cook first sailed along this section of coast in March 1770, his name for Jackson Bay was Open Bay and the two rocky islands out from the Okuru River mouth are still collectively called the Open Bay Islands. At low tide the two islands, Taumaka which is 96 feet high, and Popotai, a wildlife sanctuary, are joined by a rocky ridge. In 1809 a nine man sealing gang was dropped off on the islands by the brigantine *Active* and by the end of 1810 they had collected 11,200 seal skins which gives some idea of the number of seals before the sad slaughter started. In March 1811 the gang moved onto the mainland.

Two more lengthy trips were made out to the island and at one stage a sealskin kayak was used. It was not until late November 1813 that the gang was finally picked up by John Grono's schooner *Governor Bligh*. The sealing gang must have breathed a sigh of relief when the sails of the schooner were sighted after five years of living on seal blubber.

After a brew of tea and some sandwiches, I decided to paddle along to Ship Creek, 15 miles away. Dick would wait on the north side of Haast River in case I was too tired to continue, if not he would have a signal fire going on the beach at Ship Creek. Dick pushed *Isadora* into the surf and I paddled out to the *Lady Dorothy* and asked if the crew had heard a recent forecast. One of them shouted over the roar of the motor that the weather should stay the same for the next two days. From *Lady Dorothy's* stern a thick wire rope ran into the sea to emerge again on shore, attached to the log raft. Since the road bridges between Haast and Greymouth were reclassified unsuitable to carry the weight of the laden logging trucks, one of the Grey valley timber mills was trying sea transport as a means of bringing logs to the mill. A previous attempt had failed when the raft broke up in rough seas. Succeeding attempts were successful when the wire rope was passed through holes drilled through the logs.

I turned *Isadora's* bow in a north-easterly direction and set off for the distant township of Haast. Although I could see roof tops and aerials, it seemed to take ages to draw level with the town. Gradually the wind eased off and the whitecaps disappeared.

The wind died at about 6.30pm and the sky was cloudless. A perfect afternoon for paddling. As I neared the rocks and small islands off Tauperikaka Point I was pleased to see a thin wisp of white smoke drifting up from the beach. Dick had a signal fire going. My arms and shoulders were complaining after a two week break from paddling. The support crew were waiting on a sandy beach when I landed through a small surf next to the dried up mouth of Ship Creek; 34 miles covered for the day.

Ship Creek owes its name to the wreckage of a vessel found near here in 1867. In recent years the wreckage was identified as belonging to a large wooden clipper ship, the *Schomberg* which came to grief off the coast of Victoria during its maiden voyage in 1855. Part of the wreckage drifted across the Tasman Sea to a final resting place on a desolate West Coast beach.

A beautiful sunset, the scattered clouds tinged red in the dying sun's rays, held promise for a fine day on the morrow. While we ate dinner, *Lady Dorothy* made her way slowly north-eastwards about a mile offshore, towing the log raft to Greymouth.

Only one thing disturbed the tranquillity of the evening - sandflies. Rather than daub insect repellent over our exposed limbs, Dick and I stood in the smoke drifting up from the driftwood fire, but Ben wasn't too happy. The sandflies were getting at him so badly on his muzzle that small droplets of blood formed where he had been bitten. I even tried spreading some Dimp over his muzzle but I didn't know which was the worse of the two evils, the sting of the insect repellent or the stinging bites of the sandflies. Ben preferred to sit, rather subdued, in the back seat of the car.

As it grew dark, the sandflies disappeared only to be replaced by buzzing mosquitoes. Dick and I carried the sleeping-bags well out onto the beach and set them down beside *Isadora* where the faintest of sea breezes acted as a deterrent to the mosquitoes. Looking up at the star speckled black sky, I felt no regrets whatsoever about resuming the kayak odyssey up the West Coast.

5 February - Day 29

At dawn, the marvellous settled conditions of the day before still prevailed, a calm sea, cloudless sky and not a breath of wind. It was almost too good to be true. When Dick pushed *Isadora* out into the surf at 8am, I carried the hooks and sinker of his fishing line out to its full length and dropped it offshore. Dick would fish for an hour, then drive along to Knight Point where he would photograph the kayak going past. From this point the main road turns inland and doesn't rejoin the beach again until Bruce Bay, where we would meet for lunch. The entry in Dear diary reads: 'Waved goodbye to Dick and paddled north. The sun had just risen - no wind, almost millpond conditions. All the bluffs and small rocky islands offshore were in dark shadow; beautiful sandy beaches separated by steep rock bluffs. I could see the road winding up onto Arnott Point.'

As I neared this point, a large school of dolphins was leaping out of the sea. Before long two of them barrelled down the length of the Nordkapp, surfacing for a breath of air by the bow. Soon the whole group was playing alongside, cruising swiftly in a circle to repeat the small leaps out of the water in front of the bow. I marvelled at their timing when four dolphins all surfaced by the bow simultaneously. For 10 minutes or more, these beautiful, graceful creatures stayed around the Nordkapp, before resuming their breakfast fishing.

Seals playing by Arnott Point

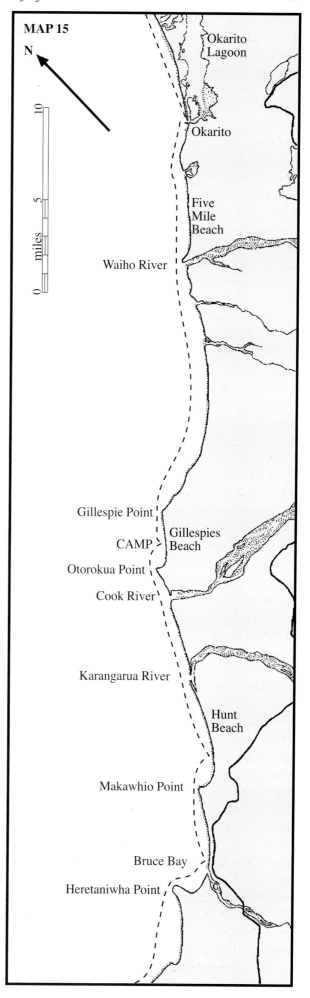

Off Arnott Point lies a rocky island with patches of green scrub clinging precariously to ledges on the steep, white-coloured cliffs. A 50 yard gap separates the island from a sandy point onshore. It took me a while to realize that the 20 or so long shiny black objects lying on the sand were not boulders but seals. Approaching the gap I noticed more groups of seals out by numerous exposed reefs, sunning themselves by floating in the sea on their backs, flippers drooping out of the water. It was only when *Isadora's* bow was less than five yards away from the nearest group, that I was spotted by one of the sun-bathing seals. It looked at me in disbelief for a fraction of a second, and then by some mysterious signal, notified all the other seals of my presence and they crash-dived, leaving only swirling eddies on the surface to mark where they had been.

One whiskery wet face popped out of the water to see what all the excitement was about, then another face and another until the whole group were all back on the surface. Beneath the kayak, the water was so clear that I could easily see the bottom, where seals were gracefully turning amongst shoals of small fish.

Only when the camera started running out of film could I bear to leave them and paddle towards Knight Point where there is a small car park and a monument on top of the sheer cliffs. Dick was waiting with the camera and we exchanged waves as I paddled past. The sea was like a millpond. The barely discernible swell enabled me to paddle in close by the shore, past cliffs and rocks to Otumoto Point.

Off the Whakapohai and Moeraki river mouths, I was intrigued to find wire cables extending out to bare, exposed rocks. A flying fox arrangement on the cables was used to moor small crayfishing boats when the sea wasn't too rough. In this weather there wasn't a boat in sight.

By the Abbey Rocks I met a small crayfishing boat, the *Nikki J* and stopped for a natter with the two fishermen.

"Have you heard a forecast?" I asked.

"It's good," replied one of the fishermen, "But the crayfishing isn't." They had four crayfish to show for the morning's fishing. *Nikki J* worked out of the Paringa River. I asked the two chaps about the coastline up to the north. They said I would be able to land at Bruce Bay without too much trouble but warned me about the surf at Gillespies Beach which could be up to 12 feet high, and the same with beaches near Karangarua River mouth.

From Abbey Rocks a sandy beach extended along to Piakatu Point. Over the next mile the rocky foreshore was eroded into weird shapes which from a distance looked like seals. I stopped paddling for a quick bite to eat and a breather before pushing on to

the mouth of the Paringa River. I then took a direct line for Heretaniwha Point which forms the southern extremity of Bruce Bay and reached it after a long slog. Despite a view of distant cars driving by the beach, two long miles remained to paddle to where Dick was waiting. It had taken six hours of steady paddling to reach Bruce Bay from Ship Creek.

Although the population of Bruce Bay swells during the whitebait season, there were only a few permanent residents. A roadside petrol station served as the local store and post office. The only other buildings were several whitebaiter's shacks. Bruce Bay had its heyday in the years 1856-66. The first goldrush to the area proved to be a duffer but despite this, a town was surveyed. After the gold and supplies ran out, very few residents remained.

As Dick and I sat out on the hot sandy beach, bowl of tea in hand, it was hard to imagine that this tranquil setting was once the scene of an ugly riot. In March 1866 a floating population of 2000 miners and prospectors gave vent to their wrath at finding a second goldrush to Bruce Bay was also a duffer. Philip Ross May in his fine book *The West Coast Gold Rushes*, describes the night and the events leading up to the riot in grim detail.

From the bay the main road left the coast, not returning again until Hokitika. Side roads led down to Hunts Beach, six miles paddle away, and from Fox Glacier township to Gillespies Beach, 18 miles up the coast. I had to decide whether my arms could sustain the paddling to Gillespies or to stop at Hunts Beach. Rather than take a plunge on the longer distance, I decided to reconsider at Hunts Beach where Dick would be waiting for me.

After Dick pushed the Nordkapp out into the surf, I had paddled only half a mile when I noticed he and Ben running along the beach. Dick was waving as if something had happened. The noise of the surf was too loud to carry on a conversation but by a combination of various hand signals it didn't take too long to realize that Dick could not find the car keys. I had removed the keys from the ignition while we were having lunch and had hidden them above the sunvisor. More hand signals followed until Dick gave the thumbs up that he knew where they were.

A 250 foot high bluff of glacial outwash material, rocks and gravel, separates Bruce Bay from Hunts Beach. At Makawhio Point, the seaward extremity of the bluff, I saw my first view of the Southern Alps from the sea. The snowcapped peaks of Mounts Cook and Tasman were dazzlingly clear; a fantastic panorama of sea, forest, mountains and sky, and not a sign of man.

Two long rides took me in through the surf at Hunts Beach. As there was plenty of daylight left and the old body remained reasonably willing, I decided to make a break for Gillespies. The fishermen on the *Nikki J* had made me wary of a 12 foot high breakers at Gillespies, so Dick agreed to light a signal fire where he thought the best landing would be.

On the way out through the surf, I smacked into or rather, was smacked by several breakers and formed a distinct impression that the waves were breaking exactly at eye level. Incredibly the sea remained calm outside with the lightest of sea breezes ruffling the surface of the gentle swell.

It was a long haul to the Karangarua River mouth where the sea lost its beautiful blue clarity, as the pale grey glacier-fed waters of the Karangarua discoloured and dirtied it. Here the sea seemed to be disturbed, a steep chop without a wind, surges appearing out of nowhere, and occasional eddies that threw *Isadora* sideways. This unusual disturbance, unlike anything I'd previously encountered, had an unsettling effect on me. But rationally I decided the cause was due either to a difference in temperature between the glacier-fed water and the warmer sea water, or just turbulence created by the river flowing into the sea. I turned out to sea and stayed there until well beyond the river mouth.

Above the forest immediately behind the beach, the cold white slopes of Mt. Sefton accompanied me along to Karangarua Bluff where I lost sight of the peak.

Off the Cook River mouth, another large glacier-fed river, I anticipated another area of disturbed seas. Sure enough, surges, a chop, and eddies accompanied an area of discoloured water off the river mouth and I kept well clear.

The sun was nearing the horizon when I rounded Otoroku Point and could see the three mile long Gillespies Beach extending away to the north-east. An orange sign post marking the road end by the beach and a thin column of smoke were clearly visible. With the knowledge that Dick had found a good landing and that I was only a mile from the beach, I found a new lease of life, powering shorewards, tiredness forgotten.

A group of people were out on a steep gravel beach fishing as I approached. Waves were dumping heavily onto the gravel but there was no sign of the 12 foot breakers, for which I was grateful. Level with Dick's signal fire, I sized up the line of dumpers momentarily, then shot in behind one large wave that was about to break. Just before the following wave hit, I broached *Isadora* sideways and bounced towards the gravel beneath the face of the broken wave, a high brace keeping me in the upright position. The retreating surge left the Nordkapp high and dry at the top of the beach and almost at the feet of the startled group of

people fishing. John Shaw had a line out for sharks when the dumper cast the kayak up on the beach, and he remarked, "At first sight, I thought you were a mermaid." When Dick lit the signal fire on the gravel, John had no idea of the impending arrival of the kayak and assumed that Dick was putting down a hangi. Mark Shaw joined us and was disappointed not to have seen the landing. The Shaw brothers were the only permanent residents at this former gold-mining field, a couple of colourful characters who were rogues when it came to trying out practical jokes on visitors.

Mark kindly offered us a bed for the night and John cut off six large steaks from the three foot long rig or spotted gummy shark that he pulled in before I arrived.

Dick cooked the shark steaks over a driftwood fire. They were delicious. Afterwards we joined the Shaw brothers and some visitors for supper. We were only in the house a few minutes when Mark told Dick and I that we both needed haircuts. Then he kept passing plates of pikelets and fruit cake to me, saying, "Eat Up, eat up. You need building up." We had a look at some of their gold samples and Mark passed Dick a tin containing a 'uranium sample.' The tin once held peanuts as the label on the outside indicated but the only way of looking at the sample of uranium was to lift the lid. Dick had an inkling that mischief was in the air and passed the tin over to me unopened. I put

Mark Shaw and Paul swap tall tales and true at Gilliespies Beach. Photo: Dick Strong

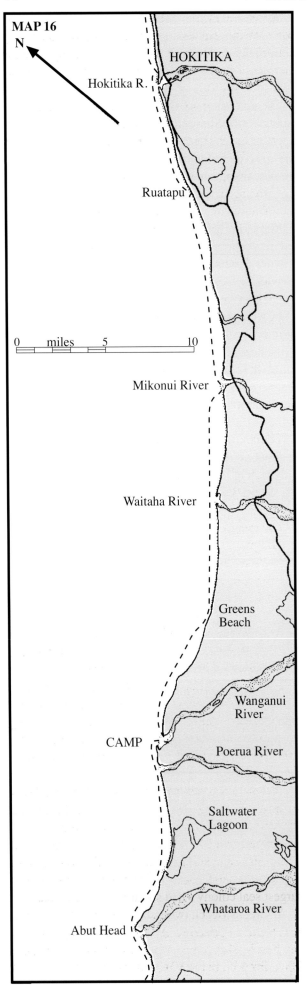

MAP 16

N

HOKITIKA

Hokitika R.

Ruatapu

0   miles   5   10

Mikonui River

Waitaha River

Greens
Beach

Wanganui
River

CAMP

Poerua River

Saltwater
Lagoon

Whataroa River

Abut Head

the tin down on a table but kept glancing at it, intrigued as to which particular rock type it was. Finally I succumbed to temptation and pulled the lid off. Zoing! A long spring shot out like a jack-in-the-box, narrowly missing my nose, much to the amusement of the troops who knew exactly what was going to happen.

After midnight we slipped away to a lovely soft bed in a nearby hut. As we left Dick noticed several coins glued to the floor in the doorway. Mark watched us like a hawk as we walked out, a playful glint in his eye. To his disappointment neither of us fell into the trap.

In our sleeping bags, Dick and I plotted ways and means of playing a practical joke on the brothers. During the evening I had offered to take out a fishing line for them in the kayak and drop it offshore. We toyed with the idea of attaching an old boot or a gumboot to the hooks once I was at sea. Unfortunately we could find nothing that would fit the bill.

Dear diary noted: 'Slept like a log.' With 11 hours of paddling and 44 miles for the day, the longest I had achieved in one day, I had every right to be tired.

6 February - Day 30

The Shaw brothers and their visitors came out to the beach after sunrise to see the Nordkapp in action. Although there was only a single line of breakers, I couldn't avoid copping a face full of cold sea water on the way out. For the third day in a row, not a breath of wind disturbed the glassy surface of the swell.

After a final wave I turned the bow to the northeast. Along the next stretch of coastline there was only one place where Dick could drive out to the coast, at the old gold mining town of Okarito, where he would have a signal fire waiting. A long 23 mile haul before lunch.

Beside a small dumping surf, I paddled 20 yards out from the beach for the next 10 miles to the Waiho River mouth. The summits of Mounts Cook and Tasman seemed to drift along the forest tops with me. At the Waiho River mouth, I found an abrupt transition from the deep blue-green of the sea to a milky grey of glacial fed waters; a sharp line curving slightly towards shore. The upper half of the Franz Joseph Glacier and the neve fields which feed the glacier, were clearly visible. There can't be many places in New Zealand where one can simultaneously see both the source and mouth of a river. I could identify the peaks of De la Beche, The Minarets, Green, Walter and Elie de Beaumont, all of which a group of us had climbed the previous winter.

Beyond the former rich goldfields of Five Mile and Three Mile beaches, stretched a two mile long section of rocky bluffs. Once beyond the bluffs I sighted the smoke from Dick's signal fire on the beach at Okarito. The day was so hot, we drank cold orange drink instead of the usual bowl of tea. The sandwiches were dry as the butter had melted into a syrupy liquid in the bottom of the food box.

There were few permanent residents at Okarito although during the height of the West Coast gold-rushes, the township supported a population of 1,250 with a further 2,500 at the goldfields of Five Mile and Three Mile beaches. The outlet of Okarito Lagoon served as a port for vessels bringing in miners and stores but shifting sand bars in the entrance caused many a vessel to founder.

Although feeling tired I decided to push on to the mouth of Wanganui River, 20 miles north of Okarito and the next place where Dick could reach the coast. He would have to walk a few miles from the road end but didn't mind carrying the sleeping bags and cooking gear. Just in case I didn't make it by nightfall, Dick would wait overnight by the river mouth until next morning.

The sea was still amazingly calm when Dick pushed me into the surf however by Abut Head, a south-westerly breeze picked up quite rapidly to 12 to 14 knots. For the first time on the trip, I was pleased by the presence of a breeze for it not only cooled me down but also aided progress. Even when the chop began capping I didn't mind for my tired muscles found sufficient energy to provide the power for a spurt to take off surfing in front of the small waves.

The sun lay low on the horizon as I paddled past Mt. Oneone and turned around a bluff towards the river mouth. I could see a towel waving from a tall driftwood pole and smoke from a signal fire. Apart from a gentle surf breaking offshore, the Wanganui River bar appeared straight forward. One small surf ride took me onto the calm waters of the river. I paddled upstream to where Dick and Ben were camped on an island in the middle of the river, well above high tide level and with a plentiful supply of driftwood.

As the sun set, the triangular shape of Mt. Oneone was silhouetted against the dying rays of the sun.

Safely inside the bar of the Wanganui River
Photo Dick Strong

After tea we lay in the sleeping bags on either side of the glowing embers of the fire, the old ship dog snuggled up alongside. We chatted for ages about how beautiful an evening it was and I said, "It's a hell of a good life."

"I could easily make it a way a life," Dick replied.

Dick's poem captures the mood of the evening spent at the Wanganui River mouth:

> A confusion of crested waves,
> Tossing, dropping.
> Whipped by wind without direction
> Creatures move in balance.
>
> The fire's warmth diffuses.
> Smoke turns in watery vision.
> Serene; as a million sounds
> Converge as one.
>
> Tide forever restless.
> Ruthless, caught in indifference.
> Silent arches glide,
> Invading tidal land.
>
> Mist envelopes starlight,
> How motionless the moments seem.
> Drifting, slowly drifting,
> To the light of home.
>
> Morning, chilled mist.
> Droplets vibrate as living mass,
> Searched by rays of light,
> As a fairy land appears.

7 February - Day 31

Before sunrise Dick had porridge simmering over a fire. The sky was cloudless but beyond the bar, a light north-easterly stirred the surface of the sea. Low tide had come and gone, leaving Dick's escape route to shore cut off and growing deeper by the minute. We packed quickly and I launched sternfirst with the skeg down. Our next meeting would be at Greens Beach, seven miles up the coast where a milling road provided beach access.

The bar looked settled but just when I thought I was in the clear, a sneaky wave reared up and doused me with a face full of cold water. For several miles I passed steep bluffs formed by glacial outwash debris. The breeze impeded progress but wasn't strong enough to create a chop. On one rocky point I passed the largest seal colony I had so far seen on the coast.

At Greens Beach two fishermen were fishing and they were surprised to see *Isadora* surfing towards the beach. Our timing was perfect for as I landed, Dick drove up in the VW. After a quick bite to eat, I headed for our next rendezvous at the Mikonui River mouth, and carried out Dick's fishing line, baited with pieces of bacon fat.

The couple fishing must have been intrigued by our meeting and only approached Dick as the kayak disappeared to the north-east. As Dick chatted to the couple, a fish took the juicy morsel of bacon fat but the line parted almost immediately. Dick wound in the line and found the hooks, trace and sinker had been removed.

As this was my fourth consecutive day of paddling, my energy reserves were running down and the distances between cup of tea stops was growing shorter and shorter. A light headwind slowed progress all afternoon and I landed at Mikonui and Ruatapu for brief spells. It was near low tide at Ruatapu where a moderate surf rolled in over an offshore bar. Along many of the West Coast beaches, a submerged sandy bar exists parallel to and about 400 yards offshore. At high water the bar has little effect on the surf but as the tide drops, the sea begins to break, leaving a calmer stretch of water between the bar and a small shore break. The only gaps in the bar are narrow rip channels or gutters.

I was so tired I felt tempted to pull out at Ruatapu but Hokitika lay temptingly close and Greymouth was in reach with one further day. Plenty of daylight remained and Dick promised to have a signal fire going by a good landing. Inside the offshore bar, I paddled along the beach searching for a lull in the sets of breakers or a gutter. During a brief lull I almost made it unscathed to the open sea but a large breakers capped over me, nearly causing a capsize. Only the tail end of a screw roll kept the kayak upright. All Dick saw from the beach as the wave broke was a paddle and two wrists above the broken water.

Inland from Hokitika the Forest Service were carrying out one of their 'Keep New Zealand Green' scorched earth burn-offs of West Coast native forest. A pall of reddish brown smoke formed a huge thunderhead cloud and slowly drifted out to sea. Smoke, drifting across the sun, acted as a filter on a camera and the sea took on a reddish brown hue.

Conspicuous features were virtually absent on a grey sandy beach along to Hokitika, just a low line of grass topped dunes behind, so I was pleased when the roof tops and forest of television aerials of the town came into view. A moderate surf was breaking on the Hokitika River bar and I kept well clear. North of the river mouth numerous small groups of people were fishing. I kept looking for smoke from Dick's signal fire but there was a problem - nearly every group of fishermen had a small driftwood fire going on the sand, with thin wisps of white smoke drifting slowly skywards. By one of the fires, a blond haired figure

stood by a black dog and I surfed in to the sand.

The evening was beautiful as we sat by *Isadora* watching the sunset turn dark yellow with smoke from the burn-off. My shoulders and arms were aching while my left arm was rather red and sore from sunburn. We unrolled the sleeping bags on the beach and Dick cooked a feed of bacon and cabbage. But before a billy of water boiled for a cup of tea, I was fast asleep. Thirty seven miles for the day.

There is little sign now of the once famous Port of Hokitika where in 1867, during the height of the West Coast gold-rushes, more overseas vessels arrived than at any other port in New Zealand. The Hokitika River was first entered in December 1854, by the 124 ton paddle steamer *Nelson*. By March 1865 so many vessels were ferrying stores and prospectors to the capital of the West Coast goldfields that the Port of Hokitika was gazetted. With numerous floods, a continually shifting bar and more often than not, heavy seas, entry to the port was often hazardous. Between the years 1865 and 1867 there were 108 strandings and 32 total shipwrecks. Three paddle-wheel steam tugs reduced the dangers of entering the river. In *The West Coast Gold Rushes* Philip Ross May describes an incident when two sailing vessels were vying for the attention of a single tug that came out to meet them. It was heading towards the schooner when an unusual signal flown by the second vessel made the tug captain change course. It was a crinoline, 'blown out like a balloon,' not to mention a number of ladies standing on a quarterdeck, waving handkerchiefs.

Once the boom was over, the port slowly fell into disuse and was closed in 1950 due to the dangerous nature of the bar, and all the navigation aids were removed.

8 February - Day 32
Dear diary: 'Woke at 0700 hours when a noisy, engine revving front end loader started carrying gravel from the beach to a nearby truck. No way of sleeping with all that noise. Still sore and not too well rested. Dick put on some porridge and had already set up a long line with several hooks baited with bacon fat. I launched at 8.15 with Dick's long line trailing astern; ran it out to its full length offshore and dropped the sinker - a large rock.'

A wave to Dick and I set off for Greymouth, the goal for the day. For the fifth day in a row the sky was cloudless, the sea glassy with a hint of a south-westerly swell. As I had once commuted for three months between Hoki and Greymouth, the landmarks were all very familiar and passed only too slowly. Between the two towns, the coast consists of a sandy-gravel beach, backed by a low line of dunes.

The only breaks in this otherwise featureless coastline are provided by the mouths of the Arahura and Taramakau rivers.

I was pleased to see the 400 foot high radio mast at Kumara Junction for it lies level with the mouth of the Taramakau River. On a topographic map, river mouths are shown as very slight projections from the coastline but when paddling around them, I always thought they projected further out than the map indicated. Waves were breaking a long way out from the river mouth so I gave the area the now traditional 'wide berth.' Past the river, the beach curved inwards toward Camerons where Dick would be waiting with lunch.

When I closed on the beach, there was neither sign of Dick nor a signal fire, just a line of wooden power poles and a clump of macrocarpa trees to indicate it was Camerons. I remained outside a line of large breakers, searching for a sign of Dick when suddenly he sprang up on the beach level with me. He and Ben had been snoozing in the sun, by the embers of a driftwood fire. By hand signals Dick indicated the surf was pretty much the same on either side of him - big dumpers. I waited for a while, sizing up the lulls between sets of large dumpers, then turned the bow towards shore. Cautiously I paddled to the rear of the breakers, waiting for a lull. I was just about to take off behind a wave when I glanced quickly over my shoulder. I was horrified to see the face of a huge swell rising up, and frantically tried to turn the bow into the face of the wave, its ugly face rearing above me. 'Here's a go,' I thought, for dumping waves usually break very quickly once their face is vertical. There didn't seem enough time to reach the wave before it broke. Luckily it held off for a fraction of a second, just long enough for *Isadora* to climb up on end and slide through the smoking crest. The Nordkapp took to the air, off the crest of the wave, and landed with a great splash. My heart beating at twice its normal rate, I took the traditional flailing out to sea escape route, pondering on the thought of continuing up to Greymouth without landing.

But thoughts of a cup of tea, a spell from making my arms go round and relief from a bursting bladder soon changed my mind. Once more I turned the bow towards the beach. Rather gingerly I paddled in, head swivelling to look for sneaky boomer waves. Dick signalled to come in and I powered in behind a small dumper onto a gravel beach where he grabbed the decklines. Just in time too for two large dumpers followed in quick succession, pushing the kayak higher up the gravel.

Throughout the trip I had been wearing a diving watch and Dick often kidded me about this, saying I would be better of throwing it away and gauging time from the position of the sun. At first when we discussed where the next rendezvous was, I would say, 'I should arrive there about 4pm' but this was pointless as Dick had no watch. So thereafter I would raise my arm in the air and say, 'I'll get there when the sun's about there Dick.'

During a lull in the dumpers Dick pushed me off for the last lap of the journey to Greymouth. He would wait at the Grey River bar. Although the distance was only half of what I accomplished during the second and third days out of Jackson Bay, there was little power left in my paddle strokes. 'Not far to go,' I reminded myself, 'Only seven miles to the bar.'

During many of the Fiordland trip training sessions on the Grey River I had wondered what it would feel like to paddle over the bar after completing a journey up the coast. The excitement at the prospect of finding out began to mount, despite the tired state of my body.

Slowly the old and so familiar sights of Greymouth came into view, the hospital, the Karoro surf club, the windsock at the end of the airstrip and I could recognize houses of friends on the hills behind the main road. For a while I couldn't identify the long, low shape lying on the horizon but from the top of several larger swell crests, I recognized the blocky stone breakwaters which form the entrance to the Port of Greymouth.

Further out to sea two fishing boats headed towards the breakwaters and for a brief time I put more effort into the paddle strokes to reach the bar at the same time, but it didn't take long to realize they

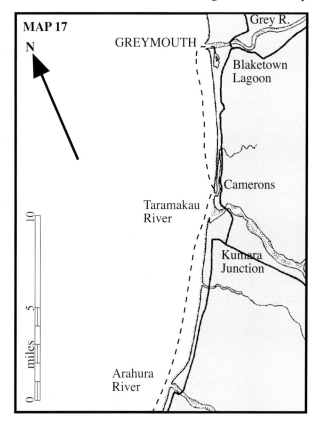

would easily beat *Isadora* to the bar, so I settled back into my normal rhythm.

Dick and Ben were waiting on the end of the southern breakwater. Excitedly I shouted and waved to him as I paddled in over the bar while Dick, in the best of naval traditions, piped me in with a shrill whistle. The bar was as settled as ever I'd seen it but the tide was ebbing swiftly which meant a real slog upstream for half a mile to the entrance of Blaketown Lagoon. This tidal inlet, a backwater off the river, offers protection to a fleet of fishing boats which work over the Grey River bar, from freshes and floods in the river and from the swell during rough weather.

Despite the strain of paddling into a current, hard against the breakwater, I found it hard to stop smiling. It felt like arriving home after a long journey. A dream had been realized. Turning the bow into the still waters of the lagoon, I eased off, content to let *Isadora* glide the remaining 100 yards to where Dick

waited on a boulder bank. Relieved to be ashore after such an easy passage across the bar, I felt tired but happy. For some time after I lurched out of the cockpit, we sat on the boulders and watched a hive of activity at the wharves. Fishing boats were waiting their turn to unload catches of tuna. It was the height of the tuna season and the port was acting host to the largest fleet of fishing boats that Greymouth had ever seen.

While Dick and I watched, what should cruise into the lagoon but *Georgina,* the boat that had escorted Max and I into Jackson Bay during the last hour of the Fiordland trip.

The trip from Jackson Bay to Greymouth had gone so smoothly that I was already thinking of the next stage up to Nelson. The 180 miles had taken five days, for an average of 36 miles per day.

We loaded *Isadora* onto the VW's roofrack and drove into town for a beer and a bath, in that order.

A calm crossing of the Grey River bar, with Dick and Ben waiting on the end of the Blaketown tiphead

Chapter 11

GREYMOUTH to KARAMEA

After a five day rest I felt ready to tackle the next stage to Nelson. I still didn't feel ready to commit myself to paddling right around the South Island, but reserved the right to pull out at any time. Dick's wife Barbara joined the support crew for the drive up to Nelson. With long black hair and striking facial features similar to that of the Peruvian Indians, Barbara had an easy going nature, a good sense of humour and a quiet zest for life.

Although I was raring to go on the morning of 14 February, sea conditions were not conducive for paddling. A heavy westerly swell broke continuously over the Grey River bar, sheets of spray hurled high above the breakwaters as waves crashed onto the concrete blocks and large boulders. Most of the Greymouth fishing fleet was safely tied up in Blaketown Lagoon.

Mid-afternoon, the VW, with *Isadora* on the roof-rack, was the only vehicle on the breakwater. The sea showed no signs of abating and we were puzzled by the sight of a fishing boat rolling towards the bar. The possibility of attempting to cross the bar appeared out of the question.

As we watched the vessel close on the breakwaters, eight cars suddenly arrived with 20 or more people. We soon discovered the reason for the sudden arrival of the crowd. The fishing boat heading towards the bar had a seriously ill crewman on board who needed hospitalization. *Okawa IV* slowed as it approached a line of breakers beyond the breakwaters, the skipper obviously sizing up his chances of entering the river.

Very occasionally a wave entered the river without breaking. Lulls were virtually non existent. With *Okawa IV* as a gauge of size, the swell was at least 10 foot high from crest to trough. As the steel-hulled vessel cautiously moved in closer, we watched silently as two large waves built up astern. *Okawa IV* was picked up by the leading wave and the boat began surfing in front of it. The bow was completely clear of the sea, exposed from keel to deck in front of the wave while amidships, white broken water surged up level with the deck railings. Just as the wave was about to break, the skipper attempted to turn out to sea. A cloud of smoke spurted from the exhaust stack as the motor was pushed to full throttle, and possibly a bit more. Broaching side on, in the crest of the wave, the boat appeared to be on the point of capsizing, but in the wave's wake she righted and pushed out to sea under full power.

The same thing happened during a second attempt when an enormous wave tried to turn *Okawa IV* into a surf ski but the skipper again turned and successfully reached the open sea. A third attempt, during a very brief lull, was successful. The boat surfed into the sheltered waters of the river in front of an unbroken wave and a pin drop silence in the crowd was broken by burst of relieved conversation. Dick, Barbara and I decided that cups of tea were in order for the rest of the day.

15 February - Day 33

We were out on the breakwater again early. Two hours earlier the tide had peaked and already the swell was occasionally breaking on the bar. I had to try now or forget paddling for the day. Provided the open sea could be reached, I was confident that despite the size of the swell, landing through surf onto the open beaches where all my training had been carried out, would be no trouble. But on my home patch, I was wrong. The mistake I made when looking down at the sea from the breakwater was to underestimate the size of the swell.

The bar was a real stumbling block in my mind. From September through to December, when I was training on the Grey River, I saw fishing vessels work out over the bar on a few occasions. The rest of the time it was too rough, due to either stormy seas or numerous spring floods. Several fishing boats have had wheelhouse windows stove in while crossing the bar. Only once had I ventured out in the Nordkapp on a reasonably calm day and was none too happy in a lumpy sea off the bar.

Wreckage of several of the vessels that came to grief while entering the Grey River is still visible at low water off the northern breakwater. In C.W.N. Ingram's book *Shipwrecks of New Zealand 1795-1970*, there are several photographs of various vessels shipwrecked on the northern breakwater. A caution in the *New Zealand Pilot* advises vessels entering the river to guard against a general northerly set of the offshore current. I would feel a lot happier when I was well clear of the bar.

I left the calm shelter of Blaketown Lagoon at 8.15am and paddled onto the swiftly ebbing, brown waters of the Grey River. Downriver, two fishing boats cruised slowly towards the bar. Inside the end of the breakwaters, the boats stopped and turned, while their skippers observed the breakers before attempting to cross the bar. Just as I was about to catch up with them, the boats turned seawards and made their break. I followed quickly but was outdistanced. Fifty yards before the tip of the breakwaters, two waves broke astern of the fishing boats and rolled upriver towards me. Frantically I changed into re-

verse gear, backpaddling furiously to avoid the clutches of the walls of approaching white broken water.

I glanced up to the tip of the southern breakwater where Dick and Barbara were watching, but as the kayak was out mid-river, it wasn't easy for Dick to signal the onset of a quiet spell.

A lull followed the two breakers and I made a sprint for the open sea. A large swell outside was steep and appeared ready to break at any time, so I kept up speed until 400 yards out. Only then did I turn and wave to the minute figures on the distant breakwater. Parallel to the swell, I pointed the bow for the grey, vertical limestone cliffs of Point Elizabeth, four miles to the north. From this point the coastline takes on a radical change of morphology from featureless gravel beaches to reef-fringed bluffs and short intervening sections of boulder or sandy gravel beaches, a much more rugged coastline.

A sharp exhalation of air astern forewarned me, however I still jumped as three dolphins shot past, surfacing simultaneously by the bow. Several times they swam so close to the hull that I lifted the paddle out of the water so as not to touch their delicate skin. If I believed in omens, then dolphins were the finest kind. Whenever they were close by, no misfortune would occur.

On the northern side of Point Elizabeth lies the sandy beach of Rapahoe where I carried out all my surf training; learning how to bring the Nordkapp in and out through the breakers and practising rolling in broken water. At high tide, surf rolls heavily against a steep bank or berm of coarse gravel, littered with driftwood. As the tide recedes, a wide gently shelving stretch of sandy beach is exposed. There is always at least one offshore bar, and sometimes a second and deeper bar where the swell breaks between half and low tide.

The size of the swell, six feet from trough to crest, worried me to the point of considering landing at Rapahoe and waiting until the seas settled. Superbly confident of landing at Rapahoe, the size and noise of the surf off the beach came as a shock when I rounded Point Elizabeth. A roaring surf, with spray fanning off tall capping waves hid all sight of the beach. The most seaward of the breakers were level with Shag Rocks, two bar waveswept rocks splatted motley white by sea birds, and the rocks lie over a mile offshore. My regrets at leaving Blaketown Lagoon grew by the minute as anxiety about landing mounted. I did not consider turning back as the condition of the bar was deteriorating as the tide ebbed. I preferred to keep paddling and take a chance of landing through the surf further to the north.

The north side of Twelve Mile Bluff would offer the next possible landing. A group of steep, scrub-covered sea stacks tended to break up a south-westerly swell. I gave them a half mile wide berth to avoid backchop off their vertical walls. The backchop added to the confusion of an already steep and frighteningly large swell. But north of the bluff, I was dismayed by the sight of a continuous line of breakers hiding all sight of the beach. I had no alternative but to push on. Any thoughts of a successful landing were fading fast.

A gravel beach a mile further north at the 13 Mile was the next possible landing. Beyond lay 14 Mile Bluff with a rocky reef extending north to 17 Mile Bluff, with a further 10 mile long sweep of gravel beach extending along the Barrytown flats where there was always a big surf. The nearest lee landing was at Woodpecker Bay, 20 miles further north. I had to either chance the surf off 13 Mile or continue for Woodpecker Bay. To push on for another five hours on a heavy swell would be inviting disaster on the cliffs and reefs south of the bay, if the weather deteriorated in that time.

From half a mile offshore, the 13 Mile Beach appeared to be the best choice for a landing. Just in case there was a better landing to the north I paddled north to 14 Mile Bluff where luckily as *Isadora* dropped over a swell crest, I caught sight of the red VW driving slowly along the coastal highway. Each time we rose over a crest I waved frantically, even holding the paddle up at arm's length so Dick would spot me. Fortunately when Dick stopped at 14 Mile Bluff, he spotted the distant kayak. Each time I glimpsed the car from a swell crest, I pointed back to the 13 Mile, trying to tell Dick where I was going to attempt to land. Dick quickly grasped my predicament and drove away slowly to search for a better landing.

While all the signalling was going on, the swell had carried *Isadora* towards the jagged rocks and reefs of 14 Mile Bluff. As I turned seawards a wave at least 10 feet high reared up between me and the open sea. Spray smoked off its crest as I paddled full tilt straight at the face of the wave, desperately hoping it wouldn't cap before I reached it. *Isadora* climbed up a vertical face of water, sliced through a white toppling crest and crashed into the wave's wake. The wave broke immediately astern with a thunderous roar - a narrow escape.

This close encounter of the worst kind turned my previous anxiety at the prospect of landing into near panic. I could see no way of getting ashore without being hammered. Mouth dry, stomach muscles knotted, my legs felt tense to the point of trembling under the strain of continual bracing.

I waited off the 13 Mile for 10 minutes until the VW returned and parked above the beach. The headlights flashed on and off, our prearranged signal for the most suitable landing.

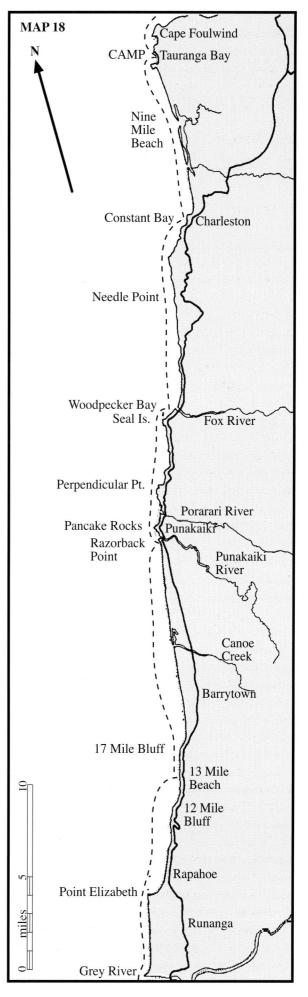

MAP 18

N

Cape Foulwind
CAMP Tauranga Bay

Nine Mile Beach

Constant Bay Charleston

Needle Point

Woodpecker Bay Seal Is.
Fox River

Perpendicular Pt.

Porarari River
Pancake Rocks Punakaiki
Razorback Point
Punakaiki River

Canoe Creek

Barrytown

17 Mile Bluff

13 Mile Beach

12 Mile Bluff

Rapahoe

Point Elizabeth

Runanga

miles

10

5

0

Grey River

The sea was almost as dark and grey as the oppressive overcast sky.

From 800 yards offshore, I cautiously headed towards where the larger sets of waves were breaking. Dear diary: 'I started in but turned out to sea rapidly when a set of large waves threatened to break. I clipped their crests just in time and escaped out to sea. There appeared no regularity in the number of waves per set, a minimum of two and as many as five. My best chance lay in hammering in during a brief lull that followed each set. I followed in closely behind a large set, hesitantly at first, but faster with all the stops out when a glance astern revealed a couple of enormous waves starting to curl. *Isadora* took off in front of a smaller wave, surfing swiftly until it broke. Then a second wave broke and carried me in another 50 yards. Ahead I could see a 200 yard stretch of broken water to the beach, which up till now had remained hidden by breakers. I had reached the offshore bar.'

Astern, the huge leading wave of the next set had broken and a towering wall of water roared towards *Isadora*. When it was only yards away I held the paddle up ready to slap in a high brace. Although buried by the breaker, the support stroke kept me upright while we bounded shorewards. In the aftermath of the wave, *Isadora* was left facing out to sea. Buried again by succeeding waves of the set, we were carried closer to the beach until at last Dick caught hold of the bow and together we dragged the kayak out of the surf.

At first I could hardly speak, my mouth was so dry. As we looked seawards from the security of shore, it was hard to credit how I'd come through the massive surf unscathed.

Dick said I had picked a quiet spell as the three waves that broke immediately behind me were the largest he saw coming in, their estimated height, 15 feet.

These had been the most anxious and worrying hours since I left Jackson Bay. For the first time I felt really conscious of being alone and totally committed on a wild sea.

Back at Dick's house, it took me several hours and numerous cups of tea to recover from the anxiety of the landing. My motivation and enthusiasm for continuing up to Nelson had disappeared somewhere in the surf off 13 Mile.

18 February - Day 34

Each morning for the next two days, we drove out to Rapahoe at 6am and looked at the surf. And that's all we did, look at the surf and return home. In that time Lyn Taylor from Christchurch joined the support crew. Lyn, attractive, long dark hair, is good natured and always ready to come up with yet another terrible

pun at the appropriate moment until we would all cry, 'Enough!' A telegram also arrived from Keith Dekkers in Nelson saying he would join me for the paddle from Karamea around to Nelson.

When my alarm went off on the third morning, I could tell from my bedroom, two miles from Rapahoe, that the sea had settled. The distant roar of surf was now barely audible in contrast to the dull roar of the previous two days. Indeed both swell and surf had settled when we arrived at 13 Mile beach. I launched into a moderate surf and reached the open sea uneventfully. After a wave to the support crew, I headed north for a rendezvous by Razorback Point near Punakaiki.

A light northerly breeze ruffled a slight swell as I passed the cliffs of 17 Mile Bluff. To the north stretched the 10 mile long gravel beach at Barrytown, where for 18 months I had worked as a geologist, so all the landmarks were very familiar. I stayed well offshore from the breakers, in the usual half mile offshore position, along to Razorback Point at the northern end of the gravel beach. On the south side of the cliffed point, the support crew were waiting and although I was tempted to push on to the north side of the Punakaiki Blowholes, I turned towards the beach for my bladder was near bursting. Reasonably sized waves were dumping heavily on the beach but I rode one large breaker sideways onto the gravel.

The dumpers seemed to grow in size during the brief period I stayed on shore, so I wasted no time in sliding back into the cockpit. But the launching proved to be a disaster. Dick pushed me off into a broken dumper but the next wave hit *Isadora* just after it had broken. It shook me and stopped progress out to sea as successfully as running into a brick wall. Before I had time to recover properly a second dumper hammered the Nordkapp and a third caused a capsize. In a dumping surf I always found it best to get out of the cockpit as fast as possible rather than attempt to roll. A struggle ensued to get my feet onto shore and pull *Isadora* out of the surge. Just when both myself and the support crew thought I was safe, yet another large dumper full of sand and gravel, reared up to a height of six or seven feet and broke over me. *Isadora* and I cartwheeled end over end, all 18 feet of kayak standing end on end for a fraction of a second, before slamming down on the gravel.

Dick ran over and helped me retrieve *Isadora* from the surge and I darted back into the surf to grab the paddle. Dear diary: 'With the paddle in one hand I was sent sprawling up the gravel by yet another dumper. Emptied the kayak of water and emptied the gravel from my ears, hair and wetsuit booties. This time we spent a little longer waiting for the right moment before Dick pushed *Isadora* into a broken wave. I took off down the steep gravel face with the retreating surge, battered through one broken wave and motored very quickly out to sea. I felt annoyed with myself for canning out and for not pushing on to the beach at Punakaiki which would have made a better landing.'

North from the Punakaiki River, cream-coloured limestone bluffs, capped by a layer of dense, moist rain forest, rise up vertically behind the coast to a height of 1200 feet above sea level. The bluffs are broken only by the vertical sided gorges of the Punakaiki and Porari rivers and Bullock Creek. The coast road, winding beneath the bluffs and along the top of steep cliffs, provides frequent views of this beautiful stretch of coastline.

Off the Punakaiki headland I could see a group of people standing on the limestone ledges, waiting for the blowholes to perform. Well out from shore, I paddled towards Perpendicular Point where limestone cliffs rise cleanly from the sea for 400 feet to the road winding around the cliff top. My next meeting with the support party would be at Woodpecker Bay, where Seal Island offers protection from the swell in its lee. A narrow gap separates the flat-topped island from shore but at low tide fishermen wade out via an exposed spit. As I approached, there was too much broken water across the gap for my liking so I continued around the tip of the island, leaving the swell behind for the calm sheltered waters of Woodpecker Bay. A gentle two foot surf was breaking onto a grey sandy beach where Lyn and Barb were waiting with lunch. If only there were more landings like this one!

The bay was named after a small river steamer, the *Woodpecker,* which anchored in the lee of Seal Island in 1866. It carried a party of miners and prospectors who were to set off the Fox River gold rush. In more recent years the steamer *Hokitika* called into the bay to load coal from the nearby Brighton Mine. The remains of coal bins and a wharf are still visible on Seal Island.

Over sandwiches and a cup of tea we agreed to meet again at Constant Bay near Charleston, 10 miles to the north. North from Fox River, sandy beaches separated by rock bluffs extend to near White Horse Creek but from here to Charleston the coastline is most inhospitable. A sharp fanglike pillar at Needle Point had me wondering if it could be climbed. Rugged brown cliffs continued along to Constant Bay, no beaches, just the swell surging through waving strands of bull kelp amongst the rocks.

With a sharp exhalation of air from astern, three dolphins shot along the full length of the kayak to surface by the bow. They were joined by another six until a total of nine dolphins were gambolling beneath *Isadora.* They soon had my undivided attention and I increased speed so they would stay with me. Surfacing at the bow, the streamlined grey mammals would curl around in tight circles to repeat the manoeuvre. My afternoon was made when all nine surfaced simultaneously, sending small waves cascading over the bow.

Gradually a south-westerly breeze came away, picking up until a light chop developed. While the dolphins were away on a side trip, I spotted a long dark shape directly in front of the bow and just below the surface, vertical tail, long thin body, two dorsal fins and a pointed snout. "Jeez, a shark!" By then I was right on top of it. Luckily it must have been asleep for the shark didn't move and I lifted the paddle out of the water so as not to disturb its slumber

I kept an eye on the shoreline's rocky bluffs in expectation of sighting the opening of Constant Bay The rugged canyon entrance opened up only when I drew level with the narrow gap in the bluffs. I watched the swell surging through the gap to see if any waves were breaking. No worries, so I paddled hard into the gap, riding in front of the swell until the spoon-shaped bay opened out. *Isadora* glided across the smooth waters of the sheltered bay and gently grounded on a sandy beach.

Gazing at the narrow rocky entrance, I had to admire the seamanship of the old mariners. The tiny natural rock harbour was first entered in 1866 by the 13 ton ketch *Constant.* The vessel, which carried a three man crew, was totally wrecked on the Grey River bar seven years later with the loss of two lives. Gazetted an official port in 1869, Charleston in its heyday was reported by the town's newspaper as receiving upwards of 200 vessels in a seven month period. For a skipper under sail, passage through the narrow entrance without assistance must have been a nightmare and one can only imagine what fare paying passengers thought of what was termed by a provincial council member in 1868 as, 'The hole in the wall.' From 1867, a number of surf boats were available for towing vessels in and out of the bay. Stores and miners were landed here for the Charleston gold rush and a short lived boom town sprang up around the shores of the bay. A few holiday cottages, a hotel and a cemetery mark the site of the once thriving mining town.

Tauranga Bay near Cape Foulwind would be my last stop for the evening. I felt tempted to stay at Charleston but the wind outside was blowing in the right direction to speed progress. Dick was fishing off the rocks as *Isadora* nosed out to sea and I called out, "How many did you catch?" A shake of the head and a rueful smile was the response.

At sea the headland on the south side of Tauranga Bay was just visible 10 miles to the north. Nine Mile Beach lies between Charleston and the headland. It is described on the topographic map as a 'gently sloping sandy beach with breakers 600 to 900 feet out.' Needless to say I stayed half a mile out from the beach, a noisy surf curtained by a veil of spray.

At 8pm the wind doubled its intensity and white-caps quickly sprang up. When the swell began capping occasionally I felt decidedly uncomfortable, especially as the headland was coming up fast. Knees locked tight in the knee rests, feet pushing hard against the foam footrest, I pushed on as hard as possible for the shelter of Tauranga Bay.

The sun disappeared behind a cloud bank on the horizon and both sea and land took on a threatening grey colour. The long hours of paddling and balancing on the rough sea were telling on me. I had to really concentrate off the headland where a single mistimed paddle stroke could result in a capsize.

Just as the light began to grow dim, the bow pointed in to the entrance of the horseshoe shape of Tauranga Bay and I was happy to escape onto calmer waters. I landed easily through a low surf onto a sandy beach where the support crew waited to grab the bow. It had been a long day, nine hours of paddling for 40 miles.

We camped at the head of the beach, by the dammed up waters of a small creek and relaxed by the warmth of a driftwood fire.

19 February - Day 35

The previous evening when I paddled into the bay, I had no idea this is one of the best surfing beaches on the West Coast. Overnight the sea lifted and large breakers extended right across the bay's entrance, tumbling half a mile to the sandy beach. The surf appeared too big to attempt leaving the bay and no easy way out was apparent. Cloud banks drifted over from the south-west, pushed by a strong breeze with intermittent drizzle. Not the most promising conditions in which to start.

Several carloads of surfies arrived with surfboards stacked three and four high on roofracks. Only two donned wetsuits and braved the surf but they didn't last long and left after copping a pounding from the breakers. Dick and I walked onto the headlands on both sides of the bay to try and chart a way out through the surf but no matter which side of the bay we looked, there seemed to be no escape from the trap.

Lyn had to return to her job and left during the afternoon. She would phone Keith Dekkers and tell him to meet us at the Karamea road end of the Heaphy Track in two days' time.

I drove into Westport to inspect the Buller River mouth. Westport lies on the eastern bank of the river which serves as a port for local coal and cement industries. In a sidewater of the river, I located the local fleet of moored fishing boats. I leant over the

edge of the wharf and called out to a group of fishermen who were chatting in the wheelhouse of one of the boats, "Have you heard the latest marine forecast?" A chap with a strong accent stuck his head out the door and replied, "It's blowing its guts out outside, and there's a big heave." He asked if I was thinking of going out and I explained about the kayak trip only to get the customary reaction. He tapped the side of his head and muttered to his mates, "He must be crazy."

20 February - Day 36

A brief entry in my diary stated: 'No change in the state of the surf and we begin to wonder if the Maori meaning for Tauranga is kayak trap. The forecast is still for moderate south-westerly winds and drizzle.'

21 February - Day 37

Although the surf looked only marginally better than the previous two days, I decided to have a crack at escaping from the bay. Offshore, a slight to moderate swell and lack of whitecaps appeared reasonable for paddling. The most feasible route lay on the northern side of the horseshoe, close to the clustered craggy rocks of Wall Islands. This would involve a half mile paddle through the slop close to the beach before I could head out seawards. At 8am Dick pushed *Isadora* into the surf and he and Barb followed my progress along shore. Twice breakers forced *Isadora* back onto the sand.

My worries at the prospect of negotiating the breakers and reefs must have been obvious. As Barb pushed *Isadora* into the surf after the second stranding, she said quietly, "The force is with you Paul." Around the driftwood fire the previous night, we talked about films we had seen. Barb and I had agreed that 'Star Wars' was a fantastic film with its forces of good and evil. One of the expressions often used was, "The force is with you." Although it is merely a saying, it seemed to make my mental attitude to breaking out of the bay a little more positive.

For the first 400 yards out from the beach *Isadora* buffeted through a series of broken waves. Less than 20 yards away on my left, waves were rearing up and breaking with a continuous roar, the noise frighteningly loud. Between this belt of breakers, which extended across the bay's entrance, and Wall Islands' reefs, a narrow channel of unbroken water led out to sea.

Several times a set of large waves came through and I felt sure they were going to break over me. As I paddled over the crest of one wave, the full length of *Isadora* took to the air. Paddling flat out, I reached the seaward end of the islands and thankfully the open sea. It had taken half an hour to escape from 'The Tauranga kayak trap.'

Relieved to be at sea again, despite a moderate swell that rolled north-eastwards, I turned the bow towards Cape Foulwind. The following swell quickly pushed *Isadora* along until we were level with the cape's automatic lighthouse. The 30 foot high concrete tower was conspicuous on top of the 170 foot high cliffs which surround the cape.

Extending north from the cape is a series of exposed rocks and jagged reefs including Black Reef and the Three Steeples. A 400 yard wide gap of unbroken water lay between the cape and the start of the broken water on the reefs. Sneaking through this I felt confident that at last I was in Buller Bay.

Without warning one of the swell crests that had just passed beneath the kayak began smoking only 20 yards in front of the bow and moments later broke in a flurry of spray. Dear diary: 'I took the traditional flailing out to sea route, before turning and heading in the general direction of the Westport Harbour entrance. Thought of a pun that had me sniggering for a while - had the wind up off Cape Foulwind.'

At the cape the coastline turns almost 90 degrees east into Buller Bay, and in the lee of the bay the swell diminished in size. It became smooth almost glassy as I closed on the tips of the stone breakwaters on either side of the Buller River mouth. I watched the Westport Harbour Board bucket dredge move out to sea and above the western breakwater, the bridge and aerials of one the large cement carriers appeared cruising downriver towards the bar. About 300 yards away from *Isadora*, the *Westport* crossed the bar. It was the largest vessel I had so far seen at sea.

Fishermen on the breakwaters must have been puzzled as the lone yellow kayak glided by the Buller River without entering and continued eastwards. I nearly pulled in for a leak at a sandy beach on the east side of the breakwater but decided to push on to the hazy distant hills where Dick and Barb were waiting on Granity beach. By taking a beeline for the Waimangaroa River mouth, I hoped to save a few mile's paddle where the coast curved inland for the next six miles to form a shallow bay. This meant venturing two miles offshore but the day was as near to perfect as I could hope for.

Dear diary: 'Quite happy to reach Granity; low tide with the surf breaking a long way out. Barb and Dick waved the orange tent from the distant beach and I had a clean run in through what looked to be a big surf. Six hours and 40 minutes from the Tauranga trap. Brew and sandwiches for lunch.' Dick told me that when they first arrived, the tide was full with surf dumping heavily onto the gravel. So while the tide remained low, I decided to push on to Waimarie. The ebb tide had exposed an offshore bar where the surf was breaking, leaving a quieter stretch of water

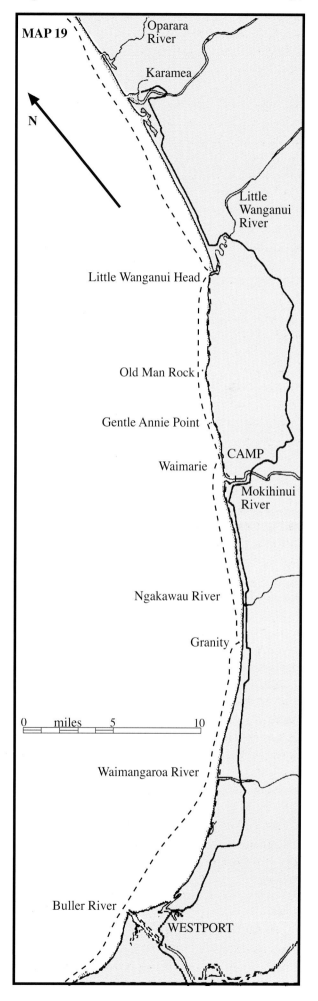

between the bar and small shore break.

The support party helped me launch and I paddled inside the bar, parallel to the main break, searching for a gap or lull in the breakers. During a brief lull I turned directly out to sea and paddled hard. Nearly in the clear I saw a six foot high wave just about to get the drop on me but thankfully it held off capping just long enough for *Isadora* to slice over its crest. In the usual half mile offshore position I passed Torea Rocks and the Ngakawau River mouth. Although the light breeze eased off, the swell increased in size as the tide came in. In sets of two or three, large waves blocked off my view of the beach. I began worrying about the impending landing at Waimarie.

This small township lies at the mouth of the Mokihinui River and here the coastal highway turns away from the beach to make its way through the ranges to Karamea. It was a logical place to stay the night. As the houses of Waimarie came into sight I strained my eyes to pick up the smoke from a signal fire but there was no sign of the VW or Dick and Barb. The lee of Cape Foulwind had been quite sheltered from the south-westerly swell but now there was no protection and the surf looked rather large. I would have preferred the company of another kayaker with the next landing coming up especially since the support crew had not spotted me.

Off the river mouth there were no gaps or low points in the line of breakers so I continued north towards Gentle Annie Point where the surf appeared to be marginally smaller. The first time I started in beachwards, a large set came barrelling through causing a rapid 180 degree turn and a fast escape to the open sea. Behind the next large set I hammered in and almost reached the sand before the following set caught up. I managed to back paddle through the first breaker but the next two hurtled *Isadora* sideways up the beach.

Dick and Barb could not see the Nordkapp offshore because of the size of the swell and the distance I stayed out beyond the breakers, but they quickly drove up when they spotted the kayak on the beach.

At a nearby isolated house, I asked for some fresh water and Dave Leavy gave us the use of his house for the night. West Coast hospitality at its best.

Another 34 miles closer to Nelson.

22 February - Day 38

The day saw an early start and I reached the open sea uneventfully after crashing through several breakers. A light northerly disturbed the surface of the swell and there wasn't a cloud in the sky. Dick and Barb were going to drive north to Karamea and along to the road end by the Kohaihai River where the Heaphy Track starts. Hopefully they would find Keith Dekkers

waiting with another Nordkapp.

Since I wanted as few encounters with the West Coast surf as possible, I aimed to paddle the 30 miles to the Kohaihai River in one go. From Gentle Annie Point to Little Wanganui Head the coast is formed by a line of bush-clad bluffs, up to 1400 feet in height, with patches of white rock exposed in cliffs and slips. Some of the larger slips had carried blocky debris down over 1000 feet into the sea.

The Little Wanganui River mouth forms the start of a long sandy beach which extends along past Karamea to the Kohaihai River, and the river bar lies hard up against the cream coloured rock bluffs of Little Wanganui Head. Despite a wild surf pounding onto Karamea beach, I nosed the bow around the headland's tip for a look at the river mouth. To my delight not a ripple was breaking over the narrow river entrance and I sneaked onto its calm waters for the quietest beaching on the West Coast since leaving Jackson Bay. Lying in the lee of the jutting headland, the bar is completely protected from the prevailing swell.

Amongst the driftwood piled on the river bank I climbed onto the remains of an old wooden fishing boat that had obviously encountered a difficult crossing of the bar. After a spell onshore to remind my legs that they actually attached to me for the purpose of walking, I put out to sea and headed north.

It would be a long walk along the beach from the Little Wanganui mouth to Kohaihai Bluff and it certainly seemed a long way in the kayak. I realized that I had lost sight of my motivation for the trip. My enthusiasm and drive had been overridden by loneliness on the long swell and the tension that mounted, wrinkling my forehead and knotting my stomach muscles, each time I faced a landing through the West Coast surf. During the paddle from Jackson Bay to Greymouth the seas had been so settled that landing was never a worry but now with the thought of the impending paddle along the rugged, inaccessible stretch of coastline north of Kohaihai Bluff, I was ready to give up.

The only relief from the monotony came from watching widely spaced landmarks drift slowly past, the house roofs of Karamea and the Oparara and Karamea river mouths. I had plenty of time for my thoughts to dwell on the landing coming up at the Kohaihai River mouth. Judging by the sight and sound of the surf breaking all the way along the Karamea beach, it was not going to be a picnic.

As I neared the river mouth *Isadora* lay so far offshore that what I assumed was an orange parka was in fact the long orange tent spread over bushes on a dune ridge behind the beach. After the usual sizing up of the sets, I cautiously nosed in to the outside line of breakers and wasn't happy to find the large swell peaking quickly and dumping heavily. Following one large set I paddled hard to be swept in sideways by two smaller breakers. Because of *Isadora's* length, in a surf over four foot high I had no option but to broach sideways in front of the breakers. Waves over this height steepen to such a degree that the kayak's bow points directly down the wave face, invariably digging in at the base of the waves. This acts as a brake, causing the stern to flip end over bow in a graceful forward loop.

The smaller breakers between two sets carried *Isadora* over the offshore bar leaving only a 100 yard stretch of broken water to the beach. Relaxed in the assumption that I had breached the worst of the shore defences, I dropped my legs out of the knee rests to let them lie on the hull. The leading breaker of the following set, larger than anticipated capsized me beneath a wall of broken water. At that stage I felt so tired and dispirited that I made no attempt to roll or right the kayak and set off swimming for the sandy shore, where Dick, Barb and Keith were watching anxiously.

Ten minutes later I was still towing *Isadora* and not making any headway over the last 10 yards to the beach. The combination of surge from the shore break and a strong rip between it and the bar prevented my feet from touching bottom. Seeing my predicament Keith and Barb stripped off and waded out to help tow *Isadora* to shore. This northern section of the West Coast certainly was not proving easy. If Keith and his enthusiasm for the next inaccessible stretch of coastline hadn't been waiting when I arrived, I think we would have returned home or at least flagged the paddling away until the swell settled down.

Keith had been waiting for two days, the time we had spent in the Tauranga Trap, and had driven up and down the coast searching for either the red VW or the yellow kayak. The previous evening Keith had slept in his car at Waimarie, less than two miles from where we had stayed. He had rented a Nordkapp in Nelson for Keith considered the best way to look at the next rugged section of shoreline along to Kahurangi Point would by kayak. He imagined us pottering along and stopping frequently for cups of tea at various points and scattered bays along the way. I didn't have the heart to tell him that because of the size of the swell, once we broke clear of the surf off the river mouth, we would probably have to stay at least half a mile offshore, not landing until we were well north of Kahurangi Point.

Keith, a builder by trade and easily recognized by his untamed reddish-brown curly hair and beard, was quietly spoken and never ruffled. He and I had remarkably similar interests in the three C's, caving, canoeing and climbing, as well as photography, skiing and music. There was only one thing that we could never agree about, the strength of a cup of tea. Keith prefers tea so weak and insipid that when milk is added, the tea goes white instead of the brown colour I prefer with a slightly stronger brew. Over the past eight years, spent in New Zealand, New Guinea and Australia, we had forged a close partnership in caves, on expeditions and on climbs. To my knowledge we were the only two people who had climbed to the highest point of New Zealand and been to the bottom of the deepest cave.

Since this was as far as the road went, Dick and Barb would have to drive back to Westport then up through the Buller Gorge to Nelson where Keith's car would be left. They would then drive the VW out to Collingwood and down the coast to the road end by the Anatori River mouth.

The Heaphy Track, one of the most popular of all tramping tracks in New Zealand, connects the West Coast with Golden Bay. Although a road between Karamea and Golden Bay has often been talked about, hopefully it will never be pushed through. There should be some places left that you can't zoom through in a car. Goldminers and prospectors discovered the route after access down the rugged coastline proved too difficult and dangerous.

A suspension bridge over the clear waters of the Kohaihai River marks the start of the Heaphy Track. The river flows into the sea by a jumbled mass of large limestone blocks at the south end of Kohaihai Bluff. High tide dams the river water, forming a broad lagoon, its tranquil surface in marked contrast to the angry, lumpy sea only 100 yards away. In this lagoon Keith had paddled round and round while waiting for us to arrive.

On a river bank overlooking the lagoon stood a caravan with an outstretched tent awning in front. It was the summer residence for Jude Grindell. Suntanned, with long rich hair, Jude had a marvellous summer existence as a Forest Service employee, counting the number of trampers who start and complete the track, and passing on advice to the daily visitors who arrive for a picnic. Already in the 1977-78 season, 2000 trampers had passed through with up to 130 on the track at a time.

At nightfall we spread out our sleeping bags in clumps of marram grass by the beach, our sleep disturbed through the night by occasional drizzle showers and the continuous background roar of the pounding surf. Sleep did not come easy for my mind drifted over the doubts that had arisen during the day; did continuing the journey justify the tension and worries of landing through the big surf; was I capable of sustaining the paddling, and why on earth did I do it when I could forget about it, call off the trip and be safe and secure at home in Runanga?

23 February - Day 39

Sandflies woke me early, sneaking though the hood of my sleeping bag. For 20 minutes I sat and watched the surf. It was huge, horrifying and breaking a long way out. I woke Keith and we drove south looking for a low section or gap in the breakers but after much indecision and procrastination, we decided the surf was too large to set off. Besides the weather didn't look promising with cloud banks drifting over from the north-west.

Mid-morning, Keith, Barb and I walked over the first graded mile of the Heaphy Track to inspect the surf of Scotts Beach. From a lookout on the northern end of Kohaihai Bluff we were able to gaze north along the spectacular coastline towards the Heaphy River mouth. A large swell broke 400 to 500 yards offshore. Large white, foaming breakers steamed in almost to the beach where on its steep sandy face, dumpers that reared up to a height of eight feet were thumping heavily. Attempting to land through that surf would be inviting a mention on the back page of a newspaper.

At Scotts Beach we met two chaps who were pouring concrete to replace the washed out foundations of a footbridge. Stocky with a long straggly beard, Peter De Vries looked after the maintenance of the southern part of the track. Peter is one of the select band of people who have walked along the coastline from Kahurangi Point to Karamea, so Keith and I were keen to seek his advice. "Once you get past the Heaphy River, there will probably be only one landing place." He told us we would paddle past the wreckage of a Japanese squid boat that was stuck on rocks by Heaphy Bluff. "The night she went aground, the seas were really huge," he explained. During a radio schedule next morning, Peter was told of a boat in trouble off Rocks Point, 10 miles north of the Heaphy River mouth. Observing three fishing boats standing off the Heaphy Bluff, Peter walked out to the beach.

A helicopter from Nelson flew down the coastline searching for the squid boat but the pilot could see nothing at Rocks Point. He continued flying down the coast and spotted the Japanese squid boat on the rocks beneath Heaphy Bluff. A line was rigged from the boat to shore, then the helicopter came in and picked up Peter. On the highest point of the boat, just out of reach of waves breaking over the vessel, 13 Japanese fishermen were clustered. A scoop net slung on a long strop beneath the helicopter, completed seven trips out to the boat to rescue the fishermen. Before they were flown to Nelson, the crew recovered at the Heaphy Hut and one chap who could speak a little English told Peter there was something wrong with the boat's radar and navigational gear. The vessel

was thought to be heading through Cook Strait for repairs when it struck the rocks.

Much to Peter and Tex's disgust (Tex was another track worker) the Government claimed the squid boat as a wreck while Peter and Tex maintained they had salvage rights. Next day they climbed out along the fixed line to ferry the Japanese crews' personal effects ashore. While they were doing this, a helicopter arrived with two chaps in white overalls, and signalled to Peter. Onshore one of the overalled figures said he was the Government Receiver of Wrecks but Peter didn't believe him and asked to see some identification. The chap had a card to prove he was the genuine article but Peter pointed out that it wasn't valid for the West Coast. "It's for Golden Bay!" In the end the Receiver of Wrecks was happy with just the squid boat's log book. A Nelson company bought the wreck and flew out everything salvageable.

As we talked a brown horse stood quietly in a patch of lupins off the track. Dan, a 23 year old gelding, was employed by the Forest Service as a packhorse and had carried loads along the Heaphy Track for the past 13 years. Dan was a scrounger of the highest order with a particular liking for biscuits. When people were picnicking at the road end, Dan ambled over and if the people didn't feed him, helped himself. Up till the previous summer, there had been two packhorses but Turner wasn't as keen on biscuits as Dan. When the two of them were carrying boxes of food along the track, it didn't take Dan long to figure out which load contained the biscuits. If Turner had them, Dan would get into all sorts of contortions to find them however if they were in his load, he would move in front of Turner. Turner would emerge from a food box with a lettuce or a cabbage in his teeth. He wasn't as shrewd as Dan.

Peter told us of the day when he set off from Scotts Camp for the Heaphy Hut with Dan carrying boxes of food on either side of the packsaddle. Dan was rather reluctant to leave the good feed around Scotts Camp and Peter had to walk on his heels in attempt to make him walk a little faster. There are occasional loop tracks that branch off the main track, circling around through groves of nikau palms to rejoin the main track. Without warning, Dan took off down one of these loop tracks, scattering tins of spaghetti and baked beans on either side as he galloped through the trees. Peter ran after him but was rapidly left behind. He stopped to listen and heard the sound of a box scraping against a tree on the main track. Quietly Peter crept back along the loop and stood behind a flax bush. Moments later, Dan came plodding slowly and silently by, placing his hooves very gently on the ground. Peter moved out from his hiding place and caught hold of the reins. What a horse!

Chapter 12

KARAMEA to NELSON

24 February - Day 40

During the night the sea settled marginally but at dawn it was still large and lumpy. Although I felt rattled by the size of the surf and not at all keen to try a break-out for the open sea, we agreed to make an attempt to leave the beach. The Forest Service staff came out to watch Keith and I get underway. As we pulled on lifejackets and sprayskirts I gave Keith last minute advice on how to cope with the West Coast breakers and explained the technique of waiting in the broken waves for a lull between sets of larger waves. At 8.30am Dick and Barb each held a kayak stern while we slid into the cockpits, pulled sprayskirts over the cockpit coamings and picked up the paddles. After one wave had broken I called, "Now!" and Dick and Barb shoved us into the surge.

For the first 150 yards out to the main break on the offshore bar it was easy going, cutting through small breakers and keeping the kayaks about 20 yards apart. Then we started hammering into the larger sets that were coming through in sets of three or four, and it was a struggle to maintain position until a lull appeared. Slowly we edged seawards, paddling quietly between sets but putting on power to crash over the larger breakers.

We crashed through two breakers of a set and I glimpsed Keith about 30 yards to my right paddling hard into the face on a high breaker, then slamming hard over into its wake. For some unknown reason, when I battered into the same wave, it swept *Isadora* backwards and I couldn't escape from the powerful drag of its surging wake. I lost 50 yards before finally breaking clear. This was just a taste of what was to come.

When I paddled out again to where the big sets were breaking, a second large wave, more powerful than the previous one, caught *Isadora* in its strong surging wake. Much of my effort with the paddle went into staying upright rather than maintaining forward momentum. After 60 yards of careering backwards, *Isadora's* stern dropped down the breaker's six foot high face. For a moment the Nordkapp stood on end before executing a bow over stern reverse loop.

Buried beneath the wave, the kayak tumbled over and over. When my head finally broke free of water, after the breaker had settled a little, I had swallowed a quantity of sea water. My glasses had been swept off but were retained around my neck by a piece of hat elastic. Rather than be buried by the following breaker, I slipped out of the cockpit, wrapped my arms around the bow and set off swimming for the beach.

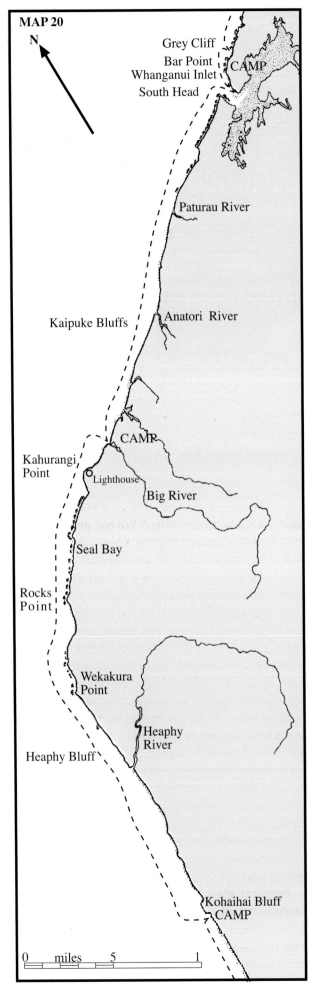

MAP 20

N

Grey Cliff
Bar Point
Whanganui Inlet
South Head
CAMP

Paturau River

Kaipuke Bluffs

Anatori River

CAMP

Kahurangi
Point

Lighthouse

Big River

Seal Bay

Rocks
Point

Wekakura
Point

Heaphy
River

Heaphy Bluff

Kohaihai Bluff
CAMP

0   miles   5   1

A long struggle ensured before I reached the shore break and I was stuffed by the time my feet touched bottom. Bedraggled and waterlogged I staggered out of the surf and the support party helped empty the cockpit of water. By now Keith was sitting half a mile offshore, beyond the farthest line of breakers and every now and then as he rode over a swell crest, we caught a glimpse of him. It was ironic that after all the advice I had given him that morning, Keith had made a clean exit whereas with my experience and 'expertise' I had canned out.

On shore we watched and waited for a lull. As Dick pushed *Isadora* into the shore break Barb reminded me, "The force is with you." This time however the expression didn't help very much. I felt even more nervous about a second capsize and doubted my ability to make a third attempt.

Amongst the broken waves I kept *Isadora* as close as possible to the large breakers and when a brief lull appeared between two sets, I paddled hard for the open sea. Fortunately I made it, after just clipping the crests of the next set before the rollers capped. At first there was no sign of Keith on the lumpy sea but I continued offshore until a yellow bladed paddle, held up on end, indicated his position. We were both relieved to see each other.

"The surf is frightening, all right!" Keith exclaimed. I agreed with him wholeheartedly. Turning the kayaks northwards we began to paddle over a steep, moderate south-westerly swell. The only good points of the day were the absence of both wind and cloud. The glare of the sun, hanging low over the ranges in the east combined with a thick pall of spray drifting over the surf, made it virtually impossible to distinguish onshore features. Beaches, bluffs and points all lay in deep shadow. I could only hope the support party had seen the two of us turn safely away to the north for we were well over half a mile offshore. Any thought Keith had of frequent stops along the coast for cups of tea had been instantly dispelled in the surf of Kohaihai Bluff.

An obvious gap in the steep forested hills behind the beach, marked the Heaphy River mouth. Here the Heaphy Track turned away from the shoreline to continue up the Heaphy River. As the Nordkapps rose and fell on the lumpy sea, we caught brief glimpses of the Heaphy Hut and the wreckage of the Japanese squid boat on rocks beneath the nearby steep bluff.

Dear diary: 'We made for Wekakura Point which Peter thought might provide a landing on its north side, but when we reached there, no way as the huge swell broke violently on both sides of the point with spray flying high into the air. A south-westerly breeze came away and freshened, pushing the kayaks along, the foreshore a boulder beach between rocky points. Coastline rises up very steeply to the forested ranges.' This stretch of coast is very similar in appearance to the Fiordland landscape, although not quite as high. The land near Wekakura Point rises from sea level to over 2,000 feet in less than a mile and a half from shore.

As the wind picked up, Keith felt more and more unstable in his Nordkapp. "There's no way of relaxing," he declared, "I feel like I'm going to tip over at any moment."

Once we rounded Rocks Point, which Captain Cook named during his first voyage to New Zealand, we could see Otukoroiti Point and a hazy outline on the horizon which had to be Kahurangi Point. Off Seal Point, a small indentation on the rugged foreshore, we rafted up briefly to look at the map and grab a bite to eat.

In contrast to the coastline to the south, Kahurangi Point is devoid of forest and especially after the bush clad coastline which I had been following for so long, it stood out like the proverbial sore thumb. What at first looked like a thin white pole on the bare projecting headland, gradually grew into the white metal tower of a 59 foot high automatic lighthouse.

The south-westerly breeze had freshened even more as we approached Kahurangi Point and with whitecaps all around we could not afford a lapse in concentration for a moment. In his younger days Keith used to enjoy deer stalking and at one stage while examining the distant shore for deer tracks, nearly capsized. Poor old Keith was none too happy. He admitted that prior sea cruises in the Nelson area, which were considered rough trips, were picnics in comparison to these seas.

To avoid the tall capping waves, breaking over shallow ground and reefs off Kahurangi Point, we increased our distance offshore by another 300 yards before turning back to the north-east.

When we drew level with the mouth of Big River, we had been paddling for seven tense hours and Keith indicated his desire to land and stretch his legs. I wasn't keen to go in as only seven miles remained to our rendezvous with the support party at the Anatori River mouth, and we were making fast progress with the following wind and swell. I wanted to avoid unnecessary landings where possible.

After some discussion we turned shorewards and inspected the surf more closely. With a near dead low tide, the large swell broke a long way out from a gently shelving sandy beach. After sizing up the sets of larger waves, we both hammered in during a brief lull and surfed through the main break without incident. In the slop, 100 yards out from the wet sandy shore, a small breaker no more than two feet high

A brief stop for a photograph off the Heaphy River mouth. Photo: Keith Dekkers

bumped into *Isadora* and I capsized, into water so shallow that my shoulders rubbed on the sand. The thought of passing through the six foot high waves of the main break unscathed only to capsize in a two footer, should have been amusing but after two capsizes in a single day, I felt really fed up. Perhaps my pride was a little damp. Keith reached shore without capsizing and ran out towards me as I towed the kayak through the shallows to where I could empty the water out. Instead of helping me, Keith attempted to take a dramatic action photograph. My tiredness and frustration boiled over. I let fly with a few choice words.

A brew of tea restored my civility. We had a bite to eat and Keith took his legs for a walk. At 5.45pm, I said, "It's time to get going." We had just two hours paddle before us to reach the Anatori River mouth. Whilst we recuperated on shore, the tide was racing in and the breakers were building in height. It would not be easy reaching the open sea.

In the slop offshore we waited for a lull. When it came we paddled hard into the breakers. Keith lay astern of *Isadora* when I took off, racing to climb over the steepening faces of the next set before they broke. The waves were peaking at seven to eight feet before toppling, a much more gripping situation than an hour ago at low tide. The leading wave of the next set appeared ready to break before I reached it but it held off just long enough for *Isadora* to climb its face and slice through the crest, slamming into the wave's wake. I paddled frantically to reach the remaining two waves of the set before they broke, cutting the last one so finely that *Isadora* became airborne. With a thumping splash, she hit the wake of the wave and I resumed hard paddling. But there were no more capping waves, I had reached the open sea.

Frequent glances astern as I moved out to the customary half mile offshore position, revealed no trace of Keith. After 10 minutes, I was sure he had capsized in the surf. I nosed into where the big sets were breaking a few times, only once catching a glimpse of Keith's Nordkapp on the distant beach. Dear diary: 'Waited until 7pm when I reckoned it would be too late to reach the Anatori before nightfall and headed back into the breakers to look for Keith. Even during the hour spent waiting offshore, the breakers had grown in size as the tide flooded. The security of the beach seemed so far away, hidden behind a wall of breakers. Waited for a lull then paddled in hard behind one set. The first big wave of the following set broke and rapidly buried *Isadora* but a high brace with the paddle kept me upright, though bouncing in front of the breaker. Twice the kayak rose up the breakers face, the second time dropping over into its wake. The second wave of the set seemed even larger but after disappearing beneath its white face, *Isadora* shook herself free to ride swiftly shorewards in the broach position. As this breaker caught up on a smaller breaker, it rose and dumped heavily, suddenly flipping me over. Four or five times I tumbled over, still in the cockpit, until I was short of breath and disorientated. I came up in the breaker's wake, gasping and coughing up water. Luckily the water was shallow enough to tow *Isadora* in. Staggered almost drunkenly onto the sand where Keith waited - this time with no camera. Certainly had not been my day at all!'

Keith had attempted four times to breach the lines of breakers but each time had been hammered beneath large waves that capped over him, causing capsizes.

So confident of reaching the Anatori rendezvous before dark, we carried only a white spirit cooker, the makings of a brew and a packet of mushroom soup in the kayak compartments. We had the usual repair and first aid kits and a change of dry clothing but not the sleeping bags. As the light began to fade, we began searching for some form of shelter.

Apart from a small mob of frisky cattle on the steep grassy hill immediately behind the beach, there was not a single sign of man. On a vantage point overlooking the river mouth we sat quietly, two rather subdued and tired kayakers, watching a colourful sunset develop with sea, sky and sand painted gold by the setting sun's rays. A strange and beautiful close to what had been a tense and gripping day.

Inland from its mouth and behind a ridge of lupin covered dunes, Big River meanders in broad curves across sandy tidal flats between steep forested hills. In a natural rock overhang at the foot of a limestone bluff, we levelled a sandy sleeping platform that would accommodate two cold, tired bodies. Our small shelter lay on the north bank of the river. As the incoming tide submerged the tidal flats, the river backed up to form a broad lagoon, its surface silent and still.

A large billy of mushroom soup heated over a driftwood fire followed by a few sweets that Keith found in his shirt pocket, were barely sufficient to satisfy our ravenous appetites. Rolled up in our parkas, with wetsuits and lifejackets for pillows, we both slept reasonably well, lulled to sleep by the very gently and soft lapping of waves as the tide encroached around our wee cave.

25 February - Day 41

We were up at first light and had a brew of tea. We walked out to the beach and looked hopefully out to sea. Disappointment! A huge surf breaking a long way out. In retrospect we should have tried to leave the beach then without letting the surf psych us out any more, but we didn't. Instead we walked along the beach to the north, back to the south, paced along to the north again, then climbed onto the hills for a better view of the surf. At one stage during the morning we carried the Nordkapps, one at a time, 400 yards north along the beach to where the breakers looked marginally smaller from our vantage point on the hill. An hour later we staggered back with them. The surf always appeared much smaller to the north or south than directly in front.

We waited until midday before making an attempt to break out through the surf, procrastination of the highest order. Mind you the surf did appear frighteningly large. The launch would have been rather amusing to an impartial spectator. With no one to steady the kayaks we had to position the Nordkapps on damp sand within reach of the highest surges. As a wave receded we had to quickly slip into the cockpits, stretch sprayskirts over the coamings and pick up the paddle before the next surge raced up the sand. If the kayaks were positioned too high up the beach, we often had to wait several minutes for a larger than average surge to float the kayaks.

Together we launched into the shore break, rising off the same wave, and paddled out slowly towards the big breakers. We decided to try and stick as close as possible to each other on the way out, so we would either reach the open sea together or capsize. Punching into the breakers, we waited for a lull but it became harder and harder to stay together, fighting to stay upright in the really big stuff. To crash through the six foot high surging breakers took all our effort and concentration. Timing was critical to make it through powerful dumping waves of this size, choosing the right moment to put on a spurt to climb up the face of a wave before it capped, or deciding to hang back and paddle through it after it had broken. To be caught beneath a wave that capped or to attempt to burst through one that had just toppled inevitably meant a capsize.

9. *Max on the boulder beach at Barn Bay, the morning after our disastrous night surf landing*

10. *Okawa 4 on her second attempt at crossing the dangerous Grey River bar*

11. *Paul on the back of the shore break at 13 Mile, after surviving a run through 15 foot high surf, visible in the background. Photo: Dick Strong*

12. *Broaching in near Razorback Point, on the West Coast, with the skeg plainly visible on the stern. Photo: Dick Strong*

The larger waves were peaking at up to 10 feet before breaking and as I clipped the top of one of these monsters, I caught a glimpse of Keith, who was about 60 yards to my right. He wasn't paddling. Just waiting with his paddle sitting on the water. The same wave that I had just crested was approaching him like a steaming express train, a terrifying mountain of water with spray rearing off its crest. Only 20 yards away from Keith, it topped with a roar. An unforgettably vivid picture is etched in my mind, of Keith waiting for this huge wall of broken water to hit. It was awesome to watch.

In its wake, I watched anxiously over my shoulder for Keith to emerge. But there was only white frothy water and empty sea. He had been clobbered.

Paddling flatstick I shot over the crests of the two succeeding waves of that large set and with a dry mouth and tightly wrinkled forehead, reached the open sea. As long minutes passed my anxiety and tension did not ease for there was still no sign of Keith. During lulls between sets, I nosed in towards the distant beach to look for him, only to rapidly retreat when another large set of capping waves steamed shorewards. From a swell crest I caught a fleeting glimpse of Keith's kayak on the beach.

A cold south-westerly breeze slowly chilled my hands until I pulled on light plastic gloves. To restore warmth to my arms, I paddled north for a while then turned and paddled back again.

An anxious hour passed. All the time without Keith breaking through, I dreaded the thought of paddling in through the surf again. Then I saw a tiny figure climb onto the dune ridge behind the beach. Keith held his yellow bladed paddle above his head and waved it several times to the north-east. It appeared he was signalling me to head on without him. Twice he repeated the signal so I paddled away for a few strokes to the north, then stopped. He repeated the signal so I turned parallel to the beach, heading for the Anatori River mouth, once more on my lonesome and not liking it at all. I hoped Keith would remember my comment before we left the beach, "If the surf is too rough off the Anatori, we may have to push on to Whanganui Inlet." The broad inlet entrance appeared feasible for a landing on the map.

The surf off Big River was the worst I had so far encountered, breakers as large as those off 13 Mile Beach and more violent than the ones Max and I had survived off Wolf River in Fiordland.

A strong south-westerly breeze pushed *Isadora* along for the seven miles to the Anatori. The coastline, rocky in places with stretches of sandy beach in between, was backed by a strip of hilly, bare, grassy pasture. Immediately south of the Anatori River mouth, lay the two mile length of the sheer bluffs of Kaipuke Cliffs.

I drew level with the river mouth but didn't seriously consider landing as huge seas were breaking a good distance offshore, obscuring all sight of the beach. From over three quarters of a mile out, I spotted the tiny red blob of the VW parked on a hillside above the river but it was little comfort to know the support crew was waiting. They could do little to help.

Just in case Dick and Barb spotted the kayak, I signalled back down the coast with the paddle, then pointed north. I was concerned that they might follow me to the north, not knowing Keith was still down by Big River. In fact Dick and Barb did not see *Isadora* for I was so far offshore on a lumpy swell, that even with a telescope the yellow kayak would have been almost impossible to spot. They had arrived at 1am after a long tiring drive from Karamea. And fortunately they were still waiting when Keith arrived late afternoon. In a marathon effort, Keith dragged his kayak five miles along the beach from Big River to Kaipuke Cliffs where he had no alternative but to take to the surf. He made a successful break-out and paddled two miles to the Anatori River mouth where he was not so lucky. He described the landing: "I made it through the first breaker but the second one flipped me over and over. The force of the water inside the breaker was so strong that I couldn't push my hand forward to reach the release strap on the sprayskirt. I had to work my hands forward beneath the cockpit coaming. Then I had trouble getting my legs out." Keith left the kayak to the mercy of the breakers and swam to shore where Dick and Barb waited. The kayak was recovered from the surf in one piece.

Several times, while paddling north-eastwards, I nosed in towards the distant shore, seeking a gap in the breakers but each time escaped out to sea as sets of large waves rolled through. By now the south-westerly breeze had created a white-capping chop on top of the swell. Where the coastal gravel road from the Anatori mouth turned inland for Golden Bay, I made a determined effort to land here but the surf was really large and I turned out to sea. No option remained but to press on to Whanganui Inlet, hopefully to reach the road end at the inlet's head and hitch back south to meet the support party. Dick and Barb would be concerned at our nonappearance and I was concerned for Keith's safety.

By my reckoning the tide should have turned by the time I reached the inlet and be on the flood, which would make crossing the bar easier. I didn't feel at all happy on the rough sea and this feeling was intensified when *Isadora* and I were buried several times by capping swell crests.

With half a mile to go to the inlet, I heard the sound of a motor astern and soon a fishing boat cruised alongside. I asked the skipper of *Bonito* the best route over the bar. He called out, "Forty yards north of South Head. We'll give you a ride in if you like. Chuck your kayak on the back of the boat." Although tempted to accept a lift, especially in view of the white line of breakers between us and sheltered water of the inlet, I replied, "No thanks, it wouldn't be ethical." The fishermen must have thought me a little daft as I waved and headed into the breakers. For the next hour I regretted my ethical decision.

The inlet's entrance is a mile wide between the cliffed and pointed summit of South Head and the bluffs of Bar Point in the north. Between these two features I could only see a white line of breaking waves and no sign of a gap of channel. I followed *Bonito*'s progress over the bar until she disappeared behind the breakers.

At the point where the fishing boat had disappeared, I cautiously approached the outside line of breakers. Dear diary: 'Big breakers. One caught me, turned the kayak out to sea and almost caused a capsize, but I rolled up only to find the sprayskirt was partially off the coaming. The cockpit was half full of water. Frantically I tried to do two things at the same time, pull the sprayskirt over the coaming before the next wave broke, and pump the cockpit dry. I managed neither before being caught in the next wave, which filled the cockpit and capsized *Isadora*. I came out and swam to the bow, my glasses dislodged and my hat missing. I started towing the capsized Nordkapp closer to the temptingly calm waters of the inlet. If the sprayskirt had stayed on, I would have been paddling easily up the inlet. Only after swimming for 10 minutes or more did I notice that I was not making progress. That relatively calm water inside the bar remained 300 yards away. Occasionally one of my feet touched a sandy bottom and I tried to drag *Isadora* in, but a powerful current was setting swiftly out to sea. In the troughs between waves I made a yard at the most, standing on tip toe, but the next wave would lift me off and we would drift backwards. I couldn't quite figure out what was going on for the tide had turned outside while in the inlet's entrance, it was still ebbing. Tired and sick of swimming and getting nowhere, I attempted to re-enter the cockpit by climbing onto the stern, working forward until astride the cockpit, then quickly sliding my legs in. In the process of doing this, the camera strap around my neck caught on something on the deck and I tugged it free without looking at the cause, until with a jerk it came free.'

What I didn't realize was that the strap had caught on the handle of the rear hatch cover. When it came free, the hatch cover had somehow come off. Almost sitting in the cockpit, I suddenly noticed that the only section of *Isadora* above water was the tip of the bow. The stern compartment had flooded. When the penny finally dropped I desperately scanned the water for the missing hatch cover, lamenting the fact that I had chosen a sea green colour for the hatch covers. Without the hatch cover there would be no more kayaking until I found a replacement.

Again I started swimming, towing the waterlogged kayak, but the cold was numbing my hands and feet. A strong northerly drift was carrying *Isadora* towards the rocks of Bar Point. In desperation I considered abandoning her to the mercy of the waves and swimming for shore. The thought was almost unbearable after all the old girl and I had been though. With the lifejacket, the buoyancy of the wetsuit and my strength as a swimmer, I was in no immediate danger, but to abandon *Isadora*, the situation was grim indeed.

Although the cockpit was flooded and below the surface, I managed to re-enter it and with water up around my neck, paddled gingerly and delicately towards shore, the tip of the bow pointing skywards and the stern three feet under. I was making headway at last. Dear diary: 'After 10 minutes I was drawing closer and closer to shore and with immense relief, I landed on a grey sandy beach. Just on dusk and I was pretty glad to be on terra firma. We were almost down at Bar Point. *Isadora* had drifted well over a mile to the north from the point of capsizing.'

Whanganui Inlet is shaped like an elongate T. A mile inside the entrance it divides into two long arms and the Pakawau to Patarau road winds around the inland side of the top of the T. Now that I was ashore, my main worry was for Keith's safety. I decided my best course of action was to paddle across the inlet and hitch a ride or walk south until I found the support party.

But my problems weren't over. Although I emptied the stern compartment before setting off, in no time choppy waves washing over the deck filled it again, and *Isadora* became unmanageable. For a while I tried dragging *Isadora* through the small surf, 100 staggering steps at a time, to where the chop eased off and I could resume paddling without the compartment filling. My eyes roamed hopefully along the sandy beach but there was no sign of neither the hatch nor my hat. Despite the rapidly fading light, I paddled up the inlet to where it branched into two arms. The road was only two miles away now, across the inlet but it became too dark to see and I paddled into a sandbank. At high tide the inlet is entirely covered, but after only an hour of ebbing tide, the bulk of the inlet's floor is exposed as broad flat sandbanks. I couldn't leave the kayak there for it would drift away with the tide but certainly did not feel like dragging *Isadora* for two miles. Not a single light was visible onshore so I turned back to a belt of dunes by the entrance to 'kip in the marram grass'. Dear diary continued: 'No tucker or water all day. Dark. Pulled the fibrefill duvet over my wet wool singlet and my feet, still in wetsuit booties, I tucked into a blue plastic rubbish bag. Parka on top and a pillow of wet woollen shirt and the lifejacket. I watched the moon rise over the eastern hills, a big beautiful yellow moon. I slept well; must have been pretty tired, but had numb feet in the morning.'

My change of clothes had been stored in the rear compartment, so I had no dry gear to put on. The lack of emergency food was an oversight on my part but oddly enough, my desire for food and water wasn't as strong as I would have expected. But I felt really tired, not just physically exhausted but emotionally drained as well. By now the support party would be really worried, not knowing my whereabouts.

Isadora was not the first vessel to come to grief on the Whanganui Inlet bar. Between the years 1865 and 1891 four vessels were totally wrecked while taking the bar. They included the steamer *Nelson* which was the first ship to successfully cross the Grey River bar. The first vessel to successfully cross the Whanganui Inlet bar was a cutter *Harriet* which picked up 10 tons of coal from the head of the inlet. The second vessel to cross the bar was seeking shelter from a northerly gale. The Brigantine *Jewess* was on a voyage from Wellington to New Plymouth when she was driven south before the gale. Her sails split, the captain at the masthead guided the vessel through heavy seas on the bar and into the welcome shelter of the inlet.

26 February - Day 42

Dawn was breaking as I walked along to Bar Point, searching amongst the flotsam and driftwood in the remote possibility that the hatch cover had drifted ashore overnight. I meandered from seaweed patch to seaweed patch to the cliffs and caves of Bar Point and was on the point of giving up when a familiar round, green object in a mound of seaweed caught my eye. I did a classic double take and boy oh boy, was I happy and relieved to find that missing hatch cover.

Minutes later as I walked back towards *Isadora*, thinking of the forthcoming paddle across the inlet to the road, I heard a distant shout. I stopped and looked up. High on a hill overlooking the sea, I could see four tiny figures climbing quickly down towards me, Keith, Dick, Barb and a stranger.

We were all excited and relieved to meet up again, faces wreathed in smiles and huge grins. When Keith asked, "Where's your kayak?" I realized the only sign of *Isadora* was the hatch cover in my hand. "Out there," I indicated with a glum face but couldn't keep up the pretence for long and related the events of the previous evening.

Once Keith had arrived safely at the Anatori River mouth, the support party loaded his kayak and drove north along a winding corrugated, dusty road to the inlet as Keith had an idea I would be waiting there. Years before he had been searching for caves in the area and knew where the road came closest to the sea. It was dark by the time they reached a farmhouse at the road end on the north side of the inlet. Local farmer Dave Ferguson was a little sceptical initially about Keith's story of a lone kayaker missing somewhere along the coast. Once the story registered, Dave was keen to set out on his trail bike but in the end decided to wait until morning. Shortly after dawn Dave led the crew over steep limestone hills until they could see down to the inlet's entrance where the solitary wetsuit clad figure was walking along the beach.

Water, food, a billy and a frying pan emerged from a pack and before long I was savouring the delights of a bowl of hot tea with hot bacon sandwiches. When Keith mentioned they'd left Dave's farm without breakfast, I was impressed. It had been a worrying evening for all.

We decided move back to Dave's farmhouse and I paddled up the north arm of Whanganui Inlet to Moki Point. Here we left the kayak high above the tide's reach and hurried across sandy tidal flats before the rapidly flooding tide cut us off.

Another cup of tea followed with Dave and his wife Marilyn in their house overlooking the inlet. Mid-afternoon we decided to reconnoitre the start of Farewell Spit and drove to Port Puponga. Here the calm, settled surface of Golden Bay provided a stark contrast to the West Coast swell. Having sought advice from local fishermen on the spit crossing, we returned to the farm. From Dave's shearing shed we followed a grass track over a low saddle to Grey Cliff where we could gaze at the sea. It was amazing to see how it had settled overnight with only a slight swell drifting in to break gently on a sandy beach below us. Motivation and enthusiasm instantly returned and I decided to bring *Isadora* around to the beach for an early start next morning. The sea appeared so settled that Keith decided to bring his kayak over on the car to Grey Cliff and rejoin the paddling. The thought of a second encounter on the bar unsettled me a little however.

At 6.30pm Barb helped me launch from Moki Point and, with the aid of an ebbing tide, I made swift progress towards the bar until I stopped to assess a continuous line of breakers which extended all the way across the inlet's entrance. Off South Head I nosed into the first of a series of breaking waves but by frequently changing course, managed to weave my way through the largest of them, taking only one drenching from a breaker.

At last I was clear of the bar. Without a large swell or nasty chop, it was almost enjoyable to be at sea again on a beautifully warm sunny afternoon. Between Bar Point and Grey Cliff the coast was rocky and fringed with reefs, and the gently shelving beach by Grey Cliff lay behind a long flat exposed reef. Although buried beneath two breakers, I reached the shore in the non-submarine position, sitting upright in the cockpit, which marked a pleasant change from the numerous upsets of the preceding days.

Dave, Keith and Dick arrived in time to watch a beautiful sunset. The television weather forecast held as much promise for fine weather next day as did the red sunset, and we slept under the stars by the end of Dave's haybarn.

Since Dave's farm was on a peninsula of land, bordered on three sides by water, he only needed one boundary fence from the inlet across to Grey Cliff. Dave ran 1,400 ewes and 200 beef cattle in summer with an additional 600 hoggets through winter. It had been such a dry winter that Dave was most apologetic there wasn't enough water for us to have a shower.

Keith at Grey Cliff; face plastered with sunburn cream

27 February - Day 43

A perfect morning, clear skies, no wind, a slight swell and a moderate surf breaking onto the beach by Grey Cliff. Dave brought a movie camera to film Keith and I launching. The previous evening we had viewed several of his movies and were impressed by their quality. We particularly appreciated one film showing the effects of gale force winds during Cyclone Ada and a second of mustering and dipping sheep. I would dearly love to see the movie that Dave took of our launching. What a sight! Keith had plastered so much sunburn cream over his face, he appeared like a Red Indian trying to be a paleface, pink spots for eyes and lips, topped by unruly ginger curly hair and a beard. Not that I looked much better. I was wearing an old striped cloth cap, courtesy of Dave, held under my chin by a piece of green fishing line, mauve wetsuit top, bleached holey woollen singlet which sagged markedly below my armpits and a red sprayskirt.

We headed into the surf at 9am and after a wave to the group on shore, we turned the bows to the northeast. The coastline was most inhospitable with no landing places. Caves and vertical sided gorges disfigured the cliffs climbing from sea to skyline.

Dick and Barb were going to drive to the Abel Tasman National Park and wait for us to arrive at Totaranui. Provided the seas and weather remained settled, there was a good chance Keith and I would arrive by evening. The distance of 43 miles out to the tip of Farewell Spit and across Golden Bay to Totaranui was certainly achievable. If we were held up, I would pass on a message from the lighthouse keeper at Farewell Spit to the park ranger.

Keith and I were enjoying gliding over a calm sea as we paddled by the small islands off Nguroa Bay but slowly an easterly breeze lifted. When we were almost in sight of the northernmost extremity of the South Island, an easterly headwind came away.

The breeze gradually gained strength until we were making only slow progress into small whitecaps. On our right lay the opening into Wharariki Beach where steep grey cliffs gave way to a low section of cream coloured sandy beach, sheltered at its eastern end by the Archway Islands. These sheer-sided islands, topped with bush, were an impressive sight with gothic archways and narrow tunnels passing through them.

By the first island, the wind was gusting strongly and our speed dropped to under one mile per hour and we struggled against a bouncy chop. We decided to pull into the beach and wait for the wind to ease. In the shadowed lee of a second island we left the swirling spray astern for calm water. A narrow tunnel led through a corner of the island to the beach and for a bit of a dag I paddled towards the tunnel's entrance. Several seals, snoozing on narrow ledges out of reach of the surge, were startled to see the yellow kayak beneath them. In a hurry to gain the shelter of the sea, one almost dropped onto *Isadora's* deck. The narrow passage acted as a wind tunnel. The wind streamed through as we inched our way into the darkness, a circle of blue sky and sandy beach beckoning us shorewards. We experienced no trouble landing through a small surf in the lee of the islands. Our best landing since leaving Karamea.

As we dragged the Nordkapps beyond the tide's reach, two middle-aged couples walked out of the dunes towards us. They stopped by the kayaks and we exchanged pleasantries about the weather and the beautiful setting of the beach. One chap asked if we were the kayakers who had paddled around Fiordland. When I answered, he asked if I remembered meeting a fisherman on Lake Brunner the previous year.

On a cold blustery day in November when I paddled around the shores of Lake Brunner, I was sur-

prised to meet Stan Eder fishing from a boat in an isolated section of the lake but grateful to accept his offer of a body warming cup of coffee. Certainly a coincidence to meet again at this isolated beach.

Stan offered Keith and I a cup of coffee and his wife gave us fresh sandwiches. He also offered to pass on a message to Dick Strong via the Abel Tasman National Park ranger that we were held up at Wharariki Beach by headwinds.

Dear diary: 'Went for a walk out to the easternmost point of Archway Islands and climbed up for a view of the sea, still choppy. Slept for a while and watched sand grains dancing along the beach driven by the wind. Tried some of the sandwiches Keith had made earlier but they were pretty dry old sandwiches. One of Dave Ferguson's farm dogs had nicked the butter out of the food box.'

By 4pm I was restless and keen to get underway. The wind had eased noticeably and swung a little to the north. Keith appeared quite happy, snoozing with his head beneath a sprayskirt but I roused him from his dreams and at 5pm we pushed off into the surf.

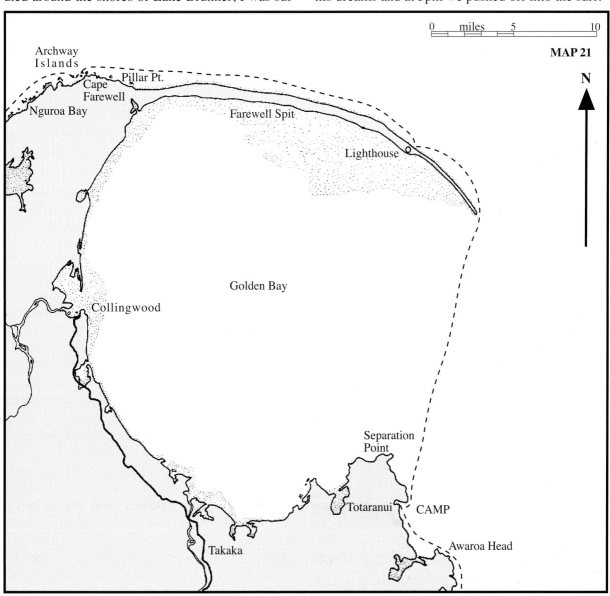

Out beyond the islands the wind and sea had settled and I was disappointed that we hadn't left earlier. We made good time over the mile out to the bluffs of Cape Farewell. The tension of the previous week had eased and I was excited to be paddling around this northern-most extremity of the mainland.

As quickly as the wind had lifted, the wind died followed by the chop. Level with the automatic lighthouse on top of Pillar Point, we saw a thin white line on the horizon which marks the start of Farewell Spit. The *New Zealand Pilot* notes:

> Farewell spit extends about 20 miles eastward and east-south-eastward from Cape Farewell; ... and is formed of drifting sand dunes, with patches of manuka scrub, marram grass and lupins, inter-spersed with numerous, small fresh water lagoons. The outer 2.5 miles of the spit, which terminates in Bush End point, is formed by low dunes up to 20 feet high. Close within the point are the lighthouse and a few buildings standing amongst pine trees. The low water extremity of the spit, which dries in patches, extends four miles south-eastward from Bush End point.

With my worries of landing through West Coast surf almost at an end, I felt an enormous load had been lifted from my mind. I was like a dog straining at the old leash, rearing to go and confident of burning up 15 miles to the Farewell Spit lighthouse before nightfall. But Keith's arms were tired and although he main-tained a steady pace, it wasn't fast enough for me. For the first hour I kept racing out in front and stopping while Keith caught up. It was soon obvious that insufficient time remained to reach the lighthouse before dark and we would have to spend a night in the dunes on shore. But that wasn't a problem as it was such a beautiful afternoon.

During the conception of the South Island trip, I had often thought of what to do at the base of Farewell Spit, whether to carry *Isadora* across the base of Farewell Spit or to paddle around its tip. A long stretch of open water lay between the tip and the Abel Tasman National Park, which would take me further away from land than I had previously paddled, but in the end I decided a true circumnavigation would have to be around the tip.

The low dune ridge and sandy beach stretching away to the horizon seemed such a contrast to the rugged forested coastline of the West Coast. No landmarks that we could use to gauge progress.

My photographs show Keith reflected on a glassy sea, his Nordkapp slicing gracefully through the water and a wave peeling back, characteristic of the finely flared bow. At the top of my voice I sang all the verses of the Boy Dylan song 'Pat Garret and Billy the Kid' and imitated Al Jolson for a rendition of the old blues number, 'When You're Down and Out'. As the saying goes, I was as happy as Larry.

As the sun dropped down to the horizon, its dying rays of rich golden yellow shimmered and sparkled on the swell. We were paddling some 300 yards offshore, outside of and parallel to a line of breakers that rolled gently against a sloping sandy beach. Two fishing boats on the horizon caught our attention, and drawing closer, we paddled over to one of the boats to seek a recent forecast.

Dolphin II cruised to a stop alongside, and one fishermen called out, "Where the heck did you spring from?"

"Te Waewae Bay"

"Where in the name of hell is that?"

At first I don't think they took me too seriously until we explained a little more about the trip. The fishermen were out checking their nets for sharks, the sort you buy when you ask for a piece of fish at the local 'greasy' shop. I asked the fishermen's advice on the forthcoming crossing of the spit and was told, "Three hours either side of high tide and you should be able to cross two miles beyond the lighthouse. The weather forecast is good for tomorrow." After thank-ing them for the advice, we turned the bows once more to the east and paddled into the growing dusk.

Dear dairy: 'Beautiful conditions, the Nordkapps gliding over the glassy swell but the light fading quickly, growing darker and darker. Drawing level with the second moored fishing boat, we contem-plated putting into shore until the moon rose before pushing on to the lighthouse. *Dolphin II* powered up from astern and the skipper called from the wheel-house, "Would you boys like a brew?" This was music to our ears and Keith and I chorused, "Yes please."'

Dolphin II moored to the stern of *Megan* and we tied the two kayaks alongside. Judging by the swirl-ing eddies around the anchor chain, a current was setting eastwards along the spit. *Dolphin II* was a 32 foot long fishing boat owned by Bob Mutts with Jerry Moat as deckhand, while *Megan J* was a 36 foot long, with a purple fibreglass hull, owned by Paul O'Connors with Tony Nicholls as crew. The fisher-men had been checking their nets for rig or spotted gummy sharks. Six nets were set, four at 500 feet in length, one of 300 feet, and a short one of 100 feet. One end of each net had a heavy anchor and a large bright red float plus a small flashing light. The nets were fed out parallel to the beach and just outside the line of waves. If set at 90 degrees to the shore, the nets picked up too much seaweed and the sharks went either over or around them. Weights held the nets on the sea-bed while small surface floats kept the net

The crew of Dolphin II *at dusk off Farewell Spit*

profile vertical. Occasionally snapper and stingrays ended up in the nets. The stingrays were set smartly back into the sea while the snapper were retained for the larder.

An offer from Paul to sleep in *Megan J's* wheelhouse was gratefully accepted. It would be better than sleeping in the dunes, although I would feel the opposite way about the decision in the morning. Bob turned on a radio to catch the 9pm forecast from Wellington. Usually forecasts were broken down into regional areas, from cape to point around both the South and North islands, but this night the marine forecast was for right around New Zealand: two anticyclones near New Zealand, with one of them centred 150 miles west of Cape Foulwind. The forecast was for: 'Fine, with seas slight to moderate.'

Since *Dolphin II* was about to set off for another net check, we pulled the two kayaks aboard *Megan J's* stern and joined the fishermen aboard *Dolphin II*. It was pitch dark now and Bob steered the boat along without a qualm. I couldn't see how he navigated, for the boat had no radar and I asked him what sort of magic he used. Bob pointed out a faint light from the automatic navigation beacon on Pillar Point and an occasional flash of light from the Farewell Spit lighthouse. This sweeping arc of light, or loom as it is defined in the dictionary of nautical expressions, was easily visible on the horizon although we were too far away to see the actual light source.

A spotlight was used to locate the first large red buoy. It was hauled on deck with the aid of a small grappling hook. The edge of the net was laid over a power block or drum, at which point Bob in the wheelhouse slipped a clutch for the drum to start rotating. All four fishermen were soon engrossed in

tasks, Bob at the wheel, steering the boat parallel to a barely visible line of floats above the net, Tony holding a spotlight on the floats and the other two retrieving fish from the net. Only five rig in the first net, a terrible catch apparently.

Thirty or so three to four foot long sharks were tangled in the mesh of the next net along with a stingray, which was immediately returned to the sea and a solitary snapper that was retained for the cooking pot. When all the nets had been checked Paul set about cleaning the catch. He used a long, razor sharp knife and I was amazed by his speed and dexterity. That he didn't lose a finger seemed a marvel. In one quick stroke he sliced off the two dorsal fins, a second stroke removed the evil looking tail, a third cut around the head followed by a slice along the belly to the tail, head and entrails flicked to the deck and the shaft of the knife was run inside the length of the body cavity to clean it. Within 20 seconds, the fish had been gutted and thrown to Jerry who washed it down with a high pressure hose. Packed in plastic boxes with ice, the fish were stored in a hold below deck.

Back on board *Megan J* we had another brew before stretching out our sleeping-bags on the wheelhouse floor. The moon had risen and after the cabin lights were extinguished, moonlight streamed in through the wheelhouse windows. What a day it had been. The trip now had a much brighter outlook. I looked forward to the next day when we would call in at the lighthouse and cross the spit. Trying to drop off to sleep I found the rolling of the boat, rocked by a very gentle swell, hard to get accustomed to.

Farewell Spit Lighthouse

28 February - Day 44

The horrible grating noise of an alarm clock shattered the depths of our sleep at 6am. Bleary-eyed, we sipped mugs of hot coffee in the wheelhouse and Paul gave us each a tin of fruit for breakfast. My stomach told me that overnight I had not grown used to the rolling of the boat, for I was at the point of feeding my breakfast to the fishes. Keith felt much the same.

It was still dark outside as we sat beneath the bright naked electric light inside the wheelhouse, but slowly the pale grey light of dawn grew, until features on shore became visible. Since the fishermen were keen to check their nets before heading home to Golden Bay, we wasted no time sliding the Nordkapps into the sea. When we climbed carefully into the cockpits, there wasn't a breath of wind to disturb the glassy surface of the gentle swell. Strangely enough as soon as I was seated in *Isadora's* cockpit I felt much better both in my stomach and head where I had the symptoms of a mild headache. Because of their high centre of gravity, fishing boats have a tendency to roll. In the wheelhouse, this rolling motion was particularly pronounced, but in the Nordkapps, seated right on the water, there was a negligible roll.

I glanced over to the anchor chain and happily noted the current still setting strongly to the east. This would hasten our progress. The fishermen said the current nearly always sets to the east along the spit apart from days when a strong east or north-east wind blowing.

We waved goodbye to Paul and Tony and glided the Nordkapps towards the end of the spit, still some six miles away. The first time ever that I had been on the sea before sunrise.

A dark red flare on the eastern horizon announced the impending arrival of the sun. Slowly and majestically it rose dull red out of the sea, growing brighter as it climbed into the pale sky. As the sun rose above banks of sea mist on the horizon, its colour changed to a golden yellow. Beneath the kayaks the water was so clear that we could easily see the sandy sea floor, 10-15 feet below but there was no sign of fish.

A light northerly breeze arose but merely ruffled the glassy swell. Half an hour after leaving the fishing boats we sighted a clump of trees on the spit. Since the only sparse vegetation growing on the dunes was marram grass and lupins, the pine trees which shelter the lighthouse buildings from the wind, stood out very clearly. As we drew closer the orange and white top of the lighthouse structure came into view above the trees and at 7.45 we landed through a small surf, level with the light.

We walked across a wide stretch of sand and through a strip of blackberries and lupins, to knock on the back door of the house closest to the light tower. Mrs. Shepherd was taken aback to find the two wetsuit clad, smiling males at her back door. "How did you get out here?" she asked. "By kayak," I replied. Visitors only arrived on Wednesdays with the mail truck. Mrs. Shepherd told us her husband Frank was sending out the morning weather, and would be back in a few minutes. When he arrived, we introduced ourselves and I said, "I bring greetings from Pauline and Robin Therkelsen at Puysegur Point." The Therkelsens had spent some time at the Farewell Spit lighthouse.

A marvellous breakfast of sausages and eggs whipped up by Mrs. Shepherd followed and Frank then took us on a tour of the lighthouse. The 88 foot high steel tower was the second lighthouse to be built on the spit. The first, a 100 foot high wooden tower with outside spiral staircase, first shone out in June 1870 and was built as a result of the numerous shipwrecks and loss of life that had occurred along the spit. When the wooden tower began to suffer from the sand blasting winds, it was replaced by the existing steel tower which began operating in 1897. Materials for the steel structure were brought out by ship, taken in through the breakers by surfboats and loaded onto horse drawn drays in the surf. The bottom two thirds of the tower consisted of open steel girders and bracing with an airy staircase. The top third was a closed in area with a dome on top surrounding the lenses of the light.

Frank took us out onto a verandah which surrounds

the dome and lent us a pair of binoculars to study the tip of Farewell Spit for the forthcoming paddle.

After dark, every 30 seconds, the light flashes for a full 360 degrees around the horizon. A section of the glass windows is coloured red. This dreaded red sector between the light and the tip of the spit, covers an arc of 34 degrees. At night if a boat passes into the shallow water on or by the spit, it sees not a white light from the lighthouse but a red one.

Frank and Dorothy Shepherd arrived at Farewell Spit lighthouse in 1946 and stayed until 1951. In those years there were three lighthouse keepers but conditions weren't as good as they are now. There was no power. Coal for the range and kerosene for lanterns and heaters were rationed, one sack of coal a week and four gallons of kerosene a month. In 1951 they left the spit to return in 1975 after spending the intervening years at various lighthouses in the North and South islands. Power was connected in November 1977 and Dorothy happily did not have to use the old coal range any more. Although there was a telephone link through Takaka to the outside world, it was a lonely existence with mail and food arriving only once a week when a truckload of tourists drove out along the spit from Collingwood. Although the work may not be as hard as in the early days, for Frank it was a seven day a week job, maintaining the light, switching it on and off, evening and morning, and sending out three hourly weather situations. The meagre salary seemed little reward for the importance of the job.

As we looked down onto their vegetable garden, Frank told us it had been a really dry summer with not enough water for the garden and barely enough to flush the toilet. As a last straw a possum breached the fence around the garden and had a field day with the young plants. Milk came from a house cow and Frank kept a few sheep for an occasional meal of fresh mutton. The middle-aged couple aimed to spend another five years at the lighthouse before retiring to Blenheim.

Keith and I were in no hurry to leave the lighthouse for the tide was flooding and the higher the tide, the less distance we would have to paddle before crossing the spit.

The effect of the night on board *Megan J* had eased to the extent that I had devoured Mrs. Shepherd's breakfast without a second thought of seasickness. For most of the two hours on shore we had been walking around and it was only when I sat in the confines of the toilet that the symptoms of seasickness appeared again. Although I was sitting still, trousers down around my ankles, the whole house seemed to be rolling gently from side to side. Apart from the second day out on the Fiordland trip, when

I felt a little queasy in sympathy with Max's seasickness, I hadn't felt seasick in *Isadora*.

After one last cup of tea and a few biscuits Frank drove us out to the beach on his tractor with Keith, Dorothy and myself riding on a tray behind. We shook hands with the Shepherds and thanked them for their hospitality. Once Keith and I cleared the breakers we turned and waved, which Frank acknowledged with a toot on the tractor's horn.

Frank and the fishermen had advised us to paddle two miles beyond Bush End Point to the last small but prominent grassy island, then to turn right at the first place we could to cross the spit. The fishermen we sought advice from at Pakawau had warned us to look out for 'boils where the tides meet and sudden waves that spring out of nowhere.' But conditions for the crossing were perfect, a clear sky, settled seas and a light northerly breeze to take the glaze off the gentle swell.

We paddled past the last small grassy island only to see a sandbank with an accompanying line of breakers extending out to the horizon. The sandbank grew lower and lower until at last it disappeared beneath small waves washing across the spit. With mounting excitement I nosed *Isadora* in close to the breakers but turned quickly away when I noticed a seagull standing in the wash, too shallow yet for the Nordkapps. One hundred yards on, the waves were breaking right across the submerged spit into Golden Bay. I decided to attempt to surf over. In front of a two foot high wave I paddled hard and took off, surfing rapidly over the submerged sandy spit into the bay. I let out a whoop of joy and photographed Keith as he surfed across. Twelve midday precisely.

Great excitement! Cook Strait at last, with the rollers of the Tasman Sea and the unpredictable weather and seas of the West Coast finally astern. Before us lay an 11 mile paddle across Golden Bay to Separation Point at the northern end of Abel Tasman National Park. Three miles further on lay Totaranui where Dick and Barb would be waiting. Golden Bay is shaped like a horseshoe with Separation Point and Farewell Spit forming the tips of the horseshoe. We set off in the general direction of Separation Point although all we could see from 11 miles away was a dark grey bulky land mass. Features such as bays and headlands were not yet distinguishable.

Beneath the Nordkapps, the sandy bottom of the bay was clearly visible and for at least a mile the water depth did not drop below two or three feet. At low tide, the whole of this area was exposed. Midway along the spit, sand and mudflats uncovered by the tide extended out into Golden Bay for as much as five miles. As such, Farewell Spit is an important bird sanctuary providing food and shelter for tens of thousands of migratory birds. These sea birds leave their Siberian and Asian homes during the northern summer and journey to the spit. At the end of the New Zealand summer they congregate in large flocks and fly back to the northern hemisphere. Because the area is so unique, public access is confined to the base of the spit, the only exception being the Wednesday tourist truck.

Despite the cooling effect of the light northerly breeze we sweated heavily in the wetsuits and for a while, to gain some relief from the sun's glare, removed the lifejackets and tied them on the fore-decks. Occasional shell beds provided the only contrast on the flat sandy sea-bed beneath us but surprisingly I did not see any fish.

After an hour of paddling we saw a grey naval vessel cruising fast out of Golden Bay heading for the tip of Farewell Spit. It passed in front of our bows about a mile away and 10 minutes later the Nordkapps rose and fell over the wash set up by the vessel's bow. Later I found it had been the *Otago* heading out to apprehend a foreign vessel that had intruded into New Zealand waters.

Halfway across the bay, the wind suddenly freshened, to the extent that we replaced the lifejackets. A short steep chop with occasional whitecaps arose.

At this stage I could just make out the red granite headland of Separation Point and we headed to the left of this to combat the effect of drift on the Nordkapps. The wind blew from the north-west while our course lay due south, thus we were drifting to the west, partly because the skegs were not deep enough, lifting right out on the choppy sea, and partly because the wind caused movement of the surface layer of the sea.

Once Keith had the knack of catching the choppy waves, he shot out in front, enjoying the speed of surfing in front of the whitecaps, but the paddling was becoming an effort as we had to concentrate on staying on course and upright on the chop.

At last we drew level with the white blob of the automatic light on Separation Point. To the south, we could see the rugged granite cliffs extending along to Totaranui and several small bays with fine sandy beaches. Around a projecting headland near Totaranui lay sheltered water and side by side we escaped from the whitecaps onto a calm sea. In less than 100 yards, we progressed from a nasty chop onto water so calm and clear that we could see the submerged reefs and rocks of the sea-bed below.

The dark golden sandy beach of Totaranui lay before the bows and both of us forgot our tired arms, and raced in to run the kayaks onto shore. It had been a four hour paddle from the spit. We didn't have to wait for a lull before landing as the single wave

lapping onto the sand was a staggering four inches high.

Dick, with Benny bounding alongside, came down to meet us. He had just dropped Barb out on the main road to catch a bus down to Christchurch. Over a cold drink and hastily put together sandwiches, we related to Dick the story of our night on the fishing boat and crossing the spit.

The headquarters of the Abel Tasman National Park was located at Totaranui and before long Bruce Millar, the Chief Ranger, arrived on a bicycle. He had a message for us from the Takaka policeman. A chap Strang and his wife were kayaking around Farewell Spit. For a few moments we thought another two kayakers were following us but finally figured the message referred to Dick Strong and his wife Barb. The message had become a little garbled in transit.

Bruce returned with some fresh fruit and vegetables and a promising forecast for the morrow. By sunset the wind had died. Low banks of cloud on the horizon turned the sun's dying rays a pale red, toning the sky and mirror like surface of the sea. A tapering, shimmering golden road lingered for a few moments, disappearing swiftly as the sun sank below the horizon. The scene was made complete by the sails of a distant yacht gliding slowly into the dusk.

1 March - Day 45

The sandflies woke us at first light, no wind, a calm sea and I was eager to go. We watched a cracker sunrise, a red orb growing and climbing into the pale pink sky of dawn. Keith didn't share my enthusiasm for an early start. He still felt tired from the previous two days.

With a good day's paddle it would be possible to reach Nelson, 40 miles away, but we decided on Kaiteriteri as our first meeting point. Dick would drive over Takaka Hill and wait for us at this seaside resort.

When Keith and I were seated in the Nordkapps on the sand, ready to go, I called to Dick, "We'll have to wait for a lull." Dick's response was to give *Isadora* a great shove backwards into the sea. The waves breaking onto the golden sand were almost two inches high.

The rocky coastline of the Abel Tasman National Park has a distinctive character and is very different from the wild West Coast. With its beautiful clear blue water, the colour and rugosity of its cliffs and the sandy beaches of its sheltered bays, we could have spent days pottering along but unfortunately my mind was registering Nelson as the goal for the day. Also I had once spent a week with a party of school-children walking along the scenic coastal track from Totaranui to Marahau so I was familiar with the area.

In the lee of Tonga Island I waited for Keith and although he was maintaining a steady speed it wasn't fast enough for me. Up to the island I had been paddling in spurts, then waiting for Keith. Travelling at his pace meant breaking my rhythm and I felt impatient to push on at my own speed. I asked Keith if he minded my paddling ahead to Kaiteriteri where I would either wait or push on to Nelson. Keith's arms were tired and he didn't want to try for Nelson by nightfall. My attitude had always been to hammer on while conditions were good.

Keith didn't say too much or show annoyance and said he didn't mind if I pushed on. I felt a bit selfish about splitting up but I was wound up like an alarm clock with all systems go. A light southerly came away just strong enough to take the glaze off the barely discernible northerly swell.

Once beyond Torrent Bay I turned into Astrolabe Roadstead, which lies in the lee of Adele Island. Two chaps fishing from a dinghy waved, also the crew of a larger fishing boat that lay moored close in by the island. Out of the lee of Fisherman Island, I could make out the white bluffs and houses of Kaiteriteri and made a beeline for them.

Expensive holiday mansions on the hill sides near Kaiteriteri were, I decided, a little out of the price range of retired kayakers. This seaside resort is protected from northerly winds, as it lies in the lee of the forested bulk of Kaka Island. The narrow rocky channel between the island and shore was so shallow that I just scraped through to glide into the midst of a fleet of pleasure boats. Sun tan seeking bodies littered the beach where the sea lapped very gently onto golden sand. Dick was enhancing his tan in front of the VW with the vigilant ship dog fast asleep in the sun beside him as I paddled in to run the bow up onto the beach.

In the motor camp that sprawls alongside the beach there didn't appear to be room to swing a cat. It was choked with caravans, camper vans, tents, flashy boats on trailers and equally flashy cars. To Dick and I, the most incredible sight on this gloriously warm, sunny day, was people sitting inside their vans and caravans watching television.

Whilst we ate lunch, Dick and I pored over the topographic map sheets and decided Nelson was within reach for the day, provided conditions stayed as good as they were. An hour after I arrived, Keith paddled in through the gap by the island. Even before he had climbed out of the cockpit I asked, "Do you want to push on to Nelson?" as I was eager to get underway. But Keith's arms and shoulders had had enough and he replied, "I'll pull out here." He had stopped for a leg stretch and a bit to eat in the National Park.

To the watching sunbathers it must have seemed like a kayak relay race for the moment Keith stepped ashore, I slid into *Isadora's* cockpit and launched backwards with the skeg down. Our next rendezvous would be at Ruby Bay, 13 miles along the coast towards Nelson. "Don't get there before we do," grinned Keith, getting in a dig at my speed during the morning.

Past boaties on their pleasure craft and fishermen out on the rocks, I powered out of the bay only to drop to my normal paddling rhythm once I was out of sight. The light northerly breeze of the morning still stirred the surface of the light swell and my destination was clearly visible on the south side of the distant Moutere Bluff. But in contrast to the impressive scenery of the morning, the coastline along to the bluff consisted of flat sandy beaches with little in the way of conspicuous or interesting features to occupy my mind or enable a check on progress to be kept. In this situation all I could do to gauge distance covered was watch the

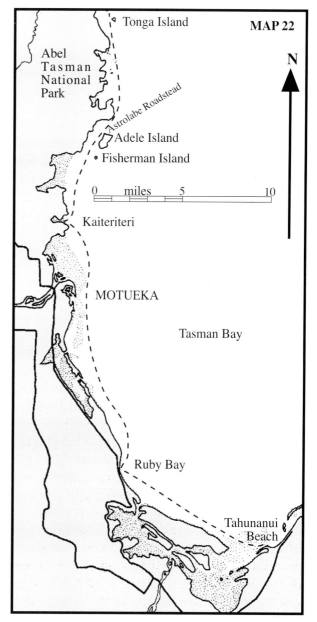

hands on my watch moving around. Afternoon haze hid all sight of Nelson and the nearby hills. Beyond Motueka I stopped for a drink of water and wished I had the food bag that remained in Keith's Nordkapp. It contained apples and two crunchie bars. My mouth watered at the thought of them.

Then the wind swung to the north and picked up in intensity, causing the chop to steepen. The white cliffs of Moutere Bluff were not too far distant but I was beginning to tire by the time I landed through a two foot surf onto the rocky beach of Ruby Bay. Dick had a brew of tea simmering over a fire while Keith had climbed up on top of the bluffs in an attempt to make out Tahuna Beach through the haze, where I hoped to complete this stage of the trip. Keith who likes really weak tea complained about the strength of Dick's brew, "It looks more like coca cola than tea." I drank two bowls of the strong tea liberally laced with sugar and asked Keith if the tucker bag was still in his kayak. "It is," he replied, "But there's only one apple left."

"What about the crunchie bars?" I questioned him.

"I ate them."

"Both of them?" I couldn't believe that Keith would have eaten all the goodies. In reply Keith nodded his head, eyes cast down on the ground. "Jeez Keith," I grunted.

We used the maps to point out the location of Tahuna Beach and decided that a tall television tower on the hills above Nelson would be a good target to steer for in order to bring *Isadora* into the beach. At 5.15pm I pulled away from Ruby Bay for the last 10 mile leg to Nelson. When the support party arrived, Keith would ring Grahame Sisson (the chap who built *Isadora*) to see if he would come out to Tahuna to meet me.

Since my course lay to the east-south-east and a northerly wind was creating a moderate chop, I stayed in line with a point a mile or so north of the distant television tower in an attempt to combat the effect of drift. Side on to the swell and chop, the Nordkapp rolled over the low waves in a not too uncomfortable motion, with only the occasional wave capping.

After an hour and a quarter half the distance lay astern. Just as I started thinking only one more hour to Nelson, the northerly breeze died to be replaced within seconds by a strong easterly headwind. "Oh no," I groaned aloud. In the time that it took this new wind to knock down the northerly swell and create its own, the sea became really lumpy and confused, waves crossing at different angles and capping steeply. *Isadora's* bow rose sharply over the waves only to crash into the accompanying troughs, burying the

bow time and time again. Painfully slow progress with only five miles to go.

During lulls I powered hard into the easterly chop, easing off as another gust approached. The strong gusts were clearly visible as dark bands on the sea, moving swiftly towards me. Gradually I crept towards the tiny clustered dots that were the houses of Nelson, until at last I could pick out cars moving along the road beneath the bluff by the northern end of Tahuna Beach.

I encountered breakers a long way offshore, for there appeared to be some form of bar or spit so I stayed well outside the broken water until I could see a clear run into the beach. The sun lay low on the western horizon as I commenced the approach through the waves. Of the support party there was no sign.

One long ride took *Isadora* in through low breakers to the gentle sandy foreshore of Tahuna Beach and out of the horrible easterly chop at last. Far along the beach to the west I could make out three figures and the silhouette of a second Nordkapp. Dick and Benny arrived first, followed by Keith and Grahame Sisson clad in a wetsuit. As soon as they had reached Nelson, Keith rang Grahame and told him I would be arriving at Tahuna at about 7.15. At the appointed time, his presence unknown to Keith and Dick on shore, Grahame sat offshore in his Nordkapp waiting to welcome me.

At one stage Keith and Dick spotted *Isadora* far out but lost sight of the Nordkapp behind the breakers Grahame grew tired and cold of waiting after 20 minutes and headed for shore. Keith and Dick sighted a Nordkapp surfing in through the breakers and, assuming it was me, jogged along only to find Grahame. Seconds later I landed 400 yards away along the beach. What a circus! Still you get that at the end of long stages on the big trips.

We were all excited and I had a great talk to Grahame about the merits of the Nordkapps. He was keen to try out some of my modifications and slid into the cockpit. "Fits like a glove," he declared. Grahame was impressed by the knee, thigh, and backrests also the foam footrest.

A beautiful evening drew this stage of the trip to a close. The setting sun turned sand and sky to gold. Our faces were flushed with sunburn and excitement. A 250 mile stage had been completed and I was almost halfway round the South Island.

Next morning I left *Isadora* with Grahame so he could carry out a few minor modifications and after saying goodbye to Keith, Dick and I headed back to the West Coast for a brief spell before commencing the next stage to Christchurch.

Chapter 13

NELSON to CHRISTCHURCH

After a week pottering around on my front verandah, I was keen to resume the trip. In the weeks while we were away, Dick's vegetable garden had become overgrown and he decided not to come on the next stage. A friend from up the coast, Bruce Annabell, offered to drive from Nelson to Christchurch and even better, offered to use his car. Lyn Taylor would join us in Nelson and the third member of the support crew would be Ben, the ship dog.

Bruce was a scrawny looking chap, with clear blue eyes, long thin straggly hair, wispy beard and moustache. He was a veritable whiz kid at fixing things, anything from television sets to cars, welding, carpentry, to his favourite occupation of tinkering with motorbikes. We had caved and tramped together in the old days. Always reliable, Bruce had a good eye for the sea and weather. The Peugeot was loaded with Bruce's kayak, and the boot and rear seat were soon filled with diving gear, compressed air tanks, food and clothes.

On 11 March, Bruce and I were at Grahame Sisson's factory in Nelson when it opened. There appeared to be lots of work remaining to be carried out on *Isadora* but I hoped to be away next day. Attached to her deck was a piece of paper with a list of seven or eight jobs still to be done. Grahame had been really busy during

the preceding week, producing kayaks and working on numerous other ingenious projects.

Grahame had taken the old bilge pump out and patched the hole on the deck where it had been. He had a bright idea for an improved pump. By changing the hinge point on the pump handle (from one end to the middle), the rubber diaphragm would now be above deck when the handle was in the normal rest position. Previously the diaphragm lay below the level of the deck and water splashing over the deck caught in the rubber cup and soaked down through the intake hose to the cockpit floor. During the Fiordland Expedition, it had been the source of most of the water that had found its way into the cockpits although we had blamed the sprayskirts for a long time. We discovered the new style pump gave an easier pumping action.

Dragging the kayak over the gravel and sand of the West Coast beaches had resulted in the yellow fibreglass gel coat of the hull wearing through in two places. Grahame mixed a brew of resin and silicon carbide and painted two narrow black strips along the keel, one each by the bow and stern.

· For us there was much to do, including making a new large skeg and a better hatch-cover arrangement. Grahame knocked up a huge shark fin-shaped skeg that would project 12 inches beneath *Isadora's* hull.

Around the fore and aft hatch openings, he fibreglassed oval-shaped coamings. The old design incorporated a recessed cover with rubber seals. Water sitting in the recesses was always a problem. Since the new coamings sat above deck level, and would be covered by canvas held on by shock cord, there would now be a dual system of keeping water out of the compartments. Grahame had sanded down the old covers so they would be retained inside the new coamings.

In the afternoon, Grahame's wife Linda, sewed up two green canvas hatch-covers, and threaded shock cord through the outside seams so they would not come off in big seas.

I worked out a system with the new skeg which would enable me to leave a beach with the skeg dangling over the stern. Once in deep water I could use a piece of elastic shock cord extending from the stern to the skeg, and a line from the skeg to the cockpit, to pull the skeg into position. For landings all I had to do was loosen the line and the shock cord would pull the skeg back out of the way.

Lyn Taylor joined us in time for the evening meal and afterwards Grahame and I went back to the factory for the finishing touches. Three coats of wax with a polish between each coat were applied to improve hull speed and to stop water absorption.

Finally, there were no more jobs. It had been a great day with much achieved. I had a last read of the *New Zealand Pilot*, and checked slack water times for French Pass, the narrow gap between D'Urville Island and the mainland.

12 March - Day 46

Before dawn we were up and ready to depart. I was impatient to leave in order to reach French Pass before 4.09pm when a brief period of slack water occurred at the turn of the tidal streams.

Grahame was keen to paddle some distance with me in one of his Nordkapps and decided Cable Bay, 13 miles along the coast to the north-east, would be far enough.

However, it wasn't until 7.15am, an hour after sunrise, that Grahame and I launched from Tahuna Beach. This meant I had one hour less to make it to French Pass by slack water. Although the sea was glassy the day wasn't all that inviting; the low grey, overcast sky was almost oppressive. We paddled out through a six inch high surf, waved to the support crew, and turned the bows to the north-east.

Only one boat cruised out through the Nelson Harbour entrance as we paddled by the long waving strands of seaweed that grow on the Boulder Bank. This seven mile long narrow bank of rounded boul-

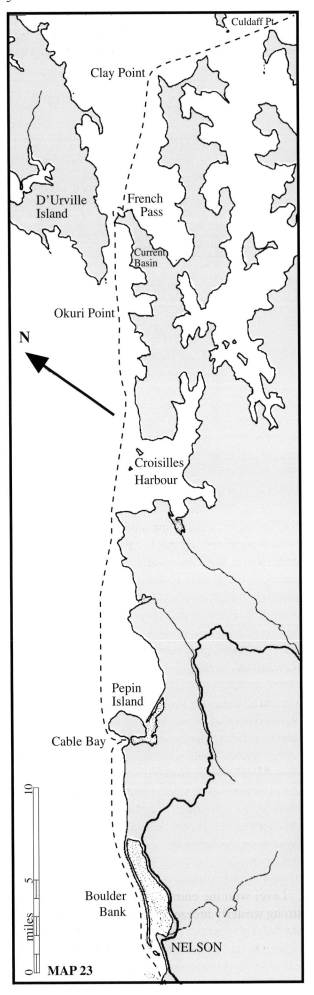

ders is an unusual natural feature along New Zealand's coastline. It protects Nelson Harbour from winds and currents. Inside the Boulder Bank is Nelson Haven, picturesque at high tide, but mossy sprawling mudflats at low tide.

Side by side, Grahame and I paddled close in by the boulders. An old chap was fishing from an anchored 14 foot long runabout. He was half asleep, leaning back in a folding chair, a hat pulled down almost over his eyes, a fishing line over the side.

As we glided quickly by his stern he opened one eye, saw the kayaks and said, "Where are you buggers going?"

Without thinking I replied, "Christchurch."

The chap's second eye opened as he sat bolt upright, a puzzled expression on his face. "Really?" he asked.

"Yep."

As we were almost out of earshot by now he was standing and staring at the departing kayaks. "Good luck," he yelled.

Nearing the rocky islands by the entrance to Cable Bay, we passed a moored yacht and suddenly Bruce shot out from behind some rocks in his kayak - ambushed! The race was on then, and the three kayaks powered in towards the sandy beach at the head of Cable Bay where Lyn waited with a brew. Grahame decided that three hour paddle was sufficient for him. I waited long enough to gulp down a bowl of tea and make a few sandwiches. Quick thanks to Grahame for all his help and at 10.30 I was underway again. Five and a half hours were left to paddle the 29 miles to French Pass. It didn't seem sufficient time. Bruce and Lyn would be waiting there in five to six hours time.

The eastern side of Cable Bay is formed by the rocky bulk of Pepin Island which is connected to the mainland by a narrow sand strip. I paddled hard out of the bay, hugging the rocky cliffs of the island, spotted white by nesting black-backed seagulls. Two boat loads of skindivers were out by the bare rocky islands off Pepin Island. Delaware Bay opened up on my right and I headed for the distant, southern-most end of D'Urville Island.

I was pleased to be hammering along at my own pace again. Despite the benefit of company with another paddler, I nearly always had to drop out of my natural paddling rhythm. Although this was fine in short bursts, it was unsettling and tiring over a long period.

Level with the entrance to Croisilles Harbour, a strong westerly breeze came away. I pulled the new shark fin shaped skeg into position, but found it was pulling to one side. Only when I partially released it did *Isadora* run true once again.

As time crept by I began to worry at the prospect of not reaching French Pass in time. D'Urville Island was now clearly visible and I could see the entrance to Current Basin, at the head of which lay French Pass.

I had never laid eyes on the 600 yard wide gap that separates D'Urville Island from the mainland. Stories of large yachts that completed 360° turns as they passed through did not add to my confidence.

The *New Zealand Pilot* has the following caution:

Vessels of moderate size can, with prudence and local knowledge, pass through French pass at slackwater or with the tidal stream. This passage saves about 15 miles in distance and avoids the heavy cross sea that is frequently met northward of D'Urville and Stephens islands. Vessels passing northward through the pass are cautioned against the eddy that sets towards Collinet point. Taking a vessel through against the stream is highly dangerous and such a vessel meeting a contrary stream should anchor to await the turn or, go round Stephens and D'Urville islands, as not only does a vessel sometimes not answer her helm, owing to the tidal stream on her bow, but there is a danger of meeting a vessel coming from the opposite direction, the vessels not being visible to each other in time to prevent collision.

The tidal streams:

attain rates of five to seven knots, and do not set directly through the narrow channel, but across, the flood stream setting in a south-westerly direction as far as the narrows and then along the shore south-south-westward of Channel point. The ebb stream sets in the opposite direction .... slack water lasts about 20 minutes. The extraordinary irregularity of the bottom, together with the narrowness of the channel accounts for the many eddies.

Once I turned Okuri Point into Current Basin, I pulled out all the stops, determined to make the most of the ebbing tide even though it appeared I wouldn't make the pass by slack water. The light westerly breeze lying astern helped push *Isadora* along. On my left the dark green forested hillsides of D'Urville Island were a pleasant contrast to the drab brown dry hillsides of the mainland.

At 4.09pm when the tidal stream turned at French Pass to flow against me, I was still two miles away. Not letting up, I paddled hard but my speed eased off as the tidal stream picked up. By 4.30 I was closing on the two white navigation towers, or beacons, that mark the sides of the main channel through French Pass. I passed a black and white chequered buoy midstream and paddled in behind the exposed reef that lies astride the centre of the pass. The main boat

Pushing into the tidal stream at French Pass.
Photo: Lyn Taylor

channel is hard up against the mainland. I was making headway all right but as I drew closer, I could see what lay before me, broken water, bands of calm water, whirlpools and eddies.

I decided it was worth trying the main channel and nosed gingerly out into the swirling eddies and whirlpools. Once across the main stream, I reached slow moving water against the rocky foreshore. This 'backwater' led right to the last major obstacle, a noisy riverlike rapid where the tidal stream first became obstructed at the eastern entrance of the pass. With the paddle almost touching the mussel-covered rocks, I hugged the shore until the last possible moment, then with a spurt of power, I hammered out into the main stream. It was like running into a sand bank. Forward speed dropped to zero but *Isadora* remained on course. Paddling at twice my normal rate, I inched my way up the 'rapid' and gradually pulled clear of the surfing tidal stream. One more smaller rapid, then calm water. Wow, what a relief!

At a sedate pace, I glided around Collinet Point to nose into Elmslie Bay, at the head of which lay a long jetty, sandy beach, and clustered houses of the isolated township of French Pass.

Tired but happy, I dragged *Isadora* up onto the beach and was reunited with the support crew. Bruce said the tidal stream was getting worse as they waited. They hadn't expected me to get through, so Bruce was all ready with the camera to record a can out. It was 30 minutes after slack water when I went through but the large skeg on the stern helped. Nine and a half hours paddling and 42 miles for the day.

While we ate tea on the beach, a helicopter landed alongside the kayak. Two chaps were conducting live deer recovery operations from D'Urville Island.

"Using the chopper must be rather dear," I commented.

Lyn sniggered and replied, "They must be rolling in dough."

Bruce, failing to find another pun, rolled his eyes and said "Jeez!"

13 March - Day 47

The goal for the day was rather ambitious. Bruce and Lyn were going to wait for me at Fighting Bay, east of Picton. This bay had the only road access to the seaward side of Marlborough Sounds. Although this was 55 miles away, and involved passing through Cook Strait, I felt confident that the distance was attainable with suitable conditions. Just in case I didn't reach the bay, I loaded a sleeping bag, primus, billy and food, apple jelly sandwiches for lunch, into *Isadora's* compartments. As well as the usual repair and first aid kits, I carried a waterproof torch for signalling after dark.

The sea was glassy at dawn. A grey overcast sky gave a washed out appearance to sea and sky.

Before 7am, I was paddling away from the beach at French Pass, heading for the distant shape of Clay Point out on the horizon. One and a half hours later I was nearing a fishing boat that was anchored off the point. Still some distance away, I counted 15 or so skindivers climbing over the side of the boat, only to find no trace of them on deck as I drew closer. The people who leaned over the deck rails were dangling fishing lines over the side for blue cod. What I thought were skindivers climbing into the boat was actually a black rubber tyre fender that was dipping in

Setting off from French Pass; Clay Point on the horizon
Photo: Bruce Annabell

13. *During the launch from the beach at Razorback Point, a huge bumper dumper wave cartwheeled Paul and* Isadora. *Photo: Dick Strong*

14. *Paul attempting the surf breakout from Tauranga Bay, south of Westport. Photo: Dick Strong*

15. Keith Dekkers and visitors on Wharariki Beach, with the Archway Islands in the background

16. Keith and lighthouse keeper Frank Shepherd on Farewell Spit, with the lighthouse in the background

and out of the sea as the boat rolled. So much for my keen eyesight.

"Great day for it," I called out to the skipper and the people fishing from the *Shangrila*. We talked about the tide, and the skipper gave me a small set of tide tables.

"You should have the tide with you after 10am," he said.

"Could you spare me some fresh water?" I asked, "I left my container back at French Pass."

The skipper passed down a half gallon jar of fresh water which I stowed between my legs. It would have been a dry day indeed but for the meeting with the *Shangrila*.

By Clay Point, the tide was disturbing the surface of the sea in the form of eddies and a few small waves but this was merely a taste of what was ahead of me. Three miles later as I approached a low rocky point, the other side of which lay the entrance to Pelorus Sound, I could see a line of whitecaps extending from the point out to sea.

'It must be a tide race,' I concluded. What unsettled me more was the sound coming from the direction of the whitecaps, a dull roaring noise as though I was drifting down a river towards a large rapid. This was to be my first encounter with a tide race, apart from French Pass and I wasn't too sure what to expect.

On my left lay the green forested Chetwode Islands. A navigation beacon sat on Ninepin Rock off the south end of the islands. The tidal flow was obviously restricted as it passed between the islands and the point I was approaching. Close in by the rocky point, I gingerly paddled through a couple of standing waves, several eddies, and with a little effort, I was in calm water again. The worst of this tide race was further out to sea.

At Culdaff Point, on the tip of Forsyth Island, I pulled in to shore, placed the skeg on, and swallowed a couple of licorice allsorts. 'The tide must turn soon,' I told myself, and the wind will probably spring up. 'Better to have the skeg already in position.'

Off the barren high bulk of Alligator Head the tide must have turned for I seemed to make better progress. Waitui Bay, between this headland and Cape Lambert, was an inhospitable looking place. Somehow I expected the Marlborough Sounds to be far more beautiful than the dry grassy hills that I saw, the drabness broken only by occasional patches of scrub. But it had been a dry summer and I was only venturing around the tips of the sounds.

Another tide race lay in wait off Cape Lambert but with the turn of tide, the force of the stream was now behind me. *Isadora's* speed picked up as we approached the line of whitecaps. She dropped down a gentle glassy slope to slice into a series of standing waves, then calm sea again.

Four miles of steady paddling led to the long, cliffed headland of Cape Jackson where a third and more violent tide race was waiting. The *New Zealand Pilot* states:

> The tidal streams around Cape Jackson are rapid and there is but little slack water. A strong eddy is formed, during the flood stream, on the western side of the cape.

North-east from the cape lay a long shoal area, the closest end marked by a 40 foot high concrete beacon.

A loud roaring sound like a large rapid or distant surf unsettled me as I neared the whitecaps at the start of the tide race. With the following tide, I rode moderate size waves swiftly through the race, bucked through several standing waves and reached calm water again. If I'd been paddling in the opposite direction it would have been a real struggle.

Now I was off the entrance to Queen Charlotte Sound with one more headland, Cape Koamaru on the northern tip of Arapawa Island, to go before I cleared Cook Strait. The cloud cover had dissipated

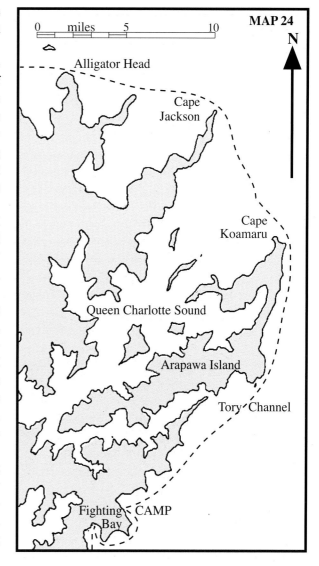

as the day wore on. It was glaringly hot. I felt dizzy for a while and stopped for a drink and a bite to eat. No sign of life anywhere. It must have been too hot even for the sea birds.

After I passed White Rocks, heading for Cape Koamaru, I hit an area of broken water, and the sea was rather lumpy despite the absence of wind. Beyond this a tide race carried me into sheltered water off the tip of this spectacular cape. With sheer cliffs and an isolated pinnacle, it was the most impressive of all the capes I passed that day.

Another area of broken water and standing waves lay in front once I turned south around the cape. A strong northerly breeze which wasn't on the other side of the cape helped *Isadora* along, but the sea was choppy. For the next seven miles the coastline consisted of steep cliffs and buttresses, the swell surging amongst fringing reefs and rocks by the shore. It was no place to linger.

Far to the south, I caught sight of one of the inter-island ferries pulling away from Tory Channel and heading for Wellington. The sea had settled markedly from the disturbed waters by Cape Koamaru. I was starting to feel at home again when a sharp noise from astern startled me. It was like the report of a rifle shot, or the sound that is made when someone slaps a paddle blade hard down on flat water.

'There's no one else out here kayaking,' I assured myself, but swung my head around to locate the source of the noise. Nothing but the sea and the sky.

Moments later, the same sound occurred again, but louder and closer this time. Quickly I turned and, to my horror, saw a huge black and white shape disappearing into the sea about 300 yards away. A tall, black, regal dorsal fin slicing down into the water. Spellbound, I watched and saw another black and white shape come partially out of the water, its belly slapping down onto the sea with the rifle shot noise. Killer whales! The one creature I hoped never to meet on the high seas and here was a group of them swimming on a parallel course. Without a second glance I took off towards shore, paddling so hard and fast, that *Isadora* was more like a hovercraft than a kayak.

My worry was not so much being eaten by a killer whale but being bumped or squashed as they landed from one of their impressive leaps. Fortunately these large mammals were not the slightest bit interested in the speeding yellow kayak and they came no closer than 200 yards, close enough for me though!

By Perano Head I started looking for a spot to land. My bladder was near bursting and I was tired and hungry. A gravel spit that extended from Arapawa Island out to the 200 foot high Ruakawa Rock served admirably. Grateful for the spell, I stretched out flat

on my back on the gravel and munched apple jelly sandwiches. I decided there was still a faint chance of reaching Fighting Bay before dark and so 10 minutes later, I was underway again, shoulders and arms aching.

Over a mile out from shore I passed the entrance to Tory Channel, and the sun soon dropped out of sight behind the hills to the west. As the evening light softened, I moved in closer to shore where there were numerous bluffs, but few if any landing spots. At 7pm I neared the entrance to Glasgow Bay. 'It would be at least another hour along to Fighting Bay,' I decided and it had been pitch black by 7.30 last night. If the sea had been calm I would have continued but it was choppy and I didn't fancy striking a reef in the dark. There was no moon so I paddled into Glasgow Bay in the fading light trying to avoid the dark partially submerged reefs. On the north side of the bay I finally found a short section of boulder beach with cliffs at both ends. It was the best I had seen, so I landed.

Dear diary. 'First thing, I dragged *Isadora* over some logs, to above high water level, and got a brew going on the primus. Found the closest thing to a level spot beneath the steep hillsides and cliffs, and levelled a sleeping bench using a piece of driftwood as a digging stick. Then back to the kayak and I got the torch out. Thought I would flash a few times just in case Bruce and Lyn were watching. I turned it on and moved my hand to and fro in front of the beam, then looked towards Rununder Point.'

To my amazement, a light flashed back at me from the headland's slopes, two miles away.

'Terrific,' I thought, 'they will know that I'm all right.' I flashed back a series of dots and dashes, and there was a return series of flashes from the headland. I counted the flashes, four, regularly spaced.

By pushing the torch beam down to the ground below me, I tried to signal that I was staying here for the night. Again the acknowledging four flashes. This time I pondered at the regularity of the returning four flashes, so I didn't use the torch but waited and watched. At the end of a minute, four flashes from the hillside and the same a minute later. It was all a little too regular for Bruce and Lyn.

I checked the map and sure enough, near the top of Rununder Point, a marine navigation light was marked. I had been signalling to a small automatic lighthouse!

A hot jelly and the remaining apple jelly sandwich toasted over the primus for tea, then I settled down in the fibrefill sleeping bag on the rocky platform, lulled to sleep by the surge washing amongst the boulders just below my ledge. It was so dark that I couldn't make out the horizon or any features at all and was glad I hadn't continued paddling.

I had been paddling for 11.5 hours, half with the

tide and half against it and had covered 51 miles, the longest distance I had achieved in a day and only four miles short of my goal. Needless to say, I slept like a log.

14 March - Day 48

I awoke at dawn and was paddling out of the bay by 6.30. The morning was still and held promise for a fine day, but out of the mile deep opening into Fighting Bay, a strong southerly breeze was stirring the sea. A large blocky pillar stood at the bay's entrance. Shaped like the head and shoulders of an ageing giant it keeps a lonely vigil.

Although tired, I was able to appreciate the beauty of this picturesque bay, with its scrub covered hill sides dropping steeply to rocky cliffs which rose above a sparkling clear green sea. On a fine white sandy beach at its head, Lyn and Ben were waiting when I arrived at 8am.

The support crew had arrived the previous evening but found a locked gate, Fighting Bay was a prohibited area. We hadn't known this was the Cook Strait Cable terminal station.

Alastair and Joan Reid were not at all put out by the two strangers who descended on them with their unusual tale. Bruce explained that I might still be paddling, despite the dark, and Alastair said he would leave all the external floodlights on.

I met Alastair and Joan and told them of my meeting with the killer whales.

"Oh, we often have killer whales come into the bay," Joan told me. Lovely!

While Lyn cooked breakfast, I soaked in a gloriously hot shower. This did wonders for my aching shoulders. After a feed and numerous cups of tea, I felt ready for another stint of paddling. The forecast was for northerly winds, at least they would push me in the right direction. I would have liked to natter to Alastair and Joan but the sunny sky and settled sea were luring me away.

The Reids, a quiet and very hospitable young couple, had joined the lighthouse service and spent 16 months at the light on Stephens Island. Despite receiving few visitors they seemed content with their caretaking job.

Out of Fighting Bay, three nitrogen-filled cables carry 200,000 volts beneath Cook Strait to feed the North Island consumers, draining the South Island's wealth of natural power.

Just after 10am *Isadora* slid into the sea, and I made sure the skeg was in position. A wave to the Reids and the support crew and I headed out of the bay. Our next rendezvous would be south of a section of coastline called White Bluffs, where there was road access to the beach.

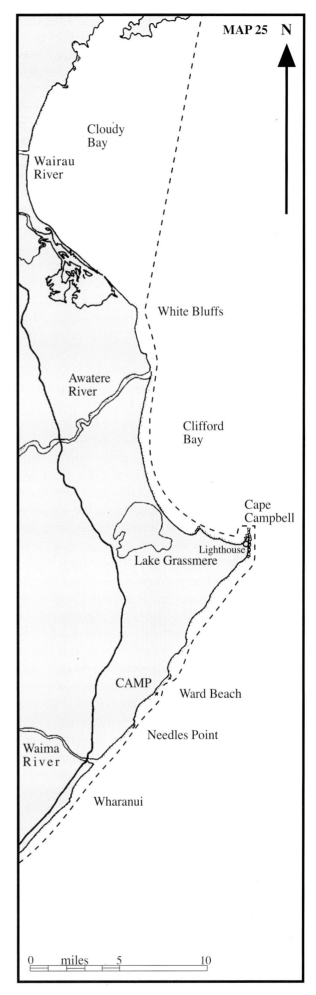

The next few hours would take me in a direct line across Cloudy Bay, at the head of which lay the Wairau River mouth with Blenheim further inland. White Bluffs were clearly visible once I was offshore, and I set course to the east of them. As the morning wore on, the northerly breeze grew in intensity, as did a northerly swell and accompanying chop. I wasn't very happy when whitecaps formed and the swell began to break.

Halfway across Cloudy Bay, and about seven miles offshore, I noticed an old, white, wooden hulled fishing boat dragging a net seawards. With following wind and seas pushing the Nordkapp along at a great clip, I closed on the boat quickly.

The skipper and deckhand were both engrossed in what they were doing and could not have dreamt a kayak would be so far out at sea. When I was only 20 feet from the stern, I yelled out but they didn't hear me over the roar of the motor. A second shout as I shot past the boat reached the deckhand and he looked up and saw the kayak with an incredible look of surprise and amazement growing on his face. He called out to the skipper in the wheelhouse but I was well out of shouting distance by now and too intent on staying upright on the lumpy sea to look around.

Half an hour later I heard a motor and the same fishing boat cruised up from astern. We were both rolling violently as the skipper yelled, "Are you all right?" With a huge grin on my face, I replied with a thumbs up sign as if I did this sort of thing every day. He was heading for the Wairau River bar and gave me some advice on rounding Cape Campbell.

"The northerly won't drop down until dark," he called. A wave in farewell and the boat turned westwards.

About 2.15pm I was level with White Bluffs. The swell had picked up in size so much that in the bottom of the troughs there was no sign of the 500 foot high bluffs. Several swell crests broke over my head completely burying *Isadora* but I wasn't too concerned. The sea didn't seem to have quite the same sting as the south-westerly swell of the Tasman Sea. I was headachy from the glare and really tired.

The steep cliffs of White Bluffs were devoid of vegetation, with only the top covered in dry brown grass. In a cutting above the beach, two miles further south, Bruce's car was easily visible. The surf was breaking a long way out from shore, but after broaching several times in the irregular breakers, I happily grounded on the gravel beach.

Having emerged from the rough surf unscathed, I received a shocking jolt from an electric fence behind the beach. Just what my tired shoulders and arms didn't need. Whilst I drank a reviving bowl of tea, we were joined by the local farmer and his wife whose

land we were on. Arnold and Phil Marfell invited us up to their farmhouse for a cup of tea and a hot shower and we ended up staying the night with them and enjoyed an excellent meal. The weather lady on the television said, "It should be fine over most of the country, with southerlies in the Kaikoura area."

Arnold and Phil Marfell, both middle-aged, had been farming for the last 22 years, running roughly 2,000 ewes and 80 cows. Their farm fronted onto the beach with a beautiful view of the sea from the farmhouse. It had been a very dry summer with little feed left for winter. The paddocks as far as the eye could see were parched and barren.

15 March - Day 49
Before 7am we were out on the beach with the Marfells who came down to watch the launching. Arnold intended ringing the lighthouse keeper at Cape Campbell to ask if Bruce and Lyn could drive out to the light as this was to be our next meeting point. After thanking the pleasant farm couple for their very kind hospitality, Lyn pushed *Isadora* out into a small surf.

A light southerly was blowing but no whitecaps as yet. If the day had been calm, I could have taken a beeline across Clifford Bay to the cape which would have saved a few miles paddle, but with the headwind I decided to hug the shore.

Two hours later, the effort of paddling into a headwind and flood tide was really beginning to tell on me so I pulled into the shore for a spell.

Just as I nosed into what looked like a deserted beach, a chap walked over the dunes carrying a fishing rod. He offered me a cup of hot coffee, which I couldn't refuse. We talked for 20 minutes or so, but the wind didn't die down. The beach and white sands of the Cape Campbell lighthouse were clearly visible from here. The fisherman gave me a push off into the surf. After the previous two days, I was most impressed with the hospitality of the East Coasters.

I estimated the wind was blowing into my face at between 10-15 knots. It was really impeding my progress.

A chap working on a drag line by the outlet of Lake Grassmere returned my wave, but there was little to relieve the monotony of slogging into the wind. The beach was devoid of interesting things to look at, and since I was hugging the shore, I could see nothing of the hinterland. Only a few small penguins, that took one startled look at the yellow kayak and crash dived, and numerous black-backed seagulls provided any interest.

I hoped to be out of the wind beneath the bluffs that extend from Mussel Point out to Cape Campbell, but to the disgust of my arms and shoulders the wind stayed in my face. On two occasions I was surprised by two foot high waves that appeared out of nowhere but at least they relieved the monotony of the paddling. At long last I approached the red roofed houses beneath the black and white banded tower of the Cape Campbell lighthouse. Lyn came out in Bruce's kayak to meet me and at midday I landed.

Peter Coleman, the lighthouse keeper, suntanned and stocky with a pale grey beard, asked us over for lunch and we met Noeline, his wife and their son Graham. Noeline provided us with delicious home-made tomato soup and fresh warm bread. Afterwards Peter took us to the top of the lighthouse and pointed out a narrow gap through the long reef off the cape where I could take a short cut.

For the last five years, Peter had tended the light on the cape and intended staying on until he retired. Before that, he was at the Moeraki light on Centre Island in Foveaux Strait, and had spent two and a half years at Puysegur Point. Four years ago, the second family left, the light service was trying to cut costs, much to the disappointment of Peter and Noeline. No female company for Noeline and no children to mix with their own, not to mention twice the workload for Peter. As he pointed out, his salary should have doubled when the second lighthouse keeper left, but it didn't. Every three hours from 6am to 6pm, he sent out a weather situation. There was no public access to the lighthouse. Food and mail arrived once a week by launch. Their three children had all completed schooling through correspondence up to university entrance level. But Noeline said she would rather be a working mother than go through correspondence again.

In 1870, a light first shone out from the top of a wooden tower on the cape. It was replaced in 1905 by the present tapering 73 foot high, cast iron tower. The light flashed once every 30 seconds and was visible for 18 nautical miles.

To the south-west the coastline was dry, dusty and almost devoid of vegetation on the brown hills. Numerous reefs and rocks were dotted along the coast, up to a mile offshore, but at least there wasn't much swell. When I first arrived, the anemometer was recording 14 knots. Slowly the wind speed eased whilst I rested at the lighthouse, nine knots at 2pm and seven knots an hour later when I was ready to start again.

I paddled north along the cape out to the narrow gap through the reef where the tide was racing, at four to five knots through the obvious channel. Bruce was out with the camera as I shot through the narrow channel, kelp covered rocks on both sides. With a turn of tide at midday, the falling tide was now moving in my favour. The *New Zealand Pilot* notes:

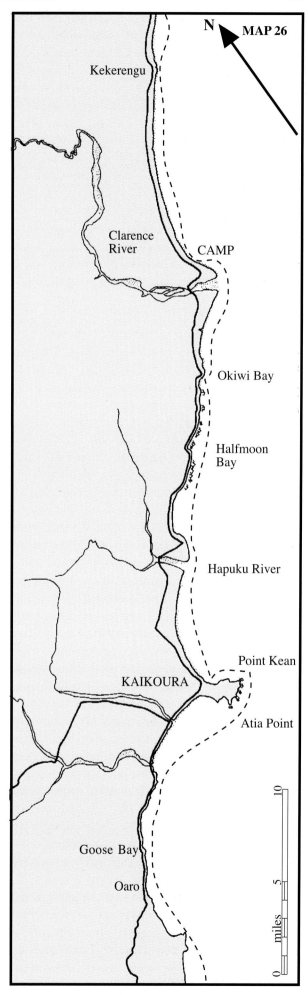

Inshore, the tidal stream sets northwards with a rising tide, and southward with a falling tide, both streams attain a rate of about 1.5 knots.

Level with the lighthouse, I spotted the Colemans on the ridge by the tower. A distant wave in farewell.

Bruce and Lyn were going to drive down the coast and wait at Ward Beach, 10 miles paddle away.

After two hours paddling I arrived at Ward Beach, tired and in low spirits. The support crew had just arrived and told me I was making good time. I thought I had been going really slowly.

The picnic area behind the beach was so dry that it appeared like part of Central Australia. A few small gum trees growing inside rusty 44 gallon drums stood near a concrete toilet block wrecked by vandals.

16 March - Day 50

I was distinctly lacking in enthusiasm. Bruce served Lyn and I a cup of tea in our sleeping bags. This was followed by porridge and bacon and eggs. But only after Bruce threatened to cart me, sleeping bag and all, down to the sea, did I suddenly rediscover my willingness to paddle.

By 7am I was underway, heading for the next meeting point at Kekerengu on State Highway Number 1. A light northerly breeze tried to push *Isadora* out to sea all morning. For the first time in many days I came in close to a main road beside which ran the Picton to Christchurch railway. Cars were flashing past, their drivers too intent on fast driving to see the Nordkapp but the driver of a goods train returned my wave providing a slight boost to morale. Anything to take my thoughts away from how tired I felt.

The brief lunch stop at Kekerengu over I pushed on to Okiwi Bay on the South side of the Clarence River fan. During the afternoon, the wind swung to the south and slowed progress. At least there was no trouble finding a landing spot along the featureless gravel beach, just a shore dumper to carefully negotiate.

A large alluvial fan has built out into the sea by the Clarence River, providing a large bump on the generally straight coastline. Extending out to sea from the fan lay a long bank of mist or cloud. As I neared the northern side of the fan I decided to flag away the paddling for the rest of the day. The southerly was too much for me. There was still plenty of daylight left but I landed in the surging wake of a dumper.

Once *Isadora* was safely disguised amongst the driftwood and marram grass behind the beach, I walked out to the highway and started hitching south to Okiwi Bay. What a sight! Wetsuit covered by a green bush shirt, face smeared with a mixture of white zinc cream and castor oil. But I soon got a lift and moments later, the Peugeot appeared driving

towards us. Frantic waving and light flashing from my driver and I rejoined the support party.

They were driving along the coast looking for me. The coast from Okiwi Bay into Kaikoura was completely enshrouded in a sea mist, with visibility down to less than 50 feet. Lyn said that from Okiwi Bay she could only hear the large surf breaking offshore although they were parked by the beach there was no sign of the sea through the dense mist. It was a 'tinny' decision on my part to pull in and land where I did because if I had continued around the Clarence River fan there would have been trouble navigating and landing in the mist. All the way to Kaikoura we drove at slow speeds, the headlights on full.

We called in at Bruce's sister's house in the town and were met by her husband Ian Milne, also a paddler, who was playing the bagpipes. What a reception. I wondered what the neighbours thought about the noise as Ian marched around the house, pipes wailing and droning. They must be used to it by now ..... or deaf.

17 March - Day 51

We were out at the kayak before 7am. Overnight the wind and mist had disappeared but the shore dumper pounded me as I left the beach. It reared up to five foot in height and jarred me from head to toe, filling my beard full of sand and small gravel. After that I had an uneventful paddle around the Clarence River fan to the rocky reefs of Okiwi Bay. Bruce slid quietly into the sea with his Scuba gear on as I approached, intent on an ambush! As I nosed in through some reefs, Bruce's goggled face suddenly rose out of the blue depths and he grabbed hold of the decklines. To distract him from capsizing *Isadora*, which I felt sure he was about to try, I gave him the waterproof camera and asked him if he would take an underwater shot of the Nordkapp.

After a reasonable break on shore I pushed on towards Kaikoura. Several seals were lying in the sun by Ohau Point and several dolphins swam by but they were not as friendly as those on the West Coast, being quite uninterested in playing around the kayak.

Bruce and Lyn waited by the Hapuka River fan, and I landed for a brew. Here I discovered why the sprayskirt had been coming off so easily since I left Greymouth. The ends of the elastic shock cord holding the sprayskirt edge over the cockpit coaming, were undone.

Bruce commented, "That shows you how often you check your gear." To which I replied, "Oh yes, it's about time for a 500 mile check." I could just imagine paddling into a seaside service station and asking the attendant for: "Two pints of hot sweet tea please! Check the blood pressure, blood sugar level, and a new set of arms please!"

The distant houses on the Kaikoura Peninsula seemed to creep very slowly towards me as I paddled so I was relieved and happy to finally land in front of the County Council offices, a very gentle surf lapping onto the beach. Fish and chips eaten beneath the avenue of pine trees marked the end of another day's paddling.

18 March - Day 52

This was to be a rest day but it didn't turn out that way. In six consecutive days of paddling, I had covered 193 miles, averaging 35 miles per day.

In a bedroom at Ian and Alison Milne's, Bruce and I had tried to sleep in, but one of the children was playing a piano in the front room and Ian was outside playing the bagpipes. It was impossible to sleep. Finally to escape the noise, we went paddling. Just a quiet paddle around the peninsula to Pinnacle Rock, which is near the first road tunnel south of Kaikoura.

Bruce, Ian and myself lined up in our kayaks on the Kaikoura beach for a racing start. On the count of three, we slid down the short gravel beach into the sea. Both Ian and Bruce were paddling 12 foot long slalom kayaks, designed for tight turning in rapids. They were not a patch on the Nordkapp for fast cruising or running true at sea.

We made good time out past the fishing wharf to Point Kean where several busloads of tourists were peering towards a few seals sunning themselves on the rocks. A slight breeze was blowing from the south-east, but the sea was calm.

We cut in closer through the kelp covered rocks and waved to Lyn and Alison. In the next two miles to the south-west, there were more craypot floats in a single area than I saw anywhere around the South Island. Small floats, large ones, multicolours and groups of them clustered together. Numerous small power boats were zapping around, lifting the pots. No wonder the crayfish are scarce off Kaikoura. The sea bed must be littered with craypots. There were a few seals on the rocks. I had to grin at the antics of a mum and her pup as they frolicked and played amongst the kelp. We chose routes through narrow channels in the reefs where the sea was surging for a little excitement. At Atia Point, on the south side of the peninsula, we turned away towards Pinnacle Rock where Lyn and Alison were waiting.

Bruce wasn't enjoying himself. And that's a gross understatement. His kayak persisted in going round in circles and would not stay on a semblance of a straight line. His arms were tired as well. I even tried tying my skeg on the hull of his kayak but that didn't help. Ian was faring better but couldn't keep up with my sedate paddling in the Nordkapp.

Finally I shot away. Bruce reckoned he would make it to the lunch stop in the end. The day was so good with a sunny sky and calm sea that I had a return of enthusiasm for paddling. I wanted to slip the leash and hammer on towards Christchurch.

When Bruce finally turned up at the lunch spot, quite a while after Ian and myself, he was paddling with only half the paddle. In desperation he had broken the paddle in half by thumping it on the deck and was quite adamant that the kayak was much easier to paddle that way.

Although Ian wanted to paddle a few more miles with his son in another kayak, I was impatient to make the most of the afternoon. After a quick bite to eat and a brew, I shot away. Bruce and Lyn were going to drive around to Claverly, north of the Conway River.

A combination of better scenery and perfect conditions enabled me to recover completely. I was glad to be out on the sea, alone but for the occasional penguin and several dolphins. I made good time by Goose Bay and Oaro to Spy Glass Point. Here I was intrigued by a crevice or chasm which passed through the tip of the point. For a brief period a southerly breeze rippled the glassy surface of the sea, but as quickly as it sprang up it faded away, to my relief.

Dark sandy beaches led to Claverly where I landed on top of a small dumper. Bruce and Lyn arrived soon after. Since it was only 5.30, I was keen to knock up another hour's paddling before dark so the support crew agreed to signal me from a road which came close to the shore, south of the Conway River.

The beautiful afternoon quickly grew dark and I was relieved to see Lyn flashing the torch alongside the car. We were now in North Canterbury, having passed the Conway River which forms the boundary between the Marlborough and Canterbury districts.

Dear diary has a lengthy description of a cold wet night spent on the beach. Despite a red sunset, it soon began blowing and by midnight pouring with rain. Bruce adjourned to the car leaving Lyn and I to try to pitch the tent. Over an inch of rain fell. By morning Ben, Lyn and I were a trifle damp. The tent had leaked like the proverbial sieve.

19 March - Day 53

A grey blustery morning with showers and a moderate south-westerly breeze. At last a rest day! At a nearby farmhouse I knocked at the back door and asked if we could make a brew in the roadside shearing shed. This was fine with Jim and Lorraine Shaw so we escaped out of the rain and set up the primus.

For a while, we sat in the car and gazed at the choppy sea, read magazines and listened to the radio. South westerly winds, returning to settled dry weather

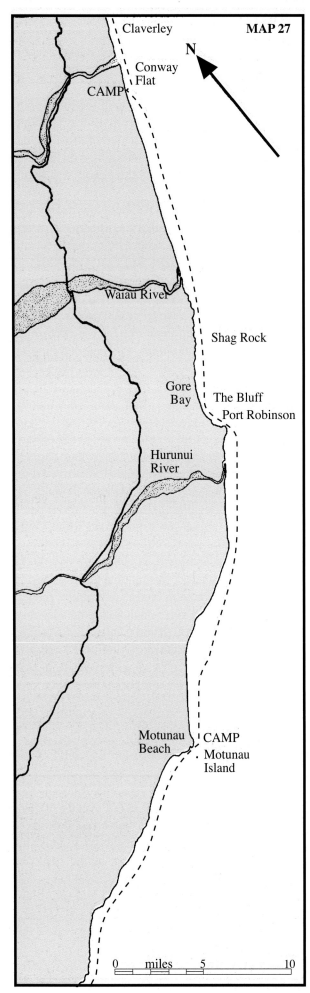

MAP 27

Claverley

N

Conway
Flat

CAMP

Waiau River

Shag Rock

Gore
Bay

The Bluff
Port Robinson

Hurunui
River

Motunau
Beach

CAMP
Motunau
Island

0   miles   5   10

next day was the morning forecast.

Mid-afternoon, Jim asked us if we would like to join him to help move a flock of 4,000 ewes. So we went along to get in the way. Jim's two children and three sheep dogs went as well on the back of the short wheel base landrover. At another farm house we picked up the farm's owner Kim MacFarland, his son Bruce with his wife and child, and another four dogs. Quite a crowd, two adults and three children in the roofless cab, five adults and seven occasionally snarling dogs on the back of the poor old Landrover. Because the summer had been so dry, the stock had to be moved often. Apart from the overnight downpour the last decent rain had been in November. Instead of the usual 5,000 bales of winter feed, there were now only 500 bales left.

Kim and Bruce said we could stay overnight in the whare by the shearing shed. I imagined an old disintegrating wooden hut, but the whare was a modern self-contained shearers' quarters with all mod cons, including a hot shower which was most appreciated. For the evening meal Jim and Lorraine invited us to join them for a mouth-watering feed of roast lamb - a most enjoyable evening with a friendly, hospitable couple.

20 March - Day 54

At the crack of dawn we ate breakfast while the sun rose slowly out to sea. The Shaw family came to watch me crash out through the shore dump. A welcome light north-easterly was blowing, and apart from a few cloud banks to the south, the sky was clear.

There was no road access to the coast again until Gore Bay by Port Robinson, 17 miles away as the seagull flies. The support party would wait for me there.

For the first few miles I passed sandy beaches with farmland behind, then steep cliffs with a narrow strip of shingle beach, with sufficient features in the form of gorges and bluffs to easily enable me to keep track of progress on the map. Near the Waiau River mouth, the breeze swung to the east and kept pushing *Isadora* towards the breakers. Once past Shag Rock with its mobs of birds nesting on tiny ledges I could see the headland called Port Robinson and the houses at Gore Bay.

On the horizon, many miles to the east of the coastline, I saw for the first time what looked like a series of pale blue coloured islands. It was easy to see why Captain Cook first called Banks Peninsula 'Banks Islands,' until the low relief Canterbury Plains were found to connect the 'islands' to the rest of the South Island.

A four foot high surf was breaking onto the sandy beach at Gore Bay. Lyn signalled me to paddle further south and I headed beachwards close by the Bluff. An exciting 100 foot ride on one wave and I caught a smaller wave onto the sand.

Lyn had bought some corn bread for making sandwiches. As Bruce munched away on a sandwich he commented, "They're really corny sandwiches." Lyn with a glint in her eyes replied, "That's amazingly funny Bruce."

It took a little prompting from Lyn before we picked up the clever pun. Not to be outdone in the competition for the most terrible pun, I said "Thanks Cobber," when Lyn passed me a sandwich. No one spotted that one until my giggles nearly caused me to choke on a mouthful of sandwich.

The first road access south of Port Robinson was at Motunau Beach, a distance of 19 miles and I hoped to reach there by evening.

Bruce was ready with the camera when I paddled out into the surf. He was always hoping to capture on film a spectacular capsize, and was most disappointed each time I made a clean exit from the beach. Since the weather forecast promised a south-westerly change in the afternoon, I didn't put the skeg on but left it tied on the deck behind.

Beneath the cliffs on the north side of Port Headland lay the remains of a shipwreck comprising a rusting steel frame and wooden planks of the old hull. According to Ingram's *New Zealand Shipwrecks 1795-1970* it may be the 87 foot long *Paroto* which, in pea soup fog one night in August 1966, stranded on the south side of Gore Bay and became a total loss.

Around the headland in Manuka Bay, a patch of green bush made a very pleasant change from the drab dry farmlands surrounding it.

Gradually a strong north-easterly breeze picked up which added to my speed, but I cursed the fact that the skeg was tied on the deck behind me. 'Banks Islands' grew into one large, long island as I progressed south-westwards.

I kept *Isadora* about half a mile offshore from the continuous line of cliffs forming the coastline. With the following wind the stern tended to swing out to sea if only I had put the skeg down. There was no way I could maintain a steady paddling rhythm as after each second or third stroke, I would have to bring the bow back in line for Motunau Island. This flat-topped, steep rocky island seemed to take ages to reach.

Between the headland north of the Motunau River and the island, reefs extended out to sea for some distance, and I had to paddle out to miss the waves breaking over them. A waving object caught my eye as the houses of the seaside fishing village of Motunau came into sight. It was Lyn signalling me to continue westwards. The river mouth was difficult to see from outside the breakers but there were two poles in the surf and I headed for them. From the river bank Bruce signalled me the direction in which to paddle in order to bring me in line with the channel inside the bar. His hand chopped down quickly when *Isadora* lay on target. Two short rides in front of breakers carried me in over the bar and I paddled up the calm, gently ebbing waters of the Motunau River.

From the river bank Bruce called, "Continue upriver and you'll find a guide waiting." Sure enough, amongst a group of moored crayfishing boats, Lyn was waiting in Bruce's kayak and together we paddled upstream to a camping ground set back on the river

Bruce helping with the launch from Gore Bay, Port Robinson. Photo: Lyn Taylor

Bruce and Lyn relaxing by the Motunau River,
map of the South Island on the ground

bank. Most impressive team work from the support crew.

Dear diary: 'I came in over the bar at 5.30, five hours after leaving Gore Bay. I felt really knackered and had trouble keeping my eyes open whilst I wrote up dear diary. We camped under the spreading gnarled branches of an ancient macrocarpa tree. The tide was well out, exposing quite an expanse of mudflats. I rang Grahame Sisson in Nelson to tell him how things were going and we had an excited rave about pumps and skegs. No pavlova as yet.'

Each evening when we camped out we always asked Lyn after the main meal, "Is the pavlova ready yet?" Lyn must have been a little tired of hearing, "Mm, the pavlova must be just about ready now." However she showed great patience with us and promised to whip one up when we arrived in Christchurch.

21 March - Day 55

At 7.15am the tide was so low that I grounded crossing the bar and had to drag *Isadora* out to the edge of the surf. Waves were breaking but they were no more than two foot high and provided no problems. A wave to Bruce and Lyn and I set off for the lunch stop at Amberley Beach. We all thought I stood a good chance of reaching New Brighton by evening.

Out beyond the breakers I found a calm sea and a light northerly disturbing the surface, not a cloud in the sky. After the hassles of the previous evening I had been silly enough to leave the skeg tied onto the deck behind the cockpit, or perhaps I was too tired to remember to put it on. The coastline consisted of cliffs and steep faces up to 300 feet above a narrow strip of beach.

The waves were breaking a long way out from shore and at one stage I was dreaming along in a steady paddling rhythm when a wave appeared out of no where on my left, steep-faced and ready to cap. I

pulled out all the stops to race directly into its face and just managed to shoot over the crest before it broke. The old pulse rate must have doubled or more and rather loudly I declared, "Jeez!" and looked around for more sneaking waves but apart from the departing wake of the breaker, there was calm sea all around.

With only five miles remaining to the end of the cliffs and start of the sandy North Canterbury beaches, the wind veered to the east and increased its intensity. *Isadora* refused to stay on a straight line and the bow kept heading out to sea as the wind swung the stern towards shore. After an hour of paddling on the left hand side and steering on the right, in desperation I tied the skeg onto the decklines by the bilge pump. But it merely drifted up to lie on the surface when I resumed paddling. I remedied this by passing a line beneath the hull to keep the skeg more or less vertical in the water beside the hull. This made little difference. Because the Nordkapp's keel is sharper by the bow than at the stern a strong following or side wind pushes the stern in the direction of the wind, whilst the bow tends to run true. The skeg projecting below the hull at the stern corrected this.

By now a sizeable chop had developed and waves were breaking over the decks. I had stayed so far offshore to miss the breakers that at Amberley Beach I nearly paddled straight past the Peugeot before spotting it in the dunes. With relief I turned the bow beachwards, and with the skeg tied back on deck, nosed in cautiously towards a mess of unruly breakers. Lulls appeared few and far between in the sets of four to five foot high breakers. The shelter of the beach seemed a long way off. I tried to sneak in between sets but one large wave broke over me. *Isadora* broached and we hurtled in sideways, the paddle straining in a high brace position on top of the surging breaker. Several waves later Bruce and Lyn grabbed one end each of the Nordkapp and steadied it while I lurched out of the cockpit. For ages I sat limply in a heap on the sand, staring out at the whitecapping choppy sea and the wild surf.

The wind didn't moderate all afternoon as we lay

Surfing into the beach at Amberley. Photo: Bruce Annabell

in the sandy dunes, and when insufficient time remained to reach New Brighton we loaded *Isadora* onto the Peugeot and drove into Christchurch for the night. Dear diary noted: 'Still no pavlova.'

22 March - Day 56

Before dawn we yawned our way out to Amberley Beach only to find I had left the sprayskirt back in Christchurch. Bruce modified his sprayskirt to fit the smaller cockpit coaming of the Nordkapp but it seemed like an ill omen. Overnight the surf had settled but it still looked large enough to cause a sick feeling in the pit of my stomach.

At 7.30 I paddled out through the shore break and waited in the slop inside the main line of breakers for a lull. When it came I paddled hard for the open sea but not fast enough. A five foot high wave creamed over my head. Such was the force in the breaker that the paddle was wrenched out of my left hand. Without its support I was about to capsize with *Isadora* shooting in stern first towards the beach.

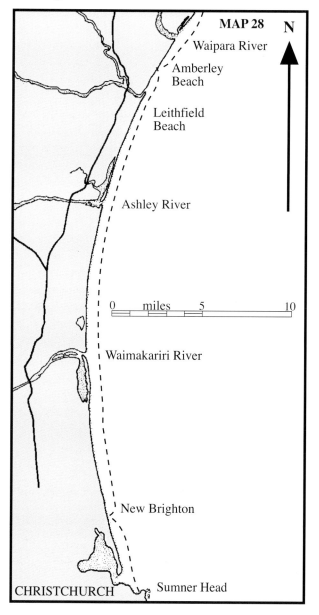

MAP 28 N
Waipara River
Amberley Beach
Leithfield Beach
Ashley River
0 miles 5 10
Waimakariri River
New Brighton
CHRISTCHURCH Sumner Head

Luckily I caught hold of the paddle and with both hands on it I righted *Isadora* and stopped the rush backwards. Once I escaped the clutches of this breaker I just managed to slice through the crest of the next wave and reach the open sea before it creamed. With a sigh of relief I turned the bow parallel to the beach and set off for New Brighton. It wasn't easy to gauge my progress during the morning as a line of dunes hid all sight of the low lying hinterland. Occasional stands of pine trees enabled me to keep a rough estimate on distance covered.

But there was no mistaking the buildings behind the beach at New Brighton and at 1pm I rode breakers in through a low surf to land in front of the surf pavilion. Pleased to be ashore, I made an immediate dash for a gents toilet.

While Bruce and I basked in the sun on concrete steps above the beach, Lyn fetched a large cake-tin from the car. Both she and Bruce were grinning like Cheshire cats. "It can't be! Is it, is it, is it a pavlova?" I stuttered. Sure enough Lyn had whipped one up for our lunch.

As we demolished the delicious pav a reporter and photographer from *The Press* arrived, closely followed by a three man television crew. We informed them that they were late as I was about to push on for the last lap to Sumner. Lyn had taken on the job of press orificer, ringing the media once I passed North Beach to say when I would be arriving at New Brighton, but they were still late. They wanted action and I obliged by paddling out through the surf, turning round and paddling back in through the breakers as though I was just arriving.

A short interview, which followed on the beach as I stepped out of *Isadora,* was terminated abruptly when the cameraman, interviewer and sound man found sea water lapping around their shoes. We had to adjourn higher up the beach, to avoid the waves. I restrained from laughing out loud at their predicament but it did seem funny. For so long I had been splashing around on the sea but when one inch of sea water lapped around the polished shoes of the television crew, it was grave cause for alarm.

Leaving the beach for the second time at 2pm I wore the proper sprayskirt and made sure the skeg was in position. An hour and a quarter later when *Isadora* glided into the concrete boat launching ramp next to the Sumner lifeboat station I called out to Lyn, "Is there another pav?" The answer came as a wet towel thrown at my head.

One more stage had been completed and only one remained. I had covered 302 miles in 10 days with one day off for inclement weather, thus averaging 30 miles per day.

Before starting the last long stage down to Te

Waewae Bay I wanted a break from paddling. However preparations to leave Christchurch for the West Coast did not run smoothly. For myself and Lyn it was like watching a Woody Allen comedy movie, although it wasn't very funny to Bruce at the time. The plan was for me to shout the support crew a restaurant type meal, catch the evening news on the idiot box, then head for the West Coast. But it didn't work out that way.

The bearing in the Peugeot's water pump was playing up and although Bruce kept pumping grease into it, water literally hosed out of it when the motor stopped. Whilst the motor was running the water loss wasn't as bad. As we were about to leave Lyn's house I topped up the radiator with a garden hose but then the motor wouldn't start. Water had sprayed onto the electrical wiring. Half an hour later the car was going in a fashion and we drove into town in a leapfrog manner, the engine alternating between two and four cylinders amidst peak hour traffic in the one way system of Oxford Terrace the motor died. Bruce drifted the car to the side of the road and fiddled beneath the bonnet. A traffic officer on a motor bike pulled up with a screech of tyres and enquired, "What's the trouble?" It was pretty obvious for water was streaming out onto the road. A can of anti-moisture spray helped to restart the engine but the traffic officer had started eyeing the warrant of fitness sticker, only 12 months since it was current. "When are you going to get a new warrant?" he asked. "Next week," Bruce replied, "I haven't been using the car very much."

Before the traffic officer could change his mind and issue a ticket, Bruce drove off and lost us in some backstreets where we cleaned and gapped the spark plugs. This made a considerable difference but it was obvious we were not going to eat at the restaurant, the booking was for an hour ago. At a friend of Bruce's, who owned a colour television set, we ate fish and chips and watched the news. For the umpteenth time Bruce topped up the radiator and pumped the water pump bearing full of grease. But then as I pulled the extendable radio aerial out, it felt tight and parted in the middle with a hard tug. "This car is jinxed," Bruce moaned as I passed him the aerial to mend.

Finally we were all set to go but when Bruce wound up the car window the glass jumped out of its track and wouldn't go up or down. Showing remarkable restraint, for a broken man, Bruce lay on the floor of the car to fix the window and said quietly, "This is the last straw." In the back seat Lyn was also showing remarkable restraint in trying to maintain a straight face. She and I were both trying hard to stifle fits of giggling.

After all that we had an incident free trip over Arthurs Pass to Runanga, stopping frequently to top up the radiator. Still as the saying goes, you get evenings like that on the big trips.

Surfing in to the beach at New Brighton. Photo: The Press

Chapter 14

CHRISTCHURCH to DUNEDIN

After a five day break, I felt ready to tackle paddling around Banks Peninsula, but first I had to find someone to drive my car and act as support crew. Lyn was back at work, Bruce had injured a knee and Dick was engrossed in his garden. On the way over to Christchurch I stopped at Arthurs Pass for a cuppa with the Park Board rangers. Pip Aplin had a few day's leave owing to him and offered to drive for up to five days. After that, another ranger, Paul Dale, could take over for a week. At least that was a start. When Paul had to return to work, I would stop for a spell and find someone else. It was a lucky break that I had stopped at the Pass as I was at the stage of considering an advertisement in a Christchurch newspaper for a driver. Pip agreed to meet me at Sumner on 29 March at 7am.

There was no doubt in my mind that Pip would be perfect in the role of support crew. After many years in the light service, two long stints on Dog Island in Foveaux Strait and the intervening time spent at the Stephens Island lighthouse off D'Urville Island, Pip felt a strong affinity for the sea. Only slightly built and sporting a sprawling curly beard, Pip never lost his sense of humour or the twinkle in his eyes.

All I had to do in Christchurch was to waterproof a set of maps for the next stage and study the coastline descriptions in the *New Zealand Pilot*:

> Banks peninsula contains the only natural harbours on the eastern side of the South island, with the exception of Otago. The peninsula is formed by a mass of rugged, and, in parts, densely wooded mountains about 3,000 feet high, which fall steeply westwards to the plains from which this promontory projects; its coast is broken and indented with numerous bays and coves.

One problem to face was the current off the tip of the peninsula for the *Pilot* notes:

> There is an almost constant current setting northward off the eastern extremity of Banks peninsula, with a rate from one to two knots according to the wind.

On the appointed morning, we met at the Sumner lifeboat station but a strong north-easterly wind was kicking up a sizeable swell with whitecaps extending as far as the eye could see. It was not a good day to start! The forecast was for continuing north-easterlies, so I flagged away kayaking for the day.

We adjourned to the Godley Head lighthouse where a friend of Pip's was caretaker. Charley Wallace, tall, bearded and gaunt looking, had a dry

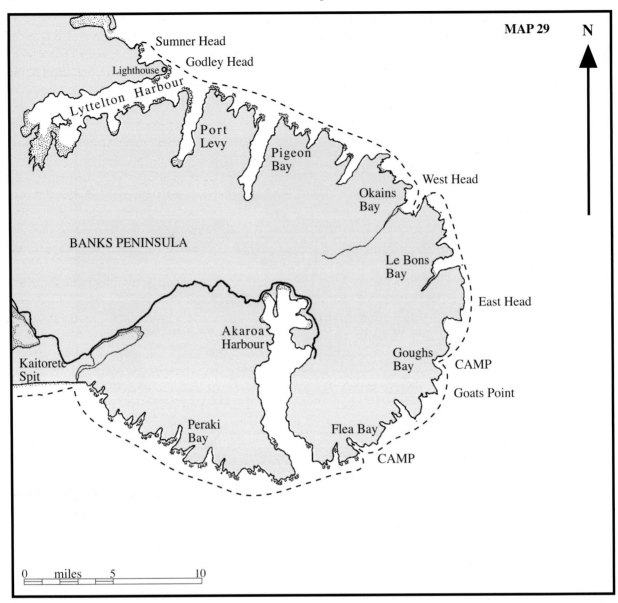

MAP 29

N

sense of humour which mixed with his broad Scottish brogue was a delight to listen to. For many years, Charley was a relieving keeper with the light service serving at many of the North and South Islands' lighthouses. Now he had an ideal occupation, with the solitude he preferred and a major city not far away. To keep vandals and intruders away from the light and installation he had three savage dobermann pinscher guard dogs, so fierce that Pip and I waited at the first locked gate for Charley to guide us in.

For the next two days the wind persisted from the north-east and we stayed with Charley. Early on the morning of 31 March I paddled away from Sumner only to turn back off Taylors Mistake. The swell was at least nine foot high from crest to trough, and I wasn't very happy when it began capping. Pip and I drove around to Birdlings Flat on the south side of the peninsula to investigate landing possibilities.

A 35 knot north-easterly wind was whipping spray off the sea. Although it was blowing in the right direction, it was definitely not a day for paddling.

When we returned to the lighthouse, with a half gallon of port, I explained to Charley, "I've developed a strong lust to port!" Charley said that our lustful thoughts would soon disappear as he was lacing the cups of tea with bromide, an old army trick to diminish the lusty thoughts of soldiers.

Charley's house had an incredible view of the sea and the entrance to Lyttelton Harbour. It was set back

Heading out from the launching ramp at Sumner

from 400 foot high cliffs that dropped sheer into the sea. Charley took us down a steep stairway to look at the light and showed us the massive tank that provided pressure to power the automatic foghorn. The actual foghorn was small and looked harmless enough but Pip assured me it was really loud. Once Charley told a visitor that he had to stand close to the foghorn to hear it. The poor chap nearly died of fright when Charley set it off.

1 April - Day 57

Charley woke us to look at the sunrise. Through his kitchen window we gazed at deep red banks of cloud. A gold-yellow band of sky on the horizon announced the impending arrival of the sun. A beautiful sunrise, but not a good weather sign, for as the saying goes, 'red sky in the morning, paddler's warning.' However, the air was still by the house, and the swell appeared to have diminished in size during the night.

At 7.15am I paddled away from Sumner, heading for a lunch stop at Okains Bay. Before driving there, Pip would return to the lighthouse to watch my progress past Godley Head.

Off Sumner Head a moderate swell was running, but I was happy enough paddling. It didn't take long to reach Godley Head but I could hardly make out the tiny figures of Charley and Pip by the light on top of the cliffs. They spotted me and we exchanged shouts across the water.

Midway across the Lyttelton Harbour entrance, there was a tall, whistling buoy. Almost at the buoy, and over a mile from Godley Head, I nearly jumped out of my skin as an incredibly deep, roaring noise suddenly echoed across the sea. Charley had set off the automatic foghorn. I threw up my arms in surrender but he let go with a second blast that reverberated across the harbour entrance. In contrast, the sound emitting from the whistling buoy was like music, similar to the plaintive cry of a sea bird.

I made good time past Port Levy but off Pigeon Bay the wind turned to the north, picking up rapidly in intensity. Twice, strong gusts barrelled past, nearly causing a capsize. The coastline was more rugged than I expected, sheer, dark cliffs climbing free from the surge up 300 feet or more, with not a show of a landing anywhere. Surfing occasionally in front of the chop, I plugged on past Long Point and felt tempted to pull into Stoney Beach to escape from the chop. However the rendezvous at Okains Bay wasn't far away so I continued by the bluffs of West Head to the bay's entrance.

A sizeable surf was smoking beachwards at the head of the bay, but there was a group of people by the dunes, one of whom was wearing a red jacket and looked like Pip. I paddled in quickly behind a large wave and caught the next one as it broke to ride some distance in the broach position until it was small enough to surf directly in front. It wasn't Pip after all but two air force chaps looking after a group of scouts for the weekend. Pip soon arrived. He had been up on the hills trying to spot the kayak!

Behind the marram grass covered dunes by the beach was a domain, sheltered beneath a grove of tall pine trees. A lovely place to stay the night but the numerous signs, 'No camping without a permit', and 'No dogs allowed' put us off. On a winding dirt road that climbed out of the bay, we peered out to East Head with Pip's telescope. A combination of wind, tide and swell was creating a sizeable chop at the entrance to the bay.

I was full of indecision on whether to continue. We drove to look at a local museum but, for the sixteenth time, I changed my mind and said, "Bugger it, may as well go and have a look." Pip replied, "Yep, I guess we're not here to look at museums." During the time on shore the tide had dropped and the surf was smaller although the wind hadn't eased. Off East Head there was a nasty chop, and I almost turned back. *Isadora* was dropping down sharply into the troughs, and from his vantage point high up on the hills, Pip lost sight of me. Only when the Nordkapp rose over the swell crests, could Pip catch a glimpse of the kayak.

One thing which kept me persevering through the lumpy sea off the head, was that the sea to the south-west appeared to be calmer. I was relieved to reach more settled seas and turned south-eastwards, the following wind pushing me along past more vertical dark cliffs to the mouth of Le Bons Bay. Here I kept well out from the cliff line to avoid a backchop off the sheer 500 foot high walls.

At the eastern extremity of Banks Peninsula the paddling was easy, the following wind seemed to be negating the northward drift of the current.

Pip was going to keep watch at the road end at Goughs Bay. If I paddled straight past the going was fine and he would drive on to Flea Bay near the entrance to Akaroa Harbour. When I drew level with Goughs Bay the sea was a little choppy, but the paddling was still easy and there remained sufficient time before dark to reach Flea Bay. There was no sign of Pip onshore. He was waiting there but because of the large surf had kept out of sight so as not to tempt me to come in just for a cup of tea.

A southerly change was forecast for the following day, but to my disgust it decided to arrive early. Not long after Goughs Bay lay astern, the north-westerly breeze died. The first indication of the southerly was a sudden gust of wind sweeping across the sea.

Then it was on me, a confounded southerly blowing strongly from dead ahead, gusting at times so hard

Leaving Goughs Bay. Photo: Pip Aplin

that I had to stop paddling and do a sculling support stroke to keep upright. Spray from the bow crashing into the chop flew back into my face. There and then I nearly turned back, but by now Pip would be well on the way to Flea Bay. Goat Point was only half a mile away, but what a struggle into the wind to reach it. Here it was even rougher for the tide seemed to be affecting the sea as well as the wind and swell. Two attempts were made to draw past the point, but it seemed pointless continuing at a snail's pace into the chop, there was no way of reaching Flea Bay before dark.

After a slow tippy turn I had a fast ride back to Goughs Bay, escorted by three dolphins who also seemed to be escaping from the southerly change. The surf was booming into the beach at the head of the bay, and I cruised along outside the breakers seeking a weak spot. At the south end the surf was dumping onto boulders while far offshore, midway along the beach, was a broken and smoking surf. It had to be the north end.

Where the sandy beach ended against the cliffs, a low rock lay not far offshore and sets of waves were breaking over it, creaming towards the beach. Behind one large set, I paddled in flat-stick, broaching right as the first wave of the next set broke behind. An exciting ride onto the sand and I was glad to be ashore in one piece.

At a nearby farmhouse, I met Cyril and Diane

Thomas who had just returned from a day of dog trialing. While Diane revived my spirits with a brew Cyril rang a farmer at Flea Bay to ask if Pip was waiting there, but no sign of him. After an hour, Cyril rang a second farmer at the head of the not so distant Long Bay. Pip had left there three-quarters of an hour earlier to return to Goughs Bay.

It had been pitch black outside for over an hour before there was a knock at the back door. Poor old Pip had been wandering along the beach lighting matches, searching for the yellow kayak. With his arms out stretched in front, Pip groped his way back towards the lights of the farmhouse, only to be stopped dead in his tracks by a waist-high, old wooden stump. Even worse was a group of large black bulls that came around to investigate the bearded figure feeling his way across the paddocks.

Cyril offered us beds for the night in the shearers' quarters, which we gratefully accepted.

2 April - Day 58

The southerly didn't ease off until after midday. Although the sky was overcast, I decided on an attempt to reach Flea Bay, eight and a half miles away.

When we were about to leave, Diane gave us some vegetables and a box of beautiful, plump tomatoes from their fabulous garden. Before moving to this farm five years ago, Cyril and Diane farmed at the head of the Rakaia Gorge. Now they were almost self-contained in this idyllic spot, with fresh fruit, vegetables and mutton. Pip and I agreed it would be a great place to settle down.

Out on the beach, Diane showed us an old wooden log which was once the mast of the *Margaret*, a 50 foot long ketch that was wrecked on the beach in 1899. Diane also told us that a whale had cruised into the bay one day and so close into shore that she could see the barnacles on its back.

Overnight the surf had settled. With Pip's help I made a clean exit from the beach. The sea was choppy at times and the grey sea and sky and sheer black cliffs presented an inhospitable picture. Near Redcliff Point I watched the shags circling overhead when suddenly a huge bird dived towards me. It was brown, with a yellow beak and a wide wingspan. Without changing its glide-path the bird flew straight at me. When it was less than 10 feet away I stopped paddling and ducked. With a wingspan of four to five feet and a body length of nearly three feet, the bird took my mind off paddling for quite a while.

From the point along to the narrow entrance of Flea Bay, I encountered steep cliffs with a surging swell and occasional caves. The lumpy sea left little time for admiring the scenery, and I was pleased to escape into the calmer waters of the bay.

By the cliffs on the west side of the bay, a 'fizz' boat seemed to be drifting with no sign of life. I paddled over to investigate. It was moored, and in a nearby cave two skindivers were searching for crayfish. A third wetsuit-clad figure sat ashen-faced on a rocky ledge. He had been seasick on the trip from Akaroa Harbour and didn't feel like diving. The two divers hadn't seen any crays because of poor visibility.

Flea Bay is a mile long but only 400 yards wide. The further up the bay I paddled, the calmer the sea became, until it was like a millpond at its head where a tiny surf was lapping gently onto a grey sandy beach. Pip soon arrived with a lukewarm feed of fish and chips bought in Akaroa. He reckoned the narrow winding road down into the bay was steeper than the swell outside.

"Guess what came out of the sky at me?"

"Seagull shit?" suggested Pip.

From my description of colour and size, we agreed the large bird I had seen may have been a giant petrel or an albatross.

"What colour is a mature albatross?" I asked.

"Albatross colour!" replied Pip.

A Toyota Landcruiser drove up in the last light of the grey evening. We met Francis and Shireen Helps, the owners of the surrounding farmland and Francis told us we could sleep in the nearby shearing shed.

Later we joined them for supper, one of the youngest and most pleasant farm couples I have met. For most of their lives they have lived on Banks Peninsula. Pip and I were impressed by Shireen's beautiful oil paintings of dead trees and tussock found on the peninsula.

3 April - Day 59

Thick clouds were scudding over from the south-west at first light and I wasn't too enthusiastic at the prospect of paddling. All the same I was away by 7am. Pip decided to wait an hour just in case I turned back, before driving around to wait at Birdlings Flat.

The sea was choppy off the entrance to the bay, with a bracing south-westerly to impede progress. Only two miles remained to the Akaroa Harbour entrance and I wasn't looking forward to crossing this as the caution in the *New Zealand Pilot* reads:

> During strong south-westerly winds there is a heavy cross sea at the entrance to Akaroa harbour, with violent baffling squalls caused by the high precipitous nature of the land. There is usually a heavy ground swell here, and loose, bad holding ground.

High above the eastern side of the harbour entrance lay the old Akaroa lighthouse, with a small automatic light close by. To the north bleak farmland and tussock rose up into the cloudbase, while to the south and west, cliffs plunged down into a grey, angry sea. When the lighthouse was manned, Charley Wallace considered its windswept site the bleakest of all New Zealand lighthouses.

The sea was lumpy and I wasn't too happy. Although the crossing of the harbour entrance went without incident, I was pleased to reach Timutimu Head on the west side. The wind had eased slightly, but the sky remained heavily overcast. A mile further on lay the southern most point of the peninsula where the dark forbidding cliffs, over 500 feet high, were pounded at their base by an impressive breaking swell.

By Peraki Bay, the sky to the south-west was ominously black, as though a squall was fast approaching. I put on all the speed I could muster. Where the road wound around the cliffs above Tumbledown Bay, the low grey line of Kaitorete Spit became visible on the horizon.

The black squally sky kept coming closer with visibility reducing fast. Since the distant spit was about to disappear in swirling cloud and mist I pulled out the compass to take a bearing on the houses at Birdlings Flat but luckily, the spit was never hidden completely from view.

Pip and Ben were waiting in front of the houses and here big breakers were thumping heavily onto a steep

Paul making a brew at Flea Bay. Photo: Pip Aplin

gravel beach. This was to be my first taste of the Ninety Mile Beach dumpers. All the way from Banks Peninsula to Timaru the coast consists of a grey shingle beach, dropping quickly down into deep water and guarded by a dumping wave, the size of which depends on the wind direction and state of the sea. This stretch of coastline forms a marked contrast to the gently shelving, golden sandy beaches north of the peninsula.

For several minutes I waited offshore, sizing up the best time to sprint for the beach. Behind one large wave I paddled hard and reached the gravel in the wave's wake. But I was too slow pulling off the spray skirt and leaping out of the cockpit. Pip didn't catch hold of *Isadora's* bow either, for the surge sucked us back into the face of the next wave. Boom! The wave broke with a jarring thump. There was so much force in the wave that the Nordkapp flipped over in a 360 degree roll and ended with the stern facing the beach. This time Pip grabbed the stern and I managed to grab the bow and together we dragged *Isadora* out of the surge.

Pip was a little disillusioned. "I'm never there on time to meet you, and even when I am, I'm no use helping you land."

Whilst Pip was waiting, he had walked over to the nearby houses to ask for some fresh water. An old lady was out weeding her front garden, her cat sitting close by. Ben saw the cat and took off, round and round the house in hot pursuit, barking his head off. Pip was about to walk away in the opposite direction,

ignore Ben and ask for water at another house. However he noticed the lady had taken no notice of the commotion. Hesitantly, he approached her but had to call loudly to attract her attention although he was only a few yards away. The old lady was deaf! Unaware that Ben had chased her cat, she happily obliged Pip with his request for water.

Since Pip's leave was finished and he had to return to Arthurs Pass by evening, I was tempted to forget about paddling for the day. Despite a threatening dark sky to the south, the sea remained reasonably settled. After much indecision I finally decided to try a stint along to Taumutu, 18 miles away at the end of the spit. At least it would be a start on the long stretch down to Timaru.

The teamwork and timing were better for the launch off the beach. Pip pushed *Isadora* into a broken dumper and a short burst of paddling carried me onto the open sea, a clean exit. Less than an hour later a southerly breeze came away, bringing with it a black, squally sky and really choppy sea. I regretted leaving Birdlings Flat.

Kaitorete Spit is a low shingle beach backed by marram grass covered dunes. It forms the southern shore of the broad expanse of Lake Ellesmere. But I could see nothing of the hinterland from the sea, just a featureless grey gravel beach with its inexorable dumpers. Only by the minute hand of my watch could I keep track of my progress, one mile every fifteen minutes, half an hour, two miles and so on.

After three hours I saw Pip and Ben waiting for me

on the beach and they jogged along with me to Taumutu. At 6pm I nosed in fast behind a dumper and Pip caught hold of the bow. A better landing than at lunchtime.

I returned to Christchurch to see Pip off and wait for Paul Dale to drive down from the Pass.

5 April - Day 60

Paul Dale and I were out on the beach by Taumutu not long after dawn. Paul was a handsome brute with a drooping, gringo-like moustache. Born and bred in Southland, he had spent the last few years as a ranger in the Arthurs Pass National Park. As he was a keen skier, conservationist, and always fit, I thought we would make a good team.

The forecast was for fresh north-easterly winds with high cloud increasing during the day. The sea was calm at Taumutu apart from the usual dumpers.

The launching from the beach didn't go smoothly. Before I had the sprayskirt pulled over the cockpit coaming, Paul had pushed *Isadora* into a broken wave. I nearly capsized as the next wave broke for it flipped *Isadora* sideways. After a brief struggle I rolled up and paddled clear of the dumpers, the cockpit half full of the water. Once the sprayskirt was in position I pumped the cockpit dry and turned south into a light south-westerly breeze which veered to the north-west after an hour and tried to push *Isadora* out to sea. Drain pipes through the shingle beach pro- vided the only gauge of progress along to the Rakaia River mouth.

At one stage I was dreaming along when I caught sight of a triangular shaped dorsal fin cutting through the water towards the kayak. Shark! The fin sank lower and lower in the water as the shark approached, to disappear as it passed beneath the Nordkapp. For the next few minutes my head swivelled from side to side, searching tor a reappearance of the shark. Luck- ily it didn't come back for a second look.

I stopped for a brief lunch stop south of the Rakaia River mouth before pushing on south-westwards. I tried to keep myself amused by singing and figuring out my exact position on the map. Mid-afternoon the wind swung to the north-east which made paddling a lot easier.

Paul flashed a mirror from the cliff top by Wakanui Creek and although he was over a mile away my attention was attracted immediately. When I drew level, he managed to swim out in his wetsuit, despite being knocked down by a large dumper. As he clung onto the decklines we agreed to meet again by the Ashburton River mouth. We had a second seaborne meeting there and as the afternoon was so good, I decided to push on to the mouth of the Hinds River.

Just on dusk Paul was waiting with the car's

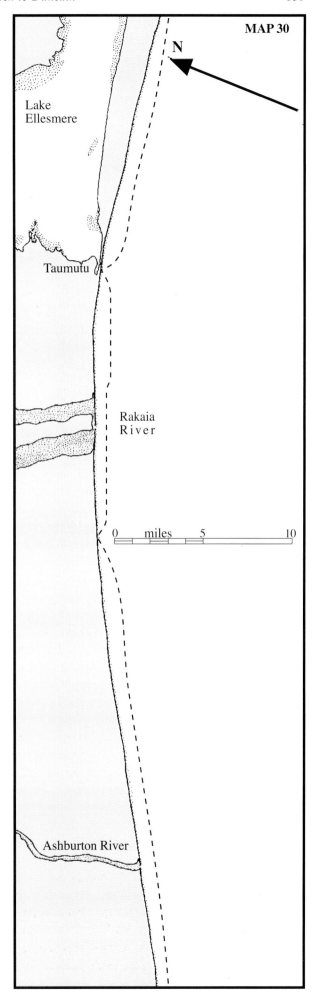

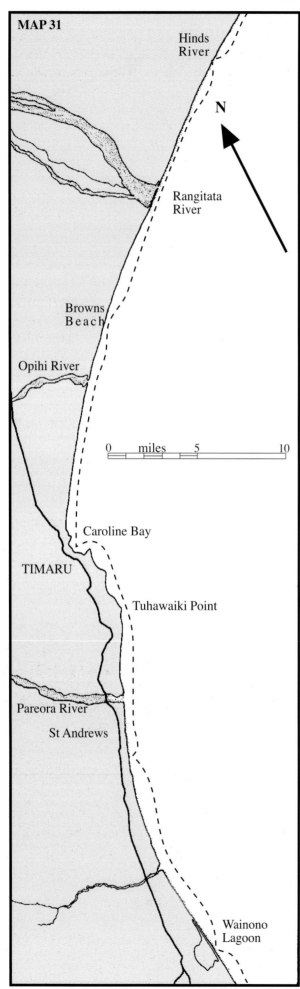

headlights switched on. The sun had set ages ago and
the beach was hard to see. Despite the monotony of
the shoreline it had been a good day, achieving 40
miles closer to Timaru.

A friend of Paul's, Brian Twiss, put us up for the
night at the wee village of fishing huts at the Rangitata
River mouth.

6 April - Day 61
A glorious morning and we were out on the beach in
time to watch the sunrise. By now Paul had developed
an eye for dumpers and the launchings into a large
shore break were being accomplished with ease.

At the Rangitata River mouth Paul and a group of
fishermen were waiting. We exchanged waves and
shouts. A brief break was taken at Browns Beach for
a brew before the long run down to Timaru. The
fishermen had warned me to give the freezing works
outlet, north of Timaru, a wide berth as sharks often
congregated there for easy meals, a seaborne take
away bar.

It was a warm sunny day and for the last hour a light
north-easterly breeze pushed *Isadora* towards the
distant houses of Timaru. Caroline Bay, on the west
side of the long breakwater which forms the harbour
edge, was to be our meeting point. There was no sign
of Paul when I coasted in to the golden sandy beach
at the head of the bay, but he soon arrived with a
thermos of tea and sandwiches which his Aunty had
made for us.

Fifteen minutes later, after I had changed into dry
clothes, a reporter and photographer from *The Timaru
Herald* arrived. They wanted action shots so I had to
climb back into wetsuit, sprayskirt, and lifejacket and
paddle in for a second arrival at Caroline Bay.

Earlier in the day, Paul had asked me if I minded a
little publicity. Apart from the arrival at Christchurch, I had made little or no effort to keep the media
informed of progress. I still had a feeling that publicity on completion of the trip was fine, but that any
earlier announcement of my intention to circumnavi-
gate the South Island would have people thinking I
was a little crazy. I didn't realize however that the
publicity in Christchurch had caught the imagination
of quite a few Canterbury people. In any case my
comment to Paul was, "If you want to keep the press
informed, its up to you. I don't mind one way or the
other." Paul thought publicity would be good for
public relations and would let people know I was
coming.

At least the reporter from *The Timaru Herald* had
a sense of humour. The photograph which appeared
in the newspaper showed Paul, myself and a third
chap who had walked over as we carried the kayak up
the beach. This chap walked up to me, shook my

hand, and as he raised his arm to describe something, the photographer snapped a photo. The title above the photograph read: 'Which way to Oamaru?' and the caption below read: 'Oamaru... certainly gentlemen. Just go back out there into the bay, turn right at the harbour, and its fifty miles on down the coast.'

While I chatted to the photographer, Paul told the reporter a few stories which I didn't hear: 'Mr. Dale said he had been observing the progress through binoculars, and on occasions he had seen sharks within three metres of the kayak. Only his laundress will know the true extent of his fright, he commented.'

When the reporter departed I was champing at the bit, all set to push on towards Oamaru, but Paul wanted to make a quick visit to the local radio station. Much arm twisting followed but it was only after a promise from Paul that there were numerous beautiful ladies just dying to meet me that I relented. I was then whisked straight to the broadcasting studio for a brief chat with the announcer.

After the bustle of the city, I was happy to escape out to sea again and paddled out of Caroline Bay at 3pm. A large cruise ship, the *Australis,* was tied up in the harbour awaiting delivery to a new owner in the United States. On the end of the harbour breakwater were several parked cars and a group of waiting people.

One woman really moved me when she wished me a safe journey and I had a special wave for an elderly lady who had to be helped out of a car to watch the yellow kayak go past. Two chaps cruised out of the harbour in a 'fizz' boat to wish me well! I could hardly believe the response from those few people after the few minutes on air at Radio Caroline Bay. It certainly changed my attitude towards the media and made the trip seem so much more worthwhile and important to finish. That people regarded the trip with sufficient interest to wish me well, gave my enthusiasm and motivation a great boost.

Paul was waiting at Scarborough and he indicated by vigorous arm movements that waves were breaking a long way out off Tuhawaiki Point. Here the north-easterly was strong and the skeg had to be released before *Isadora* would turn seawards to miss the breakers. In front of the Pareora freezing works Paul flashed the mirror, but the noise of the dumpers was too loud to allow shouted conversation so I landed. I spent only minutes on shore, enough time to say, "I'll hammer on for another hour." By the outlet of the freezing works, hundreds of sea birds, black-backed gulls, red-billed and black-billed seagulls were floating on the sea with a few hovering above the outlet.

Which way to Oamaru? Photo: Bremford Studios

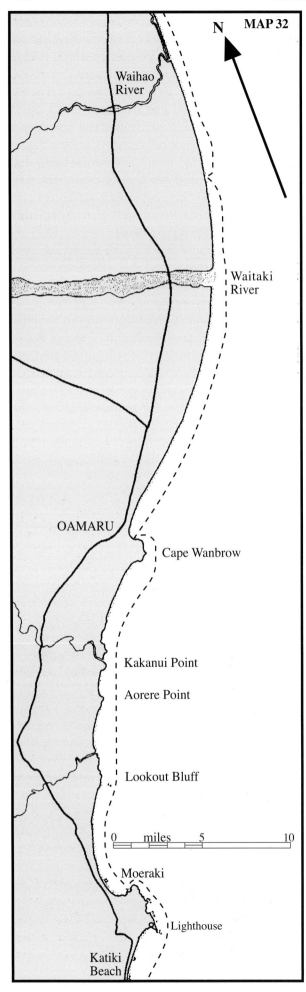

On the south side of the outlet, I paddled into large areas of an oily scum, littered with small, evil smelling, greasy fat globules. The smell was so bad that I made a conscious effort to keep my hands out of the water. The smell and scum persisted for over half a mile, and was the worst sea pollution I had so far encountered around the South Island. When it was almost too dark to see the shore I landed, and set out for the main road, having left *Isadora* secure on top of the gravel beach. Paul picked me up from the side of the road half an hour later. He had been waiting a mile further south. The tally for the day was an incredible 43 miles. We spent the night in Timaru with two keen paddlers, Adrian and Anne Higgins.

7 April - Day 62
Into the dumpers at 7.15am, just after sunrise with a clear sky, calm sea and no wind. There were very few features along the gravel beach, so I was happy to find Paul waiting by Wainono Lagoon to tell me where I was. For the first time I paddled by a group of swans on the sea, and not long after a fin in the surf gave me a fright. However there was no cause for alarm, it was a friendly old seal at play.

At the end of Ryans Road Paul waited with lunch, a delicious treat of strawberries. Our next meeting spot would be the Waitaki River mouth. Little did we know it would take three days to reach there.

Only minutes after I left the shingle beach, the north-easterly breeze died away to be replaced after a brief lull by a southerly. Rapidly, the wind picked up until it was blowing between 15 and 20 knots, creating whitecaps and a horrible chop. Speed into the whitecaps became slower and slower. The gravel cliff behind the beach had been growing in height until it was now over 40 feet high and there were very few places where it would be possible to scale the cliff.

Slogging into the whitecaps knocked the stuffing out of me, until finally I'd had enough. Spotting a slip against the cliff, which appeared feasible to climb, I landed. The beaching occurred without incident but upon leaving the cockpit I tripped into the surge and *Isadora* nearly disappeared into the next dumper.

The slip wasn't high enough for me to reach the cliff top, but I achieved my goal by climbing a drain outlet that had cut a vertical groove down the gravel face.

A farmer was moving sheep in a distant paddock and as a bedraggled wetsuit clad kayaker approached, he said, "I bet I know who you are. You're the lone paddler!" Paul had been right about the publicity. At least people knew I was coming.

Sid Blair asked me back to his farmhouse for a cup of tea and offered to drive around to the Waitaki River mouth where Paul was waiting. When we arrived there, the V.W. was parked, but of Paul and Ben there was no trace. I jogged along the cliff top to the north for a mile and was about to give up the search when a white object caught my eye. It turned out to be Paul asleep on the grass, by the edge of a 40 foot drop onto the gravel beach below, the binoculars around his neck and Ben snuggled up beside him, also asleep. The faithful, vigilant support crew were both well away in the land of nod. It seemed a pity to disturb their slumber, but I woke them and kidded Paul about his watchfulness. "Well, I was keeping watch from the edge of the cliff," he answered, "and I just dropped off."

That evening, Sid's wife Margaret cooked a mighty meal and we spent the night in a caravan by the house. Their farm, 'Walton Park', 600 acres in area, was irrigated with water from the Waitaki River. One of the stockyard railings, a 22 foot long beam, was washed up on the gravel beach in front of the farm a month after the *Manuka* was wrecked on the Otago coastline in 1929. The prevailing north-easterly current of the east coast had carried some of the wreckage this far north.

Beneath the pine trees and in sheds around the farm, Sid had a marvellous collection of old drays, tractors, ploughs and other farm implements. Sid was like me when it came to throwing out old equipment that had given faithful service. It's too good to junk and maybe someday a use could be found.

Low cloud, drizzle, poor visibility and strong south-westerly breezes set in for the next two days which became involuntary rest days. We stayed with some of Paul's friends, the Plunkets, in Oamaru. A couple who developed a taste for port, were mad keen on bridge and made us feel completely at home.

10 April - Day 63
At Walton Park, Sid joined us for the quick trip out to the cliff top. There he tied a rope around a fence-post, enabling us to slide down to the beach.

Patches of cloud, a moderate swell and a light north-easterly breeze, the day looked promising, just the old familiar, large pounding dumper to batter through. Timing would be critical to avoid a bone jarring, early morning wash. The beach consisted of a steep face of loose gravel and sand and in the aftermath of each dumper, a strong surge sucked gravel and foam noisily back into the face of the next wave. This morning, after two days of southerlies, large waves were rearing up to six feet or more before thumping like a ton of bricks onto the beach. How to feel sick in the stomach without really trying?

On top of the beach, I climbed into the cockpit, pulled the sprayskirt over the cockpit coaming, locked legs and feet into position, then nodded grimly to Paul. Dressed only in his underpants, Paul hung onto *Isadora's* stern, easing the Nordkapp down the short steep gravel face into the surge. Here we waited until a really large dumper had just broken. "Now!" I shouted. Paul gave the stern a mighty shove into the surging broken water, and then had to sprint back up the beach to avoid being caught. Yet another good launching - what teamwork!

Paul was going to wait by the Waitaki mouth to see *Isadora* safely past, and the planned lunch stop would be at Oamaru Harbour. Apart from a break where the Waitaki flowed into the sea, the coastal cliff continued uninterrupted to Oamaru giving me no chance of admiring the inland scenery. A mysterious looking object off the Waitaki mouth had me intrigued. It had four spines or rods poking skywards but it wasn't a mine, only a dead sheep floating with its legs upright. Nothing like being welcomed into Otago waters by a floating object with a sheepish grin on its waterlogged face.

At midday, I paddled in between the stone breakwaters that form the entrance to Oamaru Harbour, and headed to where Paul flashed the mirror. Sid Blair called in after dropping off a load of sheep at the freezing works, and the Plunkets came down to see the kayak. Paul cooked a scrumptious meal of fried mushrooms and bananas on the primus.

Less than an hour later, I headed out of the harbour to make the most of a moderate north-easterly breeze. I paddled into the chop and gave the reefs off Cape Wanbrow a wide berth, then turned south westwards. Paul flashed the mirror from Kakanui Point, also from Aorere Point where the surf was breaking a long way out. It was comforting to know that Paul was following my progress closely, just in case something did happen.

Isadora surfed occasionally in front of the chop, the skeg holding well, but my arms and shoulders felt really tired. From Lookout Bluff, where Paul signalled again, I headed directly for Moeraki Point, staying two miles out from shore where the famous boulders lie. At 5.15pm I came in through a fleet of anchored fishing boats to land just as the sun set. My shoulders really ached but Paul had a reviving brew waiting - 42 miles covered for the day.

Even before I had time to take off the sprayskirt, a local fisherman, John Kedzlie, walked over and introduced himself. He and his family had spotted the kayak out beyond the breakwater and followed my progress to shore. John didn't waste time with idle chatter. "Would you like a feed and a hot shower?" Both Paul and I were speechless. This Otago hospitality was pretty good. We quickly recovered the use of our vocal chords and gratefully accepted his kind offer.

John and his wife Jenny lived on the hill above the fishing fleet. A commanding view of the sea and the small Moeraki harbour was gained from their living room. For dessert, Jenny served up a fantastic pavlova left from the previous night when a couple had failed to arrive for dinner. I related the story of Lyn Taylor and the pavlova at New Brighton.

John was president of the Moeraki Fishermen's Association, and owned a 30 foot long fishing boat called *Manta Ray*, which had a plywood hull covered with fibreglass sheathing. Once the crayfishing season was over, he fished for blue cod and moki. Recently, John had tried night fishing for squid. Considering the Japanese demand for squid, he felt it was well worth a try. The squid can squirt a black inky fluid up to 30 feet once they are pulled out of the water. "Boat and crew often end up a frightful mess. One morning, a chap had six inches of the horrible stuff in his gumboot," John told us .

A special concessionaire for taking smaller crayfish (a five inch long tail instead of the normal six inches) applied between the Waitaki River mouth and the Nuggets, from the 20 June to 19 December. When John first started crayfishing from Moeraki, there were four crayfishing boats, now there were 30.

The small harbour at Moeraki lies in the lee of a three mile long rocky peninsula, with Katiki Point and the Moeraki lighthouse at the southern end and the 60 foot high bluffs of Moeraki Point at the northern end. A jetty-cum-breakwater was built out from the shore some 104 years ago, for Moeraki served as the site for a whaling station in the early days. Although the headland and breakwater protect the anchored fishing boats from easterly and southerly winds, there is no protection from the north-westerlies. In August 1975, a gale force nor-wester sprang up in the early hours of the morning and the Kedzlie family had to abandon their house at 4am. *Manta Ray* dragged her moorings at the height of the gale and by first light lay stranded on the beach, the hull full of water. The repairs cost $5,500.

Other fishermen had not been as fortunate as John. Since 1963, two fishing vessels had broken from their moorings during bad weather, and become total wrecks after being driven ashore. The first recorded wreck on the Otago coastline occurred at Moeraki in July, 1837 when a whaling industry supply vessel, the *Sydney Packet*, was driven ashore in a gale after breaking loose from her moorings. The schooner became a total wreck.

John gave me valuable advice on the next stage down to Karitane where he suggested I get in touch with another fisherman for advice on rounding Otago Peninsula. He marked on my map the position of Danger Reef, off Shag Point, and suggested a cautious approach to this area.

11 April - Day 64

Before sunrise, Paul, Jenny and her two children walked down to the beach to watch *Isadora* glide out through the moored fishing boats. John was already at sea, having set off in the early hours to seek the elusive squid.

Sticking carefully to John's instructions, I passed through the reefs off Moeraki Point and pointed the bow to the south. The Moeraki lighthouse, which is now automatic, stood on top of a gently rounded headland. As I glided by, half a mile offshore, the early morning sunlight must have reflected on the light's lenses for it appeared as though the light was suddenly switched on, a bright flash of light casting a silver trail across the glassy sea.

From this headland, I made a beeline for Shag Point, remaining two miles off shore from the gentle curve of Katiki Beach. Paul was waiting on the rocks above a natural boat harbour on the tip of Shag Point. A narrow entrance between low rocky bluffs led into the tiny sheltered harbour, choked with thick waving brown strands of bull kelp. The paddle blade wasn't pushing against the water but an intertwined mass of kelp. Paul threw a packet of sandwiches out to me and said there was ample room to pass between the shore and the waves breaking over Danger Reef. Our next meeting point would be at Karitane, over the bar of the Waikouaiti River.

Sure enough, Danger Reef slipped by on my left uneventfully, but it soon became apparent that it would be impossible to stay on a straight course. To the south, beds of bull kelp grew thicker and thicker. At first following narrow leads through the brown matted kelp beds, like a ship passing through pack ice, was a novelty. Seagulls were standing on top of the kelp, it was so thick. There was no sign of open water, either closer in to shore or further out to sea. When the leads closed off there was no option but to pick up speed and ram the bow into the kelp.

Isadora slid only a few yards before losing momentum and stopping. Like the gondoliers of Venice I used the paddle as a pole to push through to another lead. Numerous times the skeg had to be released, otherwise it acted like a brake. I'd had enough of kelp by the time I finally reached clear water off Cornish Head for my arms ached from the awkward poling movements.

Although it was low tide, the Waikouaiti River bar was easy to negotiate, with small waves breaking continuously. Paul and I found where Dave Cooper (the fisherman John Kedzlie had told us to get in touch with) lived. Dave didn't think there would be any problems on the paddle over to the entrance of

Otago Harbour. He pointed out Heyward Point, about one mile west of the entrance, but it was barely visible through the afternoon haze. Dave cooked a meal for us and, with two friends came down to the bar when it was time to push on. John and Dave, the two Otago fishermen we met, were most helpful with their useful advice and hospitality.

Instead of following the coast from Karitane along to the start of Otago Peninsula, I set off directly for Heyward Point which would save a few miles but involved my staying over four miles offshore. A moderate north-easterly was blowing, no longer from astern but now from the beam as my course was south-easterly. To correct for sideways drift, caused by the wind and chop, I aimed for a point, a mile north of Heyward Point. The lighthouse on Taiaroa Head, lying on the eastern side of the entrance to Otago harbour, became visible after an hour's steady paddling.

A large red-hulled coastal trading ship cruised out of the entrance as I neared Spit Beach. Paul was waiting on the stone breakwater, or mole, that forms the western side of the port's entrance and at 5.15pm after a long ride through a moderate surf I landed on a sandy beach next to the mole. Another 35 miles paddle lay astern.

12 April - Day 65
7.15am and I was underway. A moderate north-easterly, with its associated swell and large chop, bucked *Isadora* round considerably and it grew even rougher as I crossed the harbour entrance towards Taiaroa Head. The combination of an ebbing tide from the extensive area of the harbour, meeting the north-east swell and chop, was building a rough lumpy sea. The old familiar symptoms of running scared, dry mouth, pulse racing, body tense and a sick feeling in the pit of my stomach, were very much with me.

Although the sea was the worst it had been since leaving Christchurch, I didn't consider turning back to Spit Beach. A few of the swell crests broke over the Nordkapp before Taiaroa Head lay astern and the sheer, rugged, black cliffs to the south-east, shrouded in white spray, didn't exactly inspire any confidence.

In the sea, just below the surface, were large rounded masses of tiny moving squid-like organisms, brilliant red in colour with tiny black eyes. They had to be some form of krill.

Still absorbed in watching the clumps of krill drift by, I looked up and was startled by the spectacle in front and out to sea. It was as though someone had switched on hundreds of small fountains, all squirting jets of water up to three feet into the air. At first, I thought it was a mob of spouting killer whales, but

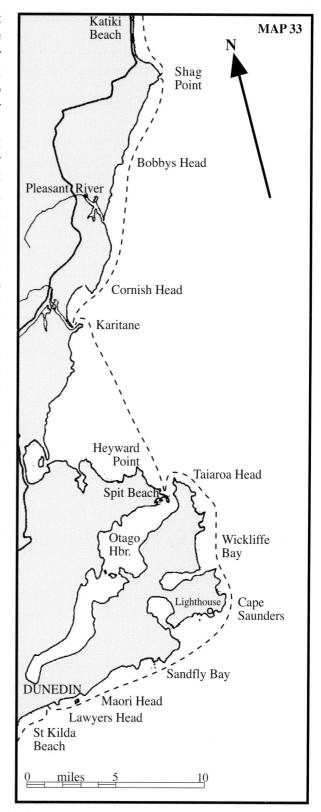

decided they were some sort of large squid 'letting off steam.' The squirts of water died away as *Isadora* approached and all that was visible of the beasts above water were dirty yellow, funnel shapes about two inches in diameter.

Off Wickliffe Bay, I decided to put into shore if the sea grew any rougher. But Cape Saunders was only three miles away; there the coast swung to the west which should allow shelter in its lee from the north-easterly. With that in mind, I headed for the cape. Fortunately, the whitecaps vanished and the sea lost some of its lumpiness by the 300 foot high cliffs of the cape. Initially, there was no sign of the lighthouse, but it soon came into view on the next steep point around to the west. I hoped to land near the light and meet the keeper, Warren Russel, but it wasn't to be. A figure waved from a house near the light-tower and I signalled that I would head into the lee of the point.

Warren climbed down through grey rocky bluffs, but there wasn't a hope of landing for the swell was rising and falling three to four feet over the kelp bedraggled rock walls. I nosed in towards a shelf but decided it wasn't worth chancing a landing in the surge. We carried on a shouted conversation over the noise of the surge.

Moments before, Paul had rung Warren asking if he had seen the lone paddler pass by. It was tinny timing for when Warren looked out through the window there was the yellow Nordkapp rounding Cape Saunders.

Progress westward became easier, for in the lee of Otago Peninsula, the chop and swell eased noticeably. A large surf was booming into Sandfly Bay and I hoped it wouldn't be like that closer to Dunedin. Inside Bird Island, the swell pattern was broken and although the sea was lumpy, only small breakers drifted into the sandy beach. It was extremely tempting to go in for it looked easy, but there was no sign of Paul.

A mirror flashed from the top of Lawyers Head - Paul had spotted me. Rather reluctant to leave a good landing astern I pushed on to the start of St. Kilda Beach. By the smell of the water off Lawyers Head, it had to be the sewerage outlet.

Any thought of landing through a large smoking surf off St. Kilda beach vanished as soon as I rounded the head. It was too big and breaking far out from shore. 'It'll have to be the St. Clair Beach now,' I decided.

Halfway along the beach, the mirror began flashing from in front of the St. Kilda surf club. 'You must be joking if you think I'm coming in here, mate,' I thought. But the flashes persisted. Presuming there must be some reason for it, I reluctantly turned the bow in towards the breakers. For a minute or so, I studied the patterns of the sets of waves, before paddling hard behind one large wave. Two succeeding waves carried *Isadora* in sideways, walls of broken water almost over my head. Smaller waves, closer to the sandy beach, enabled me to surf in front of them and reach the shore in the upright position.

The reason for all the signalling? Two television crews, a press reporter, photographer and a radio reporter all waiting on the beach. I had been conned into making a spectacular landing for them!

Surfing into St Kilda Beach, Dunedin. Photo: Otago Daily Times

Chapter 15

DUNEDIN to PORPOISE BAY

A brief excursion on the back of a motor bike into the hustle and bustle of Dunedin to cash a cheque, was almost frightening. My nose, so used to the tang of salt spray and fresh air, felt assailed by the harsh city smells. With the frantic pace of the hurrying shoppers, the budding dragsters at the traffic lights, and people too busy to chat, it was all a bit much to take. Once again I was pleased to escape out to sea, to rejoin a more natural life rhythm, governed not so much by a clock, but by the rise and fall of the sun, where each day was a high point, brought to a close by sunset.

The evening's objective was the Taieri Mouth where a small fleet of fishing boats moored in the river. Since it lay 18 miles to the south, it would be a race against the onset of darkness. The sea appeared calm out beyond the surf, with a hazy blue sky and the faintest of breezes to ruffle the water.

Low tide had come and gone. As the tide came in, the surf picked up in size, large enough for *Isadora* to become airborne over one steep wave crest on the way out. Beyond the breakers, I waved to the distant figure of Paul on the beach and turned the bow in the direction of Brighton, a small seaside resort. By the dark oppressive cliffs beneath Black Head, I turned away from shore to pass close by the scrub-covered

rock of Green Island. The coastline curved considerably down towards the mouth of the Taieri River so to save a few miles paddle I took a direct line rather than hug the coast. The river mouth was difficult to make out on the fuzzy distant coastline. Only when the small blob of Taieri Island, 102 feet high and a mile out from the river, came into view, could I pinpoint its location. A fishing boat, far out at sea, was heading for the same destination but at twice my speed and would arrive while it was still light. At my steady four knots, the chance of reaching the mouth before dark seemed to be fading as fast as the light was. Even so, I put on the power and pushed on as fast as possible with long steady strokes of the paddle.

Glancing frequently into shore, I hoped to see Paul before reaching the bar so he could guide me in. The fishing boat, now over a mile in front, had already entered the waves breaking over the bar. I watched its progress, my eyes straining to see if there was a calm passage into the river. Between Taieri Island and the shore lay a continuous line of breakers. The view from my position low on the water, was disquieting, to say the least.

The sun had long since set when, finally, I reached the first of the waves breaking over the bar. Fortunately, Paul signalled from shore with the car's head

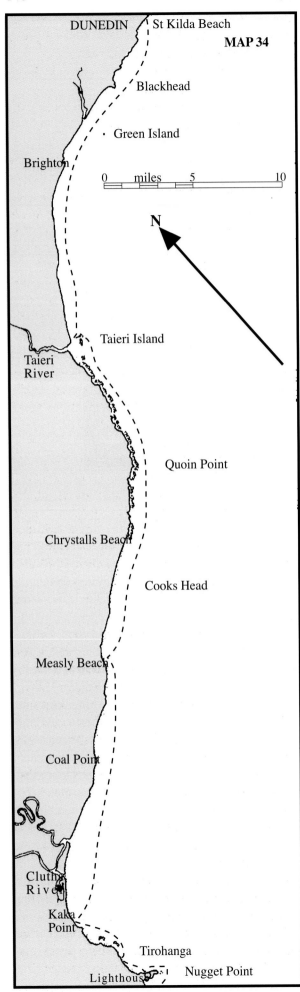

lights and I surfed into a sandy beach by the edge of
the bar. Paul told me that the bar, two or three
breakers deep, was working right across to the island.
Paddling through them in the poor light would have
been bad news.

At a wharf a short way upstream in the Taieri River
we chatted to a couple who were unloading crates of
the day's catch from their fishing boat. The fisherman
said that although there should be no problems to
watch out for down to Nugget Point, landing along
the coast would be rather difficult.

Alison Carpenter at nearby Lake Waihola, put us
up for the night, and cooked us a scrumptious meal
but we drank too much port, as usual.

13 April - Day 66

As we drove down the hill to Taieri Mouth, the sun
rose slowly out of the sea, its soft light casting a
golden glow over sea and sky. Despite this promise of
a fine day, the sky had clouded over by the time Paul
shoved *Isadora* into the surf. A light northerly breeze
began stirring the lupins and marram grass on the
dunes behind the beach. From here, Paul would drive
down to the Tokomairiro River mouth, some 16 miles
paddle away, as the seagull flies.

Once beyond the surf, I paddled due east to avoid
the breakers on the bar, until level with Taieri Island.
There I pointed the bow southwards with the 'wind
up my chuff,' as my diary noted. A white-hulled
fishing boat caught up off the island and the skipper
of the *Quest* said the sea was pretty good. Although
a southerly change was forecast, he didn't think it
would arrive until next day.

A large surf was working over the reef-fringed
coastline along to Quoin Point with farmland rising
up gently to the skyline behind, broken only by
patches of scrub. Several seals were resting on ledges
out of reach of the surge on the low rocky projection.
It was near here that I first encountered a large flock
of sooty shearwaters, brown in colour and better
known as mutton-birds. Up till now, an occasional
solitary bird had soared by the kayak, its wing tips
missing the wave crests by a hairsbreadth. Of all the
birds I had seen at sea, the sooty shearwater was the
most graceful in flight. A huge mob of birds, number-
ing well into the hundreds, sat quietly on the sea in
Isadora's path. The arrival of the kayak did not cause
the great disturbance I expected. Rather than take off
in scared flight, the birds moved only when the bow
was less than a yard away. Paddling out of the way
with swift strokes of their webbed feet or taking
briefly to the air, they were a very orderly group that
would put an English football crowd to shame.

During the morning's paddle, there were only two
feasible landing places, Watsons Beach and the end

of Bull Creek Road, both small bays reasonably protected from the swell and wind by rocky points on each side of them.

My head was throbbing from the ravages of a mild hangover, not helped by a general state of overtiredness. This would be the fourth consecutive day of paddling since passing Oamaru. As for the hangover, it could be easily remedied. The lust to port would have to taper off. However on this particular morning, it was more of a list to port than a lust. My stomach felt ready to feed the fishes as the Nordkapp approached the northern end of Chrystalls Beach, a beautiful stretch of sandy shoreline extending down to the Toko Mouth. Splashing cold sea water onto my face provided temporary relief from the nausea.

Paul flashed the headlights from the road behind Chrystalls Beach, but the sight of a large surf pounding onto the sand dispelled any thought of landing. Paul walked down the beach wearing his wetsuit and carrying a pair of flippers. 'It won't be easy swimming out,' I thought, and it was in fact quite a battle, for eight or nine minutes passed before Paul battered his way out through the buffeting of the surf. When he finally came into sight outside the last breaking wave, I'm sure we were both relieved. The second member of the support crew wasn't too happy, however. Poor old Ben, sitting forlornly on the beach, thought he had been abandoned.

Paul had some very pleasant surprises attached by a piece of rope around his neck; a thermos of hot sweet tea, the next plastic-coated map of the coastline to the south, a sealed plastic bag containing a packet of vanilla creams and .... a bag of minties. What a treat! While I savoured the refreshing delight of the tea (the recuperative powers of hot sweet tea on tired muscles and low spirits, never ceases to amaze me) Paul suggested pushing on southwards until he found a good landing.

Before resuming paddling, I waited until Paul staggered out of the surf onto terra firma, where Ben eagerly awaited his return. A mile and a half down the beach was a solitary, very conspicuous rock, 78 feet high, which poked out of the otherwise flat, sandy beach. It is named Cooks Head. The fishing boat *Quest* cruised by, dragging a trawl net back in the direction of Taieri Mouth. "Watch out for the trawl wires," called the skipper as I approached, for the thin taut wires cutting through the water behind the stern, were not easy to see. "You've got 16 nautical miles to go to the Nuggets," he called. About four hour's paddle provided the southerly change didn't arrive early.

At the meeting point off Tokomairiro River mouth the continuous line of waves breaking over the offshore submerged reefs dispelled any hope of landing.

However I had no trouble landing through a small surf off Measly Beach where an offshore reef gave a little protection in its lee from the swell.

While I recharged my energy reserves with lunch Paul took the Nordkapp out for a paddle just to see what this sea cruising was all about. He cleared the breakers all right but on the choppy sea beyond was soon upside down. The offshore northerly breeze began pushing *Isadora* out to sea so I smartly fetched the flippers from the car and waded out to lend Paul a hand.

The situation bore some similarity to the yarn about the two elderly chaps who operated a kayak hire service on the shores of a small lake. One chap looked at his watch and calls out, "Come in number 99, your time's up." A minute goes by with no sign of response from the kayak. Again he calls out, "Number 99, your time's up, come in straight away." His aged companion frowns and contemplates, "If we only have 70 kayaks, there can't be a number 99 kayak." The first chap thinks for a moment, then turns his head on its side, strains his eyes, and calls out, "Number 66, are you in trouble?" Paul wasn't really in trouble for he was making headway in towards the shore. When I reached him, we tipped the water out of the cockpit and towed *Isadora* into the beach. At this stage of the trip, I would have been most upset to see *Isadora* disappearing out to sea on her own.

By the time I reached the open sea again, the northerly breeze had come away strongly, creating quite a horrible chop offshore. It was a real slog paddling out into the chop before a turn to the southwest could be effected. Immediately behind the beach a gravel coastal road allowed Paul to keep a close eye on progress and we exchanged waves at Mitchell Rocks.

Isadora made fast progress, aided by the following wind, and my lunch-revitalized energy reserves. But off Smiths Beach, the northerly wind suddenly died. In the brief lull that followed, I anticipated what was coming. 'Here we go,' I thought, 'I bet that southerly change comes through.' By now I always expected the worst when the wind suddenly dropped. A gradual fall away in wind speed usually meant a few hours with no wind at all, but a brief lull following a sudden drop meant a strong wind change. Sure enough a stiff south-westerly wind came away, strong enough to kick up whitecaps and to whip spray off the wave crests. *Isadora*, bucking into the chop, was scarcely making headway.

Dear diary: 'Started to head into shore to escape from the chop but had quite a fight to reach Coal Point. Looked for a landing; nothing but offshore reefs and a large surf. Further along, I again tried putting in towards shore where a short section of sandy beach lay beneath the cliffed shoreline. But when two steep waves came through, spray flying off their crests, I turned out to sea. No sign of Paul either. Decided to look around the next point, down to the mouth of the Clutha River. Made slow progress, paddling directly into the wind. Made it around this next rocky point only to see a large surf smoking into a long sandy beach. Way over in the distance I could see Kaka Point which was our evening meeting place. Still a strong chop but I made gradual progress with long, slow, steady strokes. The rocky headland of Nugget Point was clearly visible and I could see the light shining out from the lighthouse there.'

The hinterland behind the Clutha River mouth was low with no hills or conspicuous features. To save a few mile's paddle, I took a direct line for the tiny houses of the distant Kaka Point township, but less than half way across, a south-westerly squall came through, bringing with it cold rain and a fall in visibility. A big mob of sooty shearwaters scooted towards me, only inches above the surface of the sea. Their fast flight was impressive, a few quick wing thrusts, a long period of low soaring flight then a few more rapid wing thrusts.

At least the rain of the squall knocked the waves down, for the whitecaps soon disappeared leaving a short steep chop. With only four miles remaining to Kaka Point, another squall approached. Darker and thicker than the preceding one, it was obvious that the cloud and misty rain were about to hide all sight of land. I took a compass bearing onto the township just in time before the visibility went completely.

For the next 20 minutes I steered by the compass to finally emerge out of the squall still on course for Kaka Point. Headlights flashed from near a church. I landed through a moderate surf, relieved to be ashore, but feeling cold and exhausted after the long slog into the headwind. Paul suggested using the last hour before dark to paddle along to the breakwater and boat landing at Tirohanga, two miles from the tip of Nugget Point.

Rather reluctantly, I put out to sea once more only to pull in at Short Bay, two miles short of Tirohanga, too tired and dispirited to continue. Thirty four miles paddle for the day.

The local postmistress and her husband drove up and asked us back to their home for a meal and a hot shower, but we had to decline. Paul had earlier rung the Nugget Point lighthouse keeper, and Eddy and Greta Norris, good friends of both Pip Aplin and Charley Wallace, had invited us up to the lighthouse for the evening.

My hands still hadn't thawed out by the time we arrived at the isolated house on the hill above Nugget Point. My handshake in greeting Eddy was numb and rather limp, not the bone crushing grasp that it should

have been after all the paddling. "You need a hot bath before anything else," declared Eddy and ushered me into the bathroom. Visibility in the bathroom, where I lay luxuriating in the steaming hot water, was soon worse than that of the afternoon's squall. With neatly trimmed beard and straight hair, both turning grey, Eddy had a distinguished look about him but still retained youthful features. His unshifting gaze and speech suggested a quality of steadiness that would be important for this isolated and vital job of light house keeping. His wit matched the colour of his hair, quicksilver. From the moment we arrived, Eddy was forever trying to pull our legs.

In contrast, his wife Greta, of slight build, with short fair hair, spoke softly but warmly and through our conversation showed a strong affinity for nature.

Eddy started working with the light service at the Cuvier Island lighthouse, only four months after marrying Greta. Three years later they moved to Puysegur Point for two years. At Puysegur, fresh food and the mail came in once every three weeks by amphibian, and often in bad weather the plane was delayed. It was in the days when helicopter venison recovery had just started. Since the three light-keepers and their families supplemented their meals with venison when the fresh food ran out, they weren't very happy when the first deer hunting helicopter landed at Puysegur Point. The pilot and shooter were told in no uncertain terms to keep well away from the vicinity of the lighthouse because of the families' reliance on fresh deer meat.

Less than a week later, another chopper flew over and appeared to be preparing to land. Eddy, the other two light-keepers and a relieving keeper, went out with their rifles (all 303s), fired off shots, leapt in the air, yelled and gesticulated for the chopper to 'clear off.' Despite the obvious hostile reception waiting on the ground, the chopper landed. Two white-uniformed naval officers, with peaked caps and scrambled eggs covering their shoulders, stepped out of the bubble. They explained that they were from the government survey ship, the *Lachlan,* to do some survey work onshore. "We thought you were someone else," explained the sheepish lighthouse keepers. The poor naval officers must have thought the four men were all a little 'light happy' or had been too long away from civilization. A two year stint at the Farewell Spit lighthouse followed, after which Eddy and Greta moved to Nugget Point where they had been for the last seven and a half years.

Greta told us it was lucky we hadn't arrived the previous evening for most likely the reception would not have been as friendly. It had not been a good day. In the morning Eddy injured himself by falling through a rotten log onto a stump. At lunchtime he parked the truck outside the house, but later when he came out, there was no sign of the vehicle. Eddy asked Greta if she had moved the truck, but she hadn't. The house is situated on top of a headland, some 400 feet above sea level, with steep slopes and cliffs all around, and a steep, winding, gravel approach road. Eddy started searching, and 400 yards down the road he found the truck facing up towards the house and sporting a burst tyre and superficial body damage. The brakes must have failed. From the car park the truck had rolled down cross country to crash into a road cutting, where fortunately it stopped. If it had rolled another 15 yards, nothing but the sea-bed would have stopped its descent. Incredibly, Eddy managed to drive the truck to town for repairs. It is not hard to imagine what sort of mood he was in by evening.

A 100 yards from the house was a building containing Eddy's weather office, a kitchen, bathroom and bedroom. These facilities were used by the relieving keeper, when the Norris family took their annual holiday. Eddy led us there and we spent a most comfortable night.

14 April - Day 67

Eddy woke us at 6am, when he came to send out the first weather situation for the day. At three hourly intervals from 6am to 6pm, he sent out barometric pressure, air temperature, wind speed and direction. The meteorological service received situations from all over New Zealand and built up a weather map and forecasts.

The equipment in Eddy's office provided a far more accurate picture of the weather situation than did our usual look at the sky and wet finger held up to feel the wind speed and direction. The anemometer registered a 14 to 15 knot wind from the west-south-west direction, the sea was flat and calm. However the forecast from the Met. Office in Dunedin, at Momona airport, wasn't very hopeful for kayaking: 'Winds 20 to 30 knots from the south-west, squalls, and moderate to rough seas.'

After breakfast we returned to the weather office. The wind had veered to the north-west, blowing at 11 to 12 knots. It was tempting to try to paddle round Nugget Point. To determine what was happening further to the south, Eddy rang the lighthouse keeper on Dog Island in Foveaux Strait. There, a south westerly had freshened during the last half hour. As a final check, Eddy rang the Met. Office at the Invercargill airport, and the same forecast was repeated. Overnight, the barograph had shown a gradual drop in barometric pressure and everything pointed towards a deterioration of the weather, so we decided to accompany Eddy on his morning walk out to switch off the light.

A steep-sided ridge to which windswept vegetation clung precariously, led out to the light. A graded track, cut into its northern slope, dropped down to a shallow saddle then climbed the narrow ridge to the light. Sturdy, chest-high fences on each side of the

On the beach at Tirohanga with Eddy Norris and his two sons. Photo: Paul Dale

track prevented Eddy from being blown away on blustery days. In front of the 31 foot high light-tower, steep grey bluffs dropped away to the sea surging 250 feet below.

Off the tip of the point are the Nuggets, eight or so large sea stacks or rocky islands with bare cliffs uncluttered by vegetation. These islands extend out to sea for almost half a mile surrounded by several smaller exposed rocks. The *New Zealand Pilot* notes:

> Off Nugget point, a north-east-going current attaining a rate of one to two knots, may be experienced.

It was fortunate that I heeded Eddy's advice and did not attempt to paddle round the point, for the Met. Office were spot on with their forecast. By the time we climbed up to the light the gentle north-westerly breeze was dying. To the south-west, grey misty squalls blotted out the coastline and horizon. Streaky bands on the water announced the impending arrival of the wind. Moments later it was there, a strong south-westerly, bringing with it rain, and not long after, whitecaps on the surface of the sea. Sheltering inside the tower, we listened as Eddy explained how the light operated. Instead of the usual bull's-eye lens, the Nugget Point light had a drum lens which threw out a sheet of light, up to 22 miles offshore. The light first shone out in July 1870 and had a 12 second sequence, a two second flash with a six second break, after which the sequence was repeated. It operated on a 110 volt system with two bulbs, mounted side by side. A reserve bulb automatically went into operation if the operating one failed.

In spite of the weather, Paul and I were keen to see the seal colony down by the tip of the point. Eddy and Greta, shepherding their two children between them, led the way down a narrow goat path through the bluffs. Greta told us there were 200 or so seals in the colony. Some on the rocky foreshore barked defiant warnings, whilst others played amongst the long strands of bull kelp. Greta pointed out a beehive-shaped sea stack where 12 pairs of gannets made their home during the nesting season. On the north side of the headland, in the lee from the south-westerly blow, hundreds of sooty shearwaters flew in wide circles, settling momentarily on the sea before continuing the circling. Eddy explained that the birds arrived in their thousands during late September for the breeding season. They departed in late April for a second summer in the North Pacific Ocean. The birds circled to build up their strength for the forthcoming yearly migration.

Late in the afternoon, although the south-westerly was still blowing strongly, I paddled *Isadora* around from Short Bay, past the boat landing at Tirohanga, to the last short section of sandy beach before the start of the rocky cliffs out to Nugget Point. The crayfishing boats based at Tirohanga were not moored at sea, but sat on wheels at the top of the beach. These wheels were not on trailers as one would expect, but were actually attached to each boat. The boats were winched down a section of flat sandy beach into the sea, with rocky reefs on both sides. Some measure of protection from the swell was afforded by a low stone breakwater on the eastern side. On completion of a day's fishing, the boats cruised in towards the beach, the wheels were folded down on both sides, then they were winched out of the water to the top of the beach, a unique and ingenious method of launching on this inhospitable shoreline.

The evening meal was washed down with half a gallon of sherry, and afterwards some fine yarns were told. Eddy's main gripe was with the idiots who were too lazy to walk out to the light, and tried to knock down the locked gate across the road up to the house, using cars like bulldozers. A second gripe concerning gates was not quite as serious. A strong, high wooden fence protected the house from high winds and kept out their two horses, one of whom, a four year old gelding, had become an expert gate opener. In spite of the latch being on the inside of the gate, the horse would spend 20 minutes or more, poking his long pink tongue through the narrow gap between gate and fence, to ease the latch up. Although Eddy kept the lawns closely mown, the horses obviously knew the old saying, 'The grass is always greener on the other side of the fence.' Car doors could not be left open otherwise upholstery and seat belts received a chewing over.

The evening forecast was discouraging, three days of southerlies. When we turned in, the wind was still blowing strongly from the west-south-west, however the barometric pressure had been slowly rising all day and at 9pm was recording 1020 millibars. This held promise for a good day on the morrow.

15 April - Day 68

Just before 6am Eddy woke us by asking, "How would you like a six knot north-easterly?" I thought he was pulling my leg again and replied unenthusiastically,

"Well, it would be nice."

"You've got it then," grinned Eddy. "The weather office have changed their minds and are forecasting three days of settled weather."

"Hellofagood," declared Paul.

Breakfast was consumed hastily and by 7.15am we were all down on the sandy beach near Tirohanga. A handshake in parting seemed such a small appreciation for the help and hospitality from this wonderful couple. I am in sincere agreement with Eddy's parting statement that, "Lighthouse keepers are the salt of the earth."

Eddy pushed *Isadora* off into a low surf. Overhead the sky was heavily overcast but the light north easterly breeze and a moderate swell held hope for a good day's paddle. I had no premonition of the near disaster that was about to occur. Because the sky was so grey, almost to the point of being gloomy, Eddy left the light going. From Tirohanga, the Norris family and support crew were going out to the light to watch my progress by the Nuggets.

I tried to take a short cut between the tip of the point and the first large sea stack, but smartly backpaddled out when the remnants of the previous day's south westerly swell broke in front, surging white and violently around the base of the stacks. There was too much heave to attempt a short cut. So I stuck to the northern side of the Nuggets until level with the most seaward of them. A Nordkapp width out from this last steep, rocky island lay a small rock, rising only three or four feet out of the surge. Around this rock on my left, the sea was breaking but not against the sea stack on my right. For the two to three minutes it took to approach, the gap was continuously clear of white water. It looked like plain sailing through it to the open sea. Although there was no logical reason to paddle through it, I decided to try the gap. An inane decision that I was immediately to regret.

As I headed into the gap, the swell was no more than four foot from crest to trough. I was halfway through and had just paddled over one crest when I saw the following swell crest, a wall of water that reared up six or seven feet in height. In the narrow gap, the water level dropped rapidly like someone had pulled out the plug. Both against the small rock and the wall of the sea stack, the face of this huge swell started to break. A fraction of a second later, the bow disappeared in the V of the surging wall of water. Then I was completely buried by the broken wave with no support for the paddle in the aerated water. With the horrifying realization that, 'this is it, the finish,' *Isadora* and I were upside down.

A second, large freak swell broke even before my head surfaced after the first one. My greatest fear was being smashed up against the rocky walls. At last the white foam disappeared and I was able to gasp a lungfull of air. With the paddle on one side of the capsized hull and my head on the other I decided not to attempt to roll but to push *Isadora* out of the gap. With the speed that only comes from staring death in the face, I was out of the cockpit had shoved *Isadora* hard to the south, and retrieved the paddle. On the south side of the sea stacks, yet another worry flashed through my mind. The two knot north-east-going current would push the kayak back onto the rocks.

It took me a while to catch up with the drifting kayak and even longer to get back into the cockpit. Four times, I managed to sit astride the cockpit only to roll over gracefully as I tried to slide my legs in. The chilling cold of the sea was starting to numb my fingers, time for extreme measures. I pulled the closed cell foam mat out from its position on the floor of the cockpit, placed it on the surface of the sea, and laid the paddle blade on top. Using this as a primitive form of outrigger, it was easy to slide my legs into the cockpit. Still retaining support from the buoyant mat, I worked the bilge pump handle to empty out the cockpit until my right arm was tired. Then I baled with a wetsuit bootie which had slipped off in the fracas.

The cockpit was now dry but I was still shaking from fright and the cold and it was a struggle to move the back rest into position. I put the sprayskirt back on then pulled on the light plastic gloves and parka to staunch the numbing cold. After a quick glance up to the distant light-tower, I paddled cautiously away to the south-west, in an attempt to stop the cold.

Apart from the foam mat, there was still one last desperate measure which could have been used. This was to take off the lifejacket and wrap it around the paddle blade. This would have given similar buoyancy to that of the mat, enabling easy access back into the cockpit. What stopped me using the lifejacket was that so many items were all attached through its top toggle, the camera, hat, whistle and compass. Removing them first and attaching them to the decklines would have taken time and there was a chance of losing them in the process.

The watchers at the light had been through 20 anxious minutes after *Isadora* disappeared from sight behind the sea stacks. Eddy and Paul both spotted the two freak swells long before I saw them. When the Nordkapp didn't reappear after the two large swells broke over the sea stacks, Paul and Eddy looked at each other grimly. Not a word was spoken until Eddy sent Paul up to the house for a telescope. Paul had been thinking of how to ring for a helicopter whilst Eddy wondered how quickly he could get a fishing boat to come round to the point.

Paul returned with the telescope just as the tip of the yellow Nordkapp came slowly into sight. By this time I was back in the cockpit and had paddled out to where they could see I was all right. It had been a worrying 20 minutes for all of us. However from my position half a mile away, I was not able to make out the figures watching from the light and had to assume they knew I was safe.

My extremities were still cold even after half an hour of steady paddling. I pulled the parka hood over my head which made a little difference and kept on wriggling my toes.

My confidence had been shattered like a piece of glass. The Nordkapp felt as tippy and unstable as the very first time I had ever sat in one even though the sea wasn't too bad, just a long moderate swell. I felt really annoyed with myself, both at the stupidity of taking the short cut when another 50 yards paddle would have cleared the rocks completely and avoided the near disaster, also at not sticking to my rule of, 'If in doubt, stay out.' But my troubles for the day were not over by a long shot. The next rendezvous with Paul was to be near the site of an old whaling station on the north side of Tautuku Peninsula, some 20 miles paddle away.

Off the mouth of the Catlins River, a light north-easterly breeze came away strongly. In no time at all it was blowing consistently between 15 and 20 knots and gusting to higher speeds. A steep, white capping chop joined the wind. The skeg was holding *Isadora* on course but the wind, blowing directly in the face of the oncoming swell, was causing a very confused and lumpy sea. The crests of the swell were peaking much higher than they would have without the wind. *Isadora* was bucking and lurching violently.

Sheltered landings are virtually nonexistent on this section of coastline. Vertical bluffs up to 600 feet high form the shoreline down to Long Point, broken only by isolated small bays where a large surf was working. Since Tautuku Bay was still a long way off and the wind showed no sign of easing, I headed in towards Jacks Bay, *Isadora* surfing in front of the whitecaps. The wind eased marginally, enough to

consider pushing on to White Head. Over the reefs off Tuhawaiki Island, the swell and chop were surging wildly, driving sheets of spray high into the air.

I gave White Head a wide berth to avoid the back chop off its cliffs, then I pointed the bow for the spray-shrouded shape of Cosgrove Island. It would have been impossible to paddle back into the wind, so there was no option left but to run for the landing in Tautuku Bay. There, at least, I knew there would be some shelter from the wind and swell. Beyond Cosgrove Island lay the flat-topped bulk of Long Point. Even from a distance of two miles, sheets of spray were plainly visible, shooting up the 200 foot high cliffs of the point, as the surging swell broke on its rocky ramparts.

Just past Cosgrove Island, the wind picked up again. I frequently resorted to support strokes to stay upright. Several strong wind gusts hit without warning. Each time I slapped the paddle blade hard down on the water to prevent a capsize. The car headlights flashed from the tip of Long Point, but there was little comfort in the knowledge that Paul was watching. Although he was less than half a mile away on shore, comfortable and warm in the car, I was struggling for survival on a wild and angry sea. It was the roughest sea I had known since leaving the West Coast.

It was difficult to rid my mind of the fate of the steamer *Manuka* which became a total wreck after running aground on Long Point one night in December 1929. Fortunately the 99 passengers and 104 crew survived a cold night in the ship's lifeboats and

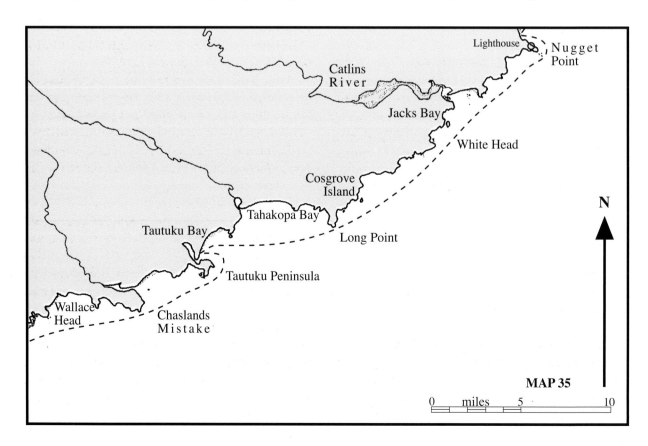

MAP 35

landed safely next morning. I hoped *Isadora* would not be the first kayak wreck on the New Zealand coastline. My morale was low.

The sea was so rough off the point that I could only glance up to the waiting support party above the cliffs, not a show of lifting a hand off the paddle to wave. To my disappointment, there was no protection from the wind in the lee of the point. A large surf smoked its way in towards the long sandy beach of Tahakopa Bay, but now the familiar old shape of Tautuku Peninsula was in sight, only seven miles to go. The wind and chop showed no signs of easing and I was feeling the strain of the intense concentration required to stay upright on the lumpy sea.

My confidence of landing safely in Tautuku Bay stemmed from a close knowledge of the area. For most of the two mile length of forest-fringed sandy beach, a large surf always breaks a good distance offshore with dangerous rips and undertows. No one ever swims or surfs there. However the extreme south end of the bay lies in the lee of the seaward projecting Tautuku Peninsula. Boats from an early whaling station once put out to sea here, where a small river enters the bay. At one time there was a jetty in the river but only a few old piles remain today. At low tide, a wide expanse of gently sloping, sandy beach is exposed and this is used for access to small holiday shacks on the peninsula.

The surf was smoking into Tautuku Bay with the north-easterly whipping spray off the breakers into a 'dream of white horses' manes. My arms and shoulders were tired, but the skeg was functioning perfectly, keeping *Isadora* running true before the following wind and chop.

There was no sign of life on the beach. I hoped Paul would be waiting to guide me through a quiet section of surf. With only 100 yards remaining before the first line of breakers, a landrover drove rapidly along the sandy beach. It stopped near the river that flows into the sea, turned out towards me and the headlights were switched on. Paul came running out into the surf wearing his wetsuit, but despite the wide expanse of breakers the waves weren't too high and I surfed into the beach.

Two friends, Sam and Linda, walked over from the landrover, but I could only wave one hand at them limply. Both mentally and physically, I was exhausted. They were amazed at the speed *Isadora* had made across from Long Point to the bay. The seven miles had taken less than an hour.

"Did you see the can out?" I asked Paul.

"We thought you stopped for a spell out beyond the Nuggets," Paul answered with a straight face, but went on to explain about the panic stations that had occurred at the light.

While Paul and Sam carried the Nordkapp up into the dunes, Linda fed me a mug of hot coffee and wrapped Sam's coat around my tired drooping shoulders. Then it was off to their house for a hot bath. As Sam drove along the beach, the sea was certainly impressive, whitecaps out to the horizon and large waves creaming beachwards, leaving a trail of spray in their wake.

Sam Samson ran the Tautuku Outdoor Education Centre, which was set back 500 yards from Tautuku Bay, in a clearing amongst cutover rimu forest. The centre catered for up to 86 high school students from the Otago district, who learned about the flora, fauna, early history, and various facets of outdoor education. Building of the centre started in 1970. Shaped like an H, the bunkrooms, showers, toilets, and drying rooms were on each of the parallel sides of the H, with the modern kitchen and large dining hall in the bar of the H. It has been financed almost entirely by donations, with no help from the Department of Education, and built with labour provided by the people of Otago, especially the service clubs. Since its conception, a Balclutha chap, Ivan Somerville, had provided the driving force behind this massive project.

Sam, whose face was mostly hidden behind a huge curly beard, had long dark brown curly hair, and looked like a whaling boat captain of yesteryear. I first met Sam in 1975 whilst on a teaching section from Christchurch Teachers' College. It was an exciting four weeks as I watched Sam teach classes of fourth formers from Otago high schools. The weekends were spent photographing the area, devising new games and projects, collecting folklore from the local district, singing and drinking.

Linda Blake, long straight dark hair, slim and beautiful, was my flatmate that year in Christchurch. Her teaching section followed mine at Tautuku and she and Sam hit it off so well that they ended up getting married. Linda worked as a botanist with the Forest Service, based in Invercargill, but her weekends were spent with Sam.

I was really happy to be back with old friends whom I hadn't seen for ages. A mouthwatering feed of roast pork for tea, was followed by Linda and Sam's first ever attempt at cooking a pavlova. Despite a rather saggy middle section, it was indeed a beauty for a first try. "We'll fatten you up on scraps from Tautuku," grinned Sam.

Over the years, Sam had built up a remarkable rapport with the farmers and old timers in the surrounding district. With their help, he had a reasonably thorough knowledge of the history of the area. The whaling station on Tautuku Peninsula commenced operations in 1839 with a catch of 11 whales but by

1845, when the station closed, the catch was down to two whales for the year. Sam had a large wall map showing the numerous shipwrecks along the South Otago coastline. The white-painted wooden figure-head from the *Otago*, which was wrecked at Chaslands Mistake in 1876, was donated to the Tautuku Centre and now stood in the foyer of the buildings. Only weeks before we arrived, the latest tragic shipwreck had occurred. One of the crib owners on Tautuku Peninsula, Doug Gillanders, put out from Tautuku Bay in his 18 foot trimaran for a day's fishing down by Chaslands. He was last seen by his wife at night-fall, only 50 yards offshore from the peninsula. Westerly winds blew offshore for the next few days while search planes flew along the coastline and ground parties checked the beaches for wreckage. A week later the damaged trimaran was picked up off Timaru by the supply vessel *Grizzly Bear*. There was no trace of the lone yachtsman.

While we were eating the meal Eddy Norris rang. It was still blowing a 35 knot north-easterly at the lighthouse and the 'glass' or barograph had showed a gradual drop all day. While Eddy and Greta were out moving a mob of sheep, another car load of idiots had knocked down their chained and padlocked gate.

Eddy promised to ring early next morning with a weather situation.

16 April - Day 69

Eddy rang at 6am, while Paul and I were forcing down the ritual bowl of porridge.

"There's two knot variable winds here at the moment and the sea is calm," said Eddy, "but the forecast is for a southerly change in the afternoon, accompanying a cold front."

"That sounds pretty good," I replied.

"Then what are you doing talking on the phone when you should be out paddling?" Eddy demanded.

Although the tide was half full, there was sufficient width of firm beach for Sam to drive along to the kayak. When a group of sea birds flew up in front of the landrover, it was obvious that the competition to find the worst pun of the trip wasn't forgotten. "Sam, you gave me quite a turn," I quipped, to which Paul responded, "That's because you're so gullible."

After a little coaxing, Paul told Sam his two terrible jokes about those small white beautiful sea birds called terns. The young tern asked mother tern when he would have a brother or sister to play with for he was rather lonely. Mother tern answered, "Very soon. You have been a good little tern, and after all, one good tern deserves another."

The second joke is even worse. A mother and son were looking out from their house at a flock of sea birds feeding in their freshly planted vegetable gar-den; "Son," said Mother, "I want you to go out there and scare those birds away. Pick up some small rocks and leave no tern unstoned." Still, as the saying goes, you get terrible puns like that from the support crews on the big trips.

In the grey light of an overcast morning conditions for paddling looked good. The sea appeared calm and only the faintest of breezes ruffled the water. Just after 7am I cut out through the breakers, waved to Sam and Paul, then set off around Tautuku Peninsula. My next meeting point with Paul would be in Porpoise Bay, near the entrance of Waikawa Harbour. Steep cliffs form the shoreline of the peninsula, gradually rising to over 100 feet at its southern-most point, on top of which a small marine navigation light was sited. Once I paddled out of the lee of the peninsula, the familiar swell was waiting to keep its daily appointment with the lone paddler. Ever since Nugget Point the Southern Ocean swell was increasingly making its presence felt. This last section of the trip wasn't proving easy.

From the tip of the peninsula, I pointed the bow towards Chaslands Mistake, an impressive, forest topped headland, with 400 foot high cliffs rising darkly out of the surge. The native forest backing the coastline between Tautuku and Chaslands Mistake almost made me think I was back on the West Coast. This was the first time since leaving the rugged Karamea coastline astern, that I had seen native forest from the sea. As such, this short section of coastline contains the last remaining stands of native forest on the whole of the East Coast. Fortunately the virgin rimu forest behind Tautuku Bay is now preserved in a scenic reserve.

Slowly, a west-south-west breeze came away, gradually picking up in intensity, to my disappointment. As well as the wind and swell, both of which I was now paddling directly into, one other factor was becoming increasingly important as I neared the entrance of Foveaux Strait, the tide. The *New Zealand Pilot* has the following note about the tides:

> With a rising tide the tidal stream sets eastward through Foveaux strait, being strongest between Bluff harbour, about 11 miles north-westward of Ruapuke island, and that island, and its influence is felt along the coast of South island as far as Long point .... With a falling tide the stream runs in an exactly contrary direction ....
>
> The strength of the tidal stream varies from half a knot to two and a half knots; in the narrowest part of the strait, between Ruapuke island and Bluff harbour, they sometimes attain a rate of three knots.

High tide would not be until approximately 10am so for the first three hours or so I would be plugging into the tidal stream.

The sooty shearwaters were out in force, sitting quietly on the sea in large flocks. An unusual visitor to investigate the kayak was a solitary, grey-headed mollymawk. The bird is similar in many ways to the black-backed gulls, both in its shape and black and white plumage. The mollymawk however, is twice as large as the gull, with a bright yellow beak and a massive wingspan. The mollymawk stayed with me for the next few miles, soaring effortlessly in broad circles, never seeming to need to flap its long powerful wings. As much as I don't believe in omens, the presence of the mollymawk was just like the dolphins on the West Coast. Whenever they were gambolling in the water by the bow, I was sure nothing bad was going to happen.

Dear diary: 'Wind freshened, and for a while I didn't think I would be able to get past where the *Otago* went aground.' On a foggy night in December 1876, the 236 foot long steamer *Otago* crashed in between two pinnacles of rock, beneath the steep, towering cliffs of Chaslands Mistake. Luckily the sea was calm, which enabled the passengers and crew to land safely next morning. It is the figurehead from this shipwreck that lies in the foyer of the Tautuku Outdoor Education Centre.

The south-westerly wind increased the height of the swell to the point that after slowly drawing past Chaslands Mistake, I was tempted to put into Teahimate Bay where the *New Zealand Pilot* mentioned a boat landing. It was slow progress across to the small rocky islets known as The Sisters.

However the wind didn't freshen further so I plugged on to the next rocky point, called, appropriately enough, The Brothers. This group of desolate rocky islands is larger, more rugged, and more exposed than The Sisters.

From a distance there appeared to be a gap or short cut between shore and The Brothers but after yesterday's performance off the Nuggets, I took the longer course around the outside of the islands. It was fortunate I did this for the swell was breaking and surging wildly on their seaward side.

Here it became apparent that the tidal stream had turned and was now setting westwards, for *Isadora* seemed to pick up speed, making faster progress by the shore. But the tidal stream, setting into the face of the oncoming wind and swell, quickly built up an even lumpier sea. Only four miles remained to Porpoise Bay where Paul and I had a system of signals arranged, to indicate the landing conditions. If he left the head lights on, the landing was fiery or no good at all, whereas three short flashes, repeated, indicated a sheltered landing.

With a mile to go to South Head, which forms the southern end of Porpoise Bay, I spotted the car headlights on top of this headland. But the swell was so large that I could only fleetingly glimpse the light from the highest swell crests. Because of this, it was hard to tell if it was a continuous signal or three flashes. It was with relief, when half a mile remained to the headland, that I saw the light flash three times, the landing was OK.

Porpoise Bay is shaped like a fish hook, with South Head, projecting eastward into the bay, forming the barb. It appeared from the map that a sheltered landing would be found at the south end of the bay, the area forming the deeply curved section of the hook by the barb.

Out to the north-east of South Head, the swell was breaking wildly over two areas of submerged reefs. The safest route to where Paul waited appeared to be inside the reefs, closer in by the sandy beach of the bay. As anticipated, the landing was sheltered with

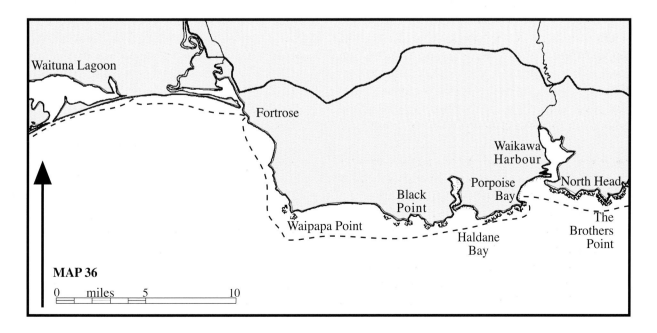

Waituna Lagoon

Fortrose

Waikawa Harbour

Porpoise Bay

Black Point

North Head

Waipapa Point

Haldane Bay

The Brothers Point

MAP 36

0   miles   5   10

Arriving at Porpoise Bay. Photo: Paul Dale

only a two foot high surf breaking onto a sandy beach. Paul had lunch and a brew waiting in a nearby picnic shelter. He was keen, almost to the point of being pushy, for me to try and reach Fortrose by evening. From there it wasn't too far to drive into Invercargill. But I wasn't so keen. Some sixth sense told me the weather was going to change. Not only that, but between Porpoise Bay and Fortrose lay the notorious reefs off Waipapa Point. I wanted reasonable conditions to attempt passing this point, not marginal conditions.

Over the narrow grassy neck of South Head, lies the smaller and less protected shoreline of Curio Bay, best known for its fossil forest. On this day, all sight of the petrified logs lay hidden beneath waves crashing over the rocks. Although the south-westerly breeze was still only slight, the visibility appeared to be dropping, the hills to the west were already swathed in cloud. However to satisfy Paul, I reluctantly paddled out into Porpoise Bay.

At first my course lay back to the east to clear the reefs off South Head, but before long *Isadora* was pushing into a seven to eight knot south-westerly breeze. Although the sea was lumpy with a fair amount of heave, it wasn't in too bad a state for paddling. But visibility was down to less than 800 yards by now and dropping. Misty squalls, coming through from the south-west, brought drizzle which reduced visibility through my spectacle lenses. When

I drew level with Curio Bay Paul was standing by the car on top of South Head, watching my slow progress.

Since the wind appeared to be picking up I stopped paddling to take stock of the situation. Even if Paul shone the headlights out from the various points to the west, I wouldn't be able to see them. The cliffs of Flaxy Head, only 500 yards away, disappeared from sight, enveloped in swirling cloud. Since the next bay to the west, Haldane Bay, was deep, over a mile wide at its entrance, and the visibility was still lowering, I decided I wouldn't be able to see across to the other side of the bay. It would be a big mistake to carry on. So I turned around, and *Isadora* ran quickly back before the wind into the shelter of Porpoise Bay.

On shore, Paul was waiting with another chap who I didn't initially recognize beneath a bundle of wet weather gear. "Hello Paul," said a familiar sounding voice, "I thought I might bump into you out here." It was John Hall-Jones, doctor, tramper, author, and noted Fiordland historian. John had driven out from Invercargill, partly to check out the sites of old Maori kitchen middens and fireplaces for a forthcoming book on the history of the Southland Coast, and partly in case he might catch up with the lone paddler. John and I first met at Cuttle Cove, the site of an old whaling station, in Preservation Inlet, Fiordland, during a caving expedition to the area.

It was a wise decision to turn back off Curio Bay. While we talked, the wind freshened and backed to the south, rising quickly to between 25 and 30 knots. Two fishing boats were making heavy weather through a mass of whitecaps towards the Waikawa Harbour entrance. If I had pushed on the situation in *Isadora* would have been rather grim.

After saying goodbye to John, Paul and I drove around the wharf in Waikawa Harbour to watch the fishing boats returning. Some of the friendly fishermen there gave me good advice on the next section of coastline along to Bluff. A local resident, Mrs. Wybrow, let us use her holiday cottage on the beach at Porpoise Bay for the night. The hot shower and comfortable beds were most appreciated.

Chapter 16

PORPOISE BAY to TE WAEWAE BAY

17 April - Day 70

At first light, a 30-35 knot south-easterly wind was driving a wild, white-capping sea into Porpoise Bay. Definitely not a day for Nordkapps. There appeared to be little chance of the wind abating so we drove into Invercargill and set up camp in Paul's father's house.

To glean as much advice as possible on what the seas would be like through Foveaux Strait, we drove to Bluff and called in at the Southland Harbour Board building. There we met Hamish Carnegie, a young Scotsman and one of the three pilots for the port of Bluff. Hamish pulled out the marine charts of Foveaux Strait, the stretch of water between Stewart Island and the mainland, and worked out the most favourable times for paddling with the tidal stream that sets westward through the strait with a falling tide. Off the notorious Waipapa Point, a favourable current would run from four hours after high tide (at Bluff) until three hours before the next high water. I noted in 'Dear diary', directions for entering and leaving Bluff Harbour's narrow entrance, and for the next stretch around to Riverton.

Direct reading instruments in the pilot's office gave us a good idea of what the weather was doing. The barograph showed a steady fall in barometric pressure while the chart recording wind speed and direction showed a steady 35 knot easterly blowing all morning.

For a closer view of the harbour entrance, we drove to the signal station at Stirling Point and introduced ourselves to watchkeeper Harry Austin. The station was manned 24 hours a day and maintained a radio and visual watch for vessels entering and leaving the harbour. Set on a large rock on the western side of the entrance, above high tide level, the station was connected to shore by a wooden walkway, 20 yards long. Circular in plan view, with a wooden catwalk around the outside, entry was through a single solid door. Inside, the appearance was dismal, high roof, faded paint on the walls, old signal flags in wooden lockers by the door, fixed windows and several small, brass portholes. An array of radio sets lay on a bench, all switched on. A signalling lamp sat ready for use.

Through the windows of the station, the seas in the strait looked horrific. Hamish had warned me to give Entrance Shoal a wide berth when entering the harbour. This area of shallow sea-bed lay square in the middle of the harbour approaches and was easily visible as a wide area of continuously breaking white water not far offshore. While we watched, the lighthouse on Dog Island began flashing. This small, flat-topped island, barely long enough to allow a light plane to land, lay three miles out in the strait.

I asked Harry if the seas ever broke around the signal station. He told us that during a decent blow in 1977, he had to wait 20 minutes on shore before dashing along the exposed walkway between breaking waves. During the remainder of his watch, which was in the early hours of the morning, high seas swept away part of the catwalk and washed away the wooden walkway. The noise of breaking seas was so loud that the radio sets were left on full volume to be heard.

Our next visit, to see how the weather forecasts were put together, was to the meteorological office at Invercargill Airport. The friendly chaps there showed us the latest weather maps. A big low was centred near Auckland with a high pressure system well to the south and two cold fronts coming over from Australia.

To while away the evening hours we decided to take in a movie. We were amused to find two out of the three Invercargill movie theatres were showing films with a definite sea flavour: 'Orca the Killer Whale' and 'The Last Wave'. We chose the latter. Fortunately I do not suffer from nightmares otherwise it may well have been a sleepless night. The film, set in Australia, was about an Aboriginal prophecy of a huge wave about to engulf the land.

19 April - Day 71

For all of the 18th, the wind showed no sign of abating. Next morning, just after 6am, I rang the lighthouse keeper on Dog Island. Jeff Harris, a good friend of both Pip Aplin and Charley Wallace, had just sent out the first weather situation for the day. He said the sea was calm with a light northerly blowing. The Met. Office forecast was for easterly winds. Conditions seemed favourable for an attempt on Waipapa Point, so we got going smartly.

It's a long drive out to Porpoise Bay and after picking up *Isadora* from Mrs. Wybrow's house, we didn't arrive at the beach until 8.30. Word soon got around that I was about to leave and by the time I was ready to launch several carloads of Waikawa residents had arrived at South Head.

Under an overcast sky, a large easterly swell, the aftermath of the previous day's strong winds, was booming into Porpoise Bay. Over the reefs off South Head, the swell broke wildly which would mean a half mile paddle back towards Tautuku before I could turn westwards.

Given a perfect day, I could reach Bluff, only 40 miles away, but a worrying obstacle was Waipapa Point, the site of New Zealand's second worst maritime disaster. From roughly 8.30am until 3.30pm, the tidal stream through Foveaux Strait would be setting eastwards, slowing progress. Paul would wait by the automatic lighthouse on the tip of the point to see me safely past, then he would drive to a sheltered landing

that we had already reconnoitred near Fortrose.

Dear diary: 'The surf wasn't too bad leaving Porpoise Bay, but the swell was. It took me half an hour to paddle out around the reefs before I could pass South Head; stayed a long way out to miss the backchop off the rocky shoreline. Could see all the cars and figures on the headland but the sea was so lumpy that I couldn't lift a hand off the paddle to wave. Stayed about half a mile out, mouth dry from worry, knees and feet locked in the brace position. The large easterly swell was frightening, not to mention the confusion added by the backchop off the 200 foot high cliffs of Flaxy Head.'

The *New Zealand Pilot* notes:

> Between South head and Waipapa point nearly 11 miles westward, the coast should not be approached by small craft, except in fine weather, owing to the irregular tidal streams.

Off the wide entrance to Haldane Bay the backchop died away. The next objective was the most southerly point of the South Island, Slope Point. Here it was obvious that the gently angling rock of the point continued for some distance out to sea below the surface, for a long line of breakers lay before me. My customary half mile offshore increased to about three quarters of a mile. But this was merely a taste of what was to come.

The tidal stream had turned and was now setting against me. This appeared to increase and steepen the size of the long easterly swell. *Isadora* began surfing down the faces of each swell only to lose momentum and almost stop as the crest passed beneath the hull. Each time this happened, the Nordkapp tipped backwards in the wake of the swell crest. From so far offshore it was difficult to estimate my speed, as the coastline didn't seem to be moving. However by lining the small white blob of the marine navigation light on top of Slope Point with the hills on the skyline, I was able to see that slow steady progress was being made.

Between Black Point and Waipapa Point, I passed a four mile long sandy beach, backed by low dunes and felt a little easier paddling by sand instead of the preceding rocky shoreline. Not that it would have been easy landing for the waves were climbing so high before they broke that all sight of shore and the hinterland was hidden. After another mile, I caught a glimpse of the top of the 44 foot high wooden tower of the Waipapa Point lighthouse. The automatic light stands some 70 feet above sea level, but despite this, it was only from the top of the highest crests of the swell that I could spot the light. I found it easier to steer by a prominent cloud that lay above the lighthouse.

I had a fair idea of what lay in store off Waipapa

Point, for an aerial photograph in Joan MacIntosh's book, *The Wreck of the Tararua*, shows two parallel reefs, roughly 500 yards apart, that extend south-eastwards for almost a mile offshore. In the early hours of 29 April 1881, the passenger steamer *Tararua* with 112 passengers and 39 crew, struck the eastern most reef. One of the passengers reached the beach through a strong surf during the morning and managed to raise the alarm. Others drowned in the heavy surf while attempting to reach shore. However as rescue ships raced to the scene that day the seas lifted. The steamer's decks were swept by high seas until during the night, the vessel suddenly disappeared beneath the waves, taking with it the remaining passengers and crew left on board. At dawn the following day, two rescue ships lay offshore, but of the *Tararua*, all that was visible were her two masts and several iron stanchions. Only 74 bodies were recovered of the 131 people who drowned. Many were buried in an area amongst the nearby sandhills which since has been known as the Tararua Acre. As a result of this tragic shipwreck, the Waipapa Point lighthouse was built.

I kept looking for a thin white line on the horizon that would show where the first reef lay. When it finally came into sight, I wasn't impressed by the sight of breakers extending out almost to the horizon. I turned south and had to keep turning south, for each time I headed back in the direction of the reefs, yet another large breaking wave reared up in front. The swell shortened and steepened as I approached the first reef with *Isadora* burying her bow frequently, obviously the effect of shoaling over the reefs on the tidal stream.

The easternmost reef was easy to spot. It lurked just below the surface, as a pale green band of water contrasted by dark coloured ocean on each side. Just merely worried up to here, I was scared between the reefs, and hoped a freak wave wouldn't rear up suddenly in front. What really put the wind up me was when the swell reared up suddenly and broke where previously there had been no breakers.

A lumpy, steep sea extended across to the second reef giving infrequent glimpses of the top of the Waipapa Point lighthouse. The second reef showed up as another pale green band in the sea, and soon I quickly passed over it. I was still really uptight and worried, for the sea showed no signs of subsiding.

Unbeknown to me, Paul Dale was watching with binoculars from the lighthouse along with the headmaster and 30 children from the Otara primary school. The children were disappointed, for I was so far out to sea that even with the aid of binoculars Paul had difficulty sighting the yellow kayak.

Weeks later, at home in Runanga, I received by mail, from the headmaster of Otara school, a book of colourful drawings by the schoolchildren showing various stages of the kayak passing the point. The text beneath one of the beautifully coloured sketches read, 'Unfortunately you could not stop at Waipapa Point. We were all disappointed but understood your reasons.' I was touched by their interest and thoughtfulness and mailed a photograph of *Isadora* for the children's scrapbook.

Far over on the western horizon the 870 foot high headland by Bluff township showed up above the swell crests and I steered for a cloud above it. My rather hopeful plan was to bypass Fortrose and use the westward setting tidal stream to carry me along to Dog Island, thereby avoiding the tide rips in and out of Bluff Harbour. I was concerned however that Paul may not have sighted *Isadora* passing Waipapa Point, so I opted for a rendezvous at a sheltered bay, one mile south-east of the Fortrose Harbour entrance. Not until I had paddled two miles beyond the point did the seas finally subside. In all probability this was the time when the tidal stream turned westwards.

At 3pm, after six and a quarter worried hours, I nosed in through a dumping surf only to face a struggle to haul the Nordkapp out of the surge and up a steep sandy beach. Although Paul had flashed the headlights from a nearby headland, there was no sign of him but as I walked up onto the headland he drove up, followed by parents, teachers and children from Fortrose school. I wasn't in much of a sociable mood, having been gripped up for the last six hours and then not being met by Paul at the beach. There was now no hope of reaching Bluff before dark since it was still 20 miles away, so I decided to paddle six miles along to Waituna, the only place on this long stretch of sandy beach where there was road access. Paul promised to wait there and shine a light out to sea for me to home in on.

A light south-easterly breeze was blowing and the sky to the south was growing really dark. With a wave to the school children I turned westwards, making good time to the Fortrose Harbour entrance with the now favourable tidal stream. Where the ebbing waters of this now disused harbour met the tidal stream, the surface of the sea was marked by a white line of small choppy waves. For a while I paddled parallel with the line, sizing it up, and then turned and crossed without incident.

Waituna trig came into sight after only an hour's paddle. This speed of roughly six knots was a marked contrast to the sluggish two to three knots during the morning. The favourable tidal stream certainly made a difference to *Isadora*'s speed.

Again there was no sign of Paul, just an unfriendly large surf booming into a steep, sandy beach. Al-

Parents, teachers and schoolchildren from Fortrose school endeavouring to spot the tiny kayak passing Waipapa Point. Photo: Paul Dale

though the roof of a shed or farmhouse was visible above the dunes, there was no sign of life. For five minutes or more I sat offshore, gauging the surf. Large waves were coming through in sets of three with the briefest of lulls between. I couldn't see a way of reaching shore without being hammered.

Apprehensively I nosed the bow towards the beach only to race out to sea when a big set came through, almost capping over *Isadora*. The skeg knocked out of position, I again set off cautiously for shore. One large set went through, breaking with a roar just in front and I set off in hot pursuit, paddling flatstick in its wake. In the brief lull that followed two smaller waves came through carrying *Isadora* shorewards until with a noise like a clap of thunder, the leading wave of the next set broke astern. However it was small enough by the time it reached me for *Isadora* to bounce sideways in front of the breaker.

Yet one final obstacle guarded the shoreline, a wave only a few yards out from the beach but rearing up rapidly to dump like a ton of bricks onto the sand. My luck held when I paddled in hard behind a large dumper and reached the sand, only to be pushed higher up the beach by the succeeding wave. Needless to say I was immensely relieved to be ashore in one piece.

Out to sea the sky had grown dark and the south-westerly was picking up in strength. Half an hour later Paul arrived. To say that I was cheesed off with him for not being there is rather an understatement.

As the trip neared completion the paddling was not getting any easier, in fact there were more objective dangers now than at any time previously during the paddle down the East Coast. The mental strain of being at sea on my own was increasing and I needed team work and reassurance from the support crew more than ever before. Although not totally reliant on the support crew, its presence when a dicey landing was coming up gave me a more positive mental attitude.

After the local farmer, Owen Hudson, offered to keep an eye on *Isadora* in one of his farm sheds, we drove back to Invercargill.

20 April - Day 72

The early morning forecast from the Met. Office, and also the situation at Dog Island were not encouraging, strong south-easterly winds, drizzle, and moderate to rough seas. Jeff Harris, the lighthouse keeper on Dog Island, had flown across to Invercargill the previous day with his wife and family for their annual vacation. His replacement as relieving keeper was, of all people, John Jeffs, who had been out at Puysegur Point lighthouse when Max and I had called in four months previously. Quite a coincidence.

The wind eased by midday but by the time we reached Waituna, it was blowing at 15 to 20 knots from the south with a mass of whitecaps out to the horizon.

21 April - Day 73

The usual phone calls were made to the Met. Office and the Dog Island lighthouse at 6am but the forecast wasn't encouraging. It was almost identical to the previous day. I had decided not to set out when John rang from Dog Island at 8am. "The sea is pretty good," he informed me. "A moderate easterly swell, light breezes, but poor visibility." That was promising enough to attempt the paddle along to Bluff.

At Waituna the surf wasn't inviting at all, a few large waves breaking well offshore not to mention a horrible, heavy, shore dump. Paul gave *Isadora* a good shove into the surge just after a boomer wave broke, and the Nordkapp showed a clean pair of heels out to the open sea, fortunately passing through the offshore break during a lull. The wind was from the south-east and visibility at times was down to less than 200 yards as drizzle patches slipped by. In case the beach disappeared from sight I set the compass on a bearing parallel to the sandy beach, and continued to make slow progress pushing into the eastward setting tidal stream.

As the land behind the beach was so low, consisting of lagoons, swampy land and low dunes, it wasn't easy to keep track of progress as only occasional clumps of trees materialized and disappeared in the light misty rain.

At one stage a flock of sooty shearwaters approached. Hundreds of birds were flying low, wing tips almost touching the sea, in a wide circle. It was fine looking at the spectacle from a distance but the birds drifted closer and finally enveloped me in the circle. It was a little like being the eye of a cyclone. I soon started to feel a little dizzy until the circling birds drifted away. Other large flocks of shearwaters sat quietly on the sea, only moving out of the way when *Isadora's* bow was less than a yard away.

My good omen appeared too, a friendly grey headed mollymawk soaring in effortless wide circles above the kayak. Despite the mollymawk's appearance, the wind picked up and veered to the south-south-west. The black and white painted shape of a trig point materialized out of the mist on shore and at least I now knew my precise location. It was the Awarua trig, seven miles from the entrance to Bluff Harbour. A mile beyond here, the coast turned more to the west which made paddling with the wind a little easier.

An hour later, when the mist cleared briefly, Dog Island lighthouse came into sight, its black and white banded tower stark against the grey sky. There was still no sign of Bluff nor what I expected to see, the tall smokestack of the Tiwai Point aluminium refinery. Between the beach and Dog Island several large oyster boats were also heading in the direction of Bluff Harbour.

At last the smokestack became visible through the moving clouds of drizzle; only a mile to go to Tiwai Rocks and the harbour entrance. A large, green-hulled oyster boat changed course, heading over to where I was paddling parallel to the shore. By hand signals the skipper indicated for me to paddle out towards them.

"It's a great day for it," I called out.

"A cracker day for it," responded one of the smiling crew, obviously a Fred Dagg fan. The skipper of the *Hirere* eased her speed away until it matched that of *Isadora*.

"I'll stick with you to the entrance," the skipper called. "Give you some shelter from the chop."

It was thoughtful of him, for indeed the paddling was easier on the starboard side of the large modern oyster boat, so long as I kept just out of the way of the *Hirere's* bow wave. In turn, all four of the fishermen on board gave me advice on entering the harbour and how best to avoid the strong tide rips that race in and out of its narrow entrance. As we drew level with the low rocky projection of Tiwai Rocks, the skipper called out, "Would you like a feed of oysters?" By vigorously nodding my head up and down I indicated my love of these shellfish. One of the crew filled a plastic bag with freshly shelled oysters, tied a light line around the neck of the bag, and lowered it over the side. The deck of the boat was six to seven feet above the water so the skipper and I manoeuvred closer together while the crewman swung the bag out like a pendulum until I could grasp it. As we were now in the harbour approaches, the friendly skipper called out final instructions to me, and picked up speed towards the harbour. Despite whatever the fishermen may have thought about the sanity of the canoeing caper, their advice was always sound and often they made a great effort to help me.

All the other oyster boats were by now well up the harbour for the *Hirere's* skipper had gone out of his way to shepherd *Isadora* to the entrance. I was most appreciative of his advice and especially for the oysters. There remained only half an hour before the flooding tide peaked at 1pm, and as the *Hirere's* skipper advised me, the entrance channel was no place to be when the tide started to ebb. The *New Zealand Pilot* notes:

> Eastward of Stirling point the ebb stream attains a rate of five to six knots and the flood stream three to four knots .... There are heavy tide rips off Stirling point and Channel rocks.

I saw Paul signal from an old navigation beacon on Tiwai Rocks. My plan was to paddle up the harbour, hugging the eastern shore then slip across the channel to Bluff township. Since Paul was close and the tide was about to turn I decided to land. Less than 300 yards inside the entrance lay a 10 yard wide section of sandy beach between two short, jutting rocky points.

I landed without incident and Paul soon arrived through a screen of flax bushes accompanied by two overall clad workers from the nearby aluminium refinery. "I wouldn't take you on in a wrist wrestling match," said one chap, looking at my bulging arm muscles. The second chap, formerly a fisherman, gave me advice on the tides and currents for the next section around to Riverton.

Paul was keen for me to push on since he had been due back at his job in Arthurs Pass several days before. But only 15 minutes later after a quick feed and a brew the ebb tide was racing out to sea with the main channel easily visible by a line of white-capping waves extending out towards Entrance Shoal. I would have to cross this tide race in order to start the paddle around to Riverton and the weather didn't look inviting. When a drizzle patch hid the Stirling Point signal station from view, less than three quarters of a mile away, I decided to finish paddling for the day.

It was four months to the day since Max and I had set out from Te Waewae Bay at the start of the Fiordland expedition.

The Tiwai Point aluminium refinery occupies the end of a long sandy peninsula with Awarua Bay on the north side. The waters of the bay run into Bluff Harbour. Since the refinery is closed to public access

Paul had to obtain permission from the top brass before he could drive out to the harbour entrance. The uniformed security guards on duty at the entrance to the refinery were really helpful, offering me a shower and a cup of tea, but Paul wanted to drop off a brochure on the Nordkapps to the shipping reporter (of all people) at the *Southland Times* building. This was a gentle con for me to be photographed, which I hated, and interviewed which over a cup of tea wasn't too bad.

Later in the afternoon we arrived at a flashy licensing trust establishment for a drink with some old friends only to be turned away from the bar because we were wearing jeans. After the hospitality of all the people we met earlier in the day, it was a bit against the old grain, so with Paul dressed in a set of tails and wearing a red top hat and myself in one of Paul's old suits, we returned to the fray where the snooty barman had no option but to serve us.

22 April - Day 74
The early morning forecast from the Met. Office was for 15 to 25 knot south-easterlies, drizzle, and a moderate sea with an easterly swell. It didn't sound too hopeful. Although it was still dark, I rang the chap on duty at the Stirling Point signal station. He told me that the sea was quiet and that if I approached too close to the rocks he would signal me with the lamp.

The tide would be dead low at 7.30am with 10 minutes of slack water on either side. During this 20

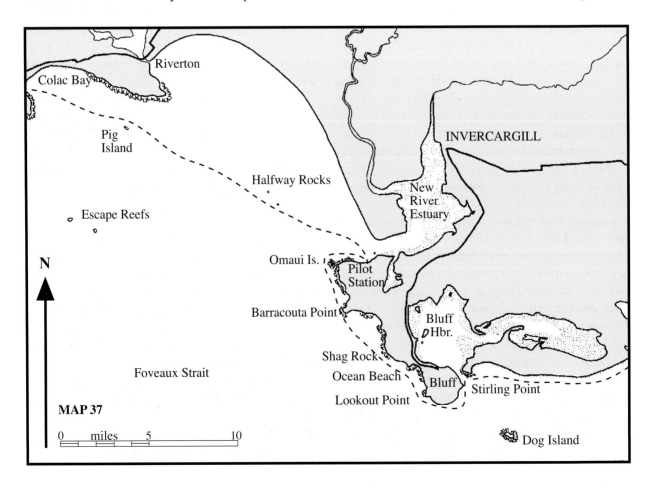

minute period when the tidal stream ceased, I hoped to make a fast exit from Tiwai Rocks across to Stirling Point and out to sea. My directions from Hamish Carnegie, the harbour pilot, and the fishermen, were to take a beeline from Tiwai Rocks to a red pillar flashing light buoy out from Stirling Point, this buoy marks the edge of foul ground between it and shore, then to keep parallel to the shoreline around Bluff headland. This course would carry me well inside Entrance Shoal.

Bluff Harbour, which serves as the port for Southland, is sheltered from the prevailing westerly winds and has several attributes including the absence of a bar and no rivers running into it, thus eliminating a silting up problem. Apart from the Bluff oyster boat fleet, numerous large overseas vessels enter the port with petroleum products and raw material for the aluminium refinery, and leave with frozen meat, wool and refined aluminium. Although full-powered vessels of moderate draught can enter at all times of the tide, the *Pilot* warns vessels of moderate power not to enter the harbour during the full strength of the tidal stream. It is the large areas of water contained in Bluff Harbour and Awarua Bay, passing through the 600 yard wide port entrance, that cause the strong tidal stream movement in and out of the harbour.

At 7.15am, with 15 minutes remaining until the tide turned, Paul shoved *Isadora* off from the small sandy beach by Tiwai Rocks. There was just enough light to see across to Stirling Point, but the flashing light on top of the red buoy was clearly visible. Our next meeting point would be near the old Omaui pilot station, near the entrance to the New River estuary.

The last minutes of ebbing tide carried *Isadora* swiftly down the channel to Stirling Point, where I passed close by the red buoy. A beautiful sunrise, the clouds tinged a light pink colour, provided a pleasant contrasting backdrop to the tall smokestacks of the refinery. Though slack water time was nearly gone, I stopped long enough to snap a photograph of the dawn.

Paddling hard around the rocky foreshore of Bluff Peninsula, I felt relieved to have left the harbour so easily and wasn't prepared for what was already building up off Lookout Point. It was a confounded tide race or overfall, like those beauties off the Marlborough Sounds only now there was one vital difference, I was paddling uphill into this one.

It was a real struggle to make headway into the standing waves on the swiftly flowing sea. *Isadora* surfed down the short faces of the waves to finally break free into smooth, fast moving water. Shallowing of the sea-bed off the point was causing the tidal stream through the strait to speed up. Eventually, however, *Isadora* drew away from the standing waves

and the effect of the tide race lessened. I headed for the sheds of the Ocean Beach freezing works, which stand astride the narrow neck of Bluff Peninsula. By paddling into this wide-bayed section of the coastline I hoped to escape the main force of the eastward setting tidal stream of Foveaux Strait. The thought of what lay in store off the next three prominent rocky points before the coast turned east to Omaui did not enthral me. If the tidal races off these were much stronger than the last one, I would have to retreat.

The sea out from the freezing works contained virtually no sign of pollution. Mind you, this wasn't surprising for it was situation normal at the works, with the highest paid workers in the country out on strike for some reason or other.

Sure enough off Shag Point there was another tidal race, only faster and stronger than the one off Lookout Point. This time I had all the stops out, with nothing in reserve, to inch my way through the standing waves and swiftly flowing water. It was like paddling up a rapid in a large river, almost reminiscent of the slog through French Pass against the tide. Finally *Isadora* broke out onto calm water again providing me with a three mile respite before reaching Barracouta Point. At least near this point, the map showed a slipway, a mile to the east of the point where I should be able to land if there was a bad tide race off the next one.

With only two days paddle remaining to reach the starting point of the Fiordland trip in Te Waewae Bay, it was certainly proving to be no anticlimax. South from Nugget Point the paddling had been as incident-prone as off the Fiordland Coast or the top part of the West Coast.

A third tide race-cum-overfall, lying off Barracouta Point, was complicated by the swell breaking over a reef. This meant a wide berth out to sea into a larger area of the race. Off the two previous points I had been able to cut in reasonably close and so avoided spending too long in the tide races.

To break through this third tide race I was right at my limit, fully extended, and could paddle no harder. To ease off the rapid powerful strokes for a second meant *Isadora* drifted swiftly backwards. Wearily but thankfully I broke out onto slower moving and calmer seas. Only Steep Head remained to pass. The next section of coast was rugged and impressive with a large surf smoking in towards a rocky shore. The sooty shearwaters were thick on the sea, apparently unperturbed by the tidal stream. A friendly mollymawk stayed by *Isadora* for a while, soaring in beautiful flight, wings flexing slightly to change direction.

Steep Head slipped slowly by and to my relief there was no tide race. There remained one final obstacle

An aerial view of Paul and Isadora *in Foveaux Strait. Photo: The Southland Times*

before reaching the old Omaui pilot station, Omaui Island, a bleak-looking, rocky island, 150 yards out from the next point. According to my rule of 'If in doubt, stay out', I should paddle round the outside of the island. There was little wind, so hesitantly I paddled towards the gap, watching carefully to see how far the swell broke out into it. Apart from a moderate tide race passing between the island and shore the conditions appeared favourable. Some hard paddling carried *Isadora* slowly through the gap onto an almost dreamy, settled sea. Sharply the coastline turned to the east along to the mouth of New River with Omaui pilot station now lying only a mile away.

For the first time since leaving Tiwai Rocks, I was able to relax my knotted stomach muscles and drop the tired legs down to lie limply along *Isadora's* hull. A soft watery sun glimmered on the gentle swell, such a contrast to the tense paddling of the last few hours. On the horizon to the north the sun reflected off what appeared to be the distant dunes behind Oreti Beach. But I was startled by the realization that the dune-like shapes were in fact tall waves breaking and rolling eastwards towards the distant beach. At first I thought the waves were breaking over the reefs of Halfway Rocks but I was soon to find out otherwise.

Paul and the trusty ship dog were waiting near the old pilot station and I landed through a low, gentle surf in front of a boulder beach. The car was some distance back down a road so we walked up to a large old rambling house nearby to ask if Paul could drive along with the lunch gear. There we met Mrs. Malcolm and her daughter Helen, who kindly asked us in for a cuppa. Mrs. Malcolm and her husband had lived at the old pilot station since Bluff took over as the port for Invercargill. The New River estuary, which was

originally the port for Invercargill, has a dangerous bar at the entrance.

Mrs. Malcolm cooked us a fine meal, then from the wide verandah of the house, pointed out Halfway Rocks, beyond which lay Riverton, although there was no sign of the town some 14 miles away over the watery horizon.

I planned to paddle in a straight line for Riverton rather than take the alternative and longer course round the curving shore of Oreti Beach. Hamish Carnegie had advised me to take the shorter and more direct route, passing Halfway Rocks on their seaward side. Within half an hour the tidal stream through the strait would turn in my favour.

Helen and Mrs. Malcolm came down to watch *Isadora* depart. The remains of the old pilot boat shed and a winch are still evident by the top of the boulder beach. From here Paul was to drive around to Riverton and keep watch from Howells Point.

I was under way again at 2.30pm but had to head almost back to Omaui Island to avoid the swell breaking over the New River bar. Only when *Isadora* was well clear of any sign of capping waves did I turn the bow in the general direction of Halfway Rocks. Although this group of reefs and rocky islands were clearly visible on the horizon from the verandah, from sea level in the Nordkapp there was no sign of them.

The size and steepness of the swell eased off when *Isadora* cleared the 300 yard wide belt of breakers out from the bar. Using the sun as a reference point I kept paddling in a north-westerly direction until at last, from the crest of a high swell, a tiny bump was visible on the horizon. The next time it came into sight, a few swell crests later, I had the compass ready and took a sight on the rocks. I found it easier to steer by a small cloud that lay directly above the rocks.

A south-easterly breeze came away half an hour later to lie directly astern but I was quite happy as long as it didn't grow too strong. Several small groups of penguins, their heads just above water, dived in a flurry when they noticed the yellow kayak approaching. I felt happy to see the now familiar shape of a large black and white sea bird gliding down towards me, the solitary, grey-headed mollymawk.

Halfway Rocks grew larger and larger until *Isadora* slipped swiftly by, about 200 yards out on the seaward side of these wave swept rocks. The tidal stream was now obviously setting west in my favour. On the open sea with no fixed reference points it was hard to gauge the Nordkapp's speed, but with the following breeze and tidal stream *Isadora* must have been making six knots or more as we passed the rocks.

The horizon out to the north-west, where sky met sea, was a bare, blue line with no trace of the 400 foot high headland by Riverton. Provided I stuck to the compass bearing there was no chance of missing Riverton unless a sudden drastic weather change occurred, which wasn't likely.

Suddenly a rather unfamiliar shape appeared gliding down towards *Isadora*. It was a light plane containing Paul and a photographer from *The Southland Times*. The passenger door had been removed and I could easily see Paul making rude gestures from the doorway as the plane flew in wide circles. After several low passes, numerous waves, and a last circuit, the plane flew off in the direction of Invercargill.

Although it was a pleasant surprise and a comfort that Paul knew my location, it felt like the plane was intruding into my lonely little world of sea and sky. A noisy trespasser into a quiet zone where the loudest sounds were the water dripping off the paddle blade, the soft splash as the blade entered the water, and the barely discernible sound of distant surf breaking. Strange as it may seem I was happy to hear the fading sound of the motor.

An hour or so later the headland and hills above Riverton came into sight on the horizon and the wind picked up a little more in intensity. Rather than put into Riverton, where I would lose at least an hour of paddling with the favourable tidal stream, I decided to push on another seven miles to Colac Bay. From there I would have a good chance of reaching Te Waewae Bay in only one more day's paddling.

In order to keep the south-easterly wind dead astern, I passed Howells Point over a mile and a half offshore. At that distance it was possible that Paul may not have sighted the Nordkapp but I felt sure we would meet up again by nightfall one way or another. Two and a half miles to the south-west of this point

lies the small, flat-topped, rocky Pig Island. I paddled in close to its lee shore, and headed in a direct line for Oraka Point at the southern side of Colac Bay. The 500 foot high headland that drops down to Oraka Point seemed almost like an island from a distance offshore, for the hinterland consists of low dunes behind the beach of Colac Bay with low lying, sometimes swampy land further inland.

Each time I had previously driven past Colac Bay a sizeable surf was rolling into shore, but I considered the western end of the sandy bay in the lee of Oraka Point would provide the best landing. Half a mile from the start of the beach a small boat lay rolling at anchor, level with a concrete ramp or slipway that projected out from the rocky reef-fringed shoreline along to Oraka Point.

The sea was quite choppy when I landed at 4.30pm, feeling relieved to be ashore and to have covered so much ground since leaving Bluff in the early morning. A young lad walked over from a nearby house and helped me carry *Isadora* up the ramp to the roadside. He asked me to accompany him back to the house, set on a hillside with a commanding view of the bay, as Olva Belsham had a cup of tea waiting. The name sounded familiar but for the life of me I couldn't think why.

Still wearing my wetsuit and parka, I walked up to the house with the boy and met Olva and some of her family friends. Standing on the carpeted living-room floor I felt a little embarrassed by the small puddles of sea-water that drained out of the wetsuit and formed around my feet, but Olva told me not to worry and passed over a reviving cup of steaming hot tea. The reason for the familiarity of her name soon became apparent. From 1945 to 1976 Olva operated a shore based radio station for crayfishing boats. Her name was mentioned in Paul Powell's book *Fishermen of Fiordland*; also, the day that Max and I set off on the Fiordland trip, Ainslie had tried to contact Olva to see if she would listen out for our radio schedules. It was yet another incredible coincidence. The bright yellow colour of the Nordkapp had been spotted by Olva a mile or more offshore with the aid of binoculars and my progress into shore watched with interest.

Olva, in a motherly manner, led me along a hallway to the bathroom and turned the hot shower on. The steaming waters did wonders for my tired arms and shoulders, after the 35 mile stint for the day. Meanwhile Paul, driving around the shore of Colac Bay, spotted *Isadora* and made his way up to the house. Paul had not seen the Nordkapp pass Howells Point since I was so far off shore by Pig Island, but assumed correctly that I was making for Colac Bay. Two friends, Anna and Helen, had come out with Paul from Invercargill, and Helen had stayed at Howells Point just in case I put in there.

After the refreshing hot shower my only desires were to set up the tent on the shore of the bay, cook a meal, and crash early for a quick getaway on the last leg next morning. However Paul wanted to spend yet another night in the big smoke and since there was no tent, no food in the car, and Helen was still waiting at Howells Point, there was virtually no option but return to Invercargill.

In my unsociable mood that night I would have been better to have stayed at the bay on my own and it turned out I would have been surprised by visitors in the early hours of the morning.

There had been an increasing tension ever since leaving Nugget Point, not only at sea with the dangers of Foveaux Strait, but with Paul. As I grumblingly pointed out, part of the essence, or magic, of the trip was meeting the local people at the landing places and camping on the beaches. Not once since leaving Banks Peninsula had we camped out.

Since I had made a promise to advise Max Reynolds and Lyn Taylor when Te Waewae Bay lay less than a day's paddle away, I made a phone call through to Christchurch. However Max, Lyn and Keith Dekkers were already on their way south after hearing an item on the radio. Bruce Annabell was also making his way down to Te Waewae Bay on a motorbike. The knowledge that these friends would be down by the next day provided a slight boost to my sagging morale.

On this night I should have been excited by the prospect that only one day's paddle remained to finish the trip, to complete the first South Island circumnavigation by kayak, that the dreams of nine months or more were about to be realised. But I wasn't. All I wanted now was for the trip to be over.

23 April - Day 75

It was still dark when we arrived at the Colac Bay concrete slipway and I was pleasantly surprised to see Keith's red station wagon parked with two kayaks tied onto the roofrack, and a small orange tent pitched nearby. My excited shouts of, "cup of tea," "load of wood" and "aardvark," familiar greetings from the old days of caving expeditions, brought three sleepy eyed figures out of the tent, Keith, Lyn and Max. Yet another coincidence that they had chosen to camp there, not knowing that this had been my landing place or that *Isadora* was hidden in a shed only 50 yards away.

The early morning marine forecast from the Met. Office was for easterly winds, but as the breeze usually picked up later in the day, I expected to find no wind and a calm sea when we arrived at Colac Bay. I was disappointed to find a 10 to 12 knot east-north-easterly blowing into the bay.

Max had brought his Nordkapp, named rather dubiously the *Good Ship Venus*, and Keith had his shorter whitewater kayak with a skeg to keep it on a straight course. However, despite their intention of joining the paddling for the final day, Max and Keith

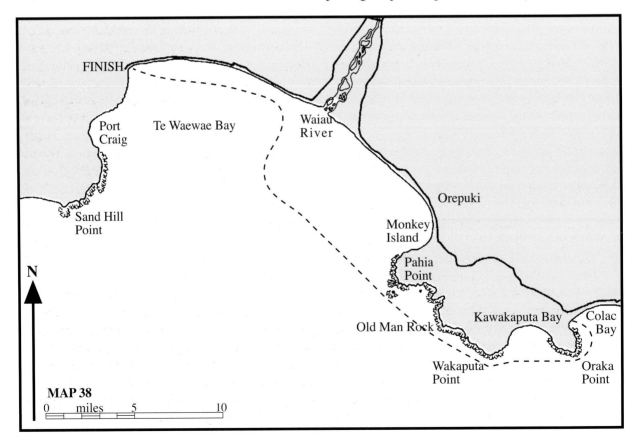

MAP 38

0   miles   5   10

had one look at the choppy sea in the grey light of dawn and decided not to join me. Instead we all agreed to rendezvous at Monkey Island, a small steep-sided island at the southern end of Te Waewae Bay where the *New Zealand Pilot* mentioned a landing for boats.

There was just enough light to make out Oraka Point when l paddled away from the concrete ramp. The wind and chop were abeam of *Isadora* for the first mile southwards to the point. Apart from the wind and light chop, the swell was small and the sky clear.

Once around the point, the sandy shore of the deeply curved Kawakaputa Bay came into view. The wind now became a curse for it wasn't directly abeam nor directly astern, but halfway between. It took a few choice words and several stops before *Isadora* would run on a straight course for Wakaputa Point on the western side of the bay.

It was almost dead low tide when *Isadora* left Colac Bay so I half expected to find tide races off each of the points along to Te Waewae Bay. Consequently it was a relief to find none off either Oraka or Wakaputa points. Off the latter the swell was breaking over reefs with steep waves toppling with a dull roar and a welter of spray. It was here that the sun crested the eastern horizon, casting a soft yellow glow over sea and shore. The most beautiful aspect of the sunrise was rays of golden light diffusing through spray that lifted off breaking waves. The light flashing from the 40 foot high lighthouse on Centre Island, five miles south-eastward of Wakaputa Point, was clearly visible. The flash of light I was seeing wasn't white but red, *Isadora* and I were in a red sector. Because there are so many reefs and shoals between the 284 foot high island and the mainland vessels are warned by the *Pilot* to pass on the southern side of it, hence the red sector.

The sooty shearwaters were again out in force, with a few inquisitive penguins, and the familiar shape of my friendly mollymawk.

Along to the next point, Old Man Rock, the shoreline was most inhospitable, reef-fringed with short sections of cliffs along the rocky coast. Old Man Rock, a large block with a finger-like projection on top, lies at the tip of a small peninsula. I became unsettled here at the sight of a 'sneaker' (a swell that reared up without warning to break in a shower of spray where previously there had been calm seas) appearing intermittently about 200 yards out from the rock. Between the area of the sneakers and shore there appeared to be enough room to take *Isadora* through but the idea of courting disaster on the last day made me turn out to sea and give the area a wide berth.

By now it was a bright sunny day, spoilt only by the

10 to 12 knot north-easterly. Pahia Point, the very last of all the hundreds of points around the South Island came into sight, a 670 foot high, scrub-covered headland. It was apparent that the rocky, reef-fringed point would not pass unnoticed for shoal areas with a breaking swell and low, wave-swept islands extended out to sea for over a mile. A possible short cut between one large island and the shore would have saved a few hundred yards paddle but again I decided a short cut wasn't worth the risk.

A hazy blue shape, darker than the clear blue sky, appeared on the horizon, my first glimpse of the mountain ranges of Fiordland, and the final destination. To my delight the wind backed from the north-east to the south-east. At this point I should have turned eastwards into Te Waewae Bay and the rendezvous at Monkey Island but the wind change and sight of the final landing spurred me on to take advantage of the following wind and make directly for the western end of Te Waewae Bay. By paddling into Monkey Island I would not only increase the distance for the day but also cut down on the chances of making the most of the settled conditions. Although I was too far offshore to see any sign of Paul on Pahia Point, I felt sure he would be watching with the aid of binoculars and would see my course change.

When I paddled past Pahia Point Keith and Max were out in their kayaks to meet me but because of the size of the swell and the numerous shoal areas with breaking waves, we did not sight each other.

For an hour the wind hastened *Isadora's* speed towards the distant mountains. Up to Pahia Point I had been feeling really tired with a dull ache in my arms and in generally low spirits. I had eaten the last of the minties and was even considering breaking into the emergency supply of glucose for some instant energy and enthusiasm. But it wasn't necessary. The wind change and sight of the western side of Te Waewae Bay in the distance, gave me a new lease of life, and the old body found a hitherto undiscovered reserve of energy. It was hard to believe that after all the ups and downs of the previous week, the day had turned out so well.

Isadora was lying about four miles offshore and level with the Waiau River mouth when the south-easterly breeze eased off and gradually died. After the last wind ripples vanished, the surface of the long, low, south westerly swell became glassy. The mollymawk which had not been far away all morning, glided down to land with a swish on the sea. I stopped paddling and let *Isadora* glide. The large bird with his white chest and black wings, used his webbed feet to paddle confidently over to within a yard of the kayak. Using slow movements I lifted the camera to photograph the bird, my good omen that had appeared each day since the Nuggets. I felt a strong affinity for, and sense of security when with the bird, rather like the relationship between the early sailors and the albatross. Several times after I paddled away the mollymawk took off only to land some distance away in the path of the Nordkapp. This close contact with the beautiful bird on the last day of the trip added to the joy and excitement that was building up in me for the final landing.

Ever since Max and I had paddled out of Te Waewae towards Sand Hill Point I had wondered what it would feel like to return from the opposite direction after paddling round the South Island, not long to wait now! Feeling quite happy and no longer tired, I pushed *Isadora* over the glassy swell with long powerful strokes of the paddle.

However, the stillness of the air was about to change. The first sign of approaching wind came when the glassy appearance of the swell closer to shore disappeared, to be replaced by a dull dark band. Then the warning traces of the wind sweeping southwards, parallel ripples on the sea. Moments later a 15 knot northerly was blowing and within 10 minutes it had turned the glassy swell into a short, steep white-capping chop. Since *Isadora* lay over three miles offshore, still on course for the mountains, I turned directly into the wind and chop, heading closer into shore just in case the conditions deteriorated further. 'So close and yet so far,' I thought, as the Nordkapp rose and fell into the chop, spray splashing back into my face.

For an hour I pushed in shorewards against the wind, then gradually, with half a mile still to go, the wind eased and I slowly turned the bow back on course for the western end of the bay. As the wind dropped my morale picked up again as did *Isadora's* speed, the kayak gliding swiftly over the swell with water creaming away from the bow. Out on the horizon, beyond Sand Hill Point, lay the desolate, steep-sided, grey shapes of the Solander Islands. I passed Rowallan Burn but could not make out the spot where Max and I had left from, four months and two days ago.

Much of my thinking revolved around this being the last few hours of solitude on the sea, that the great adventure was almost over, and what a glorious day it was to finish. I wondered if the support party had seen *Isadora* go past Pahia Point because if they hadn't, no one would be waiting. The chop died away completely to my relief and never far away, the lone mollymawk seemed to be shepherding the kayak, landing in front of *Isadora* and waiting until I had paddled past. The only thing lacking to make my day complete was my other good omen, a dolphin.

From Rowallan Burn a sandy beach forms the shoreline of Te Waewae Bay, backed by a 100 foot high cliff with forest on top. A gravel road between beach and cliff leads out to the western end of the bay. By now *Isadora* lay only 400 yards offshore and the few cars that drove along were easily visible. I had been paddling steadily now for over eight hours since leaving Colac Bay, the longest stint ever without a break on shore. Despite this I was revelling in the easy paddling on the long gentle swell, indulging in a little nostalgia and really enjoying the last hour on my own. The excitement of reaching the landing, now less than two miles away, continued to mount.

Mind you, I wasn't disappointed to see the familiar shape of the boatshed at the end of the bay come into sight, with behind it, a wall of forest rising to the skyline. 'Was it worth all the trouble?' I asked myself, but decided it definitely was, not that I would ever consider anything like it again. My day was made when, of all things, two small dolphins appeared momentarily, cutting through the sea on a parallel course.

A tiny dot appeared on the sea between *Isadora* and the distant boatshed. The dot grew larger until I could see it was Max, his red-peaked yachting cap pulled firmly on his head, powering towards me. As he came within earshot he called, "Is this the way to the South Island?" The grin on his face matched mine, ear to ear. "No," I replied, pointing in the general direction of Fiordland, "You're going the wrong way." It seemed so long ago that Max and I had set off round the Fiordland Coast in the Nordkapps and it was a fitting conclusion that he should join me for the last mile. Side by side and stroke for stroke we powered through the water towards the last landing. "There's a big mob of people waiting," Max warned me. "What say we head on out to Sand Hill Point then?" I asked.

Sure enough there was a crowd of 60 or so people waiting on the beach as Max and I nosed in towards a low line of breakers. Paul called out to watch for submerged boulders in the surf. I put on a brief burst of backpaddling to avoid the two large rocks exposed by low tide, but I caught the next wave and rode in over the rocks to the sandy beach.

Paul ran over with a large magnum of champagne and a hollow stemmed wine glass. But instead of filling the glass as I expected, he shook the large green bottle with his thumb over the neck, and sprayed the frothy contents over me, soaking my hair and beard. Then he filled the glass. Paul walked to the bow and with Max at the stern, they lifted *Isadora* waist high and staggered up the beach to the waiting people with myself still firmly ensconced in the cockpit and crying out, "You'll spill the wine, you'll spill the wine."

It was certainly a warm and rather emotional

welcome which awaited me on the beach with lots of handshakes and cuddles, a round of applause after one chap made a speech, interviews with reporters and of course the continuous filling and emptying of the wine glasses. The champagne quickly went to my head and when the television interviewer asked, "Would you go around the South Island again if you had the chance?"

"No, not even for two sticks of licorice," I replied.

Two members of the local Tuatapere Lions Club came over and introduced themselves and invited us back for a meal. "There's eight of us," I told them, but Goldie Davidson and Jack Bennett assured us it was all right.

Gradually the people drifted away until there were just the eight of us left on the beach, all a little tipsy from the champagne and faces flushed with excitement. Surrounding me were Bruce, who had arrived on his motorbike, Paul, Keith, Max, Lyn, Helen and Anna, and, of course the faithful old ship dog, Benny, who had been with the support crews since Jackson Bay. The two Nordkapps, tried and tested, now looked rather empty and lifeless on the damp sand. I raised a silent glass to *Isadora*, the dancing lady, who had been put through so much and had lived up to all my expectations. The end of a 1500 mile adventure.

For a few moments I looked out at the sea, at the distant grey shape of Stewart Island on the far horizon and the bush-clad shoreline curving out to Sand Hill Point. A beautiful afternoon, and a moment of mixed emotions, even a few sandflies turned up for nostalgia's sake. I pulled off the wetsuit and rather holey wool singlet for the last time and we loaded *Isadora* onto the car. It had been a long day with nine hours of continuous paddling to cover the last 35 miles.

Slowly we drove along to Tuatapere where *Isadora* made a brief appearance at a gala day. The Lions Club provided a tasty feed of steak and chips for us after which I gave a brief talk to the Young Leos group. Not only a feed, but Goldie and Jack filled the two vehicles' petrol tanks. I was moved by their hospitality and apologetic that there were so many of us for the meal.

With the weather coming right at last and the warmth of the reception at Te Waewae Bay, it had been a perfect day for the trip to finish.

24 April - Day 76

A quiet day when we all went our separate ways, marked only by the loss of my car keys. Despite an advertisement in the local newspaper, contacting the police and a painstaking search, there was no trace of the keys. Bruce hot-wired the car so I could return to the West Coast. Two weeks later I recovered the keys from Max in Christchurch. Somehow or other they had ended up in his coat pocket.

Still, as the saying goes, you get that at the end of the big trips.

Max Reynolds and Paul Dale carrying Isadora *up the beach at Te Waewae Bay*

The final landing and a celebratory glass of champagne from Paul Dale. Photo: The Southland Times

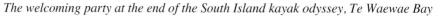

The welcoming party at the end of the South Island kayak odyssey, Te Waewae Bay

Chapter 17

EPILOGUE

The two Pauls celebrating the end of the South Island kayak odyssey at Te Waewae Bay

What did the trip achieve, apart from well developed shoulder and arm muscles? What was the motivation behind the South Island circumnavigation?

Two years of teaching outdoor education, music and maths had gradually drained me of the drive and zest for life which I used to have in abundance. My philosophy on life used to be to make the most of every available moment, spending weekends in the mountains, going away on expeditions in the holidays, always on the go. But after a day's teaching all I wanted to do was sit down in an armchair with a glass of port and relax. I felt the rather ambitious idea of a sustained kayak trip would be an excellent way to regain my self-confidence.

In retrospect, the trip was worthwhile and I am glad it was completed. It gave me the happiest state of mind that I have had for years. By the end of the trip all the mundane problems and hassles of the last two years had disappeared. The sustained daily challenge and continuous uncertainty about what lay around the next point had forced me back into a lonely but immensely satisfying reliance on my own inner resources.

The trip also gave me an opportunity to meet people who otherwise I would never have met.

Its success was due largely to the faithful support crews who cajoled, goaded, and tempted me along the coastline, providing encouragement, cups of tea, and occasional pavlovas, also the farmers, fishermen, and lighthouse keepers around the South Island who often fed us and put us up for the night.

The future? While finishing writing this book, I was training for a paddle around the North Island. I have the kayak, the equipment and the experience, so why not?

The paddle up the West Coast worries me, but to repeat an oft used expression in the book, you get a little nervous before the big trips, aye?

APPENDIX
Logistics of the Fiordland Expedition
Due to weight and volume restrictions, the gear was kept minimal and as light as possible.

Personal Gear List
1 Kayak
2 Sprayskirt & spare
3 Lifejacket
4 Paddle & spare collapsible one
5 Whistle
6 Compass
7 Light parka
8 Surfie-type wetsuit
9 Top half of wetsuit (long sleeves)
10 Wetsuit booties/sandshoes
11 Hat/helmet
12 Closed cell foam sleeping mat
13 Sleeping bag
14 Underwater torch
15 Wool singlets (2)
16 Long johns
17 Woollen shirt
18 Fibrefill duvet
19 Heavy parka
20 Nikonos camera
21 Diary
22 Length of light rope
23 Rolls of film

Group Gear
1 Small pack of flares
2 Radio
3 Tent; A-frame shape sewn in floor & zip door
4 Fly
5 Collapsible aluminium poles & tent pegs
6 Billy
7 Frying pan
8 Bowls and cutlery
9 White spirit primus
10 Fuel container
11 Water containers
12 Fishing kit
13 Plastic-covered maps
14 Fiordland Park Board map
15 Light plastic gloves
16 Gas lighters

Repair Kit
1 4 rolls of Sleek tape
2 1 square yard of woven glass cloth
3 500 mls. of polyester laminating resin
4 Small container of catalyst
5 Sandpaper

Medical Kit
1 200 mls dimethyl phallate (insect repellent)
2 Multivite vitamin tablets (200)
3 Mixture of zinc cream & castor oil (protection from sun)
4 Tube of Deep Heat
5 Forceps
6 Small pair of scissors
7 Salt tablets (100)
8 Eye drops (1 dropper bottle)
9 Paracetamol (50)
10 Lomotil (for diarrhoea - 40)
11 Elastoplast (1 yard)
12 Bandaids
13 Butterfly clips (8)
14 Brulidine cream (1 tube)
15 Suture needle and thread
16 Bactrim - antibiotic tablets (50)
17 Elastic bandages
18 Arisocot (1 tube)

Food
As with the equipment, the two considerations with choice of food were weight and bulk. The menu was as follows:
Breakfast: porridge & cup of tea
Lunch: bread/cabin bread/rye biscuits with honey, jam, salami, cheese and cup of tea
Dinner: Soup, beef curry & vegetables (dehydrated)
Apples, rice and raisins. Instant pudding or jelly
Supplemented with fresh fish, and meat for the first two days of the trip. Rather than write out the entire food list, I have listed the contents of each of the food dumps. Each item was sealed inside two plastic bags.

1 1 pkt porridge
2 1 pkt powdered milk
3 1 pkt sugar
4 1 pkt rye vita
5 1 pkt cabin bread
6 1 pound of butter
7 1 container of jam
8 1 container of honey
9 1 pkt tea
10 1 pkt baking mixture
11 1 pkt rice
12 1 pkt soup
13 1 pkt dehy. peas
14 1 pkt dehy. beef curry
15 1 pkt peanuts
16 1 pkt raisins
17 1 pkt dehy. apples
18 1 pkt. vermicelli
19 1 pkt.biscuits(raspberry cream)
20 1 pkt instant potato
21 1 pkt refresh
22 1 pkt happyade
23 1 block of cheese
24 1 bar chocolate
25 1 pkt glucose sweets
26 1 container of salt
27 1 container of pepper
28 1container of cooking oil
29 2 pkts jelly
30 1 Xmas pudding
31 1 pkt loo paper
32 3 candles
33 1 gas lighter

Day one of the Fiordland trip; the two kayaks on a beach at Sandhill Point, on the south coast of Fiordland

*Max Reynolds (09/11/1948 - 19/01/1980) in contemplative mood by the tranquil
waters of the Pandora River, Thompson Sound, Fiordland*